# A History of American Economic Thought

This vital addition to the Routledge History of Economic Thought series surveys arguably the most important country in the development of economics as we know it today – the United States of America.

*A History of American Economic Thought* is a comprehensive study of American economics as it has evolved over time, with several singularly unique features including: a thorough examination of the economics of American aboriginals prior to 1492; a detailed discussion of American economics as it has developed during the last fifty years; and a generous dose of non-mainstream American economics under the rubrics "Other Voices" and "Crosscurrents." It is far from being a standard run through of the established canon. Indeed, the role of women, the native American community, and numerous social reformers and those with alternative points of view are given as much weight as the established figures who dominate the mainstream of the profession. Generous doses of American economic history are presented where appropriate to give context to the story of American economics as it proceeds through the ages, from seventeenth-century pre-independence into the twentieth-first century packed full of influential figures including John Bates Clark, Thorstein Veblen, Irving Fisher, Paul Samuelson, and John Kenneth Galbraith, to name but a few.

This volume has something for everyone interested in the history of economic thought, the nexus of American economic thought and American economic history, the fusion of American economics and philosophy, and the history of science.

**Samuel Barbour** studied economics at Roosevelt University in Chicago and teaches community college classes and writes occasional thought pieces for publication.

**James Cicarelli** is a Professor of Economics at Roosevelt University and is co-author of *Distinguished Women Economists* and "Back to the Future of Economics."

**J. E. King** retired from LaTrobe University, Melbourne, Australia, in July 2013, and was appointed Emeritus Professor in August 2014. His continuing research interests are in the history of heterodox economic thought, particularly Marxian political economy and Post Keynesian economics.

# Routledge History of Economic Thought

# A History of American Economic Thought

## Mainstream and Crosscurrents

**Samuel Barbour, James Cicarelli and J. E. King**

LONDON AND NEW YORK

First published 2018 by Routledge

2 Park Square, Milton Park, Abingdon, Oxfordshire OX14 4RN

52 Vanderbilt Avenue, New York, NY 10017

*Routledge is an imprint of the Taylor & Francis Group, an informa business*

First issued in paperback 2019

*British Library Cataloguing-in-Publication Data*
A catalogue record for this book is available from the British Library

*Library of Congress Cataloging-in-Publication Data*
Names: Barbour, Samuel (Economist), author. | Cicarelli, James, author. |
King, J. E. (John Edward), author.
Title: A history of American economic thought : mainstream and
crosscurrents / Samuel Barbour, James Cicarelli and J.E. King.
Description: Abingdon, Oxon ; New York,
NY : Routledge, 2017. | Includes index.
Identifiers: LCCN 2017003078 | ISBN 9780415771016 (hardback) |
ISBN 9781315174365 (ebook)
Subjects: LCSH: Economics--United States--History.
Classification: LCC HB119.A2 B37 2017 | DDC 330.0973--dc23
LC record available at https://lccn.loc.gov/2017003078

ISBN: 978-0-415-77101-6 (hbk)
ISBN: 978-0-367-86453-8 (pbk)

Typeset in Times New Roman
by Taylor & Francis Books

# Contents

# Illustrations

**Figure**

**Tables**

# Acknowledgements

A work of this scope requires the efforts of many individuals in addition to those of the authors. Samuel Barbour wants to acknowledge the Economics faculty at Roosevelt University, especially Gary Langer, June Lapidus, and Steve Ziliak, as well as his co-author Jim Cicarelli, for all their support and encouragement.

Jim Cicarelli wishes to acknowledge the exceptional contributions the current and former staff members of Roosevelt University's Murray-Green Library located at the Chicago campus and the Robert R. McCormick Tribune Foundation Library located at the Schaumburg campus who together were able to locate and secure numerous resources, some quite obscure, used in developing portions of this book. A big heart-felt "thank you" goes to Ms Freeda Brook, Ms JoEllen Coney, Mr Joe Davis, Dr Lindsy Frazer, Ms Carolyn Nelson, Ms Mary Beth Riedner, Ms Renee Roth, and Ms Barbara Schoenfield and Mr Eric Wierzbicki. Ms Laura Anderson and Mr Huan Nguyen also deserve recognition for their technical assistance in preparing the manuscript for publication. A special shout-out to my co-authors, and to my friend and colleague, Dr Steven Antler.

John King gratefully acknowledges the many conversation regarding this book he had with Mr James Culham, Mr Jerry Courvisanos, Mr James Doughney, Mr Geoff Harcourt, Ms Gill Hewitson, Mr Mike Howard, Ms Therese Jefferson, Mr Peter Kriesler, Mr Alex Millmow, Mr Neil Perry, Mr Michael Schneider, and Mr Tim Thorton. Together, the authors would like to thank Ms Laura Johnson of Routledge for her assistance with this project.

This book is the result of the collective efforts of three individual authors who are, accordingly, listed alphabetically:

Samuel Barbour, Kiswaukee College and Joliet Junior College

James Cicarelli, Roosevelt University

John King, LaTrobe University, Australia and Federation University Australia

# Preface

Now that this book is in print, it is difficult to gauge which of two emotions is greater: our sense of accomplishments or our feelings of relief. Nearly seventy years have passed since the appearance in 1946 of the first volume of Joseph Dorfman's monumental, multi-volume classic *The Economic Mind in American Civilization*. At that time, the amount of American-created economic knowledge was already substantial; it has probably quadrupled since then. As important as economic thinking was in the middle of the twentieth century, for better or worse, it has become even more so. In a *New York Times* essay published in 2015, Justin Wolfers observed that "Two hundred years ago, the field of economics barely existed. Today, it is arguably the queen of the social sciences." He came to this conclusion after searching the *Times* archive for articles that used the term "economist" and compared the frequency of mention to that of other professions, specifically historian, psychologist, sociologist, anthropologist, and demographer. Tracking articles published from the late 1850s through 2014 revealed that historians held the market share of mentions with economists a distance second for the sub-period 1850s to 1900. From the beginning of the twentieth century through the advent of the Great Depression, the other social science professions began to appear on the radar screen with some regularity, but the top two spots remained historians and economists in that order. The Great Depression flipped that order of mentions as economists moved to the first rank over historians by a wide margin and have stayed there ever since except for a brief period in the late 1990s. The *Times* article reported an ever increasing fascination with the social sciences in general and the field of economics in particular, a trend corroborated in *The Congressional Record*, a verbatim account of the debates, proceeding, and activities of the United States Congress. For the period 1989 to 2014, the total mentions for the respective disciplines in the *Record* were: economists, 4,700; historians, 2,600; psychologists, 996; sociologists, 233; anthropologists, 166; demographers, 63 (Wolfers 2015). The enormous visibility of economists gives their work considerable importance, often at the expense of other social scientists whose perspectives are sometimes more cogent (Irwin 2017).

While not the sole source of the explosion in the volume of economics and the interest therein, American economists have contributed mightily to the field in the past, and continue to do so in the present as evident in the list of recipients of the Nobel Prize in Economics. The Sveriges Riksbank Prize in Economics in Memory of Alfred Nobel, the so-called Economics Nobel, has been awarded continually since its inception in 1969 to a total of 77 individuals because of multiple recipients in certain years. Of that number, 54 or 70 percent have been Americans, including several who "cannot be classified as pure Americans" (Coats 1998, 10), two who possess dual citizenship – America plus another country – and two who, strictly speaking, are not economists, all of which begs the question: Who is an American economist? This turns out to be a complicated issue but one that is tackled head on in Chapter 1 "Setting the Table." The first chapter speaks to this and other thorny matters that seemingly have little to do with core topic of this volume including the number, demographics, and literature of the American economists, and why English is the language of American economics even though other languages, notably French and Dutch were used widely in certain areas of North America that eventually became part of the United States. This chapter also discusses the philosophical leaning of American economists as well as their political inclinations. Depending on one's background and degree of knowledge of things American, especially American history, some readers may choose to skip part or all of the first chapter and go directly to Chapter 2 which marks the beginning of the book proper, that is the story of America's contribution to the growth and development of economics as an intellectual endeavor.

Aboriginal Americans had an economic mindset long before Europeans arrived in the New World and Chapter 2 explores the nature of economic thought among Native Americans prior to 1492. This is done for two reasons: first is the belief that the very survival of the European immigrants who came to America in the sixteenth and early seventeenth centuries was so dependent on successfully interacting with aboriginals that some traces of Native American economic thinking must be embedded in the DNA of contemporary American economics, if only subliminally; second, an examination of aboriginal economics can serve as a medium for investigating the interface between economics and other social sciences such as anthropology, archeology, and sociology, as well as the consideration of select economic aspects of philosophy and politics. An earlier version of this chapter appeared in *American Journal of Economics and Sociology*, Volume 71, Number 1, January 2012.

Chapter 3 covers the period 1600 to 1700 and deals with economic thought in America's protohistorical period. An anthropological concept, the notion of protohistory is defined in some detail in the chapter and then applied to American economic thought such as it was in the seventeenth century. An earlier version of this chapter appeared in the online publication *Journal of Economic and Social Thought* (Cicarelli 2016).

Economic thought in eighteenth-century America up to 1776 is discussed in Chapter 4, which covers the years 1700 to 1776 and features the works of early American writers on economic issues, notably Benjamin Franklin, considered by some to be America's first economist. This chapter introduces a format found in all subsequent chapters of the book, specifically an introduction followed by a segment on "Economy, Social, and Political Conditions," which gives a brief overview of the economic history of the time period in question as well as a glimpse of the social and political conditions in an attempt to recreate the gestalt of the era. These snapshots of history are based on the belief that "the emotional content of the hopes and fears of an earlier time is one aspect of history which often becomes harder to understand as we get further from it" (Dorfman 1959, 597). On a practical level, the historical reviews are based on the obvious relationship between much of what economists do and the economic environment in which they live at both the micro- and macroeconomic levels.

Once the historical environment is set, Chapters 4 through 8 move into a discussion of the history of economic thought in a particular time period with each chapter being divided into three parts, "Mainstream," "Other Voices," and "Crosscurrents.'" This partitioning is the equivalent of dividing the body of American economic thought as if it were a normal statistical distribution. The 'mainstream' or center of that distribution can be likened to the median plus or minus one standard deviation; 'other voices' would be that portion of the normal curve lying between one and two standard deviations of the median; finally, 'crosscurrents' would be the fringes of the distribution and represented points of view more than two standard deviations from the median or center of the state of economic thought in the time period being considered. Too many works on the history of economics take a filiopietistic approach (Furner 1975, x), beautifying the authors of works that occupy the mainstream of the discipline to the near exclusion of the contributions of those, both left and right of the center, whose insights are neglected, or at best relegated to the margins. Every effort is made in this book to give Other Voices and Crosscurrents a degree of representation proportional to their respective influence. An earlier version of Chapter 4 appeared in the *Journal of Economic and Social Thought* (Cicarelli 2015).

Chapter 5 discusses economic thought in the new nation spanning the years 1776 to 1885, a time period in which the social sciences, especially economics, began to blossom. As an end point, the year 1885 is especially important in the evolution of American economic thought for that is the year of the founding of the American Economic Association, an event symbolic of the professionalization of the discipline.

During the years 1886 to 1928 American economic thought came of age. At most four-year colleges and universities, economics became a stand-alone department offering an undergraduate degree option for liberal-arts minded individuals seeking entry-level positions in business, government, or industry. At the graduate level, select schools began offering advanced degrees in economics that reflected competing points of view in terms of topics coverage, methodology, and philosophical orientation. This 'academicization' of the discipline is the overarching topic of Chapter 6.

Chapters 7 and 8 divide the last ninety years of American economic thought into two periods of nearly equal duration. The first period, 1929 to

1973, begins with the Great Depression and ends with the arrival of an inflationary recession that lasted until the early 1980s. The combination of inflation and recession, a truly unique experience in American economic history that was once considered "theoretically impossible" by a generation of American economists reared on the Phillips curve (Okun 1977, 120). The "misery index" (Nasson 2008), a term coined by the economist Arthur Okun (1928–1980) and equal to the sum of the seasonally adjusted rate of unemployment and the annual rate of inflation, topped 20 percent in 1980 and became a particularly effective talking point for Ronald Reagan during his first presidential campaign. Stagflation, the portmanteau that captured the essence of a combination of circumstances many thought mutually exclusive, spawned a complete reevaluation of American micro- and macroeconomic thought from a variety of perspectives that collectively created "the age of neoliberalism" whose run may be coming to an end as we move deeper into the twenty-first century. An earlier, condensed version of this and related topics in Chapters 7 and 8 was explored in an essay in Vincent Barnett's *Routledge Handbook of the History of Global Economic Thought* (King 2015).

## References

Barnett, V., (Editor). 2015. *Routledge Handbook of the History of Global Economic Thought*. New York, NY: Routledge.

Cicarelli, J. S. 2015. "Economic Thought in Eighteenth-Century America Prior to Independence". *Journal of Economic and Social Thought* 2(3): 144–166.

Cicarelli, J. S. 2016. "Philosophical Origins of Seventeenth-Century American Thought". *Journal of Economic and Social Thought* 3(2): 179–195.

Coats, A. W. 1998. "What is American about American Economics?" In *The Economic Mind in America, Essays in the History of American Economics*: (M. Rutherford, Editor): London: Routledge: 9–17.

Dorfman, J. 1946; 1949; 1959. *The Economic Mind in American Civilization*. (Volumes I & II; Volume III; Volumes IV & V); New York, NY: Viking Press.

Furner, M. O. 1975. *Advocacy & Objectivity: A Crisis in the Professionalization of American Social Science, 1865–1905*. Lexington, KY: University Press of Kentucky.

Irwin, N. 2017. "What If Sociologists had as Much Influence as Economists?" *The New York Times: (The Upshot)*. March 17. Online: accessed 17 March 2017.

King, J. E. 2015. "United States of America." In *Routledge Handbook of the History of Global Economic Thought* (V. Barnett, Editor). New York, NY: Routledge: 113–129.

Nasson, R. 2008. "The Brooking's Institutions Arthur Okun – Father of the 'Misery Index'." Washington, DC: The Brookings Institution. December 17. (Online).

Okun, A. M. 1977. "The Great Stagflation Swamp." In *Vital Speeches of the Day*, 44(4): 120–125.

Wolfers, J. 2015. "How Economists Came to Dominate the Conversation." *New York Times: (The Upshot)*. January 23.

# 1    Setting the table

## Introduction

This chapter deals with a potpourri of topics that seem tangential to the main thrust of this book, and yet are integral to the story presented in Chapters 2 through 8. The disparate issues covered range from the deceptively straight-forward but nonetheless decidedly complicated question "Who is an American economist?" to an involved and lengthy response to the question "Why is English the language of American economics?" In between, there is an examination of the demographics of American economists, the scope of their discipline, and a general overview of their political preferences and philosophical leanings. Readers knowledgeable about some or all of these topics can skip what they know and focus on what they don't, or return to this chapter if motivated to do by the discussion in subsequent portions of the book.

## Who is an American economist?

The answer to this query involves breaking it down to its related parts, namely "who is an American" and "what is American economics." These two seemingly innocuous questions are anything but; consider the first question: who is an American. In order to ensure that no foreign influences would be injected into the American political system, framers of the US Constitution specified that candidates for President would have to meet three criteria: be a natural born citizen (not explicitly defined); be at least 35 years of age; and be an inhabitant of the United States for at least fourteen years. If we take July 4, 1776 as the date that the USA was established, then the eligibility of the first seven persons elected president is questionable on two counts: first, none were born in the United States strictly speaking, and second, it would be 1790 before any one of them would have lived in the country for fourteen years. The first president, a reluctant George Washington was elected in 1789, even though he was born in colonial Virginia, and the election date, April 30, 1789, was eight months shy of 1790. This "close enough" mentality also works when it comes to identifying American economists. As noted in Chapter 7 of this book, a stream of refugees fled Nazi Germany for the United States in the

1930s and 1940s, including many economists, some of whom having already distinguished themselves in the field while living in Germany. For the most part, these individuals were quickly absorbed into the American profession despite the fact that they could also be claimed by other nationalities (Coats 1998, 10). When it comes to identifying American economists, maybe a paraphrase of a response Supreme Court Justice Potter Stewart (1915–1985) gave to a question about pornography would best express our position: We may not be able to define an American economist, but rest assured we'll know one when we see one.

As for the second question – what is American economics – the answer is also somewhat nebulous. Because of the unusual circumstances involved in the creation of America as discussed in detail in the last section of this chapter, a number of hypotheses have been advanced about the "uniqueness" of American economic thinking, most of which are derivatives of the concept of American exceptionalism (Coats 1998, 11–15). A debatable hypothesis, American exceptionalism is the idea that the United States, conceived in revolution and nurtured in libertarianism, is truly different than most other countries and is a viable, indeed a superior model for other nations, emerging or existing, to emulate (Lipset 1996, 17–23). When it comes to nation building, the 'exceptionalism' of the United States is an open question, but with regards to economics it is self-evident that America economics is part of the larger, well-established Western tradition in the discipline and has been for some time. There is, however, one distinctive feature of American economics that is not nearly as evident in other Western countries, namely the continued respect and receptivity of the general public for the points of view coming from so-called amateur economists (Barber 1998, 20). A fairly recent example of this acceptance is the work of the journalist Jude Wanniski (1936–2005) whose 1978 book *The Way the World Works* became a veritable bible for the school of supply-side economics (Lewis 2006).

## The number of American economists and the scope of their discipline

Unlike pharmacy, law, medicine, and other professions, there is no licensing process for certifying someone is an economist, making a definitive census of the number of economists in the United States problematic. The publically available data on higher education and its constituent parts are inconsistent if not outright contradictory. In one US Bureau of Labor Statistics report titled "Economists" (BLS 2014), the Bureau indicates that "economists" with a typical entry-level education of a master's degree numbered about 21,500 in 2014, of whom 74 percent work, in descending order, for the federal government, consulting services, scientific research, state and local governments, and finance and insurance. This could imply that 26 percent or approximately 5,600 work in other categories, possibly teaching, but this is not stated explicitly. In another report "Economics Teachers, Postsecondary" (BLS 2015) where the typical entry-level education is a PhD degree, the Bureau indicates that total employment is 13,500, or about 1 percent of all postsecondary teachers in the US (BLS 2015a), with 11,300 of those economists in four-year colleges, universities, and professional schools, and 2,270 in junior colleges.

Higher education in the United States is a huge industry with many colleges and universities employing numerous teachers serving legions of students, but precise metrics on those three dimensions are elusive. Estimates of the number of postsecondary institutions (private, public, for-profit) range from a low of more than 4,400 (Gross and Simmons 2014, 23) to a high of nearly 7,300 (U.S. Department of Education 2016); the numbers for students served run from just over 18.5 million (Alexander 2015) to about 20 million (NCES 2016); and the total teaching and research faculty count in all higher education fields goes from 1.3 million (BLS 2015a) to just about 2 million (CAW 2012). The Coalition on the Academic Workforce (CAW 2012) estimates 25 percent of all faculty members are tenured or tenure track, while the other 75 percent are contingent positions, that is, part-time, adjuncts, full-time non-tenure track, or graduate teaching assistants. Applying those percentages to the BLS estimate of 13,500 total employment of "economics teachers, post-secondary," suggests that about 10,000 are contingent faculty, while the rest, around 3,500 are tenured or tenure-track. The tenure/tenure track number is significant because these are the economists that we expect will do much of the heavy lifting when it comes to the creation of new economic knowledge, the stuff that eventually becomes the province of the history of American economic thought.

Ironically, we probably know more about the demographics of those underrepresented in the teaching profession – Blacks and women – than those already there. Regardless of the incidence of multiple counting for the category 'Black and female,' the composition of the professorial core in economics is decidedly white and male. "African Americans make-up about 12% of the US population, but in colleges and universities, Blacks make-up an estimated 5.3% of the professoriate, a slight increase from 4% thirty years ago" (Smith 2013, 1). The extent of underrepresentation is particularly acute in economics due in part to the low production of Black economists, a problem that has persisted since the late 1980s when about 400 or 1–2 percent of all PhDs in economics were held by Blacks. In absolute terms, the number of PhDs earned by minorities, defined as Blacks, Hispanics, and Native Americans, is relatively small at about three dozen per year (Collins 2000, 146). There is probably no other field where the number of minority PhDs is so low relative to the number of undergraduates who take courses in the discipline (Simms and Swinton 1988, 67). The dearth of teaching faculty is dramatically evident at higher ranking institutions. In a 1994 study, the *Journal of Blacks in Higher Education* "found only 11 black economists teaching at the nation's 25 highest ranked universities" (JBHE 2006). Twelve years later, a census of Black economists at the country's 30 top-ranked universities, which collectively employed 935 economics faculty for an average staff size of 31, revealed little had changed. Nineteen of the top-30 institutions had no Black economists, while the remaining 11 schools had a total of 15 Black economists, with 3 being the most for any school (*JBHE* 2006). With respect to gender and race, Black males usually represent a greater proportion of Blacks in the academy than females, but economics may be an exception to this general tendency although definitive absolute numbers are hard to come by (Christian 2012, xiii).

Unlike the situation for Blacks and other minorities where supply is a contributing factor in underrepresentation, it does not appear to be the case for women. As recently as 2012 when women earned 46.2 percent of all doctorates, 32 percent of PhDs in economics went to females, down from a historic peak of 38.8 percent in 2000 (Cronin 2014), but appreciably more than the 4.2 percent in the 1950s, an era in which the environment for women in academe generally and economics in particular was especially hostile (Forget 2011, 19–20). Nevertheless, women economists, especially in academe, still face particularly stiff headwinds when it comes to career advancement in the field (Romero 2013), a journey that is even bleaker for Black women (Benjamin 1997, 9). Numerous statistical studies using a variety of analytical techniques to partition the causes of the limited success of women in the economics profession prompted this conclusion in 1995: "As other explanations fail, it becomes more likely that gender differences are the result of discrimination, either direct or subtle, against female colleagues" (Kahn 1995, 202). Anecdotal evidence suggests little has changed in the intervening 25 years (Kimball and Anonymous 2015).

Besides the sheer number of economists, oblique yet meaningful indicators of the scope and magnitude of the discipline in America are the country's plethora of associations related to the subject, and the volume of research and publications in the field. There are at least 50 societies and associations in the United States that are dedicated to the advancement of economics in general or a specific topic area therein. At the national level, the most prominent societies are the American Economic Association with over 20,000 members, and the National Association of Business Economists with about 4,600 members. Regional associations representing specific geographic areas include the Eastern Economic Association, the Southern Economic Association, the Midwest Economic Association, and the Western Economic Association, while some large-population states such as New York support state-wide groups. Numerous topic- or philosophy-specific societies exist including but not limited to the Cliometric Society, the Association of Christian Economists, the Union for Radical Political Economics, and the Cato Institute. Irrespective of orientation, membership in virtually all of these organizations is open to anyone, nationality and educational credentials notwithstanding. Naturally, some economists may be members of multiple associations, and some may not belong to any.

The substantial growth in the number of American practitioners in the discipline is also reflected in the increase in the volume of economics literature over time. In 1961 the American Economic Association began publishing a series of volumes titled *Index of Economic Journals* listing all journal articles classified by subject and in alphabetical order by the name of the author(s). Volume I of the *Index* covered the period 1886 to 1924, ran 112 pages, listing approximately 5,600 articles or roughly 150 per year. The second volume of the *Index* covered 700 articles per year for the time period 1925 to 1939, indexing 90 journals, 49 of which were fully indexed including 21 (43 percent) published in the United States. By 1968, 81 journals were completely indexed, 30 of them (38 percent) being American, with over 10,000 articles and book chapters indexed in 1968 alone. The series was discontinued in the early 1990s, having been rendered obsolete by the use of computerized databases; nevertheless, the number of economics journals continues to expand to this day with over 45 identified with American institutions such as a university or professional association. The significance of economics publications is also evident in books published. In 2013 about 309,000 books were published in the US, with about 30,000 or approximately 10 percent being in the combined fields of sociology/economics; that represented the third largest category of books printed that year, the first being 'fiction' with around 50,000 volumes and the second 'juvenile' at 32,000 (Bowker 2014). Supply-side data, specifically the 1993 National Survey of Postsecondary Faculty, also indicates that American economists are a prolific lot. The study of over 25,000 faculty members from 817 colleges and universities showed that on average each of the 368 economists surveyed produced during his or her career 10.7 refereed journal articles, 5.2 non-refereed journal articles, and 0.7 books (Hartely et al. 2001).

## American economists: their philosophical leanings and political preferences

There is little publicly-available information about the philosophical and political attitudes of economists which is too bad because there are lots of misconceptions about both aspects of those teaching the dismal science, especially among their academic peers who register as Democrats vs Republicans at far higher ratios than do economists (Langbert et al. 2016). Other academics generally perceive economists as philosophically conservative and politically Republicans, yet the available evidence, admittedly limited, suggests that neither characterization is accurate. Before reviewing the survey data, two caveats are in order: first, the sample sizes are small, and second, the samples are not necessarily random. Still, a national survey summarized in Table 1.1 of 153 academics (22 percent of whom were economists) in six disciplines at 84 American colleges and universities revealed that philosophically speaking, economists are overwhelming libertarians compared to their peer groups. This intimates that American economists are fiscally conservative but socially liberal, the latter trait apparent in the collective attitude toward same-sex marriage which 79 percent of the economist in the survey supported, the highest among the six academic groups surveyed, with Philosophy a distant second at 36 percent (Shields and Dunn 2016, 144).

*Table 1.1* Self-identified libertarians by discipline

|  | Libertarians (%) | Number |
|---|---|---|
| Economics | 77 | 30 |
| Philosophy | 29 | 14 |
| Literature | 26 | 23 |
| Political Science | 22 | 37 |
| History | 19 | 26 |
| Sociology | 0 | 12 |
| Number Responding |  | 142 |

Source: Shields and Dunn (2016, 144)

The one-sidedness in the philosophical leaning of economists is not apparent in their political preferences as registered in a 2007 survey of 1,097 academics from 26 disciplines. The 18 economists surveyed divided themselves evenly with respect to party identification: 6 Democrat, 6 Independent, and 6 Republican (Smith et al. 2008, 77). When asked if they identified with "left, liberal" only 5 economists (22.7 percent) replied in the affirmative compared to 85 percent in English (n=53), the most of any field surveyed (Smith *et al.* 2008, 76–77). This disconnect between the degree of philosophical liberalism and dispersion of political identification among economists is partially a reflection of the nature of their field. As one economist cogently put it:

> We're more focused on, 'Did you ask interesting questions? Did you do the model well? Did you understand the method?' ... It's a science thing. People's view of the science may be affected by their underlying values, but there is a common language, a common framework, a common methodology.
>
> Shields and Dunn 2016, 137

A 1950s study of 2,451 social scientists (23 percent economists) teaching at 165 American colleges and universities found that two-thirds considered themselves more liberal than those in the community at large (Lazarsfeld and Thielens 1958, 133); a majority also voted Democrat in the 1952 presidential election. Since then the entire professoriate has probably moved somewhat to the right (Gross and Simmons 2014, 32) which, given their propensity for being fiscal responsible and socially tolerant, would place the politics of the median economist in the category of 'liberal Republican,' in other words, a person who would be comfortable with the political viewpoint evident on the editorial page of *The New York Times*.

## Why is English the language of American economics?

From the perspective of the twenty-first century it is obvious that English is the language of American economics, and that the British intellectual tradition played an important if not dominant role in shaping the development of economic thought in the United States (McCloskey 2011, 61). These truths were not self-evident in the sixteenth and seventeenth centuries when North America was first discovered and explored. Then, several European countries, notably Spain, France, the Netherlands, Sweden, and Great Britain, actively competed with each other to lay claim to America or some portion thereof, and thus, its intellectual future. There was also the subliminal impact of indigenous thought and practices on American economic behavior and thinking. That topic – the nature of aboriginal economics and its effects on American thought – is explored at length in the second chapter of this book. The task at hand is threefold: first, to examine the colonization efforts of various European countries that explored the United States and identify what residual influences, if any, those efforts had on the creation of the American intellectual process, particularly economics during this country's embryonic stage; second, to identify the degrees of difference in the British approach to colonization that allowed English intellectualism to trump that of other European nations and their efforts to colonize America; third, to explore why language and cultural matter when discussing the evolution of intellectual history in general and economic thought in particular.

### Spain in America

Of the two countries on the Iberian Peninsula, Portugal seemed more likely to be the one to send the first European ship to the New World. The Portuguese had spent the better part of the fifteenth century exploring the eastern Atlantic Ocean settling Madeira in the 1420s and, in the 1440s, the Azores where they used African slaves to work the first sugar plantations established outside the Mediterranean. By 1471 Portugal had reached Ghana along Africa's Gold Coast, and in 1487 Bartholomew Diaz made the Cape of Good Hope around which Vasco de Gama traveled one year later to pioneer a new passage to India (Middleton xxxx, 6–7). But Christopher Columbus's 1492 voyage changed everything, necessitating the 1494 Treaty of Tordesillas which established the Line of Demarcation (Bourne 1904, 31–32). Portugal was given exclusive rights to New World territory to the east of the line, essentially Brazil, although the Portuguese did have a short-lived colony in Newfoundland in the early 1500s, a by-product of the voyages of the brothers Gaspar and Miguel Corte-Real (Bourne 1904, 63–65). Spain enjoyed a similar exclusivity to territory to the west of the line including Florida which Juan Ponce de Leon began exploring on behalf the Spanish Crown in 1513 (Gannon 1996, 16).

Except for the nineteen years from 1764 to 1783 when "La Florida" was under British control as called for in the 1763 Treaty of Paris which settled the Seven Years War, Spain had the longest continuous occupation of United States territory of all the European powers involved in colonial America (Gannon 2003, 18–24). For nearly 400 years beginning with Ponce de Leon's voyage and ending in 1821 when Spain complied with a provision in the

Treaty of Amity and formally ceded its Florida territory to the United States, the Spanish had a presence, either actual or legal, in America (Zeiller 2005, 174). Yet, despite the temporal span of its American occupation, Spain had negligible influence on the cultural development of the United States, certainly in comparison to that of the other Europeans interested in colonial America. Several factors contributed to this inverse relationship between the length of Spain's stay in America and its impact on American civilization.

Conditioned by their experiences in South America and Mexico, the Spanish fully expected those events to be replicated in the Southeast United States. Specifically, the early expeditions to America attracted explorers who were more interested in finding precious metals and the fame associated with such discoveries than establishing colonies (Axtell 2001, 217). When it became apparent that indigenous Floridians had no gold or silver and Florida lacked the geological profile for producing them, the treasure hunters quickly gave way to a different breed of explorers/exploiters, namely slavers seeking replacement workers for the rapidly depleting number of natives forced to toil on Caribbean plantations. The Portuguese began raiding Florida for slaves in the early 1500s and the Spanish quickly adopted the practice when it became clear that the only gold and silver to be found in La Florida was that deposited there from treasure fleet shipwrecks (Axtell 2001, 218–219). On balance the hunt for slaves produced mixed results as the Spanish found the aboriginals in the Florida territory – the Florida peninsula and the coastal regions of Georgia and South Carolina – much more difficult to subdue than the indigenous peoples of Mexico and South America. Living in densely populated and highly organized societies compared to their American counterparts, Mexican and South American aboriginals were easier to collect and coerce into slavery than the small and largely decentralized clusters of indigenous Floridians. Spanish efforts produced relatively few slaves (Zeiller 2005, 155) but so alienated the aboriginals in the Southeast that Spain's more serious attempts at colonization was virtually doomed from their inception.

In 1562 French Huguenots attempted to establish a permanent settlement near Jacksonville, galvanizing the Spanish to respond in kind as a way to protect and preserve their Florida interests (Landers 1999, 140). Under the leadership of Pedro Menendez de Aviles, the Spanish ruthlessly vanquished the French in 1565 and started a durable colony at St. Augustine (Lyon 1989, 152–154). Menendez hoped to build a permanent headquarters in Florida from which to explore the continent and, he hoped, to discover a waterway connecting the Atlantic Ocean and the Pacific, an ocean whose existence was known for some time as evident in maps in *Cosmographiae Introductio*, a 1507 book by the cartographer Martin Waldseemueller. In that book, Waldseemueller, a German priest living in France and writing in Latin, also applied the label "America" to the landmass between Africa and Asia, probably the first person to do so (Hessler 2008, 53). From 1565 until Menendez's death in 1574, St. Augustine flourished as no previous Spanish settlement in America, ultimately becoming "the oldest continuously occupied European community" in the United States, some 20 years before England's futile attempt to colonize Roanoke Island and more than 40 years before the landing at Jamestown (Chaney and Deagan 1989, 166). Though the permanent capital of La Florida, St. Augustine began to stagnate after the death of Menendez and the loss of his visionary leadership (Lyon 1989, 164). The absence of a champion, the increasing reluctance of the Spanish Crown to support American colonization, and the residual effects of earlier atrocities against aboriginals proved too much for subsequent city leaders to overcome (Axtell 2001, 219–220). The population of St. Augustine peaked at around 9,000 during Menendez's rule but thereafter declined steadily as did Spain's influence in the United States.

While having a minuscule effect on American culture, St. Augustine did play a role in the cultural development of another country, namely Cuba. Spain's relatively liberal manumission policies "eased the transition from slave to citizen and allowed the formation of significant free black society throughout the Spanish world" (Landers 1999, 2), especially in isolated St. Augustine. The city became "North America's first 'melting pot'" (Trigger and Swagerty 1996, 359). Rather than come under the control of the British at the end of the first Spanish period (1565–1763), the 3,000 inhabitants of St. Augustine, almost to a person, chose to emigrate to Cuba (Landers 1999, 3). This mass exodus was replicated in 1821 at the end of the second and final Spanish period (1783–1821) when the citizens of the city again rejected the United States in favor of Cuba (Landers 1999, 3, 246–250). Both migrations contributed to the multi-ethnicity of Cuba which is still today a hallmark of that island nation.

However marginal, Spain's contributions to American culture and intellectualism were all but erased in the late eighteenth and early nineteenth centuries when English and American scholars writing about Spanish rule in North America universally condemned it. Authors of histories, travel memoirs, and similar works were unusually vicious in castigating Spain's legacy, attributing centuries of Spanish misgovernment on the continent to "the defective character of Spaniards themselves" (Weber 1992, 336). Consumers of this literature were led to believe that the Spanish were "cruel, avaricious, treacherous, fanatical, superstitious, cowardly, corrupt, decadent, indolent, and authoritarian …" (Weber 1992, 336). Spanish historians came to call this Hispanophobia the Black Legend, a literary conspiracy rooted in Europe and fueled by the excesses of the Spanish Inquisition which began in 1478, officially ended in 1834, and was exported in the early 1500s to the New World, notably Mexico and South America (Kirsch 2008, 55). Justified or not, *la leyenda negra* eradicated the last vestiges of Spanish culture on American customs, norms, and intellectual traditions (Weber 1992, 336–337).

### France in America

In the waning years of the fifteenth century when Portugal, Spain, and England were actively exploring the New World, France, arguably the preeminent

country in continental Europe at the time (Munro 1921, 1–2), was pre-
occupied with other pursuits. For more than half a century beginning in 1494,
France was involved in the so-called Italian Wars, a series of regional conflicts
between France and other European powers, principally Spain, to control the
small independent states of Italy. Spanning the reigns of Charles VIII, Louis
XII, and Francis I, the Italian Wars were a prominent item on the French
agenda, marginalizing other state-sponsored ventures such as overseas
exploration (Bolton and Marshall 1920, 78–79). Despite official neglect, the
French were keenly aware of the New World, especially the wealth available
in both North and South America. As early as 1500, fishers from the northwest ports of France were harvesting the riches on the Grand Banks of
Newfoundland to satisfy the demand for fish created by the 153 meatless days
a year in Catholic France. In the southern hemisphere, seamen from Brittany
and Normandy dueled with the Portuguese for trading advantage with the
aboriginals living along the Brazilian coast (Eccles 1990, 1–2).

The Corte-Real brothers, Jean Deny, Thomas Aubert, and other freelance
French explorers visited various locations in the New World during the first
quarter of the sixteenth century, but not until 1524 did a crown-sanctioned
voyage take place. In that year, Francis I supported the Italian-born Giovanni
de Verrazano's expedition to the east coast of North America in search of a
more direct water route to the Far East than circumnavigating South America.
Exploring the coastline from South Carolina to Maine, Verrazano "demonstrated that North America was a vast land barrier, a geographical nuisance,
between Europe and the riches of Cathay" (Eccles 1990, 2). There was no
follow up to this voyage and the next official expedition to North America
was that of Jacques Cartier in 1534 who visited the Canadian Atlantic provinces and the Gulf of St. Lawrence with the intent of finding a northerly
passage to Asia. Though technically a failure, Cartier's first voyage induced a
return trip one year later for ostensibly the same purpose. His second voyage
took Cartier up the St. Lawrence River, which he was convinced was the
fabled Northwest Passage. Traveling on the St. Lawrence, Cartier found a
small and squalid Iroquois village at what is today Quebec and then discovered
at modern-day Montreal a sizeable and prosperous Iroquois settlement of over
1,000 individuals. Trade with the Montreal Iroquois and discussions with
other aboriginals about the mythical "Kingdom of Saguenay" where the
French would find the precious metals all Europeans so eagerly sought led to
a third Cartier voyage to North America in 1541. The purpose of what would
be Cartier's last trip to the New World was to establish a permanent French
colony and not to find a new route to the Far East, but a series of missteps
doomed the endeavor, which ended in 1542.

Some twenty years later, an earnest effort to colonize America was organized
but not before two ill-conceived and under-resourced attempts had failed. In
1555 at the suggestion of Lord Gaspar de Coligny, an ardent Huguenot who
held the title Admiral of France, a contingent of French Huguenots led by
Jean Ribaut attempted to found a colony in Brazil but the Portuguese quickly

squashed that effort (Bolton and Marshall 1920, 84). Seven years later a second Huguenot colony under the command of Jean Ribaut tried to create a permanent settlement at Port Royal Sound, South Carolina, but misfortunes beset the thirty colonists who quickly returned to France (Parkman [1865] 1996, 39–47).

Finally, in 1564 French Huguenots launched a genuine effort at colonization. Under the command of Rene de Laudonniere, three substantial ships crowded with supplies and men arrived at the St. John River and established Fort Caroline near Jacksonville, Florida, close to the Spanish enclave of St. Augustine. Not only was the scale of this operation greater than its predecessors, it was also different as evident in the inclusion of Jacques Le Moyne de Morgues, the first European artist in North America, among the colonists (Harvey 2008, 11). While the precise reason for Le Moyne's presence is a mystery, a reasonable inference is that he was there to produce artwork that would be used in marketing materials aimed at inducing other Huguenots to migrate to America. Despite all the planning, resources, and good intentions, the French effort to develop a Huguenot colony in Florida was brutally crushed by the Spanish within a year (Parkman [1865] 1996, 48–150). Nearly forty years would pass before France would again make a serious attempt to colonize North America (Munro 1921, 20–30).

At about the same time England was creating its first permanent colony in the United States, France was trying to do the same in the Canadian Maritime Provinces with limited success. In 1603 Samuel de Champlain made his first trip to North America intent on developing the fur trade, an economic magnet that drew the French to the St. Lawrence Seaway from the Atlantic coastline (Munro 1921, 155). Five years later he established a fur trading post that would become the city of Quebec and eventually the capital of New France. For the next quarter century, Champlain championed colonization of North America, yet for all his efforts, the European population of Quebec was only about 100 when he died in 1635 (Eccles 1990, 34). In 1634 the French explorer Jean Nicolet extended the boundaries of New France into Wisconsin, but French interests remained focused on the fur trade and the conversion of indigenous peoples to Catholicism and not colonization per se (Eccles 1990, 30–62). Population growth over the next thirty years remained slow, approaching 2,000 Europeans in 1663, the year Louis XIV, the only seventeenth-century French monarch with an active and enduring interest in colonizing North America, designated New France a royal colony (Munro 1921, 9, 61), Louis' declaration elevated the status of New France, which in the next ten years saw its population treble to nearly seven thousand (Munro, 79). In the early 1670s, Louis Jolliet and Father Jacques Marquette extended New France down the Mississippi River to Arkansas, and a decade later René-Robert Cavelier, Sieur de La Salle, navigated the Mississippi to its delta, enabling the founding in 1685 of Fort Saint Louis in Texas, the Louisiana colony in 1699, and the city of New Orleans in 1718 (Bolton and Marshall 1920, 99; Holbrook 1976, 103–106). The desire to acquire possessions, however, exceeded France's commitment to populate them. By the early 1690s, the population of New France was about 12,000 (Thwaites 1905, 26), and a census of 1706 showed a total population of less than seventeen thousand (Munro 1921, 206). English colonies in America by contrast had a population some fifteen times greater, with an economy proportionally advanced (Munro 1921, 14).

The propinquity of English and French colonies across much of the eastern portion of North America created a series of escalating conflicts (Eccles 1990, 63–124) that culminated in the French and Indian Wars of 1754–1763, the New World theater of the Seven Years War that involved all the major European powers from 1756–1763. The later hostilities ended with a French defeat, and in the Treaty of Paris French North American territories were divided between England and Spain with the exception of San Pierre and Miquelon, a fishing outpost on a group of tiny island in Newfoundland and still today a French possession (Thwaites 1905, 272). In 1800 under the Third Treaty of San Ildefonso, France regained possession from Spain of the Louisiana colony, but three years later Napoleon sold the territory to the United States as part of the Louisiana Purchase, effectively ending a French presence in America.

Despite their brief stay and relative small numbers, the French left a large legacy on the intellectual development of North America, particularly in Canada. The history of French Jesuits in Canada is subject to a variety of interpretations, some flattering (Munro 1921, 113–132), some less so (Eccles 1990, 39–49), but what is certain is that the Jesuits helped establish an intellectual tradition in New France and, subsequently, modern Canada. In 1635, a year before Harvard was created, the Jesuits established the College de Quebec, providing the sons of colonists an education as good as they could obtain in France (Axelrod 1997, 5). From 1632 through 1673, Jesuit missionaries in the field filed annual reports on their activities with superiors in Quebec who passed them along to church officials in Paris for final editing and printing (Eccles 1990, 40). These reports – the annual Jesuit *Relations* which are discussed in the next chapter of this book – had wide circulation among educated clergy and government officials and constitute one of the best written accounts of the lives and times of seventeenth-century North American colonists (Munro 1921, 132). The importance of French language and culture on the development of Canadian economic thought is evident in a recent book of the history of Canadian economic thinking where about 20 percent of the text is devoted specifically to this topic (Neill 1991). The significance or rather the lack thereof of French influence on American economics is explored in a sociological study of economic knowledge as it evolved in Britain, France, and the United States (Fourcade 2009). While the trajectories of economic thinking in each country are individually unique, economics as an intellectual exercise in Britain and the United States are a lot closer to each other than either is to that in France (Fourcade 2009, 7–30). Had the French and Indian Wars turned out differently, so too, in all likelihood, would have the language and scope of American economics.

### The Netherlands in America

With the defeat of the Spanish Armada in 1588, the Netherlands quickly became Europe's premiere economic power, culminating an ascendancy that began around 1500 (De Vries and Van Der Woude 1997, 665–666). Integral to becoming what some scholars consider the world's first modern economy was the formation in 1602 of the Dutch East India Company, a privately held corporation with a government-endorsed monopoly to conduct trade in Asia, principally present-day Indonesia (De Vries and Van Der Woude 1997). The planet's first multinational corporation and the first firm to issue stock, the Company was granted quasi-governmental powers in that it could wage war, negotiate treaties, coin money, and establish colonies. An instant commercial success with its ventures in the spice trade, the Dutch East India Company returned dividends between 15 and 75 percent during its early years (Bayer 1925, 135). Spurred by the prospect of finding a direct, all-water, and hence faster, less costly route to the Orient, the Company hired Henry Hudson, a British subject and seasoned navigator and explorer, to find a northeasterly passage to Asia. In April 1609, Hudson departed Amsterdam with a crew of sixteen in the *Half Moon* (Halve Maen in Dutch), a 120-ton, three-masted vessel (Johnson 1995, 87–88). Heading north with the intention of eventually turning east, the 65ft-long ship encountered a sea full of ice which led Hudson to abandon his original plan and instead sail "west in search of the elusive Northwest Passage" (Kammen 1975, 23–24). This, his third voyage to the New World, brought Hudson to Newfoundland in early July, a trip he described in his personal journal (Johnson 1995, 89–127). Traveling south along the eastern seaboard, the *Half Moon* went to Virginia then turned northward, arriving in September at the North River, now the Hudson (Jacobs 2005, 31). At 315 miles long from its source, the Hudson is a relatively short river but navigable to large ships from its southern terminus northward for 150 miles (Jacobs 2005, 2). Hudson traveled to what is now the Albany area trading with the Amerindians he encountered along the way, setting in motion a series of events that would culminate in the creation of New Netherland, a Dutch colony in America that would include the portion of New York State surrounding the Hudson, western Connecticut, New Jersey, and eastern Pennsylvania along the South River (now the Delaware).

New Netherland was part of what some writers refer to as the Dutch Atlantic World, which beside the American colony included at one time or another Dutch Brazil, Dutch islands in the Caribbean, Surinam, and parts of West Africa (Jacobs 2005, 3). Unlike the Spanish conquistadores whose prime motivation for exploration was militaristic or the English who more than any other European group sought to colonize the New World, the Dutch were first and foremost traders (Merwick 2006, 35); for them economics topped all other rationales for exploration. Within a few short years of Hudson's voyage, the East India Company established a trading post in the Albany area to acquire pelts and furs from aboriginals in exchange for light manufactures from the Netherlands. The returns on the financial investment associated with that effort, however, paled in comparison to those from Asian possessions such as the Banta Islands in eastern Indonesia, a major source of nutmeg (Major and Major 2007, 18). Interest in the Atlantic World especially New Netherland flagged, leading the Dutch government to respond affirmatively to the entrepreneurial overtures of Willem Usselinx who for years wanted to establish a company that would do in the New World what the East India Company had accomplished in the Orient. In 1621 the Dutch West India Company, a composite private/public corporation, was created to promote trade and colonization in America (De Vries and Van Der Woude 1997, 398–399). As part of its efforts at colonization, the West India Company sponsored in 1624 the migration of about 150 persons, the so-called thirty families, mostly Walloons, French-speaking Belgians who like Huguenots were followers of the Protestant theologian John Calvin (Bachman 1969, 75; Major and Major 2007, 23–24).

The thirty families established a permanent settlement on the island of Manhattan (Kammen 1975, 28), but the conflict inherent in the Company's short-term goal of profit maximization and the long-term commitments required to sustain colonization became evident. The Company vacillated between its seemingly mutually exclusive objectives, eventually putting the accent on trade at the expense of migration (Bachman 1969, 155). Whether colonization was purposeful, inadvertent, or some combination of both, the European population of New Netherland stood at a paltry 270 in 1630 some twenty years after Hudson's seminal voyage (Merwick 2006, 64). Recruiting new immigrants was always a hard sell. A direct voyage to New Netherland was long, usually about seven weeks; the return trip took about half that time because of the prevailing winds and currents (Major and Major 2007, 51; Bachman 1969, 16). Few voyages to New Netherland were direct, however. Trade priorities with Caribbean possessions and the relative safety of taking a southern route to the New World created a Dutch sailing pattern which made the American colony the last stop on a circuit that often began and ended in Amsterdam (Bachman 1969, 17). This added about five weeks to the one-way voyages of potential migrants to America.

Not only was the trip protracted, it was also dangerous. While the precise incidence of death on ships bound for New Netherland is not known, evidence indicates about a 5 percent mortality rate for passengers on voyages of comparable duration (Jacobs 2005, 46). Unlike many English transplants who consciously made one-way trips to the New World, most Dutch traders were transients keenly aware of the places to which they would return after their tours of duty (Merwick 2006, 48). Population growth of New Netherland was slow relative to English settlements which by 1630 had nearly 4,000 living in three colonies along the east coast (Norman 1988, 22). The small and relatively dispersed population of New Netherland prohibited the colony from achieving a consumer base sufficiently large enough for specialized trades such as silversmiths, printers, and furniture makers to achieve economies of scale or scope (Jacobs 2005, 472). This only exacerbated living conditions and further discouraged immigration.

In the face of dismal results, the Company changed tactics, scrapping its rule-ridden, bureaucratic system of migration in favor of a market-oriented one run by patroons, literally patron/entrepreneurs, who operated outside the corporate parameters then in vogue. The hope was "that individual initiative would achieve what a public corporation had not ..." (Kammen 1975, 31–32). This incentive-driven approach worked as the colony's population grew to about 2,000 by 1640 (Norman 1988, 22), then really began to accelerate under the leadership of Peter Stuyvesant (1612–1672), the last Dutch Director-General of New Netherland from 1647–1664 (Major and Major 2007, 59). New Netherland's population exceeded 4,000 in 1650 and hit 9,000 in the 1660s, most of whom were in New Amsterdam, present-day Manhattan (Merwick 2006, 237) This growth was somewhat deceptive as only about half the people in New Amsterdam were Dutch; the rest was a mix of Amerindians, free and slave blacks, and a variety of non-Dutch Europeans. A harbinger of modern New York City, New Amsterdam had become a bustling, ethnically diverse cosmopolitan area. Many languages were spoken in this "Dutch Colony," and official documents were at one time issued in French, Dutch, and English (Major and Major 2007, 18) As a colony New Netherland had become sustainable, but as a holding in the Dutch West India Company's investment portfolio its performance still lagged that of other New World assets (Sokoloff and Engerman 2000, 218). In 1664, recognizing the inevitability of a rapidly growing English America, which already had a population of over 70,000 (Norman 1988, 22), the Dutch provisionally ceded New Netherland to the British who administered the colony until 1673. The next year legal control of the colony was formally transferred to England under the Treaty of Westminster, thereby bringing to a close the Netherlands' 64-year experiment in colonial America. The Dutch had a short stay in America and while they did influence the culture of New York City and to some degree that of New York State, the Dutch had a minimal impact on the long-term arc of American cultural and intellectual development.

### Sweden in America

Sweden was the last of the European powers to attempt to colonize at least part of the American land mass. The first half of the seventeenth century was a time of grandiose thinking in Sweden. This was the era of King Gustavus Adolphus, Queen Christina, and Axel Oxenstierna, arguable the most influential politician in Swedish history (Johnson 1911, Vol. I, 3). The country's leadership aspired to weld the Scandinavian nations into a single state every bit the equal of England, France, or the Netherlands (Johnson 1911, Vol. I, 13). Integral to this strategy was the Mercantilist idea of national aggrandizement through trade, especially with colonial possessions. To this end, the first Swedish trading company was constituted in 1607 but quickly evaporated without producing any tangible results (Mattsson 1987, 29). Several futile attempts to form viable trading companies followed, but a workable plan did not take root until 1624 when Willem Usselinx, the former head of the Dutch West India Company convinced King Gustavus that Sweden should develop colonial interests in Asia, America, and Africa (Ward 1938, 11–13).

Sweden had come late to the idea of empire and its tardiness was matched by a lack of zeal. Fourteen years after Usselinx planted the seed, the *Kalmar Nyckel*, flagship of the New Sweden Company, landed at what is today Wilmington, Delaware, where Fort Christina was established in honor of Sweden's twelve-year-old queen. Under the leadership of Peter Minuit, who had been the head of the New Netherland colony for several years prior to working for Sweden, New Sweden was founded in March 1638 (Norman 1988, 6, 8). The cost of this expedition, the first of twelve that Sweden would launch over the next seventeen years, was 46,000 florins, more than twice initial estimates, while the cargo the *Kalmer Nyckel* brought back – mostly pelts and furs – fetched only 23,000 florins when sold in Holland a year later (Mattsson 1987, 40; Johnson 1911, 116). This sort of return on investment did not inspire enthusiasm for empire (Kupperman 1995, 89, 94). When Peter Minuit, the champion of New Sweden, died unexpectedly in 1638, interest in the colony waned. Sweden, which at the time included most of modern Finland, had a population of 850,000, small compared to France (16 million), Spain (8 million), the Netherlands (3 million), and Germany (20 million). Lacking the national wealth to underwrite a serious colonial expansion, New Sweden never really jelled as its population peaked at around 600 (Dahlegren 1988, 28). "The colonization enterprise testifies to ambitions and undertakings which can ... be said to have been unrealistic and lacking any reasonable connection to the country's actual resources" (Rystad 1988, 55). In late August 1655, the Dutch led by Peter Stuyvesant, governor of New Netherland, captured Fort Trefaldighet at modern New Castle, Delaware. One month later at Fort Christina, the governor of New Sweden signed the terms of surrender, effectively ending the Swedish presence in the New World (Johnson 1911, Vol. II, 597–605; Gehring 1995, 80). Sweden would eventually have an impact on American culture, at least on a regional basis, but that would come after the 1880s, a decade in which about 400,000 Swedes immigrated to the United States, settling primarily in the upper Midwest, especially Minnesota (Mattsson 1987, 14).

### England in America

Since English language and intellectualism have had a greater impact on the development of American thought than those of any other European convention, one might be tempted to conclude that the British approach to exploration was fundamentally different than that of other nations; it wasn't (Sokoloff and Engerman 2000, 220). The prime impulse motivating England to explore the New World was nearly identical to the one that moved other countries: to exploit the resources, human and natural, of North and South America. In 1497 King Henry VII commissioned the Italian explorer Giovanni Cobatto (known in England as John Cabot) to go on a western voyage on behalf of England. Cabot became in June of that year the second European to discover North America, landing somewhere between Labrador and Maine, with Nova Scotia being the generally accepted point of arrival (Croxton 1990–91, 42–43). For the next ninety years, English fishers and fur traders competed with their counterparts from other European countries to harvest the seafood and pelts found in and along northeast North America. Not until the 1580s did England initiate a concerted effort to create a permanent settlement in the United States. In 1584 Sir Walter Raleigh organized an expedition under the command of navigators Philip Amadas and Arthur Barlowe that sailed to Roanoke Island, North Carolina and took possession of the region, calling it Virginia in honor of the "Virgin Queen," Elizabeth I (Bolton and Marshall 1920, 110). A year later the first colonists came; they lasted about twelve months before extreme hardships drove them back to England. In 1587 a second contingent of colonists bent on establishing a permanent settlement at Roanoke arrived. Three years later the first resupply ship from England to reach the colony found a deserted village; the more than 100 men, women, and children had seemingly vanished although most had probably been assimilated into local indigenous groups (Sakolsky and Koehnline 1993).

The mystery of the Lost Colony of Roanoke Island notwithstanding, England persisted in its crown-approved efforts to colonize America, and this tenacity became one of the degrees of difference between the British approach to colonize the United States and that of other European nations. That perseverance was rewarded in 1607 with the establishment of Jamestown, Virginia in the Chesapeake Bay region. Ten years later colonial farmer John Rolfe and his wife, Pocahontas, sailed to England with the first major shipment of tobacco, and this became the second degree of separation between British attempts to colonize America and those of other countries. Tobacco was an instant commercial success, giving the Jamestown colony a renewable export with an unlimited upside. Exports reached 25 tons by 1620 and soared to six times that amount a decade later (Mann 2007, 34). Relatively overnight, Virginia had become a viable, self-sustaining economy that, in terms of the prevailing Mercantilism paradigm, completed a perfect symbiotic partnership – the agrarian colony trading with the manufacturing-oriented homeland (Carr and Walsh 1988, 145).

Thirteen years after Jamestown was settled, England established a second permanent colony in America at Plymouth, Massachusetts. As was the case for its southern predecessor, the New England colony had immediate access to an abundant supply of a cash crop that found a ready market in the homeland. The vast forests of the north satisfied a pent-up English demand for lumber that was increasingly in short supply because of the deforestation of the British Isles, a by-product of using wood to produce energy (Nef 1977). As England turned to coal from wood because of necessity, American lumber for ship-building and related industries made timber the tobacco of the north. By the mid-1660s England had two permanent, expanding, self-sustaining colonies in America, each with an economy operating within the prescribed norms of Mercantilism. The colonies, nevertheless, differed from each other in significant ways. The Virginia colony attracted a sizeable number of yeomen farmers who, dispossessed by primogeniture laws, saw the availability of free or inexpensive land in the New World as a way to recapture the lifestyle to which they had become accustomed when their fathers were alive. By contrast, many immigrants to New England were prosperous urbanites who left England to pursue religious freedom and not to escape economic insecurity (Seavoy 2006, 34). Another important distinction was the incidence of literacy which was greater in the north, consistent with empirical evidence suggesting a positive correlation between literacy and the extent of religious education and the density of population (Soltow and Stevens 1981, 22, 28). A related difference was the willingness to promote and support public education (Fischer 1989, 344–49), which was greater in some northern areas, notably Massachusetts and Connecticut (Soltow and Stevens 1981, 29), than was the case in the southern colonies. The attitude toward education was also evident when it came to founding colleges. Harvard, the first one in the north, was established in 1636; the College of William and Mary, the first such institution in the south, was founded in 1693.

Despite the many distinctions, major and minor, in values and customs, British settlers north and south shared a common characteristic that accounted for another important degree of difference between English immigrants and those from other European nations. Non-British immigrants generally had round-trip tickets to the New World as many intended to return to their homeland after making their 'fortune' in America. British settlers were usually making a one-way trip to America, believing whatever the New World had in store for them was better than what they were leaving behind (Cohen [1954] 2009, 28–29). English immigrants were determined to make the move to America work whatever the hardships and obstacles, displaying a commitment to colonization not always evident among non-British settlers. Some European immigrants, notably French Huguenots, had a similar resolve but national policies such as excluding Protestants from becoming members of the Company of One Hundred Associates, the group that founded Quebec, undermined these convictions (Thwaites 1905, 20). Actually, French Huguenots did form a permanent colony in America but it was in English America and not New France; more tolerated than welcomed, French Huguenots who had taken refuge in Germany founded New Paltz, New York in 1678.

Another minor yet significant difference between England's attitude toward colonization and that of other European nations was the matter of time horizon. Initially, all the countries exploring the New World did so with a sense of urgency preferring a quick and hefty profit on investment over sustained and/ or deferred returns. England, sooner than the other nations, developed a longer view of colonization, not exactly a long-term perspective but one longer than other European countries. This was evident in the creation of permanent American colonies in the seventeenth century and continued into the eighteenth century as reflected in the 1763 Treaty of Paris that ended the Seven Years War. During reparations deliberations, Britain was given a choice between two New World French possessions it had acquired during the conflict. England could retain the eastern Caribbean island of Guadeloupe, a well-developed agriculture area of 563 square miles or it could keep Canada whose vastness and economic potential was essentially unknown (Sokoloff and Engerman 2000, 217). After a spirited public debate Britain selected Canada, a choice that set well with the French and their here-and-now philosophy of economic return, and made equally good sense to the English given their focus on long-term development. The choice was also fortuitous for the thirteen British colonies in America that began their quest for independence just 13 years after the signing of the Treaty. The outright possession of Canada, a land mass larger than the continental United States and free of competing claims from other European rivals, notably Spain, probably diminished the resolve with which the British prosecuted the American war of independence.

## Why culture and language matter

Most scholars instinctively accept the hypothesis that Marion Fourcade's research supports: culture shapes thought including economic thought. The surprise would be if her results had suggested otherwise. Less intuitive is the notion that language influences thought. Known as the Sapir-Whorf hypothesis in recognition of its originator, the linguist and anthropologist Edward Sapir (1884–1939), and his student and popularizer of the idea, Benjamin Whorf (1897–1941), the concept is called linguistic determinism (Pinker 1994, 59–64). It attracted professional attention in the 1950s with the posthumous reprinting of Whorf's writings (Grace 1987, 117), peaking in academic interest in the 1970s. The theory then began a fall from grace as developments in cognitive psychology indicated that language had minimal effects on concepts (Pinker 2007, 124). Recently, the idea of linguistic determination has resurfaced as an active research topic in psycholinguistics among those who maintain that "the language we speak profoundly shapes the way we think ..." (Boroditsky 2009, 129). Critics acknowledge that language affects thought but remain skeptical of the proposition that it determines thought (Pinker 2007, 125). At the very least, there is consensus that language is a portal to culture, and if culture influences thinking then to some extent so does language.

Both language and culture have some bearing on thought in general and economic thought in particular, but the exact extent of that influence is difficult to measure and presupposes we can determine which of the two is the cause and which the effect (Grace 1987, 117). English language and culture certainly shaped the development of American economic thought especially during the colonial era when a majority of literate persons in the country communicated in English. Nevertheless, there was some resistance to English language, practices, and customs, especially at the regional level where the British perspective had to compete with other cultures and traditions. As the ethnic diversity of the country broadened in the nineteenth and twentieth centuries the influence of all things British diminished. Today, with less than 20 percent of Americans having any British ancestors (Fischer 1989, 6), English language and culture, while still important, are less dominant than they once were. So, for example, a history of economic thought in New York State would be remiss if it did not acknowledge the Dutch legacy. Similarly, a historical account of economic thought in Minnesota would be less than complete without recognizing the impact the 1880s mass migration of Swedes to that state had on economic thinking there. Nevertheless, the British legacy and the comprehensive scope of this book are the basic reasons this work focuses on English as the primary medium for communicating American economics. The above explanation notwithstanding, the reality is that if the competition to colonize the New World had been a horse race, handicappers would have made Spain a prohibitive favorite, with France a close second. Reasonable odds for success would have been assigned to the Netherlands, Sweden, and even Portugal; England would have been established as a prohibitive long shot. Yet, despite colonization efforts that struggled through several calamitous false starts, were grossly underfinanced and woefully inconsistent, England ultimately triumphed, proving yet again that some things cannot be explained.

## References

Alexander, B. 2015. *Higher Education Enrollments Decline Again*. Herndon, VA: National Student Clearing House Research Center (Online).

Axelrod, P. 1997. *Promise of Schooling: Education in Canada, 1800–1914*. Toronto, CAN: University of Toronto Press.

Axtell, J. 2001. *Natives and Newcomers: The Cultural Origins of North America*. New York, NY: Oxford University Press.

Bachman, C. van. 1969. *Peltries or Plantations: The Economic Policies of the Dutch West India Company in New Netherland, 1623–1639*. Baltimore, MD: The Johns Hopkins University Press.

Barber, W. J. 1998. "Remarks on 'American-ness' in American Economic Thought." In *The Economic Mind in America: Essays in the History of American Economics* (M. Rutherford, Editor). London: Routledge: 18–20.

Bayer, H. G. 1925. *The Belgians, First Settlers in New York*. New York, NY: Delvin-Adair.

Benjamin, L. 1997. "Black Women in the Academy: An Overview." In *Black Women in the Academy: Promises and Perils* (L. Benjamin, Editor). Gainsville, FL: University Press of Florida: 9–10.

BLS. 2014. "Economists." In *Occupational Outlook Handbook*. Bureau of Labor Statistics (Online).

BLS. 2015. "Economics Teachers, Postsecondary." In *Occupational Outlook Handbook* (Online).

BLS. 2015a. "Postsecondary Teachers." In *Occupational Outlook Handbook* (Online).

Bolton, H. E., and Marshall, Thomas M. 1920. *The Colonization of North America, 1492 to 1783*. New York, NY: Macmillan.

Boroditsky, L. 2009. "How Does Our Language Shape the Way We Think?" In *What's Next? Dispatches on the Future of Science* (Max Brockman, Editor). New York, NY: Vintage Books: 116–129.

Bourne, E. G. 1904. *Spain in America, 1450–1580*. (Vol. 3 in the series *The American Nation: A History*). New York, NY: Harper & Brothers.

*Bowker*. 2014. "Traditional Print Book Production Dipped Slightly in 2013." Ann Arbor, MI: Bowker. August 5 (Online).

Carr, L. G., and Walsh, L. S. 1988. "Economic Diversification and Labor Organization in the Chesapeake, 1650–1820." In *Work and Labor in Early America* (S. Innes, Editor). Chapel Hill, NC: University of North Carolina Press: 144–188.

CAW. 2012. *A Portrait of the Part-Time Faculty Member*. The Coalition of the Academic Workforce: June (Online).

Chaney, E., and Deagan, K. 1989. "St. Augustine and the La Florida Colony: New Life-styles in a New Land." In *First Encounters: Spanish Explorations in the Caribbean and the United States, 1492–1570* (J. T. Milanich and S. Milbrath, Editors). Gainesville, FL: University of Florida Press:166–182.

Christian, M. 2012. *Integrated but Unequal: Black Faculty in Predominately White Space*. Trenton, NJ: Africa World Press.

Coats, A. W. 1998. "What is American about American Economics?" In *The Economic Mind in America: Essays in the History of American Economics* (M. Rutherford, Editor). London: Routledge: 9–17.

Cohen, M. R. 2009 [1954]. *American Thought: A Critical Sketch*. New Brunswick, NJ: Transaction Publishers.

Collins, S. M. 2000. "Minority Groups in the Economics Profession." *Journal of Economic Perspectives* 14(2): Spring: 133–148.

Cronin, B. 2014. "Despite Rising Profile in Economics, Women Still Trail Men in Academia." *Wall Street Journal*. January 8. (Online).

Croxton, D. 1990–91. "The Cabot Dilemma: John Cabot's 1497 Voyage & the Limits of Historiography." *Essays in History* 33: 42–60.

Dahlgren, S. 1988. "Sweden becomes a Great Power." In *New Sweden in the New World 1638–1655* (R. Ruhnbro, Editor; translated by Richard E. Fisher). Höganäs, Sweden: Wiken: 26–41.

De Vries, J., and Van Der Woude, A. 1997. *The First Modern Economy: Success, Failure, and Perseverance of the Dutch Economy, 1500–1815*. Cambridge: Cambridge University Press.

Eccles, W. J. 1990. *France in America*. East Lansing, MI: Michigan State University Press.

Fischer, D. H. 1989. *Albion's Seed: Four British Folkways in America*. New York, NY: Oxford University Press.

Forget, E. L. 2011. "American Women and the Economics Profession in the Twentieth Century." *Oeconomia* 1(1): 19–30.

Fourcade, M. 2009. *Economists and Societies: Discipline and Profession in the United States, Britain, and France, 1890s to 1990s*. Princeton, NJ: Princeton University Press.

Gannon, M. 1996. "First European Contacts." In *The New History of Florida* (Michael Gannon, Editor). Gainesville, FL: University Press of Florida: 16–39.

Gannon, M. 2003. *Florida, A Short History* (revised edition). Gainesville, FL: University Press of Florida.

Gehring, C. T. 1995. "Hodie Mihi, Cras Tibi: Swedish–Dutch Relations in the Delaware Valley." In *New Sweden in America* (C. E. Hoffecker, *et al.*, Editors). Newark, DE: University of Delaware Press: 69–85.

Grace, G. W. 1987. *The Linguistic Construction of Reality.* London: Croom Helm.

Gross, N., and Simmons, S. 2014. "The Social and Political Views of American College and University Professors." In *Professors and Their Politics* (N. Gross and S. Simmons, Editors). Baltimore, MD: Johns Hopkins University Press: 19–49.

Hartley, J. E., Monks, J., and Robinson, M. D. 2001. "Economists' Publications Patterns." *American Economist* 45(1): 80–85.

Harvey, M. 2008. *Painter in a Savage Land.* New York, NY: Random House.

Hessler, J. W. 2008. *The Naming of America.* London: Giles.

Holbrook, S. 1976. *The French Founders of North America and Their Heritage.* New York, NY: Atheneum.

Jacobs, J. 2005. *New Netherland, A Dutch Colony in Seventeenth Century America.* Leiden, The Netherlands: Brill.

JBHE. 2006. "Almost No Black Economists at Nation's Highest Ranked Universities." *Journal of Blacks in Higher Education* (Online).

Johnson, A. 1911. *The Swedish Settlement on the Delaware, Vols I & II.* New York, NY: University of Pennsylvania.

Johnson, D. S. 1995. *Charting the Sea of Darkness: The Four Voyages of Henry Hudson.* New York, NY: Kodansha International.

Kahn, S. 1995. "Women in the Economics Profession." *Journal of Economic Perspectives* 9(4): Fall: 195–205.

Kammen, M. 1975. *Colonial New York, A History.* New York, NY: Oxford University Press.

Kimball, M., and Anonymous. 2015. "How Big is the Sexism Problem in Economics? This Article's Co-author is Anonymous Because of it." *Quartz.* January 6 (Online).

Kirsch, J. 2008. *The Grand Inquisitor's Manual: A History of Terror in the Name of God.* New York, NY: HarperOne.

Kupperman, K. O. 1995. "Scandinavian Colonists Confront the New World." In *New Sweden in America* (C. E. Hoffecker, *et al.*, Editors). Newark, DE: University of Delaware Press: 89–111.

Landers, J. 1999. *Black Society in Spanish Florida.* Urbana, IL: University of Illinois Press.

Langbert, M., Quain, A. J., and Klein, D. B. 2016. "Faculty Voter Registration in Economics, History, Journalism, Law, and Psychology." *Econ Journal Watch.* September (Online).

Lazarsfeld, P. F., and Thielens, Jr., W. 1958. *The American Mind: Social Scientists in a Time of Crisis.* Glencoe, IL: The Free Press.

Lewis, D. C. 2006. "Jude Wanniski." In *The Biographical Dictionary of American Economists* 2 (R. B. Emmett, Editor). Bristol: Thoemmes Continuum: 887–889.

Lipset, S. M. 1996. *American Exceptionalism: A Double-Edged Sword.* New York, NY: W. W. Norton.

Lyon, E. 1989. "Pedro Menendez's Plan for Settling La Florida." In *First Encounters: Spanish Explorations in the Caribbean and the United States, 1492–1570* (J. T. Milanich and S. Milbrath, Editors). Gainesville, FL: University of Florida Press:150–165.

Major, D. C., and Major, J. S. 2007. *A Huguenot on the Hackensack: David Demarest and His Legacy.* Madison, NJ: Fairleigh Dickinson University Press.

Mann, C. C. 2007. "America Found & Lost." *National Geographic* (May): 34–55.

Mattsson, A. 1987. *New Sweden: the Dream of an Empire* (translated by J. Teeland and J. Franks). Gothenburg, Sweden: Tre Bocker.

McCloskey, D. 2011. "The Prehistory of American Thrift." In *Thrift and Thriving in America: Capitalism and Moral Order from the Puritans to the Present* (J. J. Yates and J. D. Hunter, Editors). New York, NY: Oxford University Press: 61–87.

Merwick, D. 2006. *The Shame and the Sorrow: Dutch-Amerindian Encounters in New Netherland*. Philadelphia, PA: University of Pennsylvania Press.

Milanich, J. T., and Milbrath, S., Editors. 1989. *First Encounters: Spanish Explorations in the Caribbean and the United States, 1492–1570*. Gainesville, FL: University of Florida Press.

Munro, W. B. 1921. *Crusaders of New France*. New Haven, CT: Yale University Press.

NCES. 2016. *Digest of Education Statistics: 2014*. Washington, DC: National Center for Education Statistics: U. S. Department of Education (Online).

Nef, J. U. 1977. "An Early Energy Crisis and its Consequences." *Scientific American*. (Nov.): 140–151.

Neill, R. 1991. *A History of Canadian Economic Thought*. London: Routledge.

Norman, H. 1988. "A Swedish Colony in North America." In *New Sweden in the New World 1638–1655* (R. Ruhnbro, Editor; translated by Richard E. Fisher). Höganäs, Sweden: Wiken: 6–24.

Parkman, F. 1996 [1865]. *Pioneers of France in the New World*. Lincoln, NE: University of Nebraska Press.

Pinker, S. 1994. *The Language Instinct*. New York, NY: William Morrow.

Pinker, S. 2007. *The Stuff of Thought*. New York, NY: Viking.

Romero, J. 2013. "Where Are the Women?" *Econ Focus*. Second Quarter. Federal Reserve Bank of Richmond (Online).

Ruhnbro, R. (ed.). 1988. *New Sweden in the New World 1638–1655* (translated by Richard E. Fisher). Höganäs, Sweden: Wiken.

Rystad, G. 1988. "The Colonization of North America." In *New Sweden in the New World 1638–1655* (R. Ruhnbro, Editor; translated by Richard E. Fisher). Höganäs, Sweden: Wiken: 46–57.

Sakolsky, R., and Koehnline, J. (eds). 1993. *Gone to Croatan: Origins of North American Dropout Culture*. Brooklyn, NY: Autonomedia/AK Press.

Seavoy, R. E. 2006. *An Economic History of the United States: From 1607 to the Present*. New York, NY: Routledge.

Shields, J. A., and Dunn, Sr., J. M. 2016. *Passing on the Right: Conservative Professors in the Progressive University*. New York, NY: Oxford University Press.

Simms, M. C., and Swanton, D. H. 1988. "A Report of the Supply of Black Economists." *Review of Black Political Economy* 17(1): 67–88.

Smith, A. 2013. *It's Not Because You're Black: Addressing Issues of Racism and Underrepresentation of African Americans in Academia*. Lanham, MD: University Press of America.

Smith, B., Mayer, J., and Fritschler, A. 2008. *Closed Minds? Politics and Ideology in American Universities*. Washington, DC: Brookings Institution Press.

Sokoloff, K. L., and Engerman, S. L. 2000. "Institutions, Factor Endowments, and Paths of Development in the New World." *Journal of Economic Perspectives* 14(3): Summer: 217–232.

Soltow, L., and Stevens, E. 1981. *The Rise of Literacy and the Common School in the United States*. Chicago, IL: University of Chicago Press.

Thwaites, R. G. 1905. *France in America, 1497–1763*. New York, NY: Harper & Brothers.

Trigger, B. G., and Swagerty, W. R., 1996. "Entertaining Strangers: North America in the Sixteenth Century." In *The Cambridge History of the Native Peoples of the Americas: Vol 1; North America; Part 1* (B. G. Trigger and W. E. Washburn, Editors). Cambridge: Cambridge University Press: 325–398.

U.S. Department of Education, National Center for Education Statistics. 2016. *Digest of Education Statistics, 2014*. Table 105.50.

Wanniski, J. 1978. *The Way the World Works: How Economies Fail – and Succeed*. New York, NY: Simon and Schuster.

Ward, C. 1938. *New Sweden on the Delaware*. Philadelphia, PA: University of Pennsylvania Press.

Weber, P. J. 1992. *The Spanish Frontier in North America*. New Haven, CT: Yale University Press.

Zeiller, W. 2005. *A Prehistory of South Florida*. Jefferson, NC: McFarland & Company.

# 2 Economic thought among American aboriginals prior to European contact

## Introduction

American economic thinking began thousands of years prior to the arrival of Europeans and the purpose of this chapter is to explore the nature of economic thought among indigenous Americans prior to 1492, a task easier to describe than to execute as will be explained shortly. Additionally, the subject matter of this chapter allows for a partial investigation of the interface between economics and several other disciplines – notably anthropology, archaeology, history, philosophy, psychology, and sociology – the sort of intellectual cross-fertilization that was once fairly common but in the era of academic specialization is now comparatively infrequent.

## Intellectual history without documents

The history of economic thought is a sub-discipline of intellectual history, broadly defined as the story of ideas and the people who create them. Ideas develop in context. A basic tenet of intellectual history is that an analysis of thinking and the processes producing it require an understanding of the thinkers' cultural environment. Within this framework, the thinking of persons who create ideas are typically revealed through the written word, that is, transcribed speeches, personal journals, or published works. In the lexicon of cultural anthropology, this is an *emic* viewpoint or the participants' description and/or interpretation of their culture, institutions, and values (Pike 1954, 8–28). The usual path to discovery in the field of intellectual history does not work for pre-Colombian aboriginals as native-American societies were preliterate by modern standards (Posner 1980, 1). Indeed, in all North America prior to 1492, only the Olmecs, Mayans, and Zapotecs in Mesoamerica developed true writing (Driver 1969, 50–51). Of these civilizations, the Mayans are considered the most advanced but their writing did not go beyond ideographic glyphs, comparable to ancient Egyptian and Chinese, and has only recently been deciphered (Coe 1992). Indigenous societies of the 50 United States had an oral tradition used mostly for the intergenerational communication of philosophical truths and societal norms and less for how-to knowledge or factual information. Prior to 1492 none of these groups had a written language. In the absence of a written legacy that reveals the Amerindians' self-described approaches to economics in theory or practice, an intellectual history of their economic thought must build on information derived from first-hand European accounts and a rich and growing body of data drawn from archaeology and anthropological interpretations thereof (Trigger 1968, 1–5). This is an *etic* focus or the observers' interpretation of a society's culture and institutions, a view point that may be subject to ethnocentric biases and other limitations (Pike 1954). Archaeological discoveries and their anthropological interpretations offer circumstantial evidence about the lifestyles of preliterate societies from which inferences about the practices, institutions, and thought patterns of said societies can be made. Specifically, economic anthropology is the sub-field that considers the central issue of anthropology – human behavior within a network of social relationships and cultural influences – through the lens of economics. There are two major approaches in economic anthropology, formalism and substantivism.

The formalist approach is associated with mainstream economics and is based on what some scholars consider the three universals of the human condition: scarcity, trade-offs, and opportunity costs. Consider the so-called "20/80 rule," that is 20 percent of the causes produce 80 percent of the effects. Formalists put the three universals in the 20 percent of causes producing 80 percent of the effects when it comes to economic behavior. By invoking *ceteris paribus,* formalists marginalize the other 80 percent of the causes and conclude that the three universals shape the choice system human groups develop to allocate limited resources among competing uses. This is a pure etic focus which assumes that the prevailing neoclassical synthesis – rational agents (humans) seek to maximize satisfaction and achieve a stable equilibrium given steady preference functions and sufficient information – can be applied to all peoples regardless of the time, place, or social context in which they exist (Pryor 1977; Schneider 1974).

Substantivists see things differently. Some substantivists, notably culturalists, reject the formalists' notions regarding the very universality of scarcity, trade-offs, and opportunity costs (Elardo and Campbell 2007). Other substantivists accept the presence of the universals but question their importance. These substantivists would argue that in many societies, some or all of the three universals are in the 80 percent of the causes producing 20 percent of the effects. In such instances the universals are relatively insignificant in achieving the fundamental questions of what to produce, how, and for whom. In much the same way that small variations in DNA can create vast biological diversity, substantivists believe a myriad of factors, some seemingly inconsequential, created aboriginal economies, and those systems can only be appreciated from an emic perspective or a least a focus that is empathetic to circumstances prevalent when economies emerged. Rejecting the *a priori* reasoning of formalists, substantivists maintain that each preliterate economy is an entity unto itself and needs to be studied accordingly. By imposing the neoclassical synthesis of mainstream economics on these primitive systems, formalists minimize the differences between preliterate economies rather than celebrating their distinctions, which is precisely what substantivists do (Dalton 1961; Sahlins 1972; Herskovits 1940, 1952).

The first salvo in the formalist/substantivist debate was probably fired in 1941 when the mainstream economist Frank Knight published in the *Journal of Political Economy* a review critical of Melville Herskovits' substantivist book *The Economic Life of Primitive People*. In 1957 Karl Polanyi crystallized the substantivist approach in his classic essay "The Economy as Instituted Process." A decade later Harold Demsetz did the same for the formalist viewpoint in an article published in the *American Economic Review*. The intensity of the formalist/substantivist debate has varied over time, burning white-hot in the 1960s, then cooling for a while only to reemerge in the early twenty-first century, less spirited than previously but just as profound. The rift is still there and the once purely academic debate has taken on the overtones of an ideological dispute. Either-or disagreements often lead researchers to seek out instances that confirm their position rather than seeing what is there, and "while many of the arguments seem models of good sense, the total effect has been to confirm everyone in his original prejudice" (Sahlins 1972, xiii).

Enter cultural materialism. Attributed to Marvin Harris, cultural materialism "is based on the simple premise that human social life is a response to the practical problems of earthly existence" (Harris 1979, ix). Not so much a school of anthropology as a way to develop a science of culture, cultural materialism rejects the near dogmatic approaches of formalism versus substantivism for a more eclectic view, placing "no restrictions on methodological techniques as long as they conform to the need for public and replicable operations in conformity with general epistemological principles of the scientific way of knowing" (Harris 1979, 290). Rather than rejecting out-of-hand one approach over another, cultural materialism is more inclusive, regarding as worthy any scholarship that contributes to the scientific of culture, believing that "*both* emic and etic analyses are essential for a thorough understanding of sociocultural phenomena" (Murphy and Margolis 1995, 4).

Consider the nature of human nature, an issue at the crux of the formalists-substantivist-culturalist debate (LeClair and Schneider 1968; Cook 1973; Wilk 1996). Formalists see humans as "naturally uncooperative and self-centered beings who view life as a zero-sum game (Schneider 1974, 26). Given this 'natural' disposition, a market system is perceived as the most effective means of harnessing human economic so as to promote the social good. Substantivists/culturalists view humans as cooperative and magnanimous, qualities that speak to a non-competitive economic system as one most likely to further self-actualization and social well-being. The obvious popularity of market-system economies seems to give some credence to the formalists' view of human nature, but substantivists, claiming intellectual hegemony, argue that this is matter of learning not preference, as they believe economic behavior is acquired not innate (Rodrigues 2004). By contrast formalists see economic behavior as integral to the human condition and inherently innate. This dichotomous question – Is economic behavior innate or acquired? – has other answers including both.

Reasoning by analogy, consider the case of language: Is it innate or acquired? Science indicates (Pinker 1994) that humans are hardwired for language, making it innate, but the specific language or languages a person speaks are essentially environmentally determined, that is, acquired. As Charles Darwin put it, language is "an instinctive tendency to acquire an art" (Pinker 1994, 20). Economic behavior is instinctive as all persons or groups confront choices and resource allocation. Economics is the study of that aspect of human behavior, and not as is often perceived, the study of the type of society, individualistic or communalistic, in which that behavior takes place (Burling 1962). How choices are made about consumption, production, and distribution within the context of society is essentially learned or acquired. In the spirit if not the letter of cultural materialism – and a paraphrase of Darwin with a dash of Alfred Marshall ([1890] 1964, 1) – economic behavior is an innate tendency to become proficient in the ordinary business of life. Taking an either/or approach causes a hardening of intellectual arteries and inhibits the search for a science of culture.

Reflecting the ecumenical spirit embedded in cultural materialism, this chapter draws on the collective scholarship of economic anthropologists of whatever stripe and merges those findings with contemporary written accounts of European colonials and the research of archaeologists, historians, demographers, biologists, and others who have studied aboriginal peoples. The goal is to create a holographic representation of pre-Columbian Amerindians from which can be extracted meaningful generalizations about their economic thinking (Jennings 1993, 90–97). This model of economic thought has to be representative of an admittedly diverse indigenous population, so diverse that at least 250 "mutually unintelligible languages" were spoken before 1492 in what is now the United States (Johansen 2005, 3). This chapter is essentially an inductive empirical analysis designed to infer the underlying patterns of economic thought among pre-contact Americans (Trigger 1968, 3–4). In terms of descriptive statistics, this approach is equivalent to a measure of central tendency such as the mean, a parameter whose value "represents" an entire population even though no single bit of information in the data set being summarized may in fact be equal to that parameter. The idea is to tease a broad yet accurate model of Amerindian economics from a multitude of sources about aboriginal life styles, customs, practices, and policies. The thinking is that understanding the infrastructure and structure of pre-Columbian societies would make it possible to induce the underlying philosophical precepts and values that were at the core of American economic thought prior to 1492. Moving from actual conditions and behavior to discovering the principles that motivate actions is full of difficulties that require several caveats to appreciate.

First, early descriptions of indigenous societies are sometimes problematic and must be accepted with discretion. Amerindians may not have left written accounts of their economics but early Europeans who visited the so-called New World kept logs and journals that directly or indirectly described the economic lifestyles of Western hemisphere aboriginals. These writings represent quasi-emic viewpoints in that the observers were contemporaries of the participants. "To understand long-ago Indian lives, one cannot avoid accounts of the first literate people who saw them," but as historical records "colonial reports leave much to be desired" (Mann 2006, 280). Many of those early writers considered indigenous peoples to be less than human, frequently using the term "savages" to register contempt or loathing, a descriptor that was not always a pejorative. Even authors who viewed aboriginals through a prism of admiration use the work "savages" in their empathetic descriptions (Morton [1637] 1967).

Beside the nomenclature issues, the motivations for these early authors are sometimes problematic. Much of what the first Europeans said about the New World had less to do with a sense of history and more with career advancement, derelictions of duty, or both as evident in the story of Gaspar de Carvajal, a Dominican priest credited with authoring the first description of the Amazon Riven and the indigenous people inhabiting its banks (Mann 2006, 280–286). On an unauthorized six-month voyage down the Amazon to the Atlantic Ocean, Carvajal created a paper trail to justify his caper. He wrote extensively of frequent and hostile encounters with native river people, including a battle with Amazons – "tall, topless women who fought without quarter and lived without men" (Mann 2006, 284). Because of this and other improbable anecdotes, Carvajal's peers challenged the accuracy and purpose of his manuscript, which was not published formally until 1894.

The *Jesuit Relations*, a landmark set of reports and narratives written between 1610 and 1791 by French Jesuit missionaries at their stations in New France, a land area that today traverses Canada and the US, are a counterpoint to Carvajal's journal. Originally produced in Paris as annual volumes, the *Relations* were translated and edited by R. G. Thwaites in a series of 73 texts published from 1896 through 1901. The standard academic bromide about the *Relations* – that they are "invaluable as historical sources for French exploration and native relations and also as a record of the various indigenous tribes of the region before the influence of settlers and missionaries changed them" (Columbia Encyclopedia) – is half right. Scholars generally agree that the journalistic *Relations* contain reliable reports compared with much of what was previously written about other indigenous peoples of the Western Hemisphere. However, the claim that the Jesuit portrayals of Amerindians were made before colonial influences had changed these aboriginals is suspect. "The discovery of America by Christopher Columbus initiated the most dramatic and far-reaching cross-fertilization of cultures in the history of the world" (Driver 1969, 554). The impact and influences were large and immediate, especially to the population of Amerindians, the dramatic decline of which has to be understood so one can appreciate why a discussion of aboriginal economics deals with the time period prior to 1492.

Estimates of the pre-Colombian population of the United States vary, ranging from a low of one million (Johansen 2005, 44) to a high of 12.5 million (Dobyns 1966, 415), with a generally accepted figure of 2.5 million (Driver 1969, 63). By the first third of the seventeenth century when the Jesuits began writing their reports, the aboriginal population was about 500,000 or roughly 20 percent of the commonly accepted 1492 level. Depopulation of this magnitude also occurred in Mesoamerica where the population fell to around 5 million from the consensus peak of 25 million in basically the same time period (Mann 2006, 94). The experience in Hawaii tends to corroborate their sudden population declines, declines that some critics claim have been exaggerated in magnitude and duration. From 1778 when Captain James Cook and his English expedition visited the islands, the Hawaiian population dropped to the 40,000–50,000 range within twenty-five years or about 20 percent of the pre-contact peak estimated at 300,000 (Fuchs 1961, 4). As was the case in North and Central America, this decimation of population was attributable to three factors – disease, demoralization, and warfare with colonials – of which first was by far the most devastating (Trigger and Swagerty, 361–369).

A thousand years of contacts between the humans living in Asia, Africa, and Europe with each other and all sorts of viruses and microbes had enabled the peoples of those continents to acquire immunity to a number of terminal diseases or at least the ability to co-exist with many deadly pathogens. By contrast, the ancestors of American aboriginals developed in isolation after the Bering ice bridge vanished some 5,000–25,000 years ago. Human migration is a primary cause of epidemics, and "when migrations take place, those creatures who have been longest in isolation suffer most, for their genetic material has been least tempered by the variety of world diseases" (Crosby 1972, 30). Having entered the cul-de-sac of the New World before the continental intermingling of peoples 'inoculated' large portions of the planet's inhabitants against epidemics, indigenous Americans were particularly vulnerable to many Old World diseases, major or minor. To be sure the New World was not a disease-free zone. Evidence indicates that smallpox had visited South America before the Spanish, and tuberculosis had plagued parts of the United States before Hernando de Soto's disease-carrying expedition of 1539 (Shaffer 1992, 82). Colonists and their livestock, especially pigs (Mann 2006, 97–99), transmitted a deadly combination of human and zoonotic diseases to Amerindians. Even measles, a childhood nuisance in Europe by the sixteenth century, could create havoc on indigenous peoples. Traveling the same route along the Mississippi River where less than 150 years earlier de Soto had found some 50 aboriginal villages, the French explorer René-Robert Cavelier de la Salle found fewer ten during his 1662 voyage (Mann 2006, 98). In a tragic twist of history, Amerindian medicine may have exacerbated the depopulation problem; sweating lodges, a common therapeutic among aboriginals for treating a number of everyday aliments, probably hastened the spread of many communicable diseases, particularly smallpox (Bruce 1896, 188).

The devastating effects of colonial diseases were uneven, having greater impact on the well-being of sedentary, agricultural-based aboriginal societies than on the health of less well established tribes of nomadic hunter/gatherers. This means that the native cultures colonials observed and described in their journals and logs were different in degree if not kind from pre-Columbian indigenous societies. Early written accounts of these peoples, however important, must be respected for their limitations as well as their insights. The value of such writings is heightened when their contents are cross-referenced with the physical evidence that archaeologists have amassed, which brings us to a second caveat about reconstructing ancient cultures. Cultural materialism has a strong affinity for archaeology because of the latter's inherently scientific process of discovery (Harris 2001, 145–146; 647–681). Based on material culture defined as the structures and objects people make and use, "archaeological data don't deliberately mislead readers" (Kehoe 2002, 1). Nevertheless, archaeological evidence has its limits. On May 30, 1539, Hernando de Soto and his fleet of ten ships landed near Tampa Bay, Florida. The expeditionary force consisted of six hundred soldiers, two hundred horses, and an "ambulatory meat locker" of three hundred pigs (Mann 2006, 97–98). In search of gold and other forms of instant wealth, the expedition spent four years wandering through the Southeast visiting a land area ten states now occupy. The voyage of this private army was well documented and, in geologic time, took place yesterday, figuratively speaking. Yet, despite knowing exactly where to look for artifacts, archaeological verification of the journey is virtually nonexistent (Kehoe 2002, 53).

The last caveat concerning the methodology of this chapter deals with replication, a cornerstone of any science, be it physical or social. Economics is not the physics of social sciences; never has been and never will be. If there is a scientific metaphor for economics it is probably meteorology, a discipline were predictions are couched in probabilities, not mathematical certainties. It would be audacious to claim that other scholars traveling the terrain this chapter covers would come to the same conclusions exactly. There is, however, an expectation that if researchers, genuinely committed to "seeing what is there," were to mine the currently available stocks of knowledge about indigenous peoples, they would identify, more or less, the same basic set of behavioral propensities that were generally but not necessarily universally evident in the economic thinking of American aboriginals prior to 1492. This chapter now turns to the application of the methodology described above to the world of American aboriginals as it was prior to 1492. First to be considered are the material conditions of pre-Columbian America, that is, the kinds and quantities of resources available to indigenous Americans. Following that is an examination of the institutional arrangements that governed consumption, production, distribution, and exchange/ trade in the aboriginal world, all of which, in turn, serves as a backdrop for an interpretative exploration about the nature of aboriginal economic thought.

## Material conditions

The standard categories of resources or factors of production – human (labor), natural (land), capital (building, tools), and know-how (technology) – were evident to one degree or another in every Amerindian economy, whether that economy was centered on hunting/gathering, agriculture, or a combination of the two. Before considering the magnitude of human resources (population) in pre-1492 America, a few words are in order regarding the origins of these peoples. While the genetic origin of indigenous Americans is a matter of debate and may never be known with certainty, people who were the common ancestors of present-day Chinese and Japanese are the likely biological sources of Amerindians (Crosby 1972, 23). In the late Pleistocene (Ice Age) when oceans were 400–500 feet below current levels, these Asians crossed a land bridge over the Bering Strait pursuing the big game they hunted for food and clothing (Smith 1999, 59). An obvious exception is Hawaii whose first inhabitants probably came from French Polynesia, possibly Tahiti, about 1,500 years ago (Fuchs 1961, 4). There is general but not universal agreement that there were two major periods of migration to North America. The first or earlier one came about 30,000–50,000 years before the current era (BCE) and the second between 5,000–20,000 years BCE (Driver 1969, 4). Other theories suggest that some migrants to the New World came by sea from Polynesia or Africa, but the prevailing view is that the bulk of pre-Columbian peoples who populated the West Hemisphere from Alaska to Patagonia came from Asia (Cameron and Neal 2003, 91).

At the dawn of the sixteenth century, total population of the United States was 2.5–3.0 million, with more than 90 percent living in the forty-eight contiguous states. This population total had been remarkably stable over a long stretch of time as population growth among indigenous Americans – around one-twentieth of 1 percent per year – was probably comparable to that of other pre-literate, pre-Columbian peoples (Haub 1995). For the country as a whole, overall population density was less than one person per square mile, ranging from a high of about fifty persons per square mile in Hawaii to a low of approximately one person per every four square miles in Alaska. By comparison, European countries at about the time of contact had a total population estimated at 81 million, with population densities ranging from 30–90 persons per square mile (Zambardino 1980, 2). In the forty-eight contiguous states, population density was at most one person per square mile; "Population density varied directly with the productivity of the economy; it was greatest in those areas that practiced settled agriculture and lowest where the inhabitants still lived by hunting and gathering" (Cameron and Neal 2003, 91). One exception to this general rule was the Pacific Northwest where ready access to abundant fisheries permitted a population density higher than that found in the farming regions of the Eastern United States (Driver 1969, 94).

With the exception of Hawaii, which had a well-developed feudal system with a king (or two) for each major island (Barnes 1999, 13–15), Amerindians lived in stateless societies where the household or clan of related persons was the basic social, political, and economic unit (Wilk 1996, 15). Clusters of households sometimes joined to form kinship groups, kinship groups combined to become tribes, and tribes banded together to create nations or confederacies (Driver 1969, 306–307). Among California plant gatherers, the village was the fundamental social and political unit, and tribes were "mere loose aggregates of villages which recognized no central authority" (Linton 1943, 48). The size of the different population groupings varied greatly depending on a number of factors such as climate, topography, the availability of arable land, and the methods of producing foodstuffs. In arctic Alaska the hostile environment meant that hunting was just about the only source of food, and inhabitants lived principally in kinship groups of at most several families. In the forty-eight contiguous states, tribes of a few hundred to several thousand were evident, depending on the importance of agriculture in the supply of food. Generally, tribe size varied directly with the extent to which farming provided for nutritional needs (Driver 1969, 81). Confederacies were rare. The Iroquois Confederacy of five tribes located primarily in New York State had a maximum population of 15,000–25,000. Cahokia, a virtually urban area on the eastern bank of the Mississippi River near St. Louis, Missouri, had a maximum population estimated at 30,000–40,000. Life expectancy among indigenous American at the time of contact was about 35 years, roughly the same as that of the Europeans who came in the 1500s.

As with most preliterate peoples, the division of labor among Amerindians was based primarily on gender and age (Schneider 1974, 45). Men did most of the hunting, fishing, land clearing, and community defense. In over half the areas that aboriginals occupied, hunting, gathering, and fishing supplied nearly all the food stuffs consumed (Driver 1969, 84). Women were engaged chiefly in household management and agriculture, which in some regions of the US provided 80 percent or more of the diet (Driver 1969, 85). Everyone was expected to work and usually did so in communal groups, be it 100 or so men engaged in an organized hunt, a group of women tending to their personal gardens or the tribal plots, or both sexes working together on tasks dependent on gender cooperation (Bruhns and Stothert 1999, 33). While universal contribution to the work effort was expected, exemptions were made for the infirm, the very young, and the aged. The gender-based division of labor was common with notable exceptions. Role reversal was manifested in societies where agriculture displaced hunting/gathering as the prime source of food (Driver 1969, 81), or where a task was always assigned via custom to one gender or the other. For example, among the Navahos and Pueblos of the Southwest, men did the farming in addition to their other duties. Some scholars hypothesize that some gender-based divisions of labor were a way to economize on information searches in situations where determining individual comparative advantage was difficult to ascertain due to the communal nature of work (Posner 1980a, 612).

The economic success of Amerindians required a large and growing endowment of human capital (knowledge) which, in the absence of written language, had to be communicated from one generation to the next by word and/or deed (Smith 1999, 68–69). This reservoir of information dealt with all aspects of indigenous life and its extent and complexity may best be exemplified by considering food. Aboriginal Americans ate from a smorgasbord of around 1,500 species of plants, about 2 percent of which were cultivated. They consumed about 1,000 species of animals. Taking plants and animals in combinations of twos and threes yields an enormous number of dishes and respective recipes (Driver 1969, 89). When multiplied by various methods of preparation and preservation, the human capital of just processing food becomes staggering. Similar stores of aboriginal human capital were present in life's other basics – construction of dwellings, assembly of clothing, fabrication of tools – as well as the intergenerational transfer of societal customs, norms, values, and history. That aboriginals lived close with the natural world is obvious, however, that coexistence had become the basis of a long-standing myth, namely that indigenous peoples lived "in sacred natural harmony of and with Nature" (Mann 2006, 247). Traceable to such luminaries as Henry David Thoreau, this notion embraces the idea that aboriginals, being unwilling or unable to control their natural surroundings, left the Earth pretty much the way they found it. Amerindians did manifest an extraordinary reverence for nature and especially the landscape. Nonetheless, they actively transformed the natural resources at their disposal, altering the environment within the parameters of their preferences and technology. At the time of first contact, "native Americans *were* living in balance with Nature – but they had their thumbs on the scale" (Mann 2006, 252).

Almost without exception indigenous societies across the forty-eight contiguous states shaped their environments using a variety of techniques, especially fire. Except for the dog, American aboriginals had no domesticated animals; nevertheless they still practiced animal husbandry on wild game by burning undergrowth, which increased the number of herbivores and the predators that fed on them, the basic food stuffs in the Amerindian's agricultural supply chains. Fire played a particularly significant role in farming as practiced in the Eastern third of the country. The agricultural implements native Americans had – pointed sticks and hoes – could not break the hardened sod that covered the prairies and other areas of open land in the contiguous states. Opportunity costs made it more economical "to clear woods than to till the tough soils of open county" (Driver 1969, 80). Burning was the principal but by no means only method used to create spaces for indigenous garden farming or horticulture, as cultivation using only hand tools is often called. In the American Southwest resource management focused on water or rather lack thereof. Large, intricate irrigation systems were common in southern Arizona dating from the year 800 CE (Driver 1969, 78, 437). Second only to agriculture in terms of food productivity per acre, fishing was also a managed activity in the Pacific Northwest where weirs and traps boosted yields of fisheries above what they would have been otherwise. The active management and administration of natural resources gave rise to externalities that were fairly evident in small, household-centered communities. These externalities, in turn, led to the development of property rights as a way to internalize the costs and benefits created (Demsetz 1967, 350–353).

Amerindians created a variety of rights that applied to land as well as to other forms of property, tangible and intellectual. These rights were typically embodied in social customs and norms which served as a *de facto* legal system, thus minimizing information costs in a world of stateless societies with no formal mechanisms for arbitrating disputes and enforcing compliance (Posner 1980, 32–34). Property rights pertaining to land frequently depended on the type of use, local ecology, and the prevailing techniques of exploitation (Linton 1943, 42–54). Farm land was often covered by usufructuary rights, that is, an individual, family, kinship group, or tribe had exclusive rights to usage as long as cultivation was seasonally continuous (Posner 1980, 32–33). Usufruct or possessory rights could be transferred within the group working a particular tract of land according to established lines of inheritance, be they matriarchal, patriarchal, both, or simply kinship group (Driver 1969, 271). Possessory rights lapsed if cultivation ceased or was suspended even for a single growing season. Given the abundance of land relative to the low population density, most agricultural-centered communities abandoned land as soon as its productivity began to wane. Left to fallow, a plot could change hands if a new individual or group began to work the land others once 'owned' (Linton 1943, 49). Although clans in some California tribes had indefinite claims to privately held hunting lands, ownership of land in hunting-based societies was generally communal. Individual ownership of an area that migrating game roamed made little economic sense as organized group hunts worked best on land held in common (Linton 1943, 43). Similar logic for communal property rights held sway among the Eskimos who hunted large sea mammals along the Arctic Coast. In contrast to the quasi-private ownership implied in usufruct rights, the Navaho system of land tenure was more individualistic; a household that first cultivated a specific garden plot could retain use rights indefinitely (Linton, 52). Aboriginal land rights could also be seasonal in that during the summer when economies of scale could be realized, property rights could be communal. Private or household rights prevailed in the winter when food was relatively scarce "and the best chances of survival were gained by solitary or familial hunting and gathering" (Bailey 1992, 189).

The elaborate array of land rights that Amerindians followed was replicated for other forms of property (Driver 1969, 269–270; 283–285). Portable capital goods such as teepees, tools, canoes, and other objects used exclusively or nearly so by a single individual or family were mostly regarded as private property. Stationary or fixed capital goods such as permanent shelters, fishing weirs, and shared hunting grounds were subject to communal rights of ownership and use. Intellectual rights for such items as songs, dances, and family crests were also recognized; ownership and exclusivity of use could be restricted to a specific person, clan, or a larger group. Within a given tribe or comparable group, a single individual might exercise a variety of rights such as private ownership of tools, family ownership of housing, communal owner-ship of farm lands, and "the right to sing a bear song at a public ceremony" by virtue of having slain a bear (Driver 1969, 270). That they respected "almost all conceivable structure of rights" was also good economics (Bailey 1992, 183), an inescapable conclusion if one sees much of economic behavior as just common sense.

The material conditions in pre-contact America in terms of land and labor can be characterized as relatively plentiful, but compared to European norms, American aboriginals had limited stocks of capital. Still, what they did have was used efficiently and effectively.

> Without steel and iron tools, wheeled vehicles, gunpowder, large sailing ships, or keystone arches or domes, Native peoples with the present-day borders of the United States maintained extensive trade routes, practiced irrigated agriculture using dams and canals, and built cities that supported populations estimated in the tens of thousands.
>
> (Barrington 1999a, 5)

One of the most important capital assets virtually every Amerindian used for part if not all of the year was a house. Permanent dwellings ran the gamut from Eskimo domed houses built of snow blocks and meant to shelter a solitary family to the spacious Iroquois longhouse whose typical wood frame and shingles enclosed some 20,000 cubic feet, providing space for several families often from a single clan. Tools were another important item of personal capital and included the stone axe and other implements related to agri-culture; instruments used in the fabrication of textiles and clothing (Bruhns and Stothert 1999, 145); canoes, rafts, and boats, especially those used in long-distance trading; and the indispensable bow and arrow. The latter proved especially durable even after contact. European muzzle-loading rifles were very awkward for hunting, and even the availability of breech-loading guns and cartridge munitions did not displace the bow and arrow, which became obsolete "only after the repeating rifle appeared" (Driver 1969, 512).

In addition to stocks of private or restricted-use capital goods, indigenous Americans had civil or public capital goods that were communally owned and/or operated. The Pueblos brought sustainable agriculture to the arid Southwest through the construction of elaborate irrigation works (Johansen 2005, 35). Unlike other tribes that typically settled on or near rivers or other waterways for transportation and trade purposes (Hoebel 1954, 127), the Pueblo had to build an extensive system of roads to ship surplus food stocks to trading partners. On the Pacific northwest coast weirs were used to harvest fish, especially salmon and other migratory water game. Although technically private capital, weirs were *de facto* public capital goods as other households or village members were seldom denied use (Driver 1969, 87–88). In the East,

Iroquois typically surrounded a cluster of 30 to 150 longhouses with a wooden palisade consisting of small or midsized tree trunks aligned vertically with no spaces in between (Fenton 1985, 7). For defensive purposes, palisades were bona fide public goods. American aboriginals compensated for their dearth of capital with a level of technical know-how that allowed them to exploit their respective environments with minimal effort that yielded surprisingly fruitful results. By observing the consequences of lightning-caused fires, Amerindians stumbled onto a variant of the Schumpeterian notion of "creative destruction" (Schumpeter 1950, 81–86) and came to understand that managed fires could create more than they destroyed.

> Firing broadened the margins of natural grasslands, in some areas adding thousands of square kilometers of grazing for bison or deer … [thus maintaining] … favored game populations higher than natural environments would have provided.
>
> (Kehoe 2002, 27)

In some parts of the country, hunting was consciously monitored – especially the taking of smaller, non-migratory mammals – to prevent depletion. Conservation was also evident in the Pacific Northwest where the harvesting of trees was subject to "sustainable yields" to insure continued growth (Johansen 2005, 34).

Amerindians were particularly skilled botanists when it came to the domestication of wild plants for human consumption. The core of the food supply in the Americas was the 'three sisters' – maize, beans, and squash – all of which originated in Mesoamerica. Aboriginals in America adapted and refined the 'sisters,' often planting them together "to maintain nitrogen and phosphorus through bacteria and fungi roots" (Kehoe 2002, 44). The botanical prowess of Amerindians was evident in their large number of cultivated originals including pumpkins, blueberries, and green beans (Driver and Driver 1967, 4). The Mississippians of Cahokia in the American Midwest created what modern scholars refer to as Woodhenge, 48 vertically-positioned wooden posts, each 20–30 feet high, spaced evenly apart along the circumference of a precise circle some 410 feet in diameter (Shaffer 1992, 54; Wittry 1969). A play on the name Stonehenge, Woodhenge marked solstices, equinoxes, and other astronomical events important to agricultural cycles and the dating of festivals and other social ceremonies.

To be sure, aboriginal science and technology were pre-Newtonian, not in the significance of their accomplishments but in their outlook. Amerindians did not yet believe "that the external world was subject to a few knowable laws, and was systematically capable of productive manipulation" (Rostow 1971, 4). Nevertheless, indigenous Americans were inventive within the context of their environment. For example, the Iroquois had an ingenious way of making axes, arguably the most important tool in stone-age technology (Stites 1904, 45). First a blade was fashioned from slate or other hard stone, then chipped and polished to give it a sharp edge. Next, the blade was inserted into a vertical slit make in a 4–5-inch diameter hardwood sapling growing in the forest. In two or three years, the axe maker would return to the tree, cut it down, and carve an axe from the sapling, its wooden handle and blade a single piece ready for immediate use. The process insured that the blade was attached to the handle as permanently as any space-age adhesive can affix one surface to another. Given the time and energy invested in making them, axes became a lasting addition to the tribe's capital stock even though they were privately owned.

Aboriginal Americans did not think of themselves as having dominion over nature, nor were they its mindless servants. Neither above or below nature, aboriginals were part of the landscape, which to them was more than infinite, it was eternal (Wilson 1999, 24). As was true of most preliterate societies, pre-Columbian technological change was marked by long periods of constancy occasionally punctuated with a breakthrough that could be characterized as revolutionary (Smith 1999, 72–73). Indigenous peoples of America had no notion of progress comparable to that of the Westerners who enter their world after 1492 (Waters 2004, xix). Amerindians' reluctance to initiate change was the result of two factors: first, the incentive to change was low given the abundance of their environment, and second, the high opportunity costs associated with failure discouraged experimentation (Smith 1999, 67–68; Schneider 1974, 185; Posner 1980, 10–11). Aboriginal technology proceeded slowly, adhering to the adage that "necessity is the mother of invention." Indigenous Americans neither avoided change nor created it systematically. They did adapt and adjust to change whether exogenous such as meteorological or geological events, or endogenous/induced changes that come with breakthroughs or scientific discoveries.

The institutions of consumption, production, and distribution were as nearly as stable in the indigenous, pre-Columbian world, as were the states of science and technology. Supply chains in primitive economies have few links; "Production is for the benefit of the producers" (Sahlins 1972, 77). In advanced economic systems consumption, production, and distribution are easily compartmentalized and each can be discussed independently of the others. Consumption, production, and distribution in preliterate economic systems occurred almost simultaneously; there was little separation in time or space between these activities. Accordingly, the discussion that follows braids together the three basic processes to reveal the economic thinking that Amerindians invoked when addressing the fundamental questions of what to produce, how, and for whom.

Thomas Hobbes' use of the New World as an example of a stateless society where life is "solitary, poor, nasty, brutish, and short" spoke to the life after 1492 not before (Hobbes [1651] 1985, 107–108). As recently as 1570 the population of the United States was nearly 100 percent indigenous. When *Leviathan* was published in 1651, the country's population was 85 percent indigenous and 15 percent non-indigenous. The 50/50 split came around 1750.

About 75 years later the aboriginal population had fallen to 2 percent (Barrington 1999a, 8), Alexis de Tocqueville in his penetrating analysis of nineteenth-century American culture wrote "one must go more than a hundred leagues into the interior of the continent to meet with an Indian. These savages have not only withdrawn, they are destroyed" (de Tocqueville [1835] 2000, 308). Prior to contact, life for Amerindians was the antithesis of the Hobbesian depiction.

With two exceptions, pre-contact Amerindians lived in a veritable Garden of Eden largely of their own making (Mann 2006, 320–323) although some scholars challenge the idea that pre-1492 America was a gastronomical cornucopia (Fagan 2005, 237–263). The exceptions were Hawaiians who lived *in* the Garden of Eden literally, and indigenous Alaskans, especially those near the Arctic Circle, whose lives resembled that of Hobbes's characterization. Inexhaustible supplies of acorns, beechnuts, wheat, oats, squash, all sorts of berries, and other vegetable food stuffs, some cultivated, most growing wild, were readily available to the vast majority of Amerindians. These sources of nutrition were supplemented with ample stocks of protein in the form of millions of bison, pronghorns, elk, deer, mountain sheep, passenger pigeons, and unimaginable quantities of fish (Mann 2006, 318). The bounty was a direct result of the skill with which indigenous Americans managed their environments over the long haul despite periodic mistakes. This abundance of consumables created a truly affluent society "in which all … people's material wants [were] easily satisfied" (Sahlins 1972, 1). As was the case for most pre-literate peoples, Amerindians adopted a Zen approach to consumption, "that human material wants are finite and few, and technical means unchanging but on the whole adequate" (Sahlins 1972, 2). This produced a standard of living that was easily attainable, astonishingly stable, and more than ample. The economic conundrum of unlimited wants pitted against limited means was not a puzzle indigenous Americans had to solve.

In the areas of production and distribution, Amerindians appear to have adhered to a standard communist platitude: from each according to his or her abilities, to each according to his or her needs. However, "Aborigines were not at all Marxians" (Dalton 1978, 143). When it came to dividing the fruits of their labors, American aboriginals embraced the Golden Rule, treating others as they would like to be treated, understanding that this ethic applies to the basic wants and needs all people share but not to personal idiosyncrasies or deviant behavior (Binmore 2005, 129–130). Distribution systems in most primitive societies usually follow one of three types: reciprocity, redistribution, or pooling. Reciprocity is generally synonymous with gift giving or social exchange between equals with the expectation of deference or obligations in return the value received (Schneider 1974, 248; Sahlins 1965, 141). Redistribution is exchange among unequals where wealth gravitates to a political or religious center to be redistributed to people in return for obedience and/or explicit services rendered (Schneider 1974, 249). Pooling, as the name implies, is within the group (Sahlins 1965, 41). While the primary division is among those responsible for creating the output, pooling transcends a strict distribution proportioned according to the relative productivity of the producers; rather, it divides output according to the needs of all including elderly, children, and the incapacitated regardless of their contribution to the production process (Sahlins 1965, 94).

Amerindians operationalized the innate sense of human fairness inherent in the Golden Rule, which embodies the principle of reciprocity (Haidt 2006, xi) because of the absence of two conditions – privacy and anonymity – in pre-Columbian society. The communal life of indigenous Americans made solitude a situation seldom experienced (Posner 1980, 6). Additionally, the relatively small populations of societal clusters or groups meant everyone literally knew everyone else, so social persuasion was sufficient to insure compliance with established tribal norms. As we shall discover in the case studies of the relatively complex Cakohia and Iroquois societies that conclude this chapter, implementing reciprocity and redistribution systems required more elaborate societal arrangements than were found in the majority of Amerindian enclaves or tribes.

Production patterns among American aboriginals mirrored those scholars have observed or inferred among many primitive societies regardless of location (Sahlins 1972, 41–148). As was the case for many preliterate peoples, the most important consumer good among Amerindians was leisure. Labor supply schedules for both women and men were backward bending to such an extent that primitive economies regularly operated well within their respective production possibilities frontiers (Sahlins 1972, 17). Although work assignments were gender based, males and females could occupy "all specializations, crafts, and statuses" depending on local clan customs and practices (Bruhns and Stothert 1999, 140). Work itself was intense but sporadic, seldom occurring more than two or three days in a row, and from four to six hours per day for women and men alike (Sahlins 1972, 14–27). Among Amerindian tribes that had a well-developed agrarian sector, work occupied about four months per year (Bruce 1896, 175). Since exceeding subsistence requirements was a near certainty (Sahlins 1972, 32), individuals did not often contribute to their maximum abilities. Rather, the effort of the median worker – female or male – apparently set a standard that others used as a benchmark in determining their personal contributions to the communal work effort. This equity-based norm was relaxed in emergencies such as a drought-induced shortfall of food. Diminishing returns was the only real hardship Amerindians had to confront with any regularity. Because they relied so heavily on the largesse of nature, indigenous Americans living in even a small to modest population cluster would deplete the productivity of the resources within convenient range of their base location (Sahlins 1972, 33). Relocation of villages was frequent, taking place every five to fifteen years depending on the abundance of the local flora and fauna and the population of the group. Productivity was contingent on mobility, and for food gathering peoples who had yet to invent the wheel, the ability to migrate from one location to another necessitated certain practices: "minimum necessary equipment, elimination of duplication, and ... infanticide, senilicide, [and] sexual continence for the duration of the nursing period ..." (Sahlin 1972, 34).

Chayanov's Rule confirms indirectly the willingness in particular and preliterate peoples in general to exchange productivity gains for additional leisure time instead of other options such as a higher standard of living (more consumer goods) or a growing population. Although A. V. Chayanov developed his hypothesis after observing peasant farm families in twentieth-century Russia and not primitive societies (Chayanov), anthropologists have applied his finding to preliterate, hunter-gatherer cultures (Sahlins 1972, 87–92). Succinctly put, Chayanov's Rule states that "Intensity of labor in a system of domestic production for use varies inversely with relative working capacity of the producing unit" (Sahlins 1972, 91). While some dispute this interpretation (Tannenbaum 1984), when applied to American aboriginals this rule implies a choice of decreasing or at least holding constant work effort as productivity increased. In other words, indigenous Americans consciously chose their ideal of living well and all that it implied – underproduction, more leisure, and a near constant quality of life on a per capita basis – even when other options were clearly attainable (Sahlins 1972, 34). This would seem to imply that Amerindians lacked a sense of adventure, which was certainly not the case. While basically self-reliant, indigenous Americans were not autarkical. Economic interactions among and between aboriginal groups was the rule not the exception. Exchange – trade/transfers among individuals related or at least known to each other – involved socially expected sharing, what anthropologists call reciprocity (Schneider 1974, 154), or balanced reciprocity, the exchange of equivalents (Sahlins 1965, 147–148). Reciprocity differs from pooling in that the latter is an entitlement *within* a family whereas the former is a custom-dictated social exchange *between* groups (Sahlins 1965, 141). For example, reciprocity could be assistance freely given in the course of everyday neighborly relations – a pure gift (Hyde 1979) – of the redistribution of food stuffs from an individual family to the larger group in celebration of a special event such as a wedding. This sort of exchange was predicated on the understanding that those receiving the materials had an obligation to reciprocate in kind if when a comparable situation in reverse should arise.

Less personal than generalized reciprocity, balanced reciprocity was more of an economic *quid pro quo* exchange, that is, the simultaneous exchange of equivalent goods (Sahlin 1965, 148). The use of credit, though uncommon, permitted one-sided transactions with the promise of future payment in accordance with terms agreed to in the present (Firth 1964, 29). In balanced reciprocity, individuals who were especially proficient in the production of a specific good or service would exchange their surplus with those whose relative productivity and hence surplus lay in producing other products. The principle of comparative advantage was at least as crucial to these exchanges as any social expectation (Sahlins 1965, 148). Balanced reciprocity encouraged specialization, which in turn created more exchange opportunities. In contrast to exchange, trade involved strangers, that is, people outside the everyday circle of social interactions. Virtually every aboriginal group in North America engaged in trade except Polar Eskimos who had no contact with other tribes and they thought were the only people on Earth when discovered by John Reed in 1818" (Driver, 211). Trade was undertaken for economic, political, and social reasons, and it is impossible to weigh the relative importance of each factor. The principle of absolute advantage was the primary economic motivation for trade as Amerindians sought to acquire things not generally available locally.

> Certain materials, because of their high quality for manufacturing purposes or because they were of intrinsic beauty, were in great demand and were traded over wide areas. Jadeite, obsidian, fine flint, and pipestone (catlinite) were in demand for the manufacture of tools and implements; marine shells, quartz crystals, copper, mica, mineral paints, turquoise, and feathers were wanted for ornaments and ceremonial objects. Salt was an important item of trade, as were wild and cultivated food products and furs and hides.
>
> (Martin et al. 1947, 67)

Some examples of these long-distance exchanges included the Mohave of Arizona traveling to the California coast to obtain dentalium shells, which in turn, were exchanged for Hopi textiles (Martin *et al.* 1947, 67), while on the plains and prairies, hunting tribes traded meat and hides for the agricultural products of farming tribes (Driver 1969, 214).

The economic trading of material goods, especially bulk items, was subject to a propinquity factor – the volume of trade was inversely related to distance. Since indigenous Americans had no draft animals nor did they make practical use of the wheel, human backpacking was the foremost means of transporting goods over land. Unearthed wheeled pull-toys indicate that North American aboriginals were aware of the wheel, but they had not transferred the technology to the world of work, something that occurred in the Old World some 5,000–6,000 years BCE (Driver 1969, 212). Water transport was the preferred method for moving hefty items, and diffusion – the relaying of products from one region to another – came into play when rivers or lakes were not available (Driver 1969, 220).

The political and social reasons for trade were certainly as important as the economic motives. Politically, trade was a way to cement alliances, buy-off potential enemies, or settle disputes. Socially, trade was an integral part of exogamy – the requirement that persons seeking spouses must marry outside their kinship group. More than an incest taboo, exogamy was a cultural practice that nearly all preliterate societies the world over invoked (Posner 1980, 41–42). It served several objectives such as facilitating trade as well as the obvious benefit of promoting genetic diversity (Posner 1980, 41–42). Whatever the purpose, trade revealed two obscure yet important facets of indigenous American societies. First, Amerindians had overcome a basic human instinct – the fear of strangers (Seabright 2004, 4–5). Second and more important, the willingness to trade meant that indigenous Americans trusted strangers and expected to encounter a reciprocal disposition (Seabright 2004, 27–28). For better and for worse, this outlook played a significant role in the relationships that emerged between Amerindians and European immigrants during the sixteenth and seventeenth centuries.

An intriguing question that arises when discussing aboriginal trade is what role, if any, money played in the process. Although barter was the general method of exchange, the pervasiveness of wampum throughout the contiguous states had fueled speculation that Amerindians used primitive monies to facilitate trade. Wampum – in this context a generic reference to strings of baubles fashioned primarily from sea shells – was a medium of exchange, store of value, and unit of account in the trade between indigenous peoples and European immigrants that began in earnest in the early 1600s and flourished during the next 50–100 years. Wampum became so widely accepted that exchange rates were established between it and various country-issued monies that circulated in the United States during much of the seventeenth century (Martin *et al.* 1947, 68). That Amerindians were quick to take to the use of money in the seventeenth century suggests that they had used it before contact with Europeans, but there is no concrete evidence for this inference (Einzig 1966, 170–174). An alternative explanation to the dispersion of wampum throughout the contiguous states may rest in the realm of human curiosity and not trade per se. Amerindians were inveterate explorers and used much of their considerable free time finding out what was on the other side of the next hill or beyond the next bend in the river. The drive to explore was so strong it seems almost a certainty that if people from the Old World had not discovered the New, sooner or later, people from the New World would have discovered the Old. Trade in lightweight artifacts was one way to verify discovery. Wampum offered proof of having been somewhere new and different, an ideal validator of adventure, a souvenir whose relative scarcity gave it special meaning and enhanced the prestige of anyone who could accumulate it in significant amounts.

## The economic mind of American aboriginals prior to 1492

Despite the absence of a written legacy, we can still infer the economic mind of American aboriginals from the way that they grappled with the ordinary business of life. In the mid-1930s at the depths of the Great Depression when confidence market-driven price systems had all but evaporated and proponents of command-type economies were popping up everywhere, the noted American Margaret Mead and some colleagues initiated a research project that sought to determine where on the competition/cooperation spectrum did primitive societies lie (Mead 1937). Economics was one of the dimensions on which a number of primitive societies were assessed, reflecting the desire to ascertain what the 'natural' inclination of humans is when it comes to organizing an economy as opposed to the 'learned' system they had been taught to accept. The anticipated outcome would show what, in their pristine state, humans preferred, command or choice, cooperation or competition, communal economic systems or individualistic ones. The actual findings were messy and inconclusive, in part because the researchers had preconceived notions of what they would find. No single operational model then available proved sufficiently robust to explain primitive economics, for in such cultures economic behavior is batched with political, social, and psychological behaviors, making it difficult to tease out the principles of choice that guide primitive economies.

Even today, a single handle for describing the economic mind of aboriginals remains elusive. The basic supposition of cultural materialism – that human behaviors are forged in the struggle for existence – seems barely applicable to pre-contact Americans whose survival, by and large, required a minimal effort hardly indicative of a struggle. As illustrated in Table 2.1, ancient Amerindians turned upside-down the idea of scarcity, a fundamental tenet of modern mainstream economics. Orthodox economics presupposes that human societies confront a world where resources are limited but wants are not, giving rise to perpetual scarcity. In preliterate aboriginal societies, the reverse was often true – resources were unlimited but wants were finite if not fixed. The rationality of indigenous peoples may not have been bounded but their desires were. In this state of material well-being as shown in Table 2.1, the multiple, independent sources of the supply of all resources creates redundancies, which means that the loss of any one source does not jeopardize a society's ability to satisfy its limited wants (Daily and Ellison 2002, 5–8). In terms of contemporary economic models, this is tantamount to a society operating perpetually with its production possibility frontier.

Those seeking a theoretical construct for characterizing primitive economies in general and indigenous American economies in particular would do well to consider *Administrative Behavior*, the seminal work of Nobel Laureate Herbert A. Simon (1916–2001). In the preface of this book, Simon notes that the body of economic theory "has reached a state of Thomistic refinement having great intellectual and esthetic appeal but little discernible relation to the actual or possible behavior of flesh-and-blood human beings" (Simon 1976, xxvii). Modern, mainstream choice theory assumes that humans have a complete and consistent set of preferences, full knowledge of available

*Table 2.1* States of material well-being

| Wants | Resources | |
| --- | --- | --- |
| | Limited | Unlimited |
| Limited | Subsistence | Redundancies |
| Unlimited | Scarcity | Abundance |

options, the skill to calculate the consequences of any decision, the ability to select the optimal alternative, and perfect foresight. Since their conditions are rarely satisfied in the real world, rational or purposeful behavior is bounded or limited, and choice becomes a matter of satisticing behavior rather than optimizing behavior (Simon 1976, 80–84; 240–242). In short, good enough trumps the ideal.

Viewing American aboriginal economic thinking through the Simon prism of bounded rationality helps bring cohesion to what otherwise would be an almost dizzying array of competing descriptions. Consummate pragmatists, Amerindians discovered what worked and stayed with it. In their societies, effectiveness – doing the right things – was more important than efficiency – doing things right. Consumption, both its level and composition, was easily sustained, making resource scarcity practically nonexistent. Production methods remained nearly static over long stretches of time as did the patterns of distribution. Trade was as much a political and social phenomenon as an economic one. Technological change came in fits and starts. Productivity gains were usually taken in expanded leisure time and not more consumption or investment, or increased population. Doubling roughly every 1,400 years, population levels were remarkably constant. So was the average life expectancy of pre-contact Amerindians as investing in health care was a low priority. If early nineteenth-century scholars knew as much about primitive peoples as we do today, Malthusian population theory would have encountered pointed criticism instead of widespread acceptance.

Following the directive of their god as stated in The Bible, European immigrants who came to America after 1600 were growth oriented.

> And God blessed them, and God said unto them, Be fruitful, and multiply, and replenish the earth, and subdue it: and have dominion over the fish of the sea, and over the fowl of the air, and over every living thing that moveth upon the earth.
>
> (Genesis 1:28)

By comparison, indigenous Americans had maintenance economies. The present was a near photocopy of the past and a picture of the future. Pre-contact aboriginals seldom initiated change, thereby minimizing the need to adjust to it. In Simonesque fashion, a few time-honored heuristics or rules-of-thumb guided Amerindian economic behavior with respect to resource allocation. Within the context of bounded rationality, choice making was considered 'good enough' if the results were satisfactory, reasonably efficient, and above all practical to implement. Herbert Simon was of the opinion that satisficing was the behavior of humans who did not have the wits to optimize (Simon 1976, xxviii). The design of Amerindian life suggests another possibility, one focused more on desire and will and less on know-how and learning.

In a very real sense, Amerindians chose to live a lifestyle that the ancient Greek philosopher Epicurus espoused (Panichas 1967; Lillegard 2003). With few exceptions, indigenous American societies applied the Epicurean maxim of minimizing harm while maximizing happiness to themselves and their environment. Egalitarianism was the norm in aboriginal cultures, tranquility the ideal, and moderation in all things the expectation. There was nearly universal belief that "living prudently in deep appreciation of modest pleasures, was not just the route to happiness, it *was* happiness" (Hecht 2004, 41). The purposeful moderation of Amerindian culture stressed communal responsibility, respect for individual liberty, and the cultivation of friendship over personal aggrandizement. Taken *in toto*, American aboriginal life operationalized a philosophical system that Epicurus could only wistfully imagine. It is no coincidence that Thomas More's Utopia – the fabled commonwealth free of hunger and homelessness, an egalitarian state where everyone is caring and cared for – is set in the New World (Johnson 1932, 5). This is precisely the impression early European explorers and immigrants were left with after experiencing the New World first hand (Fox 1993; Logan and Adams 2002).

## Two case studies: Cahokia and the Iroquois

In order to show in some detail the diversity of aboriginal economics, this chapter concludes with two case studies, the first being Cahokia, a prosperous, urban enclave that was located on the east bank of the Mississippi River across from is now St. Louis, Missouri.

In *The Wealth of Nations* Adam Smith postulated that the level of development of the 'savages' of North America in the late eighteenth century was equivalent to that of the peoples of England at the time of Julius Caesar or about 50 BCE (Smith [1776] 1937, 327). What he didn't know, what he couldn't know was that about 500 years before the publication of *Wealth* there was in the American heartland a metropolitan area with a population equal to that of contemporary London at the time, and a standard of living higher than that in any part of thirteenth-century England (Johansen 2005, 31). At its pinnacle at around 1250, Cahokia and its nearby towns had an estimated 15,000–40,000 inhabitants (Pauketat 2009, 2; Shaffer 1992, 85–86), making it the largest urban center in the United States until 1790 when the population of Philadelphia officially exceeded 28,000 (Milner 1991; Gregg 1975). Located near present-day East St. Louis, Illinois, Cahokia was the center of a vast zone of trade and commerce that used the major river systems of the American Midwest and Southeast to transport food stuffs and manufactures over an area about the size of Western Europe (Barrington 1999b, 86–102). What began as a simple settlement around the year 800 had become by 1200 the closest thing to a nation-state in pre-contact America. By 1500, the 'city' that took half a millennium to develop was all but abandoned. Seventeenth-century French who journeyed to the area found only a small tribe of Cahokians living nearby and named the site after this group (Shaffer 1992, 52). For the next 250 years Cahokia became part of the hidden history of North America. Not until the twentieth century did researchers, led by archaeologists, come to appreciate the size, scope, and significance of Cahokia (Pauketat 2009, 51–98).

Mississippian, the tribal group that settled Cahokia, was an Amerindian civilization that flourished in the Midwest and Southeast for approximately 1,000 years from 500 to 1500 CE (Muller 1983). Mississippian settlements were generally situated along the banks and/or at the confluence of important rivers (Kehoe 2002, 170). In the case of Cahokia that site was the American Bottom, a 125-square-mile area formed by the intersections of the Mississippi, Missouri, and Illinois Rivers near St. Louis, Missouri. In colloquial jargon, a bottom is a low-lying flood plain where exceedingly fertile yet light soils are deposited, precisely the type of soils Amerindians would find easy to work given their stone-age farm tools and implements (Shaffer 1992, 61–62). The ecological environment of the American Bottom – sandy loam, ample rain, moderate temperatures, and a long growing season – make a perfect location for growing maize, which was present in the eastern woodlands since year zero (Bruhns and Stothert 1999, 86).

For several hundred years, aboriginal life patterns in and around the American Bottom did not differ appreciably from those in other parts of the contiguous states. Around 700–800 CE, a quantum shift in the economics of the region began. Some attribute this change to influences from Mesoamerica where the rise of maize-base agrarian systems created a level of prosperity and economic development that manifested itself in a variety of ways, most notably the construction of significant public structures, especially tiered, flat-topped pyramids (Jennings 1993, 56–67; Johansen 2005, 31–32). Others attribute the similarities between Cahokia and Mesoamerican cultures to coincidence, the by-product of independent origination.

> Despite striking similarities to features of cultures in Mexico and elsewhere, there is no scientific evidence that several Mississippian trademarks – flat-topped temple mounds, calendric systems, and ceramic styles – were the result of anything other than independent invention. No Mexican artifacts have ever been found in the American Bottom or in any part of this country outside the Southwest.
>
> (Mink 1992, 13)

Regardless of the origin, the nature of economic practice and thought in Cahokia changed profoundly beginning around 800 CE.

Prior to this transformation, agriculture at the clan level was slowly developing in the American Bottom with pooling as the primary method of distribution. When they occurred, surpluses were used to establish reciprocity relationships. In the last quarter of the first millennium, production for sustainment of the given populace gave way to production for trade with outside groups. Redistribution began to coexist with reciprocity (Potter 1969, 159), and technological and institutional changes befitting a growth-oriented economy began to emerge (Barrington 1999b, 87). Food in particular and many goods in general were produced expressly for trade and not just local consumption. Specialization of production became the norm and genuine interdependency replaced self-sufficiency. Cahokia focused on the production of maize, which came to account for 50 percent of the diet, the principal but not the sole crop grown in excess of local demand for the purpose of exchange. Seeking their own comparative advantages, other centers and hamlets within a 25-mile radius of Cahokia specialized in the production of manufactures (hoes), crafts (baskets), or other non-food stuffs (clothing) that were traded for maize, beans, squash, and the other agricultural products grown in the American Bottom (Barrington 1999b, 89; Shaffer 1992, 54, 62).

Cahokia used its strategic location to become the largest and most important Mississippian trade center. The Mississippi and Illinois Rivers gave Cahokia direct access to the north–south exchanges, while the proximity to the Missouri and Ohio Rivers, and entry to the Tennessee River, a major tributary of the Ohio, facilitated east–west trade (Shaffer 1992, 61). Using interconnected waterways, the Mississippians developed an intricate trading system between themselves and the other tribes that stretched from the Gulf coast to the upper Midwest and from the eastern edge of the Rocky Mountains to the coastal Southeast. Cahokia was the nexus of this system; other major centers were located in Mississippi, Alabama, Georgia, and Missouri (Barrington 1999b, 92–93; Shaffer 1992, 62–65; Stoltman 1991, 93–347). Social and cultural changes began to occur in conjunction with the evolution of the Mississippian economy.

At Cahokia, the egalitarianism customary among Amerindians gave way to a "four-tiered socio-political hierarchy" that brought structure, organization, and planning to society (Mink 1992, 60). Research evidence indicates that at the top of this social pyramid were a theocratic chief and his close relatives, the visionaries of the system. Next came the priestly advisors, an elite class of managers who directed the third rung of society – heads of family clans – in the daily agrarian, manufacturing, and construction activities. Last were the commoners who toiled in the fields, backpacked soil used to build mounds, and produced the goods and services that supported themselves and those in the other classes (Mink 1992, 20, 44). As the economy grew, communal living arrangements gave way to private housing. "By far, the most common buildings at Cakohia were single-family dwellings" (Mink 1992, 31). The residences for the top three tiers of society ranged from generous to opulent; commoners lived in modest yet spacious homes. Hunting and gathering was always a part of Mississippian life, especially for commoners, regardless of the general level of prosperity attained. With the increasing volume and variety of trade, the specialization of production became more pronounced, and implicit contracts were almost certainly developed as Cahokia and its trading partners had to increasingly trust each other to fulfill their mutual obligations (Barrington 1999b, 90–92).

The signature expression of Mississippian culture was mound building. At Cahokia alone there were an estimated 120 conical and pyramid mounds of varying size, the grandest being Monks Mound, so named for the French Trappist Monks who settled in the area in the early 1800s (Mink 1992, 68). Once a four-tiered, flat-topped pyramid, Monks Mound – a significant portion of which still exists and is the centerpiece of Cahokia Mounds Museum at Collinsville, Illinois – is noteworthy for its sheer size. With a volume in excess of 800,000 cubic yards, it was built in stages over 250–300 years (Shaffer 1992, 60) as part of a vast ceremonial complex capable of accommodating over 40,000 people (Scarre 1999, 141; Johansen 1999, 43). When completed Monks Mound was greater in extent than the pyramid at Giza in Egypt (Kennedy 1994, 12). Indicative of their ethnocentric biases, nineteenth-century European writers, believing that Amerindians lacked the engineering savvy to erect such structures, attributed construction of mound complexes to, alternatively, "the Chinese, the Welsh, the Phoenicians, and the lost nation of Atlantis ... various biblical personages," and the Vikings (Mann 2006, 254).

For economists, mounds have an added dimension of importance beyond being an indicator of prosperity. Their very existence implies the presence of "a system of taxation or tribute" necessary to marshal the labor and other resources required to design, build, and maintain these public works (Barrington 1999b, 86). The mystery, one of many about Cahokia, is whether these resources were forthcoming because of coercion or cajoling. Coercion is consistent with scholars who believe that the elite in primitive societies relied on the authority of their social status to redistribute resources as they deemed fit. However, evidence suggests that the heads of centers such as Cahokia were not autocratic leaders. If taxation begets representation (Ross 2004), leaders of Cahokia eventually discovered that authority alone was not enough to mobilize the resources necessary to do what they wanted. Major decisions that had community-wide implications were often reached after consulting with those involved (Griffin 1990, 70). Cajoling is a distinct possibility especially among those researchers who think that a nascent market economy may have been operational at Cahokia (Potter 1969, 152–153), a level of sophistication other scholars believed is embroidered (Griffin 1983; Muller 1983).

If the amount and scope of trade originating in or passing through Cahokia was as significant as some have suggested, and Amerindians were truly pragmatic decision makers, then the view that the unfettered interplay of demand and supply governed Mississippian exchange has some merit. Barter works best when the variety of items exchanged is relatively small so that the number of pair-wise terms of trade – real prices – is tractable. A growing and increasingly diverse pool of traded goods can complicate exchange to point where those responsible for establishing the barter ratios are overwhelmed. At Cahokia, the uneven flow of goods coupled with the absence of a prescribed class of traders (Griffin 1990, 10–11), exacerbated the problems inherent in escalating volume and variety. Letting market forces determine barter (exchange) ratios could very well have been the default solution to a vexing problem. Conceivably, command and market economics could have coexisted in the American Bottom, with a command system guiding consumption, production, and distribution of the products made in and for Cahokia and its immediate environs, and market forces establishing the prices of goods that passed through Cahokia on their way to other destinations. This would imply a medium of exchange, an innovation Mississippians were capable of, given the vast territorial expanse of their influence and the ready availability of seashells and other lightweight, durable materials with no intrinsic value (Jennings 1993, 64–65). Clearly the incentive to create a genuine medium of exchange would have been compelling. Someday this and other mysteries surrounding Cahokia may be resolved. About 90 percent of Mississippian sites have been destroyed because of highway construction, farming, and residential and commercial developments (Barrington 1999b, 90). However, of the remaining sites, only about 1 percent has been examined scientifically and may yet reveal details about the inner working of Cahokia (Mink 1992, 60).

What we do know for sure is that an urban center which reached its pinnacle around 1250 was all but abandoned a century later. Many theories have been advanced about the demise of Cahokia, all of them equally plausible. A number of scholars believe that environmental factors – a prolonged drought, a major earthquake, the impact of the Little Ice Age on agricultural productivity – either individually or collectively doomed Cahokia (Kehoe 2002, 171; Shaffer 1992, 81–83). Other hypotheses point to self-inflicted wounds with malnutrition associated with an over-reliance on maize in the diet, deforestation of the area surrounding Cahokia, and depletion of the fertility of the American Bottom due to excessive cultivation as the culprits (Shaffer 1992, 81–83; Mann 1992, 262–265). Less popular but just as likely are quality of life issues. Being in a flood plain only about half of Cahokia's six square miles were high enough for year-round habitation (Mink 1992, 26). This gave the city a population density that was high even by modern norms. With 5,000 cooking fires burning continuously, pollution was undoubtedly a problem, to say nothing about the hygiene and sanitation conditions associated with congestion. Cahokia may have been a victim of its success as an increasing scale of operation probably demanded efficiencies associated with a system of writing to record inventories and a system of mathematics to count those stores, technical breakthroughs Mississippians were unable or unwilling to develop. Life may have become unbearably complicated and people may have left Cahokia in search of a more palpable version of the Epicurean life. Other Mississippian centers, less intense commercially and noticeably smaller than Cahokia flourished well into the sixteenth century (Hudson 1976, 82–97), suggesting that the leisure/work trade-off expected in the American Bottom may have ultimately been deemed too dear. Voting with their feet, alienated inhabitants disenchanted with the rising levels of organizational discipline required to make Cahokia work, probably migrated to other settlements where there was less command and more choice.

Unlike Cahokia which was all but defunct at the time of contact, the Iroquois Confederacy was a vibrant league of five tribes located on or near the eleven, glacier-etched Finger Lakes of central New York State. Beginning in the sixteenth century, Europeans interacted with the Iroquois, often writing first-hand accounts of these experiences that proved valuable in understanding the life, culture, and customs of the Haudenosaunee as the Iroquois 'nations' collectively referred to themselves. Such narratives, while informative, must be approached with caution. Even if first-person descriptions were the unvarnished truth, accepting them as such would be tantamount to assuming European contact did not alter aboriginal behavior when clearly it did. In the case of the Iroquois, many sixteenth- and seventeenth-century European accounts portray them as particularly warlike. Ironically their confederacy was formed to mitigate conflict not enable it. Indigenous peoples in general and the Iroquois in particular came to realize early after European contact that their way of life, if not their very existence, was in jeopardy. Iroquois aggressiveness toward Amerindians and certain Europeans after contact was in part a manifestation of this realization (Quain 1937, 245; 275). The rise of uncharacteristically hostile behavior took an obvious toll on Europeans. Less obvious was the boomerang effect that violence had on the Iroquois, particularly warriors. Research suggests that they became increasing susceptible to what was probably post-traumatic stress disorder as revealed in the Iroquois' Freudian-like custom of interpreting dreams (Wallace 1958).

First-hand accounts of the Iroquois also suffered from the ethnocentric biases of their authors, many of who perceived Amerindians as less than human. In part this pejorative view can be dismissed as the expected reaction when a 'civilized' society encounters a 'primitive' one. Equally likely, the alleged 'inferiority/backwardness' of Amerindians was a convenient rationale for those wishing to subjugate and exploit indigenous peoples. Whatever the motivation, stereotyping aboriginals of North and South America persisted even after the publication of *Sublimus Dei*, the papal bull Pope Paul III issued in 1537 declaring indigenous peoples to be human, rational beings with souls capable of salvation, and expressly prohibited their enslavement (*Papal Encyclicals Online*). Of course, many direct-observation descriptions of the Iroquois were sensitive and sympathetic, sometimes too much so. *League of the Haudenosaunee, or Iroquois*, published in 1851, is still regarded as "the most comprehensive single treatment of the Haudenosaunee" (Johansen and Mann 2000, vii). The book's author, anthropologist Lewis Henry Morgan, a "friend and champion of the Iroquois," embellished the already embalmed history of the confederacy, creating in the process "an empire for the Iroquois that never existed" (Jennings 1984, xvi, xvii). Regardless of their points of view, first-hand narratives of the Iroquois must be triangulated with other sources of information if a reasonably accurate portrait of the Iroquois is to emerge. Specifically, historical analyses, including the Iroquois' own oral tradition, need to be cross-referenced with anthropological interpretations of archaeological research to insure that written accounts of the Iroquois square with the physical evidence. This also applies to interpreting the economic mind of the Iroquois.

Economic thought among the Iroquois was similar to that for most Amerindian groups as described above, save for that as practiced at Cahokia. Still, Iroquois economic philosophy had some singularly unique aspects as revealed in their economic practices and institutions. To appreciate the subtle but significant nuances of Iroquois economic thought, especially when compared to the general norms that prevailed among other groups, some background information is necessary to give context to the discussion, beginning with the origins of the Iroquois which are still unsettled (Kehoe 2002, 198–200). The prevailing view is that the ancestors of the Iroquois appeared in central New York sometime between 3200 and 2400 BCE (Funk 1983, 323). The first tribes or nations that would ultimately form the Iroquois confederacy – Cayuga, Mohawk, Oneida, Onondaga, and Seneca – were well established by the year 1000 CE (Funk 1983, 323). A sixth nation, the Tuscarora, was added to the league or confederacy in the 1720s after having been expelled from North Carolina (Shaffer 1992, 89). Dating of the confederacy is a keenly debated subject with some scholars positing the exact date of formal unification as August 31, 1142 (Mann and Fields 1976), while others favor the time span 1350 to 1550 (Stites 1904, 40–41; Hodge 1975, 618–619). Notwithstanding these differences the consensus is that the confederacy was in place and functioning prior to sustained contact with Europeans, which for the Iroquois came in the sixteenth century, although some speculate initial contact with Norse explorers may have occurred some five hundred years earlier (Johansen 2005, 40–42). At the time of sustained contact, the population of the Iroquois has been estimated between 1,000 and 70,000 (Morgan [1851] 1901, 23–25), with contemporary estimates coalescing at around 15,000 (Hodge 1975, 619), organized in villages of 100 to 400 families or approximately 500 to 2,000 inhabitants each (Bruhns and Stothert 1999, 124; Johansen 1999, 122).

As with most preliterate peoples, the Iroquois were well aware of the benefits of genetic diversity; exogamy served as the initial impetus for contacts among the independent and largely insular tribes that eventually formed the confederacy. The biological motivation for interactions did not prevent feuds between the tribes, modest conflicts by European standards but still a source of friction. At some point in time, possibly during the era of Deganawidah, an Iroquois prophet who preached a message of peace and camaraderie, the league came into being, facilitated in part by the realization that exogamy created clan lines that stretched across the five tribes (Fenton 1985, 14–15; Grinde 1977, 3–4). Because of the impact of exogamy, the Iroquois confederacy became a kinship state, a matrilineal system headed by clan mothers where each tribe member had family relations in every tribe in the league (Johansen 2005, 37). Tribal affiliation and clan membership became the warp and woof of society, forming the basis of the confederacy's relational economic system (Frey 2009, 1–8). With its gender-based schemes of production and power, the tribe defined a person's life purpose; clan membership, in turn, became the basis of peaceful contacts and interactions – social, political, and economic – across the Iroquois league. The two characteristics defined the individual's rights and responsibilities to the group and vice versa. Equally important from an economic perspective, the confederacy became the medium for the ascendency of women, who in Iroquois life attained status well beyond the customs prevalent in many other Amerindian societies.

To be sure, women always remained secondary to men who administered the confederacy with the assistance of and significant input from women, especially some distinguished clan mothers. Over the centuries, however, the status of all women increased appreciably, due in large measure to the ascendancy of agriculture, which was essentially women's work. Prior to European contact, agriculture had already gone from being an insignificant contributor of nutrition to the primary source of diet in the individual tribes and the confederacy as a whole, accounting for two-thirds of the foodstuffs the Iroquois consumed (Johansen 1999, 122). Cognizant of the ever increasing contribution of women to general societal welfare, the Iroquois rewarded these efforts the only way they could, with elevated levels of status and greater political influence; increasing women's "wages" was not an option. Rising confederacy income did not translate into higher per capita income as the Iroquois did not stray far from their notions of social egalitarianism and personal moderation. Instead, increasing prosperity was demonstrated in communal property – more and better longhouses – or in public goods such as palisades for villages vulnerable to attack from the outside.

The designation of status, the real measure of income (economic wellbeing) in Iroquois culture, was another matter. There, the distribution was decidedly uneven and based in part on one's contributions to society. As a group, women became beneficiaries of this practice (Stites 1904, 87). Unlike Europe at the time of contact where income and wealth tended to gravitate to power, in Iroquois society, particularly for women, power gravitated wealth or at least those responsible for its production. In this sense, Iroquois economic thinking was a precursor of modern market economics, where, theoretically, reward is related to marginal contribution, if not of the individual then at least for a well-defined group that is obviously the source of significant improvements in societal well-being.

Another fascinating aspect of Iroquois economics and thus of their economic mind was the use of wampum as money. Among Amerindians in general, wampum served an array of functions. In diplomatic affairs involving either different aboriginal groups or between indigenous peoples and European colonists, wampum was a "medium of communication" with the strings of beads or seashells arranged in patterns to record what was agreed upon, by whom, and when (Grinde 1977, 8; Foster 1985, 103–108). Certain shell patterns may have been designed to elicit phonetic sounds, making some wampum belts precursors of writing (Johansen 2005, 24–25). Wampum was also a mnemonic device that allowed Amerindians to preserve accounts of important events and dates in the histories of specific tribes (Druke 1985, 88–90). Other wampum strings served as credentials for those negotiating treaties or symbols of tribal leaders (Grinde 1977, 8). There is ample evidence that after European contact wampum served as money in commercial transactions between and among aboriginals and colonists, but there is no incontrovertible proof that it was used as money prior to the arrival of Europeans (Einzig 1966, 170). However, circumstantial evidence is overwhelming in support of the hypothesis that indigenous Americans in general and especially the Iroquois used wampum as a medium of exchange, unit of account, and a store of value.

European explorers who visited the United States intermittently during the sixteenth century observed that the inhabitants of the New World, notably the Iroquois, used wampum to facilitate the exchange of goods in much the same way that gold and silver were used in the Old World (Stites 1904, 83). Wampum also played a role in settling debts such as the payment of ransoms and fines (Einzig 1966, 172), and the resolution of what today would be described as wrongful death suits (Hodge 1975, 616). That personal prestige was directly related to the quantity an individual possessed indicates that wampum served as a unit of account (Stites 1904, 68). Finally, wampum was an important if not the primary store of value in the treasuries that each of the five tribes and the Confederacy as a whole kept (Einzig 1966, 172). Other commodities in those treasuries included animal pelts and skins, corn meal, dressed meats, and other goods that could be used to pay tribal or league expenses (Stites 1904, 69).

The greatest legacy of the Iroquois may be the imprint it had on the economic and political behavior of European colonists during the seventeenth and eighteenth centuries, and ultimately on the development of the political economy that evolved into the American economic system. In the multi-layered strata of the geology that is Amerindian scholarship, a thin vein of research hypothesizes that indigenous peoples, particularly the Iroquois, played an instrumental if not a pivotal role in the development of American political thinking. Scholars who subscribe to this line of reasoning contend that the study of aboriginal cultures influenced the natural law philosophies of John Law and Jean-Jacques Rousseau, which in turn, shaped the thinking of such American luminaries as Benjamin Franklin and Thomas Jefferson (Grinde 1977, 19–23). Direct observation of Iroquois political practices reinforced these European perspectives among those who crafted the Declaration of Independence and the Constitution, making the Iroquois as responsible for the American body politic as the so-called founding fathers (Johansen 1982). The case that to some degree the origins of the American system of government emanated with the Iroquois is captivating if not convincing. Parallel reasoning suggests that a corresponding hypothesis can be made for aboriginal economics being an important source of American economic thinking. That is, Iroquois economic thought served as the template for an economic system that emerged during the colonial period of America and became institutionalized over the subsequent 350 years of practice.

The Iroquois had successfully balanced the yin and yang of personal liberty and social responsibility, of tribal sovereignty and confederacy collectivism, and of private prestige or wealth and the expectation of sharing. America's prodigious philanthropy can be viewed as a modern equivalent of 'the gift,' an Amerindian custom of redistributing personal wealth to promote social well-being. Similarly, tribal independence coexisted with the idea of confederacy in much the same way that state rights can prevail in a federal system. As Benjamin Franklin so cogently put it in his 1754 tongue-in-cheek remarks in support of the Albany Plan of Union:

> It would be a strange thing ... if Six Nations of ignorant savages should be capable of forming such a union and be able to execute it in such a manner that it has subsisted ages and appears indissoluble, and yet that a like union should be impractical for ten or a dozen English colonies to whom it is more necessary and must be more advantageous, and who cannot suppose to want an equal understanding of interest.
>
> (Grinde 1977, 35)

"The link between past and present is as certain as it is at times indiscernible" (Klein and Cooke 1975, xiii). Our existing canon of cherished beliefs and accepted truths owes more to the thoughts of distant predecessors than we can possibly imagine or ever hope to comprehend (Cohen 1952, 183).

# References

Bailey, M. J. 1992. "Approximate Optimality of Aboriginal Property Rights." *Journal of Law and Economics* 35: 183–198.

Barnes, P. 1999. *A Concise History of the Hawaiian Islands*. Hilo, HA: Pteroglyph Press.

Barrington, L. (Editor). 1999. *The Other Side of the Frontier*. Boulder, CO: Westview Press.

Barrington, L. 1999a. "Editor's Introduction." In *The Other Side of the Frontier*. (L. Barrington Editor). Boulder, CO: Westview Press: 1–50.

Barrington, L. 1999b. "The Mississippians and Economic Development Before European Colonization." In *The Other Side of the Frontier*. (L. Barrington Editor). Boulder, CO: Westview Press: 86–102.

Binmore, K. 2005. *Natural Justice*. New York, NY: Oxford University Press.

Bruce, P. A. 1896. *Economic History of Virginia in the Seventeenth Century*. New York, NY: Macmillan.

Bruhns, K. O., and K. E. Stothert. 1999. *Women in Ancient America*. Norman, OK: University of Oklahoma Press.

Burling, R. 1962. "Maximization Theories and the Study of Economic Anthropology." *American Anthropologist* 64(4): 802–821.

Cameron, R., and L. Neal. 2003. *A Concise Economic History of the World (From Paleolithic Times to the Present)*. (Fourth Edition): New York, NY: Oxford University Press.

Chayanov, A. V. 1966. *The Theory of Peasant Economy*. Homewood, IL: Irwin.

Clark, G. 2007. *A Farewell to Alms*. Princeton, NJ: Princeton University Press.

Coe, M. D. 1992. *Breaking the Maya Code*. New York, NY: Thomas and Hudson.

Cohen, F. 1952. "Americanizing the White Man." *American Scholar* 21(2): 177–191.

*Columbia Electronic Encyclopedia*. 2005. www.cc.columbia.edu/cu/cup/.

Cook, S. 1973. "Economic Anthropology: Problems in Theory, Methods, and Analysis." In *Handbook of Social and Cultural Anthropology* (J. J. Honigmann, Editor). Chicago, IL: Rand McNally: 795–860.

Crosby, Jr., A. W. 1972. *The Columbian Exchange: Biological and Cultural Consequences of 1492*. Westport, CT: Greenwood Publishing.

Daily, G. C., and K. Ellison. 2002. *The New Economy of Nature*. Washington, DC: Shearwater Books.

Dalton, G. 1961. "Economic Theory and Primitive Society." *American Anthropologist* 63: 1–25.

Dalton, G. 1977. "Aboriginal Economies in Stateless Societies." In *Exchange Systems in Prehistory* (T. K. Earle and J. E. Ericson, Editors). New York, NY: Academic Press: 191–212.

Dalton, G. 1978. "The Impact of Colonization on Aboriginal Economics in Stateless Societies." *Research in Economic Anthropology, Volume I* (G. Dalton, Editor). Greenwich, CT: JAI Press.

Demsetz, H. 1967. "Toward a Theory of Property Rights." *American Economic Review* 57(2): 347–359.

de Tocqueville, A. [1835] 2000. *Democracy in America* (translated, edited, and with an introduction by H. E. Mansfield and D. Winthrop). Chicago, IL: University of Chicago Press.

Dobyns, H. F. 1966. "Estimating Aboriginal American Population." *Current Anthropology* 7(4): 395–416.

Driver, H. E., and Driver, W. 1967. *Indian Farmers of North America*. Chicago, IL: Rand McNally.

Driver, H. E. 1969. *Indians of North America* (Second Edition, Revised), Chicago, IL: University of Chicago Press.

Druke, M. A. 1985. "Iroquois Treaties: Common Forms, Varying Interpretations." In *The Founders of America* (F. Jennings). New York, NY: W. W. Norton: 85–98.

Einzig, P. 1966. *Primitive Money* (Second Edition). Oxford: Pergamon Press.

Elardo, J. A., and A. Campbell. 2007. "Choice and the Substantivist/Formalist Debate: A Formal Presentation of Three Substantivist Criticisms." In *Choice in Economic Contexts: Ethnographic and Theoretical Enquires* (Research in Economic Anthropology 25, D. Woods, Editor). Amsterdam: Elsevier: 267–284.

Fagan, B. M. 2005. *Ancient North America: The Archaeology of a Continent* (Fourth Edition). New York, NY: Thames and Hudson.

Fenton, W. N. 1985. "Structure, Continuity, and Change in the Process of Iroquois Treaty Making." In *The Founders of America* (F. Jennings). New York, NY: W. W. Norton: 3–36.

Firth, R. 1964. "Capital, Saving and Credit in Peasant Societies: A Viewpoint from Economic Anthropology." In *Capital, Saving and Credit in Peasant Societies* (R. Firth and B. S. Yamey, Editors). Chicago, IL: Aldine: 15–34.

Foster, M. K. 1985. "Another Look at the Functions of Wampum in Iroquois-White Councils." In *The Founders of America* (F. Jennings). New York, NY: W. W. Norton: 99–114.

Fox, A. 1993. *Utopia, An Elusive Vision*. New York, NY: Twayne.

Frey, D. E. 2009. *America's Economic Moralists*. Albany, NY: State University of New York Press.

Fuchs, L. H. 1961. *Hawaii Pono: A Social History*. New York, NY: Harcourt, Brace & World.

Funk, R. E. 1983. "The Northeastern United States." In *Ancient North Americans* (J. D. Jennings, Editor). San Francisco, CA: W. H. Freeman: 303–371.

Gregg, M. L. 1975. "A Population Estimate for Cahokia." In *New Perspectives in Cahokia Archaeology.* (J. A. Brown, Editor). Urbana, IL: Illinois Archaeological Society, Bulletin No. 10: 126–136.

Griffin, J. B. 1983. "The Midlands." In *Ancient North Americans* (J. D. Jennings, Editor). San Francisco, CA: W. H. Freeman: 242–301.

Griffin, J. B. 1990. "Comments on the Late Prehistoric Societies in the Southeast." In *Towns and Temples Along the Mississippi* (D. H. Dye and C. A. Cox, Editors). Tuscaloosa, AL: University of Alabama Press: 5–15.

Grinde, D. A. 1977. *The Iroquois and the Founding of the American Nation.* San Francisco, CA: Indian Historian Press.

Haidt, J. 2006. *The Happiness Hypothesis.* New York, NY: Basic Books.

Harris, M. 1979. *Cultural Materalism: The Struggle for a Science of Culture.* New York, NY: Random House.

Harris, M. 2001. *The Rise of Anthropological Theory* (Updated Edition). Walnut Creek, CA: Altamira Press.

Haub, C. 1995. "How Many People Have Ever Lived On Earth." *Population Today.* (February): Population Reference Bureau (prb.org).

Hecht, J. M. 2004. *Doubt, A History.* San Francisco, CA: HarperCollins.

Herskovits, M. J. 1940. *The Economic Life of Primitive People.* New York, NY: A. A. Knopf.

Herskovits, M. J. 1952. *Economic Anthropology.* New York, NY: Knopf.

Hobbes, T. [1651] 1985. *Leviathan* (with an introduction by H. W. Schneider). Indianapolis, IN: Bobbs-Merrill.

Hodge, F. W. (ed.). 1975. *Handbook of American Indians North of Mexico, Part 1.* Totowa, NJ: Rowman and Littlefield.

Hoebel, E. A. 1954. *The Law of Primitive Man.* New York, NY: Atheneum.

Hudson, C. 1976. *The Southeastern Indians.* Knoxville, TN: University of Tennessee Press.

Hyde, L. 1979. *The Gift.* New York, NY: Random House.

Isaac, B. L. 2005. "Karl Polanyi." In *A Handbook of Economic Anthropology* (J. G. Carrier, Editor). Cheltenham: Edward Elgar: 14–25.

Jennings, F. 1984. *The Ambiguous Iroquois Empire.* New York, NY: W. W. Norton.

Jennings, F. *et al.*, (eds). 1985. *The History and Culture of Iroquois Diplomacy.* Syracuse, NY: Syracuse University Press.

Jennings, F. 1993. *The Founders of America.* New York, NY: W. W. Norton.

Johansen, B. E. 1982. *Forgotten Founders.* Ipswich, MA: Gambit Publishers.

Johansen, B. E. (ed.). 1999. *The Encyclopedia of Native American Economic History.* Westport, CT: Greenwood Press.

Johansen, B. E. 2005. *The Native Peoples of North America, A History, Vol. I.* Westport, CT: Praeger.

Johansen, B. E., and B. A. Mann, (eds). 2000. *Encyclopedia of the Haudenosaunee (Iroquois Confederacy).* Westport, CT: Greenwood Press.

Johnson, E. A. J. 1932. *American Economic Thought in the Seventeenth Century.* London: P. S. King & Son.

Kehoe, A. B. 2002. *America Before the European Invasions.* London: Longman.

Kennedy, R. G. 1994. *Hidden Cities: The Discovery and Loss of Ancient North American Civilization.* New York, NY: The Free Press.

Klein, M. T., and J. E. Cooke. 1975. "Editors' Introduction." In *Colonial New York* (M. Kemmen). New York, NY: Oxford University Press: xi–xix.

Knight, F. H. 1941. "Anthropology and Economics." *Journal of Political Economy* 49(2): 247–268.

LeClair, E. E., Jr., and H. K. Schneider, (eds). 1968. *Economic Anthropology: Readings in Theory and Analysis.* New York, NY: Holt, Rinehart, and Winston.

Lillegard, N. 2003. *On Epicurus.* Belmont, MA: Thomson/Wadsworth.

Linton, R. M. 1943. "Land Tenure in Aboriginal America." In *The Changing Indian* (O. La Farge, Editor). Norman, OK: University of Oklahoma Press: 42–54.

Logan, G. M., and R. M. Adams, (eds). 2002. *Thomas More: Utopia* (Revised Edition). Cambridge: Cambridge University Press.

Mann, B. A., and J. L. Fields. 1976. "A Sign in the Sky: Dating the League of the Haudenosaunee." *American Indian Culture and Research Journal* 21: 105–163.

Mann, C. C. 2006. *1491.* New York: Alfred A. Knopf.

Marshall, A. [1890] 1964. *Principles of Economics* (Eighth Edition). London: Macmillan.

Martin, P. S., G. I. Quimby, and D. Collier. 1947. *Indians Before Columbus.* Chicago, IL: University of Chicago Press.

Mead, M., (ed.). 1937. *Cooperation and Competition Among Primitive Peoples.* New York, NY: McGraw-Hill.

Milner, G. R. 1991. "American Bottom Mississippian Cultures: Internal Development and External Relations." In *New Perspectives on Cahokia* (J. B. Stoltman, Editor). Madison, WI: Prehistory Press: 29–47.

Mink, C. G. 1992. *Cahokia: City of the Sun.* Collinsville, IL: Cahokia Mounds Museum Society.

Morgan, L. H. [1851] 1901. *League of the Hodenosaunee or Iroquois.* New York, NY: Burt Franklin.

Morton, T. [1637] 1967. *New English Canaan.* Reprinted as *New English Canaan of Thomas Mortan* (with Introductory Matter and Notes by C. F.Adams, Jr. [1883]): New York, NY: Burt Franklin.

Muller, J. D. 1983. "The Southeast." In *Ancient North Americans* (J. D. Jennings, Editor). San Francisco, CA: W. H. Freeman: 372–419.

Murphy, M. F., and M. L. Margolis. 1995. "An Introduction to Cultural Materialism." In *Science, Materialism, and the Study of Culture* (M. F. Murphy and M. L. Margolis, Editors). Gainesville, FL: University Press of Florida: 1–4.

Panichas, G. A. 1967. *Epicurus.* New York, NY: Twayne.

*Papal Encyclicals Online.*

Pauketat, T. R. 2009. *Cahokia, Ancient America's Great City on the Mississippi.* New York, NY: Viking.

Pike, K. L. 1954. *Language in Relation to a Unified Theory of the Structure of Human Behavior.* Glendale, CA: Summer Institute of Linguistics.

Pinker, S. 1994. *The Language Instinct.* New York, NY: W. Morrow.

Polanyi, K. 1957. "The Economy as Instituted Process." In *Trade and Market in the Early Empires* (K. Polanyi *et al.*, Editors). New York, NY: Free Press: 243–270.

Posner, R. A. 1980. "A Theory of Primitive Society, with Special Reference to Law." *Journal of Law and Economics* 23(1): 1–53.

Posner, R. A. 1980a. "Anthropology and Economics." *Journal of Political Economy* 88(3): 608–616.

Potter, J. W. 1969. "The Mitchell Site and Prehistoric Exchange Systems at Cahokia: AD 1000±300." In *Explorations into Cahokia Archaeology* (M. L. Fowler, Editor). Urbana, IL: Illinois Archaeological Society, Bulletin No. 7: 137–164.

Pryor, F. L. 1977. *The Origins of the Economy: A Comparative Study of Distribution in Primitive and Peasant Economies.* New York, NY: Academic Press.

Quain, B. H. 1937. "The Iroquois." In *Cooperation and Competition Among Primitive Peoples* (M. Mead, Editor). New York, NY: McGraw-Hill:240–281.

Rodrigues, J. 2004. "Endogenous Preferences and Embeddedness: A Reappraisal of Karl Polanyi." *Journal of Economic Issues* 38(1): 189–200.

Ross, M. L. 2004. "Does Taxation Lead to Representation?" *British Journal of Political Science* 34(2): 229–249.

Rostow, W. W. 1971. *The Stages of Economic Growth* (Second Edition). Cambridge: Cambridge University Press.

Sahlins, M. 1965. "On the Sociology of Primitive Exchange." In *The Relevance of Models for Social Anthropology* (M. Banton, Editor). London: Tavistock Publications: 139–236.

Sahlins, M. 1972. *Stone Age Economics.* New York, NY: Aldine.

Scarre, C., (ed.). 1999. *The Seventy Wonders of the Ancient World.* New York, NY: Themes & Hudson.

Schneider, H. K. 1974. *Economic Man, The Anthropology of Economics.* New York, NY: Free Press.

Schumpeter, J. A. 1950. *Capitalism, Socialism and Democracy* (Third Edition). New York, NY: Harper.

Seabright, P. 2004. *The Company of Strangers.* Princeton, NJ: Princeton University Press.

Shaffer, L. N. 1992. *Native Americans Before 1492.* Armonk, NY: M. E. Sharpe.

Simon, H. A. 1976. *Administrative Behavior* (Third Edition): New York, NY: The Free Press.

Smith, A. [1776] 1937. *The Wealth of Nations.* New York, NY: Modern Library.

Smith, V. L. 1999. "Economy, Ecology, and Institutions in the Emergence of Humankind." In *The Other Side of the Frontier.* (L. Barrington Editor). Boulder, CO: Westview Press: 57–85.

Stites, S. H. 1904. *Economics of the Iroquois.* Bryn Mawr, PA: Bryn Mawr College Monographs, Vol. 1, No. 3.

Stoltman, J. D. (Editor). 1991. *New Perspectives on Cahokia: Views from the Periphery.* Madison, WI: Prehistory Press.

Tannenbaum, N. 1984. "The Misuse of Chayanov: 'Chayanov's Rule' and Empiricists Bias in Anthropology." *American Anthropologist* 86(4): 927–942.

*The Bible.* 1997. *Authorized King James Version* (with an Introduction and Notes by R. Carroll and S. Prickett). Oxford: Oxford University Press.

Trigger, B. G. 1968. *Beyond History: The Methods of Prehistory.* New York, NY: Holt, Rinehart and Winston.

Trigger, B. G. and W. R. Swagerty. 1996. "Entertaining Strangers: North America in the Sixteenth Century." In *The Cambridge History of the Native Peoples of the Americas, Vol. I, North America* (Part 1) (B. G. Trigger and W. E. Washburn, Editors). Cambridge: Cambridge University Press: 325–391.

Wallace, A. F. C. 1958. "Dreams and Wishes of the Soul: A Type of Psychoanalytic Theory among the Seventeenth Century Iroquois." *American Anthropologist* 60: 234–248. Reprinted in *The Americans on the Eve of Discovery* (H. E. Driver, Editor). Englewood Cliffs, NJ: Prentice-Hall: 69–79.

Waters, A. (Editor). 2004. *American Indian Thought.* Malden, MA: Blackwell.

Wilk, R. R. 1996. *Economics and Cultures: Foundations of Economic Anthropology.* Boulder, CO: Westview Press.

Wilson, J. 1999. *The Earth Shall Weep: A History of Native America*. New York, NY: Atlantic Monthly Press.

Wittry, W. L. 1969. "The American Woodhenge." In *Explorations into Cahokia Archaeology* (M. L. Fowler, Editor). Urbana, IL: Illinois Archaeological Survey, Bulletin No. 7: 43–48.

Zambardino, R. A. 1980. "Mexico's Population in the Sixteenth Century: Demographic Anomaly or Mathematical Illusion?" *Journal of Interdisciplinary History* 12: 1–27.

# 3 Economic thought in America's protohistorical period

## Introduction

Anthropologists define protohistory as (1) a period between prehistory and history, a time when the existence of a preliterate culture is noted in the writings of other societies, or (2) a transitional period between the advent of literacy in a civilization and the writings of the first historians (Trigger 1985, 116; Trigger and Swagerty 1996, 326). For American aboriginals, the sixteenth century, basically the period from 1492 to 1600, satisfies the first definition. For colonial America, the seventeenth century or roughly 1607 to 1700, fits the second meaning as will be shown presently.

At first glance, summarizing seventeenth-century American economic thought would seem to be an easy task as so little formal writing and publishing of any kind was produced in America during this era. Therein lies a paradox. Early American colonists, whose numbers grew to approximately a quarter million by the century's end from less than a thousand at its beginning (Cassedy 1969, 14–15, 62–63), were busy if not consumed with answering the basic economic questions of what, how, and for whom at the individual and societal levels (Johnson et al. 2003). The practice of economics was extensive even if writing about economics was not. Some economic-thought historians ascribe the dearth of bona fide economics to the start-up cost of forming a new society: "Adventurers, colonizers, planters, agriculturalists, merchants, governors or soldiers as a rule are neither highly reflective nor philosophical in method" (Johnson 1932, 11). The reality is that the absence of a well-developed body of knowledge for posterity, be it economics or whatever, is a major by-product of a protohistorical period. Indigenous Americans were preliterate and, understandably, did not create a written legacy. Colonial Americans came from literate countries, but the vast majority of these immigrants, especially the large number who came in the first substantial waves of migration in the mid-seventeenth century, could neither read nor write. These early colonists did not create a rich written legacy for future generations, nor could they access the works of the few fellow colonists who did. Recognizing this is crucial to seeing the 1600s as the literary time-bridge between the prehistory of the sixteenth century and the first thoroughly historical era in America, the eighteenth century.

On the premise that "nothing can be understood apart from its context" (Crosby 1972, xiii), this essay begins with a circular flow model of the production, transmission, and consumption of knowledge in early colonial America as a way of making the case for considering the seventeenth century as America's protohistorical period. Once the notion of a protohistorical period is accepted or at least entertained, the chapter examines, interprets, and evaluates the economics of New England Puritans, one group whose rich written heritage allows inference of their economic thinking, thinking that was complete, consistent, but in the end had limited impact on America economics in the seventeenth century or beyond despite the efforts of modern scholars to suggest otherwise. The chapter concludes with an investigation of other seventeenth-century authors whose output, while nowhere near as voluminous as that of the Puritans, was more influential in shaping colonial economic behavior and ultimately the arc of American economic thought.

## Knowledge, ideas, influence, and protohistory

Capitalizing on Europe's fascination with the New World, books and pamphlets by English visitors or immigrants to America appeared almost as soon as England began a sustained effort at colonization. Examples included Captain John Smith's *A Description of New England* (1616) and *Good Newes from New England* (1624) by Edward Winslow, leader of the *Mayflower* pilgrims. Opportunities for place-bound Brits to see American aboriginals for themselves – Pocahontas and her husband, the colonist John Rolfe, and their son Thomas, visited London in 1616 – only heightened New World curiosity (Foreman 1943, 8). Awareness of America's indigenous people became so commonplace in England, the term "indian" found its way into Shakespeare's *The Tempest,* first performed in 1611 (Vaughan 1965, 24). Hoping to exploit Europe's New World interest, colonists, particularly Puritans, crafted publications meant to induce others to migrate to America, and/or persuade policy makers to support colonization (Geller and Gomes 1975, 16). Works such as John Winthrop's *A Modell of Christian Charity* (1630) probably had the desired effect; the question we need to explore is what impact did these writings have on the Puritans' colonial contemporaries living in America, and thus indirectly, the trajectory of American thought, particularly as it applies to economics?

To get a handle on this issue, consider Figure 3.1, a simple circular flow model of written knowledge in which the "product market" represents the consumption of information and the "resource market" describes its production. In the product market literate persons demand or buy written information and the printing industry supplies or sells it. In the resource market, the roles are switched; literate individuals supply or sell manuscripts and printing firms demand or buy material to publish. We need to appreciate the scope and complexity of both the product and resource markets in this model to gauge the influence seventeenth-century American writings had in the American colonies, and then contrast that with the status and weight such writings enjoy in modern intellectual history if we wish to avoid some of the common myths associated with literacy (Graff 2011).

Consider the demand side in the product market, in short, the state of literacy in colonial America, understanding that the seventeenth century is a veritable "cul-de-sac of inadequate data" (Price 1984, 19). Since the lack of data makes evaluating the incidence of literacy in seventeenth-century colonial America in terms of the modern definition of literacy impossible (Soltow and Stevens 1981, 4), modern researchers have used the evidence of testators' signatures or marks as a proxy measure, reasoning that "signatures on wills approximate the literacy not only of the sample but of the population" (Lockridge 1974, 7). Other literacy scholars, recognizing that this approach has shortcomings "as it uses a biased sample and an ambiguous measure (Lockridge 1974, 4), have studied signatures and marks "attached to deeds of conveyance, depositions and jury inquests" as a way to assess the degree of general literacy (Bruce 1910, 450–459), arguing that signers of these documents were likely to be drawn from a wider swath of the population than property-owning will-makers (Soltow and Stevens 1981, 56). Even though signature evidence is thought to overstate a population's literacy (Grubb 1990, 455), the cumulative results of numerous signature-base measures of colonial literacy provide a clue as to the status of reading and writing in seventeenth-century America (Soltow and Stevens; Bruce).

In the first third of the century when immigration was minor and mainly ideologically driven, literacy was relatively high, about 75 percent for men, considerably less for women, and well above that for the general populations of England and Western Europe. From 1630 to 1680 when motivation for migration became more economic and less philosophical, the new colonists were more representative of the European populations from where they came, and literacy rates fell to about 30 percent for men and less for women (Cressy 1987, 98). By the end of the seventeenth century literacy for colonial men and women began to rise. This increase was due to a number of factors notably the rise of education, especially religious education (Morison 1936, 56–79, 83–87), increasing population density, and the broad ascent in the general level of prosperity (Perkins 1980, 39). Increasing population in America's northeast created the economies of scale that permitted formation of public school systems, another boost to literacy (Soltow and Stevens 1981, 30). In the southern colonies, the physical dispersion of the population because of the expanding plantation economy put the emphasis on home schooling rather than formal education, contributing to regional differences in literacy rates, which were lower in the south than the north (Bruce 1910, 293). By mid-century conservative estimates are that at least 40 percent of male colonists and two-thirds of female colonists could *not* write their own names (Cressy 1987, 217). Though the rising tide of prosperity elevated literacy across colonial America during the latter part of the seventeenth century (Grubb 1990, 477), true literacy in America by century's end was confined primarily to scholars, clergy, and gentlemen of means (Steinberg 1959, 165). Using signature evidence indicates that by 1700, the pool of literate persons in the American colonies was small, about 30 percent of the adult males in the north, less in the south, and still less when the total population of men and women of all races is considered (Lockridge 1974, 14–15). The consumption of reading material was understandably negligible, a conclusion reinforced in probate records showing that book possession was rare even among the well-to-do. Personal libraries were tiny, usually in the single digits with a high probability that at least one of those volumes, if not all, was the Bible (Bruce 1910, 410–441; Morison 1936, 138).

The anemic demand side of the product market in Figure 3.1 seems downright robust compared to the supply side. The 1636 founding of Harvard College in Cambridge, Massachusetts led to the establishment of the first printing shop in colonial America in 1639 to produce imprints for the school as well as the general public (Thomas [1810] 1970, 4). In the southern colonies, the first print house began around 1680 in Williamsburg, Virginia (Bruce 1910, 390, 402): it began producing imprints in earnest in 1693 when the College of William and Mary, which operated as a "grammar school until well into the next century" opened (Dorfman 1946, 27). During the early phase of the printing industry in America – 1640–1669 – about five imprints per year were produced (Soltow and Stevens 1981, 41). By the end of the century printing houses had been established in a number of colonial urban centers including Boston, New York, and Philadelphia, but the overall level of output for the period 1639–1700 remained small, less than one thousand imprints (Weeks [1916] 1996, 2), consisting mostly of legal notices, broadsheets, and religious pamphlets, the majority of which appeared in the last decade of the century (Evans [1916] 1941). The short supply of paper, which in the seventeenth century and through the first half of the eighteenth century was

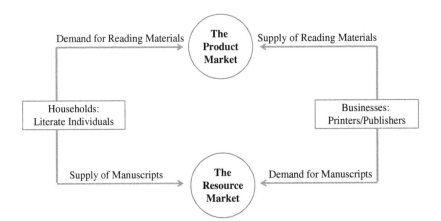

*Figure 3.1* The circular flow of the printed knowledge/information industry in America during the pre-historical period

produced using fibers extracted from linen and cotton rags and not wood, also inhibited the development of a colonial printing industry (Weeks [1916] 1996, 3, 60–72). Granted that during the protohistorical period most printing jobs originating in America were outsourced to Europe (Thomas [1810] 1970, 5), and most reading materials used in the colonies were imported (Cressy 1987, 232–233), the conclusion is inescapable: the product market in Figure 3.1 was diminutive and so was its economic and social influence within the colonies.

While reasonably operational in the major urban areas of England and Western Europe during the seventeenth century, the circular flow model of knowledge production and distribution in Figure 3.1 was basically nonexistent in colonial America because of an economic 'catch-22.' On the demand side of the model's product market, individuals were hesitant to acquire literacy skills due to the paucity of available reading material. On the supply side of the product market, printers were unwilling to exploit the economies of scale intrinsic in mechanical printing given the dearth of readers. Without viable demand and supply conditions in the product market, there was no derived demand to drive the resource market, creating an economic stalemate that persisted in colonial America until the eighteenth century. Compounding this situation was the absence of publishing intermediaries; "Publishers, in the modern sense of the word, did not exist in the English-speaking world until the eighteenth century" (Morison 1936, 124). This was especially evident in the newspaper industry. The first attempts to publish newspapers in England date to the late 1500s (Thomas [1810] 1970, 9), but sustained publishing success was not achieved until 1620 (Copeland 1997, 14–15). By contrast, the first newspaper in the American colonies appeared in Boston in 1690. After one issue *Publick Occurrences Both Forreign and Domestick* ceased publication, suppressed for political and religious reasons (Copeland 1997, 11, 14). Not until 1704 and the appearance of the *Boston News-Letter*, a weekly broadsheet with a typical print run of 250 in a town with a population of about 10,000, did America witness the continuous operation of a successful newspaper (Mott 1945, 12). The *News-Letter* survived until December 1719, the same month Boston got its second newspaper and Philadelphia got its first (Copeland 1997, 14). Papers in the southern colonies appeared later suggesting a north–south pattern of development, but the spatial reality of the seventeenth century gave an east–west progression, or more accurately, a coastal–interior settlement pattern, and not a north–south one. The South as a geographical expression did not emerge until well after independence (Bridenbaugh 1970, vii–viii).

One group of American immigrants, however, was intent on communicating with others, present and future. American Puritans, particularly in New England, "were highly self-conscious about their achievements and began interpreting themselves for posterity as soon as they arrived in the New World" (Morgan 1964, 3). Published New England Puritans included John Winthrop, William Pynchon, John Cotton, and Anne Bradstreet, while numerous others produced hand-written journals and diaries. Most of this voluminous output met with indifference among British scholars (Cressy 1987, vii), but has been mined to near exhaustion by twentieth-century American scholars creating a variety of interpretations of New England Puritans ranging from the conceptual narratives of the incomparable Perry Miller, his equally eminent protégé Edmund Morgan, or the neglected Samuel Eliot Morison, to the eclectic methodologies of the new social historians – "cliometricians, interdisciplinary social theorists, and critically minded social democrats" – whose views of historical scholarship are both complementary and sometimes contradictory (Henretta 1979, 1295). As a result of these modern efforts we probably know more about American Puritans then they knew about themselves (Greene and Pole 1984, 8); we certainly know more about New England Puritans than their contemporaries living in other American colonies. The accumulated body of work has yielded unimaginable insights into a distant culture but not without some consequences, largely unintentional.

First, inherent in the study of intellectual history is the analysis of written documents and those who create them, which in seventeenth-century America means accentuating the views of clerics and political officials, a distinct minority that had the time and talent to write, as opposed to the largely illiterate mass of immigrants who had neither (Trigger 1985, 341). Second, "the rich and extensive writings ... on New England culture ... especially Puritanism" has given the latter "a disproportionate importance in the history of seventeenth-century America" (Bailyn 1955, 75), to the near exclusion of other shapers of American culture. Yet, however exaggerated the significance of Puritans – the radicals of their time – may be, they cannot be ignored (Grigg 2008). As recently as 1776, "Puritanism provided the moral and religious background of fully 75 percent" of European immigrants living in America (Ahlstrom 1972, 124). Rather than downplaying the influence of the New England Puritans on the development of the American mind, their importance must be calibrated, contextualized, and put in perspective with other prominent contributors whose modest written legacy underestimates the magnitude of their impact, especially as it pertains to economic thought.

## Puritan economic thought

In 1930 Max Weber published *The Protestant Ethic and the Spirit of Capitalism*, a work which helped popularized the view that Puritanism in general, and that practiced in New England in particular, was a religious precursor of the market economics Adam Smith 'preached' in *The Wealth of Nations* (Parks 1996, 15–16). The reality was more complicated than that (Frey 1998). To be sure, certain aspects of Puritanism parallel Smith's economic thinking such as the idea of harnessing self-interest to advance the social good, although Puritans clearly distinguished morally acceptable self-interest from sinful self-centeredness (Frey 2009, 13). On the other hand, certain tenets of Puritanism – just price, the sin of usury and other Scholastic precepts – were antithetical to pure market economics (Appleby 1978, 14). As no Puritan ever penned a tract explicitly focused on the sect's economics, Puritan economic thought has always been a matter of inference and interpretation, especially speculative processes, given that the group's economics was embedded in its religion, itself a manifestation of Puritan philosophy. Contemporary scholars often have difficulty coming to terms with Puritan thought, "not because of its profundity but because of its simplicity" (Miller [1939] 1967, 161.

> Its [Puritan thought] fundamental ways of regarding things being utterly foreign to our manner of thinking, or seeing; to us it seems highly abstract and over-intellectualized, yet in its day the doctrine had for Puritans among its many virtues that of easy comprehensibility. It can indeed be stated very compactly. When God created the world, He formed a plan or scheme of it in His mind, of which the universe is the embodiment; in His mind the plan is single, but in the universe it is reflected through concrete objects and so seems diverse to the eye of human reason; these apparently diverse and temporal segments of the single and timeless divine order are the various arts; the principles of them are gathered from things by men through the use of their inherent capacities, their natural powers; once assembled, the principles are arranged into series of axiomatical propositions according to sequences determined by the laws of method.
>
> (Miller [1939] 1967, 161)

Like nested Russian dolls, the three interrelated aspects of Puritan thought – economics, religion, and philosophy – are conceptually distinct yet inexorably related, requiring an appreciation of both the philosophy and the religion if one hopes to understand their economics.

The philosophical roots of Puritanism can be traced to William Perkins (1558–1602), a Cambridge University theologian and a moderate during the English Reformation (Wright 1940, 171). Writing in Latin during a period of limited literacy, his influence was restricted largely to his peers, namely, intellectuals, academics, and other clerics. Still, the power of his prose to explain the "knotty problems that troubled the consciences of the time" (Wright 1940, 196), made Perkins as important to England as John Calvin was to Western Europe. Many of his students used their careers to spread his message. Principal among these was William Ames (1576–1633), Perkins' protégé and the one especially instrumental in shaping seventeenth-century Puritan religious thinking as it evolved in England and was practiced in New England. Ames operationalized Perkins' philosophical precepts into a useful, every-day religion that served as a practical guide to ethics (Sprunger 1972, 257) teaching "men what to believe and how to act" (Haller [1938] 1957, 25). His writings, many of which appeared in English before those of Perkins, had a profound impact on ordinary Puritans, particularly those who migrated or considering migrating to the New World. Indeed, Ames's *The Marrow of Theology* (1627), which initially appeared in Latin but was quickly translated into English, became the primary divinity text at Harvard College from its founding in 1636 and well into the eighteenth century (Maloy 2008, 105).

Less dogmatic than many of his peers, Ames gave Puritanism a degree of flexibility often lacking in purely philosophical approaches, reworking Scholastic doctrines to make them more applicable to contemporary life (Boughton 1987, 203); in the process he inadvertently crafted a religion that was especially adaptable to the unanticipated realities of the New World (Davis 2005). Ames's "theological treatises ... were to reign supreme in New England for a century and a half" (Morgan 1963, 74), but in England he was dismissed. Unable to coexist with the established English church, he began in 1610 a self-imposed exile in the Netherlands that lasted until his death (Sprunger 1972, 27).

However important Perkins and Ames were to Puritanism in general, John Robinson (1575–1625) was the minister most instrumental in bringing the religion to New England (Tyler 1904, 150–163). A "rigid Separatist who saw the English church as polluted throughout" (Sprunger 1972, 19), Robinson studied at Cambridge during a time when both Perkins and Ames were there. After graduation and several ministries, he became pastor of a Separatist group in Scrooby, a small town in Northern England. Robinson was apparently a gifted preacher with substantial influence among his followers (McNeill 1954, 335–336) during a period when Puritans placed a premium on the spoken word (Haller [1938] 1957, 19), due in part to the low rates of literacy (Lockridge 1974, 15). Indeed, Puritans considered preaching "the principal means ordained by God for instructing people in the great truths revealed by the Scriptures" (Morgan 1963, 7), which would explain why William Perkins' most enduring work was not one of his philosophical tracts but rather *The Art of Prophesying* published posthumously in 1607 (Emerson 1990, 17).

Using his powers of persuasion, Robinson convinced his flock to migrate to the religiously tolerant Netherlands, first to Amsterdam in 1607 then settling in Leiden in 1609, where Robinson became the leading Separatist outside of England (Sprunger 1972, 37). Being mostly merchants, the Scrooby group initially encountered some serious problems adjusting to life in the commercial republic of the Netherlands, but within a decade became sufficiently comfortable in their new, liberal surroundings to achieve a level of prosperity comparable to that which they had left behind. For Robinson, convinced that Puritanism was not just the right way but the only way, the Puritans' new life had become too tolerant and too comfortable. Having "no intention of tolerating other sects" (Miller 1933, 64), Robinson believed that Dutch hegemony would eventually absorb the Scrooby congregation, rendering the Separatist movement meaningless. As the author of *A Justification of Separation from the Church of England* (1610), Robinson had no truck with the institutional arrangement that gave political officials authority over church affairs, but as a Puritan, he was favorably disposed to the reverse situation – church officials running the government – and was especially partial to laws providing that only church members could vote or hold elected office (Morgan 1965, xxix).

To thwart the religious hospitality of the Dutch and simultaneously promote the idea of creating a Puritan theocracy, Robinson began to call upon his congregation to consider relocating to the New World, there to erect a "new state … in accordance with Puritan ideals" (Miller 1933, 100). In the fall of 1620 a small portion of Robinson's followers, heeding their leader's appeal, went to London with the intent of voyaging to the New World to establish "the Puritan dream of a godly Utopia" (Haller 1957, 189). In London, the thirty-three Puritans joined a group of "strangers," essentially non-Puritans seeking to migrate to the New World for economic reasons. This bizarre combination of the righteous and the opportunistic boarded the *Mayflower* and, after one false start, the 102 passengers and a crew of 30 departed for their destination on September 16, 1620. Following nearly two months at sea, the ship anchored in what is now Provincetown Harbor of Cape Cod, making Robinson the "pastor of the Plymouth pilgrims" (Emerson 1990, 51) and bringing Puritanism to what would become Massachusetts. What was this variant of Calvinism that Perkins conceived, Ames refined, and Robinson preached, all about, and what economic thinking was embedded in the philosophy of this religion?

Puritanism was a retro radical movement as it sought to recapture the Christianity of the past (McGrade 2003) rather than take the faith in a new direction (Geller and Gomes 1975, 13). Following the lead of William Perkins, Puritans looked upon the Bible "as the ultimate authority" in all matters concerning human life (Wright 1940, 184). Committed to building a society based on biblical precepts as interpreted by St. Augustine and filtered through the writings of Thomas Aquinas and other Scholastic thinkers (Miller [1939] 1967, 66), the Puritans worked toward updating medieval teachings for life in the seventeenth century (Boughton 1987, 194–203). This was especially true of the Puritans who migrated to Massachusetts where they relied heavily on preaching to deliver their message given the low rate of literacy (Stout 1986). In the process, the so-called New England Yankee was created (Bridenbaugh 1981, 77–78), a mythical persona formed when religious idealism came to terms with 'Yankee' realism, "a product of native condition, created by a practical economics" (Parrington 1927, 3–4). This wisdom born of necessity is evident in the Puritans' attitude toward the Scholastic notions of just price and usury.

Functioning markets in which the dynamic interactions of buyers and sellers set prices that influenced choice making were operational in England and its colonies long before the publication of Adam Smith's *Wealth of Nations* (Appleby 1978, 20–23). Commodity markets were well established throughout the seventeenth century, and factor markets, particularly for labor, while less evident, were clearly emerging at the time Puritans landed in Massachusetts (Jones 1996, 118–120). Initially, Puritans followed Scholastic teaching about pricing as evident in the infamous Keayne trial (Valeri 2010, 37–71), in which Robert Keayne, a Boston merchant, was assessed a hefty fine and given a severe tongue lashing for repeatedly taking advantage of shortages to "overcharge" his customers (Morison 1936, 8). Eventually, Puritans figured out how to be pious and profitable (Valeri 2010, 90); ever the Yankee, they equated the "just price" with "the common market price," a proto-market economics that was a practical concession to reality and well within the norms of conformity expected of everyone, Puritans and non-Puritans alike (Bercovitch 1993, 72–79). Similarly, usury or interest-bearing, business-to-business loans were considered an acceptable and appropriate aspect of commercial life, although when lending to the poor, Puritans believed that one should neither demand nor expect a return beyond the principal (Frey 1998, 1578). Plainly, with respect to just-price and usury, Puritans were "attuned to the commercial needs of the times" (Dorfman 1946, 12). While Puritans paid lip service to Scholastic economics, they embraced wholeheartedly a basic tenet of Scholastic society, namely, mutual interdependency of individuals and the collective responsibility of all to promote the common good (Langholm 1998, 101). Acceptance of this proposition was evident in the covenants or contracts Puritans believed to be the foundation of social order, although the impact of Scholasticism on the development of Western economic thought is a matter of debate as evident in Schumpeter (1954, 82–107), Blaug (1985, 29–31), Zuniga (1997), and Casey (2010).

Rightly or wrongly, Puritans believed that endemic to medieval society was the notion that every individual "was placed by God's command in a particular station in life" (Morgan 1965, xv), a covenant or spiritual contract the Puritans dubbed 'the calling.' In Puritan microeconomics, there is a person for every job and a job for every person; the calling is the process that determines who does what, that is, the life activity by which each individual earns a living for one's self while simultaneously promoting social wellbeing. Finding one's special place required each individual to study God's word (the Bible) and examine one's "God given capacities and opportunities" to discern what that calling was (Morgan 1965, xvi). Those who selected the correct calling were rewarded accordingly, while those who could not decipher the Almighty's message or chose to ignore it, would never know prosperity. Puritans expected everyone to work and work hard, but hard work alone was not sufficient to prevent poverty. Having no truck in a labor theory of value, Puritans subscribed, if only implicitly, to the principle of comparative advantage. For Puritans, poverty was the result of following a sub-optimal calling. By simply reassessing their life choices and discerning one's true calling, the poor could alter their financial status for the better. Coupling a person's unique abilities with society's occupational needs promoted the common good as well as personal well-being, for when the good of the self is optimized so too is that of society as a whole (Frey 1998, 1575). Believing that on Earth God's work was surely their own, Puritans, were not averse to tweaking the system of callings as reality dictated; the staffing of the teaching profession was a clear example of this.

During the seventeenth century and throughout much of the eighteenth, brawn trumped brains as the human attribute most necessary for the survival of colonials. Thinking and reflection were no substitutes for a strong back and the willingness to work endless hours using primitive tools to create a pasture, till the rocky New England soil, or build a crude home and hearth. Yet not all those expected to shoulder their burdens, namely men, were physically endowed for the task. Some had genetically-based physical disabilities while others were simply too slight for the demanding physical labor that early colonists had to endure in establishing a permanent presence in the New World. Nevertheless, even physically disabled Puritans had a calling, a commitment to serve self and the community through work. Applying a bit of human ingenuity, the Puritans matched God's design with theirs. This was surely the case when it came to staffing the growing educational system and its ever increasing need for teachers, a perfect 'calling' for men with physical limitations (Elsbree 1939, 34). This became a common practice in New England as well as in other colonial areas such as New York and Philadelphia. Begun in the seventeenth century, the calling of frail men to the teaching profession continued well into the next century illustrated in the person of the spindly Ichabod Crane, the main character in Washington Irving's classic short story "The Legend of Sleepy Hollow," set in the 1790s and first published in 1820. When the quantity supplied of men, disabled or not, was insufficient to match that being demanded, Puritans turned to women to fill the growing teacher shortage (Elsbree 1939, 68). During this period of American history, the old saw "those that can do, those that can't teach" was an apt description of clever resource management and not merely a catty remark.

The calling was part of a larger, grand covenant that imposed a variety of mutually interdependent obligations on each person in a Puritan society, creating a microeconomics that was essentially the by-product of prescribed social expectations. As revealed in scriptures, this social contract spelled out the proper behavior of all individuals to self and others, mimicking a religious commune; even the ostensibly individualistic choice of an occupation was in reality a social decision "in which one's vocation was service to the community, not purely service of the self" (Frey 2009, 15). Embedded in this complex social matrix was a relational economic system based on a network of reciprocal duties that applied to everyone, including leaders and their followers.

> God approved of rulers, called them to office, and endowed them with the sanction of His authority; but He did so, as with other callings, indirectly: He called rulers to office through the consent of their people. It belonged to the people to establish government, define its purposes, place rulers in charge of it, and submit to those rulers as long as they fulfilled their offices properly. To achieve all these ends, the people must engage in a second, subsidiary covenant, not with God but with each other and their perspective rulers.
>
> (Morgan [1965], xxiii)

The Puritan system of economics, which was as much ecclesiastical as it was economic, required unflinching compliance with social norm and a willingness to work hard, with the accent on the later; disobedience was intolerable and indolence forbidden (Rosano 2003). In this saintly yet secular culture, cloistered monastics "were actually viewed as following an unproductive, even antisocial, calling" (Frey 2009, 16).

The "distinctly theological" system of Puritan microeconomics was strictly medieval, but their macroeconomics was *au courant.* The seventeenth century was the golden age of Mercantilism, at least in colonial America (Johnson 1932, 139–149). Building on the policy recommendations of Thomas Mun as reflected in his *England's treasure by forraign trade*, written in 1623 and widely circulated among British politicians but not formally published until 1664 (Appleby 1978, 37), the English established trade patterns with colonial America that were mutually beneficial and eagerly accepted by all parties involved – "the colonial providers of raw materials and the metropolitan producers [England] of finished manufactures …" (McCusker 1996, 362). The American colonies, including New England, found ready markets in England proper and its Caribbean colonies for their furs, fish, ship masts, tobacco, and other agricultural products, and were happy to buy, in turn, British-made capital goods and consumer durables (McCusker and Menard 1985, 97, 118). In the eighteenth century Mercantilist economics would become a contributing factor to the American war of independence, but in the seventeenth century it was the basis of a welcome and thriving symbiotic relationship (Munck 1989, 379).

Given the state of Puritan economic thought, clearly not on a par with what the English economist William Petty was producing at approximately the same time, two questions arise about its impact: How well did the Puritan economic system actually perform, and what legacy did that system and its underlying philosophy have on the long-term development of American economic thought? For an answer to the first question, let's start with the Plymouth colony, the first explicit attempt to create an American settlement based on Puritan principles. As a theocratic beachhead, Plymouth was doomed before the Puritans disembarked from the *Mayflower.* The strangers (non-Puritans) on board, mostly farmers representing about two-thirds of the 100 or so passengers who survived the Atlantic crossing, were driven by dreams of the prosperity to be had in the blossoming agriculture belt of northern Virginia, the original destination of the *Mayflower.* Believing that those dreams were not likely to be realized in the wilderness that was Massachusetts, technically part of the Virginia Colony (Tyler 1907, 291), the strangers initially refused to disembark. After nearly two months on a tiny ship with a bunch of religious zealots, they demanded that a binding contract, a "covenant" protecting secular as well as religious rights, be agreed to before landing; otherwise the strangers would remain on the ship for the return trip to England (Dorfman 1946, 30–31). Painfully cognizant of their lack of agrarian skills, the Puritans quickly agreed to the strangers' demands and the Mayflower Compact was struck. Often portrayed as a cosmic document that "laid the groundwork for democracy in America" (Yero 2006, 18), the

Mayflower Compact was more likely the first manifestation in what is now the State of Massachusetts of O'Neill's dictum – all politics is local, named in honor of Thomas "Tip" O'Neill (1912–1994), a former speaker of the United States House of Representatives (O'Neill 1987, 25–26).

Neither the Puritans nor their religion thrived in Plymouth. Within a year of their first landing, half of the colonists who came to Plymouth had perished. Initially under-resourced and later poorly resupplied, the Plymouth settlement nearly suffered the same fate as the "Lost Colony" at Roanoke or the abandoned Sagadahoc colony in Maine; yet, Plymouth survived, just barely. Ten years after being settled, Plymouth had a population of about 300 living in "primitive comfort within small frame houses built along two intersecting streets" (Bailyn 1955, 4). The Mayflower Compact created an open society at Plymouth, at least as open as prevailing seventeenth-century English mores would allow. This meant that the Puritans, who had little use for other Protestant sects, even separatists' ones (Ver Steeg 1964, 78–79), could not build their utopian theocracy at Plymouth. So, in 1629–1630 the Puritans initiated a bigger and better-financed effort to create a religious state in the New World. In less than two years 17 ships brought over 1,000 colonists, who established "what would become the city of Boston upon their arrival in Massachusetts Bay" (Carter 2008, 44). However, what set this endeavor at colonization apart from its forerunner at Plymouth was not just its size or its resources but its leader, John Winthrop, the champion of the Puritan ideal whose force of will was the single most important factor in the founding and success, however limited, of the Massachusetts Bay Colony (Morgan 1964, vii, 174).

Winthrop (1588–1649) came to the New World as governor of the Massachusetts Colony, a position he was elected to on four separate occasions and held for 12 years. He and many of the early Puritans who travelled with him (Emerson 1990, 35) came to America with one purpose in mind: to create a society consistent with biblical precepts that would be both "ciuill and ecclesiasticall." Boston was to become a "Citty upon a Hill," a paragon of piety, politics, and prosperity that would serve as a shining model of nation building for England, if not all of western Europe (Miller 1953, 4–5). For Winthrop and those who accompanied him, the idea was "to make New England a beacon to the world, not a refuge from it" (Morgan [1944] 1980, 173), and for the first dozen years in Massachusetts it appeared as though they would succeed. The period from 1630 to 1642 witnessed a 'great migration' from England to New England as some fifteen to twenty thousand people made the crossing with a fair share settling in Boston, the center of Puritan America (Morgan 2007, 60). These immigrants brought with them, in ascending order of importance, their human capital, their aggregate demand, and their money supply. The ships that transported the migrants also carried many of the products colonists needed but could not produce, while on the return trip took fish, lumber, and other New England exports to consumers in the Caribbean, England, or both, thereby completing the mercantilist cycle of trade (Morgan 2007, 60). The duration and magnitude of this spurt of economic growth was unprecedented in Colonial American history, but in 1642 these halcyon days came to a bubble-bursting end when the very engine of prosperity – immigration – stalled, and America experienced what was possibly its first recession (Carnes 2007).

The ostensible cause of this economic downturn was the English Civil War, a series of armed conflicts that began in 1642 and occurred on and off for nearly ten years. The war resulted in a number of prominent changes in English life including the creation of a social climate more hospitable to Puritans and other separatists' groups; this, in turn, diminished the significance of the political and religious reasons for migrating while simultaneously elevating the import of economic factors. On that score, New England was an inferior destination compared to the agricultural-rich areas in Pennsylvania, New Jersey, Maryland, Virginia, and other points along coastal America south of Boston (Galenson 1996). At its peak, New England was the destination for just over 30 percent of those immigrating from England (Smith 1972). After the English Civil War, that proportion dropped as even second- and third-generation New England Puritans began migrating south, causing net immigration to New England to turn negative in the 1680s and 1690s (Cressy 1987, 68–69; Smith 1972).

Other contributing causes to the decline of the Puritan ideal included but were not limited to: a growing perception among the elder founders of Puritan New England of "a great and visible decay of godliness" and the increased "manifestations of pride" (Miller 1956, 7); conflicts with American aboriginals (Schultz and Tougias 2000); a lack of intensity on the part of immigrants during the second half of the seventeenth century to push the Puritan agenda (Bailyn 1986, 9); the impractically of the communal system of work and rewards (Parks 1996, 19); the growing importance of the shipping-services industry and the corresponding decline of the resource-intensive export industry (Anderson 1975, 8–23): the increasingly unpopular, class-identifying sumptuary codes (North 1988, 41–58); the nearly perpetual internecine conflicts between John Winthrop and virtually everyone who disagreed with him (Morgan 2007, 145–152); and the Salem witch trials, symbolic of the "death throes of a passing era" (Middleton 2002, 181). Even though 'blue laws,' statutes prohibiting commerce on the Sabbath, and other vestiges of Puritan economics survived well into the twentieth century in parts of New England, the influence of Puritan economic thought, never appreciable, gave way to Yankee realism by the end of the seventeenth century, a convergence in economic thinking more in tune with the practices prevailing in most other areas of Colonial America (Johnson 1932, 128–133).

## Other voices

If modern scholars have exaggerated the importance of Puritan contributions to the scope of American economic thinking, then they have done so at the expense of others whose writings have influenced, albeit subliminally, the arc of economic thought in America. Two authors whose seventeenth-century ideas affected and/or were subsequently confirmed by later American scholarship are Captain John Smith (1580–1631), the soldier of fortune, and William Penn (1644–1718), the English political philosopher, real estate developer, and ardent Quaker. Of the two, the inclusion of Smith as part of the American economics tradition is the more difficult case to make on at least two counts. First, there is the matter of national identity. Some historians (Morison 1936, 3) believe much of what Smith wrote, even that about the American colonies, belongs to "English rather than American literature." Alternatively, others note that Smith was "a member of the first ruling council in Virginia, and subsequently its president; the acknowledged savior of the colony [Jamestown] during its first two years; [and] the first principal historian of Virginia, ... and a lifelong proponent of English settlement in America" making his "credentials as an American ... impressive" even though he spent more time in England than the colonies (Vaughan 1975, viii). Second and more problematic are the questions surrounding the veracity, accuracy, and motivation of his writings, which have been "violently attacked by some ... and as stoutly defended by others ..." (Arber and Bradley [1910] 1967, iii). The episode with Pocahontas is probably more fact than fiction (Mann 2007), but the stories of his exploits in Asia Minor are implausible if not downright unbelievable (Tyler 1907, 27). Notwithstanding his shortcomings, Smith was the person most instrumental in getting England to colonize America, not because of what he did, but rather because of what he wrote (Walter).

Smith published "eight books about his adventures, and those on his explorations in the New World were long regarded as authoritative" (Gerson 1978, 1). The first book that Smith wrote about the New World to be well received among the literati of England, a relatively large number compared to that in Colonial America but still an anemic proportion of the total population, was *A Description of New England*, which appeared in 1616. The book found a ready audience among politicians and venture capitalists, two groups extremely important in the organization and resourcing of new colonies in America. Credited with inspiring the *Mayflower* voyage (Chatterton 1927, 260–62), the book reflected Smith's infatuation with the power of New England the place; his exquisite descriptions of the countryside and sea shore indicated a singular degree of wonder and affection for the American landscape (Gallager 1994), especially remarkable for someone who during his lifetime had seen a con-siderable portion of the then known world. He also envisioned an economic future for New England, one built on fish in much the same way that tobacco proved a path to economic viability for the Virginia colony. His efforts to market New England to English movers and shakers was also self-serving in that "establishing an identity for New England was indistinguishable in Smith's mind from advancing himself as the man most capable of its settle-ment" (Woodward 2008, 93). When it became apparent that that was not likely to happen, Smith approached his subsequent writings about the New World from a broader perspective, one that emphasized long-term economic growth and development and not short-term returns and profit often associated with colonization.

In 1624 Smith released *The Generall Historie of Virginia, New England & The Summer Isles*, his "largest and most influential book" (Vaughan 1975, 176). A compilation of some of his earlier works – some of which were rewritten and/or revised for this volume – coupled with contributions from other authors, the book was more cathartic and less commercial than his previous publications. While absent of any concise and coherent testament of economics, *The Generall Historie* has interspersed throughout its pages cogent references to what modern economists would recognize as a theory of economic growth and development. From the earlier failures at Jamestown and the experiences of other European nations in the New World, Smith had come to the realization that colonization was a long-term process that depended on the commitment of capital, physical and human, and the availability of natural resources, which when blended together, could provide sustained economic growth and development, the cornerstone for establishing a viable society in America or for that matter anywhere. He had also come to understand that quantifiable inputs were a necessary but not a sufficient condition for economic progress, as an examination of past failures at sustainable colonization by England and other countries convinced him of the importance of trust in the economic equation, a conclusion that anticipated the scholarship of Francis Fukuyama by some three hundred years.

> Where there was no honesty, nor equity, nor sanctitie, nor veritie, nor pietie, nor good ciuilitie in such a Countrey, certainly there can be no stabilitie.
>
> (The Generall Historie, 148).

This sentiment represents quite a metamorphosis for someone who at times during his life seemed unable to distinguish right from wrong. As with most great individuals, Smith is a conflicted and complicated person; nevertheless, he is arguably "the most vivid personality of American literature before Benjamin Franklin" (Emerson 1993, 116).

If Captain John Smith merits inclusion in a history of American for what he wrote, than William Penn deserves recognition for what he did, and to some extent for what he didn't do (Geiter 2000). Because of an old friendship and debts the Crown owed his father, Penn received a royal charter in 1681 making him the proprietor of 45,000 square miles in the New World that included most of present-day Pennsylvania (named for Penn's father), northern Delaware, and western New Jersey (Bronner 1978). In 1682 Penn came to America intent on achieving three important goals. One of his objectives was to acquire legal title to some of the lands in his proprietorship, specifically riverfront properties along the rivers separating eastern Pennsylvania from Delaware and New Jersey; this meant purchasing the property from resident aboriginals (Forrest 2001). The acquisition process took Penn nearly two years to complete, and by all accounts he treated indigenous Americans with dignity and respect, paying fair prices for their lands (Peare 1957, 246–247, 250–251). A second major goal of his first visit to colonial America was to create a Quaker utopia in Pennsylvania that would "show a society founded and operated along the lines of Quaker ideals not only could work but was the answer to mankind's ills" (Endy 1973, 349). John Winthrop and the Puritans came to the New World to create the scaffolding for a temporary society that would ultimately serve as a model for nation building in the Old World; Penn saw his Quaker enclave as a permanent refuge from Europe, with Pennsylvania being as different from Massachusetts as Quakerism was from Puritanism.

In a sense Puritanism and Quakerism were more alike than different in that both were bible-based Protestant sects. However, Puritans were partial to the Old Testament with its negative reinforcement, exclusivity of membership, and limited redemption; by contrast, Quakers favored the New Testament and its notions of positive reinforcement, inclusiveness, and the prospect of universal salvation. In Massachusetts, Puritan values translated into inhibiting norms that encouraged conformity and stifled initiative. This would not be the case in Penn's "holy experiment" where Quaker principles would insure democracy and justice, inclusion, and creativity. In 1684 Penn, the real estate entrepreneur, returned to England to recruit Quakers and non-Quakers from all of Europe to migrate to his religious utopia (Hull 1970). Before his departure he wrote *Framework of Government*, a genuinely democratic blueprint for governing Pennsylvania in his absence, which takes us to the one important thing he didn't do.

John Winthrop was the champion of the Massachusetts colony; he was also a micromanager. They were called Puritans for a reason and Winthrop was inclined to see himself as being among the purest of the pure. For almost twenty years he made the major strategic decisions in the Massachusetts colony, that is, the what and the why; he also made most of the tactical decisions – the how. As both chief executive and day-to-day manager, Winthrop institutionalized decision-making in Massachusetts, leaving little wiggle room for those who governed after him. Penn was the visionary of Pennsylvania and probably would have become a micromanager if he had the opportunity; he chose instead to return to Europe to people his utopia, trusting that the managers he left behind would follow the spirit if not the letter of his principles as described in *Framework*, a document that ultimately served as an inspiration for the United States Constitution (Peare 1957, 294–295). Penn stayed in Europe fifteen years and during this time there arose in Pennsylvania the inevitable conflicts that occur when the mixture of "low politics and high ideals" clash (Kammen [1972] 1980, 146). Using their discretion, resident managers in Pennsylvania devised commonsense compromises "between Penn's radical vision and the tradition-bound expectations of the early settlers" (Dunn and Dunn 1982, 2). The result transformed lofty values into workable ethics, and did so within the guidelines Penn prescribed in *Framework*. Naturally, there were gaps between practice and principles. As a group,

Quakers were almost uniformly outspoken in their denunciations of slavery, yet the record clearly indicates even William Penn owned and traded slaves (Endy 1973, 356). The acute labor shortage in Colonial America led some to tolerate the supposedly intolerable (Jernegan 1931, 30–35). Still, when Penn returned to his proprietorship in 1699 for a two-year stay, he found a prosperous, pluralistic society whose political system embraced his concept of democracy, whose economic practices were aligned with his business-oriented thinking, and whose social norms were in tune with his puritanical inclinations as reflected in his 1682 essay *No Cross, No Crown* (Morgan 1983).

Penn's third objective in visiting his proprietorship in 1682 was to establish the city of Philadelphia, a planned community complete with a commercial hub that would serve as the economic engine driving the Pennsylvania colony (Forrest 2001), an engine fueled by trade, both domestic and international (Dunn and Dunn 1982, 18). When Penn returned to England in 1684, Philadelphia was more dream than reality; upon his return to America in 1699, presumably a permanent relocation, he found that the population of Pennsylvania had grown to 18,000, of whom about 3,000 lived in Philadelphia. Though he had intended to live out his years in the colony, Penn returned to England in 1701 to put his crumbling financial affairs in order; he never succeeded, and on July 30, 1718 he died penniless (Dunn 1986). If he could have returned in seventy years he would have found Philadelphia a vibrant, thriving city with a population of 30,000 and a hub of science and letters comparable in many respects to the major centers in Europe.

> In 1787 Philadelphia was unquestionably the intellectual capital of the United States. It was not simply that Philadelphia was much larger in population than New York or Boston; it was the distinction of its citizens that made the city a magnet for foreign visitors and the obvious meeting place for men of thought, as Alexander Hamilton put it, continentally, men who could see beyond the boundaries of their town or parish or county or state. It was the city of Benjamin Franklin, the very symbol of the Enlightenment, of Benjamin Rush, America's best-known physician, of David Rittenhouse, America's leading astronomer, of Charles Willson Peale, painter and promoter, of William Bartram, the country's foremost botanist. It was home of the American Philosophical Society, the only significant learned society on the continent. It had a flourishing theater, where, despite lingering objections from Quaker moralists, ladies and gentlemen could laugh at a farce or weep at a tragedy. It had eight newspapers and two monthly magazines (the *Columbian Magazine* and the *American Museum*). It had Peale's Museum with a display of waxworks, paintings, and scientific curiosities, the eighteenth-century prototype of the Smithsonian. It had Gray's Tavern, with the most elaborate landscape gardens in the country, complete with waterfalls, grottoes, and Chinese pagodas. Philadelphia was the place to be, the place to go.
>
> (Morgan [2009], 130–131)

Despite his extensive publications – more than "fifty books, pamphlets, and broadsides ... which he published at his own expense" (Dunn 1986, 41) – William Penn did not add in a material way to the development of economics as an intellectual pursuit. Nevertheless, the implementations of his visions for Pennsylvania and Philadelphia were instrumental in fashioning the America version of laissez-faire, that paradoxical blend of public and private interests designed to foster business development and promote economic growth on the local, regional and even the national level. This public/private paradigm became the model of economics, at least as it evolved in the eighteenth century America (Johnson 1932, 243–261), and that alone is sufficient to include Penn among those who have contributed to the American strain of economic thought.

## References

Ahlstrom, S. E. 1972. *A Religious History of the American People.* New Haven, CT: Yale University Press.

Anderson, T. L. 1975. *The Economic Growth of Seventeenth Century New England: A Measurement of Regional Income.* New York, NY: Arno Press.

Appleby, J. O. 1978. *Economic Thought and Ideology in Seventeenth-Century England.* Princeton, NJ: Princeton University Press.

Arber, E., and Bradely, A. G., (eds). [1910] 1967. *Travels and Works of Captain John Smith.* New York, NY: Burt Franklin.

Bailyn, B. 1955. *The New England Merchants in the Seventeenth Century.* Cambridge, MA: Harvard University Press.

Bailyn, B. 1960. *Education in the Forming of American Society.* Chapel Hill, NC: University of North Carolina.

Bailyn, B. 1986. *The Peopling of British North America.* New York, NY: Alfred A. Knopf.

Bercovitch, S. 1993. *The Rites of Assent: Transformations in the Symbolic Construction of America.* New York, NY: Routledge.

Blaug, M. 1985. *Economic Theory in Retrospect* (Fourth Edition). Cambridge: Cambridge University Press.

Boughton, L. C. 1987. "Choice and Action: William Ames's Concept of the Mind's Operation in Moral Decisions." *Church History* 56(2): 188–203.

Bridenbaugh, C. 1970. *Myths & Realities: Societies of the Colonial South.* New York, NY: Atheneum.

Bridenbaugh, C. 1981. *Early Americans.* New York, NY: Oxford University Press.

Bronner, E. B. [1962] 1978. *William Penn's "Holy Experiment:" The Founding of Pennsylvania, 1681–1701.* Westport, CT: Greenwood Press.

Bruce, P. B. 1910. *Institutional History of Virginia in the Seventeenth Century.* New York, NY: Putman.

Carnes, M. C. 2007. "Editor's Preface." In Edmund S. Morgan's *The Puritan Dilemma: The Story of John Winthrop* (Third Edition). New York, NY: Pearson/Longman: ix–x.

Carter, M. S. 2008. "Puritan Life." In *British Colonial America: People and Perspectives* (J. A. Grigg, Editor). Santa Barbara, CA: ABC Clio: 41–58.

Casey, G. N. 2010. "The Major Contributions of the Scholastics to Economics." *Mises Daily*. December 3. (Online).

Cassedy, J. H. 1969. *Demography in Early America: Beginnings of the Statistical Mind, 1600–1800*. Cambridge, MA: Harvard University Press.

Chatterton, E. K. 1927. *Captain John Smith*. New York, NY: Harper.

Copeland, David A. 1997. *Colonial American Newspapers: Character and Content*. Newark, DE: University of Delaware.

Cressy, D. 1987. *Coming Over, Migration and Communication between England and New England in the Seventeenth Century*. Cambridge: Cambridge University Press.

Crosby, A. W. 1972. *The Columbian Exchange: Biological and Cultural Consequences of 1492*. Westport, CT: Greenwood Press.

Davis, J. C. 2005. "William Ames's Calvinist Ambiguity over Freedom of Conscience." *Journal of Religious Ethics* 33(2): 335–355.

Dorfman, J. 1946. *The Economic Mind in American Civilization, 1606–1895*. New York, NY: Viking Press.

Dunn, R. S. 1986. "Penny Wise and Pound Foolish: Penn as a Businessman. " In *The World of William Penn* (R. S. Dunn and M. M. Dunn, Editors). Philadelphia, PA: University of Pennsylvania Press: 37–54.

Dunn, M. M., and Dunn, R. S. 1982. "The Founding, 1681–1701." In *Philadelphia, a 300-Year History* (R. F. Weigley, Editor). New York, NY: W. W. Norton: 1–32.

Elsbree, W. S. 1939. *The American Teacher: Evolution of a Profession in a Democracy*. New York: American Book Company.

Emerson, E. 1990. *John Cotton* (Revised Edition). Boston, MA: Twayne.

Emerson, E. 1993. *Captain John Smith* (Revised Edition). New York, NY: Twayne.

Endy, Jr., M. B. 1973. *William Penn and Early Quakerism*. Princeton, NJ: Princeton University Press.

Evans, C. [1916] 1941. *American Bibliography, A Chronological Dictionary of All Books, Pamphlets, and Periodicals Published in the United States of America, Volume I, 1639–1729*. New York, NY: P. Smith.

Foreman, C. T. 1943. *Indians Abroad, 1493–1938*. Norman, OK: University of Oklahoma Press.

Forrest, T. J. 2001. *William Penn, Visionary Proprietor*. (eBook): xroads.virginia.edu.

Frey, D. E. 1998. "Individualist Economic Values and Self Interest: The Problem in the Puritan Ethic." *Journal of Business Ethics* 17: 1573–1580.

Frey, D. E. 2009. *America's Economic Moralists*. Albany, NY: State University of New York Press.

Friedman, D. D. 1980. "In Defense of Thomas Aquinas and the Just Price." *History of Political Economy* 12(2): 234–242.

Fukuyama, F. 1995. *Trust: The Social Virtues and the Creation of Prosperity*. New York, NY: Free Press.

Galenson, D. G. 1996. "The Settlement and Growth of the Colonies: Population, Labor, and Economic Development." In *The Cambridge Economic History of the United States, Volume I, The Colonial Era* (S. L. Engerman and R. E. Gallman, Editors). Cambridge: Cambridge University Press: 135–207.

Gallager, W. 1994. *The Power of Place*. New York, NY: HarperPerennial.

Geiter, M. K. 2000. *William Penn*. Harlow: Pearson Education.

Geller, L. D., and Gomes, P. J. 1975. *The Books of the Piligrims*. New York, NY: Garland.

Gerson, N. B. 1978. *The Glorious Scoundrel, A Biography of Captain John Smith*. New York, NY: Dodd, Mead.

Graff, H. J. 2011. *Literacy Myths, Legacies, & Lessons.* New Brunswick, NJ; Transaction.

Greene, J. P., and Pole, J. R. 1984. "Reconstructing British American Colonial History: An Introduction." In *Colonial British America* (J. P. Greene and J. R. Pole, Editors). Baltimore, MD: Johns Hopkins University Press: 1–17.

Grigg, J. A. 2008. "Introduction." In *British Colonial America: People and Perspectives* (J. A. Grigg, Editor). Santa Barbara, CA: ABC-CLIO: xi–xxiii.

Grubb, F. W. 1990. "Growth of Literacy in Colonial America: Longitudinal Patterns, Economic Models, and the Direction of Future Research." *Social Science History* 14(4): 451–482.

Haller, W. [1938] 1957. *The Rise of Puritanism.* New York, NY: Harper & Row.

Henretta, J. A. 1979. "Social History as Lived and Written." *American Historical Review* 84(5): 1293–1322.

Hull, W. I. 1970. *William Penn and the Dutch Quaker Migration to Pennsylvania.* Balitmore, MD: Genealogical Publishing.

Jernegan, M.W. 1931. *Laboring and Dependent Classes in Colonial America, 1607–1783.* Chicago, IL: University of Chicago Press.

Johnson, E. A. J. 1932. *American Economic Thought in the Seventeenth Century.* London: P. S. King & Son.

Johnson, M., Medema, S. G., and Samuels, W. J. 2003. *Foundations of the American Economy, Volume I, The American Colonies from Inception to Independence.* London: Pickering & Chatto.

Jones, E. L. 1996. "The European Background." In *The Cambridge Economic History of the United States, Vol. I, The Colonial Era* (S. L. Engerman and R. E. Gallman, Editors). Cambridge: Cambridge University Press: 99–133.

Kammen, M. [1972] 1980. *People of Paradox: An Inquiry concerning the Origins of American Civilization.* Ithaca, NY: Cornell University Press.

Langholm, O. 1998. *The Legacy of Scholasticism in Economic Thought.* Cambridge: Cambridge University Press.

Lockridge, K. A. 1974. *Literacy in Colonial New England.* New York, NY: W. W. Norton.

Maloy, J. S. 2008. *The Colonial American Origins of Modern Democratic Thought.* New York, NY: Cambridge University Press.

Mann, C. C. 2007. "Jamestown, the Real Story." *National Geographic.* May: 32–55.

McCusker, J. J., and Menard, R. R. 1985. *The Economy of British America, 1607–1789.* Chapel Hill, NC: University of North Carolina Press.

McCusker, J. J. 1996. "British Mercantilist Policies and the American Colonies." In *The Cambridge History of the United States, Vol. I, The Colonial Era* (S. L. Engerman and R. E. Gallman, Editors). Cambridge: Cambridge University Press: 337–362.

McGrade, A. S., (ed.). 2003. *The Cambridge Companion to Medieval Philosophy.* Cambridge: Cambridge University Press.

McNeill, J. T. 1954. *The History and Character of Calvinism.* Oxford: Oxford University Press.

Middleton, R. 2002. *Colonial America, A History, 1565–1776* (Third Edition). Malden, MA: Blackwell.

Miller, P. 1933. *Orthodoxy in Massachusetts, 1630–1650.* Cambridge, MA: Harvard University Press.

Miller, P. 1953. *The New England Mind from Colony to Province.* Cambridge, MA: Harvard University Press.

Miller, P. 1956. *Errand into The Wilderness*. Cambridge, MA: Belknap Press.

Miller, P. [1939] 1967. *The New England Mind, the Seventeenth Century*. Cambridge, MA: Harvard University Press.

Morgan, E. S. 1963. *Visible Saints: The History of a Puritan Idea*. New York, NY: New York University Press.

Morgan, E. S., (ed.). 1964. *The Founding of Massachusetts: Historians and the Sources*. Indianapolis, IN: Bobbs-Merrill.

Morgan, E. S., (ed.). 1965. *Puritan Political Ideas, 1558–1794*. Indianapolis, IN: Bobbs-Merrill.

Morgan, E. S. [1944] 1980. *The Puritan Family, Religion & Domestic Relations in Seventeenth-Century New England* (New Edition). Westport, CT: Greenwood Press.

Morgan, E. S. 1983. "The World and William Penn." *Proceedings of the American Philosophical Society* 127(5): 291–315.

Morgan, E. S. 2007. *The Puritans Dilemma: The Story of John Winthrop* (Third Edition). New York, NY: Pearson/Longman.

Morgan, E. S. 2009. *American Heroes: Profiles of Men and Women Who Shaped Early America*. New York, NY: W. W. Norton.

Morison, S. E. 1936. *The Puritan Pronaos: Studies in the Intellectual Life of New England in The Seventeenth Century*. New York, NY: New York University Press.

Morison, S. E. [1930] 1964. *Builders of the Bay Colony*. Boston, MA: Houghton Mifflin.

Mott, F. L. 1945. *American Journalism: A History of Newspapers in the United States through 250 Years, 1690–1940*. New York, NY: Macmillan.

Munck, T. 1989. *Seventeenth Century Europe, 1598–1700*. New York, NY: St. Martin's Press.

North, G. 1988. *Puritan Economic Experiments*. Tyler, TX: Institute for Christian Economics.

O'Neill, T. 1987. *Man of the House*. New York, NY: Random House.

Parks, L. A. 1996. *Capitalism in Early American Literature*. New York, NY: Peter Lang.

Parrington, V. L. 1927. *Main Currents in American Thought*. New York, NY: Harcourt, Brace & World.

Peare, C. O. 1957. *William Penn, A Biography*. Philadelphia, PA: J. B. Lippincott.

Perkins, E. J. 1980. *The Economy of Colonial America*. New York, NY: Columbia University Press.

Price, J. M. 1984. "The Transatlantic Economy." In *Colonial British America* (J. P. Greene and J. R. Pole, Editors). Baltimore, MD: Johns Hopkins University Press: 18–42.

Rosano, M. J. 2003. "John Winthrop, John Cotton, and Nathaniel Niles: The Basic Principles of Puritan Thought." In *History of American Political Thought* (B.-P. Frost and J. Sikkenga, Editors). Lanham, MD: Lexington Books: 25–43.

Schultz, E. B., and Tougias, M. J. 2000. *King Philips's War: The History and Legacy of America's Forgotten Conflict*. Woodstock, VT: Countryman Press.

Schumpeter, J. A. 1954. *History of Economic Analysis*. New York, NY: Oxford University Press.

Soltow, L., and Stevens, E. 1981. *The Rise of Literacy and the Common School in the United States, A Socioeconomic Analysis to 1870*. Chicago, IL: University of Chicago Press.

Smith, D. S. 1972. "The Demographic History of Colonial New England." *Journal of Economic History* 32(1): 165–183.

Smith, Captain J. [1616] 1898. *A Description of New England*. London: H. Lownes.

Smith, Captain J. [1624] 1907. *The Generall Historie of Virginia, New England, & The Summer Isles*. Vol. 1. New York, NY: Macmillan.

Sprunger, K. L. 1972. *The Learned Doctor William Ames: Dutch Backgrounds of English and American Puritanism*. Urbana, IL: University of Illinois Press.

Steinberg, S. H. 1959. *Five Hundred Years of Printing*. New York, NY: Criterion Books.

Stout, H. S. 1986. *The New England Soul: Preaching and Religious Culture in Colonial New England*. New York, NY: Oxford University Press.

Thomas, I. [1810] 1970. *The History of Printing in America*. New York, NY: Weathervane Books.

Trigger, B. G. 1985. *Natives and Newcomers: Canada's "Historic Age" Reconsidered*. Kingston, Ontario: McGill-Queen's University Press.

Trigger, B. G. and Swagerty, W. R. 1996. "Entertaining Strangers: North America in the Sixteenth Century." In *The Cambridge History of the Native Peoples of the Americas, Volume I, North America, Part 1* (B. G. Trigger and W. E. Washburn, Editors). Cambridge: Cambridge University Press: 325–398.

Tyler, L. G. 1904. *England in America, 1580–1652*. New York, NY: Harper.

Tyler, L. G., (ed.). 1907. *Narratives of Early Virginia, 1606–1625*. New York, NY: Scribner's.

Valeri, M. 2010. *Heavenly Merchandize: How Religion Shaped Commerce in Puritan America*. Princeton, NJ: Princeton University Press.

Vaughan, A. T. 1965. *New England Frontier: Puritans and Indians, 1620–1675*. Boston, MA: Little, Brown.

Vaughan, A. T. 1975. *American Genesis, Captain John Smith and the Founding of Virginia*. Boston, MA: Little, Brown.

Ver Steeg, C. L. 1964. *The Making of America: The Formative Years, 1607–1763*. New York, NY: Hill and Wang.

Weber, M. [1930] 1958. *The Protestant Ethic and the Spirit of Capitalism*. New York, NY: Scribner's.

Weeks, L. H. [1916] 1996. *A History of Paper Manufacturing in the United States, 1690–1916*. New York, NY: Burt Franklin.

Woodward, W. W. 2008. "Captain John Smith and the Campaign for New England: A Study in Early Modern Identity and Promotion." *New England Quarterly* 81(1): 91–125.

Wright, L. B. 1940. "William Perkins: Elizabethan Apostle of 'Practical Divinity'." *Huntington Library Quarterly* 3(2): 171–196.

Yero, J. L. 2006. *The Mayflower Compact*. Washington, DC: National Geographic Society.

Zuniga, G. 1997. "Scholastic Economics: Thomastic Values Theory." *Religion and Liberty* 7(4) (Online).

# 4 Economic thought in eighteenth-century America prior to independence

## Introduction

Discussing the state of American economic thinking in the eighteenth century might seem a bit pretentious given that the century witnessed the publication of *The Wealth of Nations*, arguably one of the most notable events in the history of Western economic thought. Compared to the active, organized, and sometimes competing schools of European thought – mercantilism, physiocracy, laissez-faire, invisible-hand market capitalism – the state of American economics from 1700 to 1775 was truly primitive. Yet, as the 1978 Nobel Laureate in Economics Herbert A. Simon once observed "Advances in human knowledge even more than other events, cast very long shadows before them" (Katz 1989, 264). This cogent insight certainly applies to American economic thinking prior to the revolution, and provides a revealing preview of what the country's economics would look like after independence. Before discussing pre-revolutionary economic thought per se, this chapter begins with an overview of economic, social, and political conditions as a way of giving historical context to the development of American economics during the colonial period prior to independence.

## Economic, social, and political conditions, 1700–1775

The first 75 years of the eighteenth century were a period of consistent, sustained economic growth, thanks in large measure to a steadily increasing colonial population that grew at a rate slightly in excess of 3 percent per year (McCusker and Menard 1985, 9). Overall human head count in America – colonial plus aboriginal – was probably less in 1700 than it was in 1600 because of the dramatic drop in the indigenous populations due mainly to the adverse effects of the human and zoonotic diseases associated with European immigrants and their livestock (Menard 1996, 254–255; Jennings 2000, 21). By 1700 the decimation of native peoples which had been so precipitous was more than offset by the growth of colonial populations – domestic and immigrant. From about 250,000 at the beginning of the eighteenth century, the colonial population of America increased tenfold on the eve of independence to about 2.6 million, the composition of which was "1.95 million whites, 520,000 blacks, and 100,000 or fewer Native Americans" (Perkins 1980, 2). The colonial population was also becoming more diverse as the proportion of immigrants from England steadily decreased to about 60 percent in 1770, the other 40 percent coming from a variety of European countries and Africa (Kammen [1972] 1980, 203). From about mid-century on, the impact of immigration on the size of America's population had waned and the domestic birth rate became responsible for about 95 percent of population growth (Perkins 1980, 2).

The American workforce prior to independence was not only getting larger, it was also getting better. The broad implementation of compulsory education for a variety of religious and secular reasons (Jernegan 1931, 84–91) produced an appreciable deepening of the human capital embodied in the colonial population. This was particularly evident in the relatively densely populated coastal areas such as those around Boston and Philadelphia, which could sustain a large and growing number of private and public grammar and secondary schools (Seybolt 1935; [1935). While not as high as along the sea coast, the incidence of schooling rose steadily during this time period for children living in the comparatively less populated interior (Seavoy 2006, 28). The overall growth in education had a dramatic impact on the literacy rate as evident in development of the newspaper industry in America. The first continuous publication of an American newspaper began in Boston in 1704. Fifteen years later Boston got its second newspaper and Philadelphia got its first. Thereafter in rapid succession, newspapers appeared in other coastal urban centers: New York, 1725; Maryland, 1727; Charleston, 1732; and Virginia, 1736 (Copeland 1997, 14; Mott 1945, 12). Printing and widespread literacy took longer to arrive at interior settlements; the first newspaper in Vermont began publishing in 1781 (Thomas [1810] 1970, 586).

Notwithstanding the large commercial plantations in Maryland, Virginia, and South Carolina that were exporting tobacco, rice, and sugar to England and its other New World possessions, 80–90 percent of the colonial population depended on the activities of small-scale agriculture for their livelihood (Seavoy 2006, 1). These farms were generally self-sustaining but not necessarily self-sufficient as there were extensive networks of farmers' markets and barter arrangements for farm-to-farm trade. Most of these exchanges did not occur in formal markets so measures of national output or its dual, national income, are rough approximations. Nevertheless, rigorous and reasonable analysis of available data has yielded credible estimates for national income statistics for 1700–1775 (Jones 1980). For the timeframe in question, per capita income in colonial America grew at rates ranging from 0.3 to 0.5 percent per annum (Jones 1980, 78). Given the rate of population growth, this implies that gross domestic product was increasing at a minimum of about 3 percent a year for the 75-year period, which translates into a doubling every 20–25 years without interruption. A favorable tailwind gave additional momentum to this seamless expansion: "No major famines, epidemics, or extended wars intervened to reverse or even slow down appreciably the tide of vigorous economic expansion" (Perkins 1980, ix). This period of growth transformed the American colonies into a developing nation from an undeveloped one.

> From 1700 to 1774, ... aggregate output multiplied almost twelvefold. At the start of the eighteenth century, the size of the colonial economy was a mere 4 percent of the mother country's; yet on the eve of independence the percentage had risen to over one-third, and the colonies were gaining steadily.
>
> (Perkins 1980, ix)

Despite being one of the longest periods of uninterrupted growth in American economic history, the years from 1700 to 1775 were not without problems, two of the more prominent ones begin the quantity of money and the supply of labor. With respect to money, the long held conventional view was that glitches with the American money supply were a by-product of British mercantilism (Kammen 1970, 48; Bailyn 1955, 182–183).

> The colonies – as a debtor region – were confronted with a continuous adverse balance of payments, and their available specie was repeatedly drawn away to creditors in Europe. The scarcity of specie in America gave birth to a widespread belief that prices of colonial products were ruinously low because money was wanting. Commercial rates of exchange were unfavorable to the debtors; and, when the prices of their products fell in response to European commercial conditions, they were hard pressed to find the means of paying their debts
>
> (Nettels [1934] 1964, 8)

A more contemporary stance is that the colonial supply of money was just about right to sustain the robust rate of growth the American economy experienced over the 1770–1775 period. If this was not the case, that is, if the conventional view were correct, the colonies would have experienced a general and persistent decline in the price level; that did not happen although regional liquidity problems often occurred and were sometimes acute (Perkins 1980, 102). For some modern scholars, the underlying issues about the supply of colonial money were more a matter of political control than economics (Perkins 1980, 116). Whether real or imagined or something in between, matters surrounding the institution of money and its many facets were frequent topics of those few Americans writing about economics in the eighteenth century prior to independence.

The second major economic concern in eighteenth-century colonial America was the persistent shortage of labor due in large measure to the "unfettered access to abundant land" (Matson 2006, 28). Most immigrants came to America to become farmers; even transplanted merchants regularly gave up their craft to enter agriculture once they had acquired enough wealth to purchase a farm and with it, the sense of security that accompanied land ownership (Nash 1986, 344–345). To cope with the labor shortage which was particularly acute in the seventeenth century and the early portion of the eighteenth century before population growth eased the situation somewhat, the colonies developed an elaborate system of servants, i.e., contract workers who bound themselves to a single employer for a fixed period of time in return for free transportation to America.

> There were three main classes of servants. One who entered into such a contract with an agent, often the shipmaster, was called an indentured servant. The shipmaster reimbursed himself, on arrival in America, by selling the time of the servant to the highest bidder. The second class included the "redemptioners," or "free-willers." They signed no contract beforehand, but were given transportation by the shipmaster with the understanding that on arrival they were to have a few days to indenture themselves to someone to pay for their passage. Failing this, the shipmaster could sell them himself. The free-willer then was at a great disadvantage. He had to bargain in competition with many others, and was so much at the mercy of the buyer or the shipmaster that laws were passed by several colonies limiting his time of service and defining his rights.
>
> (Jernegan 1931, 47)

All told, "roughly half the Europeans arriving before 1776 owed a term of servitude in exchange for their ocean passage" (Rockman 2006, 335). A third category of servants included those forced into servitude such as prisoners and convicted criminals. This was the smallest class of servants amounting to no more than 10 percent of the roughly 500,000 servants who came to America prior to independence (Tomlins 2006, 150). The practice of shipping felons to the Americas was relatively short lived as several colonial governments were successful in persuading the British to discontinue the practice (Jernegan 1931, 48–49).

The twin magnets of high wages and cheap land continued to attract immigrants to America as the eighteenth century progressed but in reduced numbers, diminishing the effectiveness of servitude as a means of dealing with the labor shortage (Bailyn 1986, 60–61). That plus the frequent turn-over of servants working on fixed-length contracts led colonists, particularly plantation owners in the West Indies and America's southern colonies, to seek an alternative supply of labor (Koo 2008, 82–83). Slavery began in the British West Indies in the 1620s, and about fifty years later in colonial America. More slaves were imported into the West Indies than America (Dunn 1984, 165), but the rate of population growth among American slaves exceeded that among the slaves in the West Indies. As a result, at the time American independence was declared, there were about 350,000 slaves in the West Indies compared to 500,000 in the mainland colonies. Of the total American slave population, about 90 percent lived in the southern colonies while the rest were scattered in the Mid-Atlantic and New England regions (Dunn 1984, 165), where a combination of social forces and economics discouraged the practice. Ultimately, the institutions of slavery and issues surrounding the supply of money played prominent roles in the American story; the control of the money supply was a contributing factor to the seminal event in eighteenth-century America, the War of Independence, while the moral, political, and economic ramifications of slavery were instrumental causes of the watershed event in nineteenth-century American history, the Civil War.

## Eighteenth-century American economics

Any examination of American economic thought in the eighteenth century must include a discussion of Benjamin Franklin (1706–1790), arguably one of the most fascinating people on the planet during that century, and certainly the "one commanding name in [the] American economic discussion" of pre-revolutionary literature (Seligman [1925] 1967, 126). Born in Boston into a family of limited means, Franklin was the fifteenth of seventeen children Josiah Franklin fathered in two marriages. Though essentially self-educated, Franklin was sent to the Boston Latin School at age eight as preparation for a life in the clergy but family finances, or rather the lack thereof, forced an end to his formal schooling after two years. He worked for his father, a maker of candles and soap, until age twelve at which time he was indentured to his older brother James, a printer. The quid pro quo for this arrangement was that James would teach his younger brother the trade and in return, Franklin pledged nine years of service, this at a time when white servitude, though still popular, was declining as black slavery was increasingly becoming the predominant form of bound labor in colonial America (Dunn 1984; Galenson 1981). After five years of almost continuous friction between himself and his brother James, Franklin absconded from his apprenticeship, fleeing to Philadelphia in 1723 to begin a new and what would prove to be a remarkable life.

Franklin arrived in Philadelphia an "unkempt urchin," with few possessions save for "a Dutch dollar and a change of stockings in his pants" (Connor 1965, 10). Being a skilled printer, he eventually found work in what he personally considered his life's primary occupation as evident in his last will and testament which begins "I, Benjamin Franklin, Printer …" (Seeger 1973, 4). In 1729 after several years working for others, he bought and published the *Pennsylvania Gazette*, and turned what was a regional publication into the largest circulating newspaper in colonial America. The paper ultimately became the forerunner of the *Saturday Evening Post*, which is still in publication. In 1733, Franklin created *Poor Richard's Almanack*, an annual publication which appeared continually until 1758. The *Almanack* had a peak circulation of about 10,000 (Van Doren 1938, 109), equivalent to about 2 percent of the literate population in the American colonies, making it, in relative terms, comparable to the 2.7 million circulation of *The Saturday*

*Evening Post* in its heyday (Bruccoli 1996, 14). By 1750 he left the publishing industry, but not before arranging sales of his literary properties in a way that provided him and his family a comfortable standard of living for the rest of their days.

Franklin was a printer by necessity; he was a polymath by choice. A voracious reader from an early age, he amassed a personal library of over 4,000 volumes covering a variety of topics and subjects including science, literature, and politics (Seeger 1973, 7). More than just a consumer of knowledge, he also created it. In the 1740s he performed many ingenious experiments in physics and electricity, the results of which he often shared via correspondences with like-minded thinkers in colonial America and other parts of the world as was the practice among scholars at that time (Brands 2000, 193). His efforts produced a number of important inventions such as the Franklin stove and the lightning rod, technological breakthroughs that diminished appreciably the incidence of household fires, the scourge of eighteenth-century urban areas. Eschewing patents, he readily made his inventions available to society as a whole, a gesture that reflected his personal but unarticulated belief in knowledge as a public good (Labaree et al. 1964, 192). The 1751 publication of *Experiments and Observations on Electricity* cemented his international reputation and helped make him "the only American whose name was widely known outside America before 1776 ..." (Forde 2003, 80). It was no fluke that in 1747 when the Royal Swedish Academy of Sciences sent the agricultural economist Peter Kalm, a protégé of Carl Linnaeus, to North America in search of seeds and plants that could be commercially transplanted, literally the first person Kalm contacted upon reaching colonial America was Benjamin Franklin (Benson 1937, 17; 625).

Given his eclectic interests it was inevitable that Franklin would at some point in time train his reasoning powers on economic issues; he did so at the age of 22 when he examined one of the most stubborn problems of life in colonial America.

> In the pre-revolutionary period there were only a few economic topics that attracted attention. These were agriculture, trade, taxation and currency, of which the most important, as well as the most contentious, was the last (Seligman [1925] 1967, 122).

On April 3, 1729, Franklin published the small pamphlet *A Modest Enquiry into the Nature and Necessity of a Paper Currency* (Franklin [1729] 1911, 335–358), which first appeared as an essay in the *Maryland Gazette* on December 17, 1728 (Carey 1928, 7). The purpose of the piece was to endorse the use of paper currency as a way to deal "with the perennial insufficiency" of a circulating medium of exchange in the American colonies. The latter situation arose because international traders in the colonies were obliged to ship gold and silver overseas to settle accounts, leaving an inadequate supply of money available to support the growing volume of internal trade in

America, which at the time lacked an indigenous supply of precious metals (McCusker 1978, 117).

To cope with the persistent shortage of a circulating medium of exchange, trade in the American colonies relied on a combination of barter, commodity monies such as sugar and tobacco, overvalued gold and silver coins, and paper currency (McCusker 1978, 117–121). The last method – paper money – was clearly a superior option compared to the other solutions of the problem, each of which lacked convenience especially when comparing the value of one commodity to another. Franklin wrote: "To remedy such Inconveniences and facilitate Exchange, men have invented MONEY, properly called a *Medium of Exchange,* because through or by its Means Labour is exchanged for Labour, or one Commodity for another" (Franklin [1729] 1911, 345). Thus, Franklin introduced his labor theory of value, a concept he borrowed from William Petty's (1623–1687) *A Treatise of Taxes and Contributions*, published in 1662. As Petty reasoned and Franklin eloquently explained, the amount of labor (time) embedded in the production of a commodity determines its comparative value vis-à-vis other commodities; the medium of exchange "whether Gold, Silver, Copper, or Tobacco" merely measures worth and facilitates trade but does not create value per se (Franklin [1729] 1911, 345). A side-by-side comparison of relevant passages from the works of Petty and Franklin reveals just how much the latter lifted from the former (Wetzel 1895, 30–31). Using contemporary norms one could argue that Franklin plagiarized Petty, but given the literary milieu of the early eighteenth century, such a conclusion would be hasty and inappropriate.

The term plagiarism "had no currency in English before the late sixteenth century" and was then an issue involved more with the production of literary material than its appropriation by other writers (Loewenstein 2002, 87). England's first copyright law – the Statute of Anne – was adopted in 1710; it was less about defending the intellectual property of authors and more about protecting the commercial interests of stationers (a catch-all term for publishers, printers, and booksellers) from those who would pirate their imprints (Loewenstein 2002, 13–14). For authors "plagiarism didn't become a truly sore point ... until they thought of writing as their trade" (Mallon 1989, 3–4). In England, that did not occur until the middle of the eighteenth century (Pitcher 2000), when a variety of factors combined to make writing a viable career choice (Pitcher 2000, 1).

> Increases in literacy, the growth of cities, falling paper prices, the influx of international capital, the end of pre-publication censorship, and above all, the newfound willingness of authors to make their work public transformed British literary culture from a courtly coterie into a thriving marketplace.
> (Greene 2005, 1).

A comparable transformation of writing from an avocation to a viable livelihood did not occur in America until the nineteenth century. "Franklin was not an original economist and would never become one" (Brands 2000, 133), so he did what any self-respecting intellectual of his era would do when writing in a field outside his areas of expertise: he grafted the best economics then available and adopted it for his purposes. Petty may have been the first to advance a labor theory of value, however opaquely, but Franklin's explanation of the theory was more accessible to the general reader, which is probably why Karl Marx regarded both as originators of the concept (Marx [1867] 1906, 59).

While William Petty was the major source of Franklin's economics (Spiegel 1991, 124, 131), Franklin drew his inspiration for the essay on money from his personal experience and observations. Growing up in Massachusetts the first American colony that began using paper money as early as 1690, Franklin was exposed to a lively and continuous debate on the topic as reflected in the approximately 30 pamphlets printed in the colony and distributed in Boston from 1682 until his departure for Philadelphia in 1723 (Carey 1928, 1). About half of these leaflets were published during Franklin's apprenticeship as a printer; indeed, two of the pamphlets were printed in James Franklin's shop (Carey 1928, 1; Davis 1911, 414–442). The positions expressed in the essays circulating in Boston represented the spectrum of viewpoints, from those in manufacturing and commerce who generally supported paper currency as a way to boost business, to those opposed to the idea such as lenders and others fearful of the possibility of devaluation. These competing perspectives tampered Franklin's enthusiasm for paper money and made him mindful of the need to create a prudent supply of currency subject to an orderly rate of growth to accommodate an expanding economy (Franklin [1729] 1911, 342–345). There is no indication in his writing that he fully appreciated the potential of runaway inflation or the economic harm that it could produce (Hutchison 1988, 140). For Franklin, the benefits of paper currency far outweighed the risks, a position reinforced in 1723 when Philadelphia began its own experiment with paper money accompanied by a noticeable uptick in the overall level of economic activity in the city, a boom he directly attributed to the increase of money in circulation (Carey 1928, 5).

After *A Modest Enquiry* appeared in print, Franklin did not revisit the field of economics in any meaningful way until 1751 when he published *Observations Concerning the Increase of Mankind and the Peopling of Countries*, an essay "in which he emphasized the tendency for population to increase when subsistence was available, but with none of the menace proclaimed nearly half a century later in Malthus' first essay" (Hutchison 1988, 245). Contrary to Malthus' fatalism, Franklin noted that colonial population and American prosperity seemed directly related, with the former doubling every 25 years for an annual rate of growth of about 2.5 percent. "By 1775 the population of the 13 colonies had reached 2.5 million, compared with only 250,000 in 1700, a tenfold increase" (Lemon 2001, 119–21). During that time period, the population in America grew from one-tenth to about one-third of that of Britain (Lemon 2001) due primarily to a high domestic birth rate and immigration, both voluntary and forced (slavery). That the colonial population would soon exceed England's (which it did by 1820) was obvious to all, so much so that colonists were prone to tell anyone who would listen "that in thirty or forty years ... the North American colonies would form an independent country" (Olsson 1970, 13). For Franklin, believing as he did that population growth drives economic expansion, an independent America would be both more populous and more prosperous than Great Britain (Carey 1928, 2–6).

Over the next three decades Franklin published several works that touched on economics or economic issues including: *The Interest of Great Britain Considered with Regard to her Colonies and the Acquisition of Canada and Guadeloupe* (1760), in which he makes use of the principle of the division of labor; *On the Price of Corn and Management of the Poor* (1767), where he excoriates export taxes; and *Reflections on the Augmentation of Wages which will be occasioned in Europe by the American Revolution* (1788), an annunciation of his version of a theory of the high wage economy (Seligman [1925] 1967, 127). In 1876 an assessment of these works and other economic writings of Franklin led one historian of American economics to conclude: "Of Franklin then it must be said, that he not only did not advance the growth of economic science, but that he seems not even to have mastered it as it was already developed," a criticism softened somewhat with the rationalization that "little more can be said for any of our public men or writers during the period of Franklin's activity" (Dunbar 1876, 7).

The reality was that the state of American economic thinking throughout much of the eighteenth century was embryonic compared to what was going on in other parts of the world. At about the time Franklin was publishing *A Modest Inquiry*, several universities in Prussia and Sweden were establishing academic chairs in political economy (Stapelbroek and Marjanen 2012, 19). None of America's universities taught economics as a stand-alone course, and if economic matters such as fair price or usury were discussed at all, it was usually in the context of a class on moral philosophy (Conkin 1980, ix). If positive economics is the economics of what is or can be, and normative economics is what ought or should be, than policy economics is about program or plans to narrow the gap between the two. The habit of making policy recommendations that promote the welfare of the whole was the thrust of Franklin's economics (Kammen [1972] 1980, 127), or rather his political economy as the expression was commonly used in the eighteenth century.

> The word *political* in *political economy* did not refer to the policy implications of economic theory or to the interaction of economic analysis and governmental action. Rather, *political* designated a universe of discourse. Political economy included those universal principles applicable to a national economy, to a single sovereign entity. It set off the public scope of political from the more limited field of domestic economy, and thus from those principles applicable only to a single household or firm.
>
> (Conkin 1980, ix)

Since his purpose was promoting societal welfare, be it of Philadelphia or that of the entire nation, Franklin was way too practical to let consistency interfere with his economic thinking. "His inconsistencies were many, but they were the inevitable accompaniments of his diverse loyalties and journalistic habits" (Dorfman [1946] 1966, 178). As a young man he argued against Mercantilism and its system of tariffs but later in life he saw the virtue of protectionism as a way to insulate the commerce of an emerging nation from the rigors of competing with merchants in well-established countries. This apparent contradiction was Franklin's eighteenth-century version of "import substitution" (Mott and Zinke 1987, 114). The first economist he read was William Petty from whom he borrowed a labor theory of value, but in the 1760s, trips to Paris and meetings with leading physiocrats convinced a mature Franklin that agriculture was the ultimate source of wealth (Hutchison 1988, 246). In the short essay *Positions to be Examined* published in 1769, he wrote:

> Finally, there seem to be but three ways for a nation to acquire wealth. The first is by *war*, as the *Romans* did, in plundering their conquered neighbors. This is *robbery*. – The second by *commerce*, which is, generally, *cheating*. – The third by *agriculture*, the only *honest way*; wherein man receives a real increase of the seed thrown into the ground, in a kind of continual miracle wrought by the hand God in his favor, as a reward for his innocent life, and his virtuous industry.
>
> (Franklin [1769] 1859)

For a mellowed Franklin, the value and dignity of an agriculture-based economy trumped that of a manufacturing-based system regardless of amount of back-breaking effort involved or the diminished level of prosperity attained (Carey 1928, 168–169). As he had done with other economic thinkers, Franklin mimicked the ideas of the physiocrats, but he did so creatively.

> While European in his general philosophy, Franklin was American in his economic views, and simply adopted those parts of French philosophy which were fitted to the conditions of his country. His general economic ideas were of the laissez-faire type in the sense in which they were held by his French friends, but he was a pioneer of American economic thought, bringing optimism into the discussion of population and the wages problem, and basing his opinions on the peculiar features of the American economy of vast spaces.
>
> (Normano 1943, 37)

Always pragmatic, "Franklin's political economy was motivated throughout by a vision of the good society to which sound economic policy should lead" (Mott and Zinke 1987, 116). For him, this meant a strong middle class and a "society without extremes of conduct and of wealth or poverty" (Mott and

Zinke 1987). This "Happy Mediocrity" as Franklin called it, smacks of the modern concept of 'optimal,' the idea singularly responsible for contemporary economics being dubbed the "Goldilocks" science.

Given the sum total of his economics, whether derived from Franklin's standalone pamphlets or passing remarks embedded in his other writings, a legitimate question can be posed: Was Benjamin Franklin America's first economist? Some scholars respond with an enthusiastic yes: "Franklin, then, deserves a place in the history of early economic literature, and especially in the history of American economics. He is the first American who deserves to be dignified by the title Economist" (Wetzel 1895, 56). Other writers describe his economic contributions with more muted admiration (Dorfman [1946] 1966, 178–195). The point is debatable but the significance of Franklin to economics in particular and American life in general is not.

> Benjamin Franklin personified the transformation of Britain's mainland colonies into the first modern society. Most of the major transformations that occurred in America between 1680 and 1770 unfolded before him – the colonies' massive population growth, the maturation of colonial politics, the creation of a slaveholding culture even outside the southern colonies, immense domestic and international expansion, the growth of a rich secular life and material culture, the evolution of diverse, sometimes baffling modern religious pluralism.
>
> The aphorisms of Franklin's *Poor Richard's Almanac* made sense of that transformation. In Franklin's hands ... life became something to be shaped, reshaped, then reshaped again – "Lost Time is never found again" – "God helps them that helps themselves" .... These aphorisms tamed and disciplined an expanding, aggressive, and calculating society. They did not guarantee a moral society or even a good society. But they channeled behavior that might drift toward pure greed, asserted the virtue of labor over status, and bypassed traditional European emphasis on family inheritance, political deference, and vengeful religious dogmatism. In *Poor Richard's Almanac,* many Americans could see what they were becoming and what they wanted to be.
>
> (Butler, 247)

That Benjamin Franklin still commands our attention validates his importance; American economics is fortunate to be able to trace its roots to him.

## Other voices

Benjamin Franklin was probably the most significant political economist in colonial America from 1700 to 1775 but he was not alone. There was a small but vocal cadre of political economists during this time period galvanized into action by the debates swirling around paper currency and the institution of land banking. Through self-published pamphlets and the modern equivalent of letters-to-the-editor, many writers, most anonymous, argued the pros and cons of land banks and paper money, especially in New England where a tradition of conventional banking and an allegiance to hard (specie) money were particularly strong (Newell 1998, 143). Boston, where paper money was a source of contention since first being introduced in 1690, was the epicenter of this debate (Bailyn 1955, 185–189).

Like nature, economic activity abhors a vacuum, and in the absence of a domestic supply of gold and silver, American colonists sought a solution to the shortage of money in the one thing they had in great abundance, land. Usually organized and operated by various colonial governmental units, land banks created loans in the form of provincial paper currency lent to borrowers who used their land, farms, homes, and other types of real estate as collateral (Thayer 1953, 145). Along with a limited quantity of specie money, the land-backed paper currency circulated as a medium of exchange and fueled economic growth, especially in the middle colonies where "a moderate volume of money issues on the security of good land in a region whose agriculture was highly profitable gave value and stability to the currency" (Thayer 1953, 146). This was not the case in New England, especially in the Boston area where a combination of poor quality land and an oversupply of currency generated inflation, which proved to be bothersome for traditional bankers, merchants involved in international commerce, and similar creditors who despite their preference for hard money were often obliged to accept depreciated paper currency in the settlement of debts (Michener [2003] 2011, 8).

Many Massachusetts residents contributed to the literary debate over the efficacy of land banks and paper money including William Douglass and Hugh Vance, two pamphleteers who together "created the most comprehensive body of analysis in the entire paper money debate" (Newell 1998, 219). Of the two, Douglass was clearly the more well known in the New England colonies then and to history now. Born about 1691 in Gifford, Scotland to a family of some means, he studied in the Netherlands and France, and eventually earned a medical degree from the University of Edinburgh, "at the time the best medical school in Great Britain" (Lemay 2006, 98). Douglass immigrated to England's New World colonies in 1716, settling in Boston in 1718 where he stayed until his death in 1752. At a time when most American 'physicians' were trained via apprenticeships, Douglass claimed he was the only professionally educated doctor in Boston, a fact that was probably true and something he never let his associates forget (Bullock 1897, 266). A self-proclaimed rationalist, he rejected the blind acceptance of doctrine in favor of empirical-based reasoning. As was the case among educated individuals of this era, his intellectual interests were many, including history. His book *A Summary, Historical and Political, of the First Planting, Progressive Improvements, and Present State of the British Settlements in North America* was cited three times in *The Wealth of Nations* (Smith [1776] 1937, 972). His many accomplishments and generous philanthropy led to the small village of Douglass, Massachusetts, about 15 miles south of Wooster, being named in his honor.

By contrast, Hugh Vance's biography is not nearly as well documented as that of Douglass. Vance (1699–1763) was born in Boston to a well-respected Huguenot family. His educational background is something of a mystery, although he did spend some time in Stockholm as a young man. In adulthood, he became a stalwart within the Boston merchant community, serving on a number of citizen committees in the 1730s and 1740s and was elected to public office, all of which "indicates that he enjoyed the respect and confidence of his fellow citizens" (Wilhite 1958, 148). Unlike Douglass who amassed a sizeable fortune during his life, Vance the merchant had limited success despite his extensive involvement in civic affairs; "in his old age, after a career of activities on his own and in town affairs, he was adjudged a bankrupt" in 1758 (Davis 1910, 20). While his business acumen may have been wanting, Vance's economic thinking as evident in his 1740 pamphlet *An Inquiry into the Nature and Uses of Money; More especially of the Bills of Publick Credit* was rich in prescient observations. An ardent enthusiast of paper currency, he began his essay supporting soft money with a fledgling theory of value that would resonate with modern economists.

> All things in use in the world, whether they have real or accidental Value, or Price in the Market, from the same causes, *viz.* either from the *Plenty* or the *Scarcity* of the Commodity to be sold, or from the greater or smaller number of *Buyers;* but more fully and clearly expressed by means of any change in the *Proportion* between the *Quantity* to be sold and the *Demand* for that *Quantity.* By the *Quantity to be sold*, we must understand the present Quantity of goods that the *Sellers* are inclined or forced to part with; and by the Demand, the present quantity of goods, which the *Buyers* are under obligations at the same time to purchase…
>
> (Vance [1740] 1911, 374)

In this passage, Vance exhibits an instinctive appreciation of price determination via the interaction of demand and supply; applying his insight proved more difficult than expressing it. Further along in his essay Vance reasons that the price level and the amount of money in circulation are not necessarily related (Vance [1740] 1911, 379), a proposition that becomes the linchpin of his measured and reasoned "defense of paper currency against the charge of inflation" (Newell 1998, 219).

Long a champion of hard money, William Douglass in his 1740 pamphlet *A Discourse concerning the Currencies of the British Plantations in America: More Particularly to the Province of Massachusetts Bay in New England* launched a rebuttal to Vance's position. Save for an appreciation of Gresham's Law (Wilhite 1958, 143), Douglass, a man long on opinions but short on logic, relied on polemics to discredit his adversary, a tactic he had employed in 1721 when arguing against inoculation as an effective treatment for smallpox during a potential epidemic in eastern Massachusetts (Dorfman [1946] 1966, 155). Despite his medical credentials, local Boston politicians went ahead with an inoculation program, disregarding Douglass' tradition-bound professional judgment in favor of experimental pragmatism (Carr 2008, 306–307). Never publically admitting that his initial opinion was wrong, Douglass reluctantly accepted the effectiveness of inoculations (Copeland 2000, 13–24). Given his propensity to consider himself the smartest person in the room, any room, Douglass used the same heavy-handedness to discredit Vance's argument while promoting his fundamental belief in hard currency even though "he had no basic or complete theory of money" and otherwise "contributed nothing of importance to any other phase of economic theory" (Wilhite 1958, 144).

Considered *in toto*, the Douglas/Vance debate illustrated the adage "where one stands depends on where one sits." The haughty Douglass reflected the point of view of British-oriented "foreign" merchants, namely importers and exporters who dealt in international commerce where specie money was the preferred medium of exchange, while Vance, a "native" merchant spoke for those engaged in trade within the colonies where paper currency worked just fine (Dorfman [1946] 1966, 158). The difference between the two positions was more about Douglass' style and station than Vance's substance and insight. In part because they wanted to believe that Douglass and those of his ilk represented the popular view, the British enacted the Currency Act of 1752, restricting future emissions of paper currency in the New England colonies. In 1764 the British extended the Currency Act to all colonies in North America, a move that backfired as it made currency autonomy a contributing factor of the American Revolution. Some historians (Greene and Jellison 1961) have argued that a 1773 amendment to the Currency Act mitigated the restrictions on the issuing of paper currencies in the American colonies, thereby diminishing the significance of currency sovereignty as a cause of the War of Independence. The amendment, however, was most likely too little too late; by 1773 the arrow had already left the bow.

## A crosscurrent

Through the first 75 years of the eighteenth century, there was no uniquely American body of economic thought per se. American economics of the time was a stew of Old World thought seasoned with aboriginal practices and "dyed by the geography, physical aspects, and environment of the New World, as well as by its lack of history and traditions of its own" (Normano 1943, 28) Yet during this unprecedented period of continuous prosperity, there was a call for reforming American economic practices and thought, a plea that would become a persistent echo in the evolution of American economic thinking, recurring in varying degrees of intensity and duration from the eighteenth century to the present. The point of tension that pits a crosscurrent against the main stream often involves the quintessential problem of democracy: the frictions between libertarian views and a communitarian outlook; balancing the rights and responsibilities of the individual with the needs and aspirations of the community (Normano 1943, 30–31). Pinpointing the origins of this constant and contentious struggle is debatable, but certainly a leading candidate for this contrariness in American economic thought can be found in the writings of John Woolman (1720–1772).

Woolman was born into a pioneering Quaker family who had established a homestead in western New Jersey not far from Philadelphia (Whitney 1943, 18–20). Well educated considering the norms of the time, Woolman performed many tasks for his community as an adult – schoolteacher, surveyor, will writer, estate executor, peripatetic preacher – but his primary vocation was as a tailor, "a useful occupation … [that] would provide him a 'plain' living … but not great wealth and luxury," those temptations that "lead men astray from the path of righteousness" (Dorfman [1946] 1966, 196). Early in his life, Woolman experienced a crisis of conscience when he had to write a bill of sale for his employer who was selling a slave (Shore 1913, 45). The obvious contradiction of Quaker philosophy and slavery struck Woolman as insidious and ultimately inspired him to publish in 1754 the abolitionist tract *Some Observations on the Keeping of Negroes*, a pamphlet printed by his friend Benjamin Franklin (Shore 1913, 69–70). The abolition of slavery was one of the two main aims of his life; the other was "the readjustment of human relations for the relief of the laboring classes" (Gummere 1922, v). In the mid-1750s, Woolman began to keep a journal, a common practice among many of his literate contemporaries. His journal was part diary, part philosophy, and part travelogue as it provided detailed descriptions of his many travels in colonial America and abroad. Woolman was certainly no economist, but when passages from his journals (Woolman 1922) are combined with those from his other publications such as *A Plea for the Poor*, written in the mid-1760s but not formally published until some thirty years later (Gummere 1922, 401) one can infer his "radical Christian view of economics" (Sazama 2003, 190).

Although neither man followed a career path in agriculture, Woolman like Franklin was a firm believer in and a strong supporter of an agrarian-oriented economics system (Rosenblatt 1969, 89–94). Ever the practical humanist, Franklin was fundamentally but not exclusively an agrarian; Woolman, the idealistic spiritualist, saw husbandry as the only true purpose of human labor;

> I know of no employ in life, more innocent in its nature, more healthy, and more acceptable in common to the minds of honest men, than husbandry …
> Labouring to raise the necessaries of life, is in itself an honest labour, and the more men there are employed in honest employment, the better.
> (Woolman 1772, 464)

As the eighteenth century unfolded, subsistence farming was increasingly giving way to commercial agriculture where economies of scale and ever increasing farm size created a consolidation of economic power and, invariably political clout. Woolman saw the consequences of this tectonic economic shift as devastating to the human spirit.

Wealth desired for its own sake Obstructs the increase of Virtue, and large possessions in the hands of selfish men have a bad tendency, for by their means too small a number of people are employed in things usefull, and therefore some of them are necessitated to labour too hard, while others would want business to earn their Bread, were not employments invented, which having no real use, serve to please the vain mind ...

The mony which the wealthy receive from the poor, who do more than a proper share of business in raising it, is frequently paid to other poor people for doing business which is foreign to the true use of things ...

To be busied in that which is but vanity, & serves only to please the unstable mind, tends to an alliance with those who promote that vanity, and is a snare in which many poor tradesmen are entangled.

To be employed in things connected with Virtue, is most agreeable with the Character and inclination of an honest man.

While industrious frugal people are borne down with poverty, and oppressed with too much labour in useful things, the way to apply mony, without promoting pride and Vanity, remains open to such who are truly Sympathize with them in their various Difficulties.

(Woolman, 1763: 402–403).

In Woolman's implicit labor theory of value some scholars see the thinking of a latent socialist (Ripley [1917] 1931, 87), but that conclusion is a stretch. Woolman never wrote for the abolition of private property or "government restrictions to limit wealth" (Rosenblatt, 84). His message was saintly, his tone non-threating, his economics "moderate, self-regulating, and benevolent capitalism" (Rosenblatt 1969). His position in the history of American economic thinking is secured not because of his economics, but rather for his opposition to the prevailing economic paradigm of his time. He was a harbinger of what would become a recurring phenomenon in the subsequent story of American economic thought.

## References

Bailyn, B. 1955. *The New England Merchants in the Seventeenth Century.* Cambridge, MA: Harvard University Press.

Bailyn, B. 1986. *The Peopling of British North America.* New York, NY: Alfred A. Knopf.

Benson, A. B., (ed.). 1937. *Peter Kalm's Travels in North America, The English Version of 1770.* New York, NY: Dover.

Brands, H. W. 2000. *The First American: The Life and Times of Benjamin Franklin.* New York, NY: Doubleday.

Bruccoli, M. J. 1996. "The Man of Letters as Professional." In *F. Scott Fitzgerald on Authorship* (M. J. Bruccoli and J. S. Baughman, Editors). Columbia, SC: University of South Carolina Press: 11–22.

Bullock, C. J. 1897. "Introduction: The Life and Writings of William Douglass." *Economic Studies* 2(5): 265–290.

Butler, J. 2000. *Becoming America: The Revolution Before 1776*. Cambridge, MA: Harvard University Press.

Carey, L. J. 1928. *Franklin's Economic Views*. Garden City, NY: Doubleday, Doran & Company.

Carr, J. R. 2008. *Seeds of Discontent: The Deep Roots of the American Revolution, 1650–1750*. New York: Walker & Company.

Conkin, P. K. 1980. *Prophets of Prosperity: America's First Political Economist*. Bloomington, IN: Indiana University Press.

Connor, P. W. 1965. *Poor Richard's Politicks*. London: Oxford University Press.

Copeland, D. A. 1997. *Colonial American Newspapers: Character and Content*. Newark, DE: University of Delaware Press.

Copeland, D. A. 2000. *Debating the Issues in Colonial Newspapers: Primary Documents on Events of the Period*. Westport, CT: Greenwood Press.

Davis, A. M. 1910. *Two Forgotten Pamphleteers in the Massachusetts Currency Controversy, 1720–1740*. Cambridge, MA: Massachusetts Historical Society.

Davis, A. M., (ed.). 1911. *Colonial Currency Reprints, 1682–1751*. New York, NY: Burt Franklin.

Dorfman, J. [1946] 1966. *The Economic Mind in American Civilization, 1606–1865, Vol I*. New York, NY: August M. Kelley.

Dunbar, C. F. [1876] 1904. "Economic Science in America, 1776–1876." *North American Review*. Republished in *Economic Essays by Charles Franklin Dunbar* (O. M. W. Sprague, Editor). New York, NY: Macmillan: 1–30.

Dunn, R. S. 1984. "Servants and Slaves: The Recruitment and Employment of Labor." In *Colonial British America: Essays in the New History of the Early Modern Era* (J. P. Greene and J. R. Pole, Editors). Baltimore, MD: The Johns Hopkins University Press: 157–194.

Forde, S. 2003. "Benjamin Franklin: A Model American and an American Model." In *History of American Political Thought* (B.-P. Frost and J. Sikkenga, Editors). Lanham, MD: Lexington Books: 80–92.

Franklin, B. [1729] 1911. "A Modest Enquiry into the Nature and Necessity of a Paper Currency." In *Colonial Currency Reprints, 1682–1751* (A. M. Davis, Editor). New York, NY: Burt Franklin: 335–358.

Franklin, B. [1769] 1859. "Positions to be Examined." In *A Select Collection of Scare and Valuable Economical Tracts* (J. R. McCulloch, Editor). London: Lord Overstone: 202–205.

Galenson, D. W. 1981. *White Servitude in Colonial America*. Cambridge: Cambridge University Press.

Greene, J. 2005. *The Trouble with Ownership: Literary Property and Authorial Liability in England, 1660–1730*. Philadelphia, PA: University of Pennsylvania Press.

Greene, J. P., and Jellison, R. M. 1961. "The Currency Act of 1764 in Imperial-Colonial Relations, 1764–1776." *The William and Mary Quarterly*. Third Series: 18/4: 485–518.

Gummere, A. M. 1922. "Preface." In *The Journal and Essays of John Woolman*. Philadelphia, PA: Macmillan: v–vii.

Hutchison, T. 1988. *Before Adam Smith: The Emergence of Political Economy, 1662–1776*. York, NY: Basil Blackwell.

Jennings, F. 2000. *The Creation of America*. Cambridge: Cambridge University Press.

Jernegan, M. W. 1931. *Laboring and Dependent Classes in Colonial America, 1607–1783*. Chicago, IL: University of Chicago Press.

Jones, A. H. 1980. *Wealth of a Nation to Be.* New York, NY: Columbia University Press.

Kammen, M. 1970. *Empire and Interest: The American Colonies and the Politics of Mercantilism.* Philadelphia, PA: J. B. Lippincott.

Kammen, M. [1972] 1980. *People of Paradox.* Ithaca, NY: Cornell University Press.

Katz, B. S. 1989. *Nobel Laureates in Economic Science, A Biographical Dictionary.* New York, NY: Garland: 264–276.

Koo, K. S. 2008. "Slave Life in Colonial America." In *British Colonial America: People and Perspectives* (J. A. Grigg and P. C. Mancall, Editors). Santa Barbara, CA: ABC-CLIO: 81–97.

Labaree, L. W., Ketcham, R. L., Boatfield, H. C., and Fineman, H. H., (eds). 1964. *The Autobiography of Benjamin Franklin.* New Haven, CT: Yale University Press.

Lemay, J. A. L. 2006. *The Life of Benjamin Franklin. Volume 1. Journalist, 1706–1730.* Philadelphia, PA: University of Pennsylvania Press.

Lemon, J. T. 2001. "Colonial America in the Eighteenth Century." In *North America: The Historical Geography of a Changing Continent* (Second Edition, T. F. McIlwraith and E. K. Muller, Editors). Lanham, MD: Rowman & Littlefield: 119–139.

Loewenstein, J. 2002. *The Author's Due: Printing and the Prehistory of Copyright.* Chicago, IL: University of Chicago Press.

Mallon, T. 1989. *Stolen Words: Forays into the Origins and Ravages of Plagiarism.* New York, NY: Ticknor & Fields.

Marx, K. 1906 (1867). *Capital, A Critique of Political Economy.* New York, NY: Modern Library.

Matson, C. 2006. "A House of Many Mansions: Some Thoughts on the Field of Economic History." In *The Economy of Early America: Historical Perspectives & New Directions* (C. Matson, Editor). University Park, PA: Pennsylvania State University Press: 1–70.

McCusker, J. J. 1978. *Money and Exchange in Europe and America, 1600–1775: A Handbook.* Chapel Hill, NC: University of North Carolina Press.

McCusker, J. J. and Menard, Russell R. 1985. *The Economy of British America, 1607–1789.* Chapel Hill, NC: University of North Carolina.

Menard, R. R. 1996. "Economic and Social Development of the South." In *The Cambridge Economic History of the United States, Vol. I, The Colonial Era* (S. L. Engerman and R. E. Gallman, Editors). Cambridge: Cambridge University Press: 249–295.

Michener, R. [2003] 2011. "Money in the American Colonies." *EH. Net Encyclopedia* (R. Whaples, Editor). Economic History Association.

Mott, F. L. 1945. *American Journalism: A History of Newspapers in the United States Through 250 Years, 1690–1940.* New York, NY: Macmillan.

Mott, T., and Zinke, G. W. 1987. "Benjamin Franklin's Economic Thought: A Twentieth Century Appraisal." In *Critical Essays on Benjamin Franklin* (M. H. Buxbaum, Editor). Boston, MA: G. K. Hall: 111–127.

Nash, G. B. 1986. "The Early Merchants of Philadelphia: The Formation and Disintegration of a Founding Elite." In *The World of William Penn* (R. S. Dunn and M. M. Dunn, Editors). Philadelphia, PA: University of Pennsylvania Press: 337–362.

Nettels, C. P. [1934] 1964. *The Money Supply of the American Colonies before 1720.* New York, NY: Augustus M. Kelley.

Newell, M. E. 1998. *From Dependency to Independence: Economic Revolution in Colonial New England.* Ithaca, NY: Cornell University Press.

Normano, J. F. 1943. *The Spirit of American Economics*. New York, NY: John Day.

Olsson, N. W. 1970. *Pehr Kalm and the Image of North America*. Minneapolis, MN: James Ford Bell Library.

Perkins, E. 1980. *The Economy of Colonial America*. New York, NY: Columbia University Press.

Pitcher, E. W. R. 2000. *An Anatomy of Reprintings and Plagiarisms: Finding Keys to Editorial and Magazine History, 1730–1820*. Lewiston, NY: Edwin Mellen Press.

Ripley, W. [1917] 1931. "Philosophers and Divines, 1720–1789." In *The Cambridge History of American Literature, Book I* (W. P. Trent, *et al.*, Editors). New York, NY: Macmillan: 72–89.

Rockman, S. 2006. "The Unfree Origins of American Capitalism." In *The Economy of Early America: Historical Perspectives & New Directions* (C. Matson, Editor). University Park, PA: Pennsylvania State University Press: 335–361.

Rosenblatt, P. 1969. *John Woolman*. New York, NY: Twayne Publishers.

Sazama, G.W. 2003. "On Woolman's 'Conversations,' Ethics, and Economics." In *The Tendering Presence, Essays on John Woolman* (M. Heller, Editor). Wallingford, PA: Pendle Hill Publications: 190–206.

Seavoy, R. E. 2006. *An Economic History of the United States from 1607 to the Present*. New York, NY: Routledge.

Seeger, R. J. 1973. *Benjamin Franklin: New World Physicist*. Oxford: Pergamon Press.

Seligman, E. R. [1925] 1967. *Essays in Economics*. New York, NY: August M. Kelley.

Seybolt, R. F. 1935. *The Public Schools of Colonial Boston, 1635–1775*. Cambridge, MA: Harvard University Press.

Seybolt, R. F. [1935] 1970. *The Private Schools of Colonial Boston*. Westport, CT: Greenwood Press.

Shore, W. T. 1913. *John Woolman, His Life and Our Times*. London: Macmillan.

Smith, A. [1776] 1937. *The Wealth of Nations*. New York, NY: Modern Library.

Spiegel, Henry W. 1991. *The Growth of Economics Thought* (Third Edition). Durham, NC: Duke University Press.

Stapelbroek, K., and Marjanen, J. 2012. "Political Economy, Patriotism and the Rise of Societies." In *The Rise of Economic Societies in the Eighteenth Century* (K. Stapelbroek and J. Marjanen, Editors). New York, NY: Palgrave Macmillan: 1–25.

Thayer, T. 1953. "The Land-Bank System in the American Colonies." *The Journal of Economic History* 13(2): 145–159.

Thomas, I. [1810] 1970. *The History of Printing in America*. New York, NY: Weathervane Books.

Tomlins, C. 2006. "Indentured Servitude in Perspective: European Migration into North America and the Composition of the Early American Labor Force, 1600–1775." In *The Economy of Early America: Historical Perspectives & New Directions* (C. Matson, Editor). University Park, PA: Pennsylvania State University Press: 146–182.

Vance, H. 1740 [1911]. *An Inquiry into the Nature and Uses of Money; More especially of the Bills of Credit*. In *Colonial Currency Reprints, (VIII)* (A. M. Davis, Editor). Boston, MA: The Prince Society: 365–474.

Van Doren, C. 1938. *Benjamin Franklin*. New York, NY: Viking Press.

Wetzel, W. A. 1895. *Benjamin Franklin as an Economist*. Baltimore, MD: Johns Hopkins Press.

Whitney, J. 1943. *John Woolman Quaker*. London: Harrap & Co. LTD.

Wilhite, V. G. 1958. *Founders of American Economic Thought and Policy.* New York, NY: Bookman Associates.

Woolman, John. 1922. *The Journal and Essays of John Woolman* (A. M. Gummere, Editor). Philadelphia, PA: Macmillan.

Woolman, John. 1763. "A Plea for the Poor." In A. M. Gummere, *The Journal and Essays of John Woolman* (1922): 402–437.

Woolman, John. 1772. "Conversations of the True Harmony of Mankind and How it May be Promoted." In A. M. Gummere, *The Journal and Essays of John Woolman* (1922): 460–473.

# 5 Economic thought in the new nation, 1776–1885

## Introduction

The first one-hundred-plus years of the so-called long nineteenth century – defined as 1776 to the start of WWI (Engerman and Gallman 2000) – is arguably the seminal period of transition in what is still the relative short history of the United States. During this time period, America fought a civil war, some of whose implications are still unsettled today. It is also the time span during which the United States was transformed into a continental nation, moving from 13 colonies scattered along its eastern seaboard to a country of 38 separate states stretching from the Atlantic to the Pacific Oceans, and from the Canadian border to that with Mexico. This epic transformation from a cluster of colonies into a nation – the term "the United States" morphed into a singular noun from a plural one midway through the period (Wiltse 1961, 191) – was reflected in virtually every aspect of American life and thought, including economics. This chapter examines the evolution and development of American economic thinking from the declaring of independence to the founding of the American Economic Association in 1885, an event that can be viewed as the beginning of the modern era of American economic thought.

## Economic, social, and political conditions, 1776–1886

Growth, the attribute evident in virtually every aspect of the American experience during the nineteenth century, was nowhere more apparent than in the sheer geographic size of the country. In 1803 the Louisiana Purchase nearly doubled the area of the United States to 1.6 million square miles. Subsequent treaties, some almost byzantine, plus arranged acquisitions, forced trades, voluntary swaps, and flat-out land grabs involving Great Britain, other Western European countries, Mexico, and Russia (Seavoy 2006, 88–90), brought the area of the country to approximately its current size of about 3.5 million square miles. Among the more significant of these acquisitions were Florida (1819), Texas (1845), Oregon (1846), California (1848), and Alaska (1867), all of which were acquired in a span of fifty years (Wiltse

1961, 82–83). The rapid physical expansion of the country seemed to validate the "manifest destiny" hypothesis, the notion that America was preordained to become a continental power (Nichols 1961, 41–42). The American columnist John L. O'Sullivan (1813–1895) coined the phrase in 1845 in an article he wrote for the *United States Magazine and Democratic Review*, but the term itself did not become part of American historiography until the twentieth century (Sampson 2003, 194–195).

For the time period under examination, the size of the US population grew at a faster rate than the country's land mass. Pre-census population history places the American population at about 2.5 million in 1776; by 1886 census data indicates that population had grown to about 58 million, a 23-fold increase (Historical Statistics, A 1–8). "In most colonies in the seventeenth century, males outnumbered females by a substantial margin" (Price 1988, 303), making biological reproduction of the population impossible; consequently, immigration became critical for population growth. In the late 1700s the US population grew at a rate in excess of 3 percent per year, due largely to high fertility rates and immigration. Birth rates fell throughout the nineteenth century, but population continued to grow, propelled by a combination of declining mortality rates and accelerating international immigration (Haines 2000, 280–287; 194–203). In the 1820s for example, records indicate that 140,000 internationals came to the US, most from countries in northern and western Europe; in the 1880s immigration rose to 5.2 million, chiefly from the same European locations (Haines 2000, 196). In the first two decades of the twentieth century, immigration numbers rose again, but the principal sources of migrants shifted to countries in eastern, central, and southern Europe (Wiebe 1967, 14). Over the long nineteenth century, immigration accounted for about 25 percent of US population growth (Haines 2000, 203).

While many "push and pull factors" stimulated immigration, the empirical evidence suggests that the strongest influence was the relentless growth of the American economy and the opportunities that that created (Haines 2000, 195). During the war for independence (1775–1783), America's national income fell sharply; indeed "it was not until the first decade of the nineteenth century that per capita income ... reached the level achieved in the colonies in 1774" (Menard 1996, 294). During the next quarter century economic recovery was steady and accelerating so that by 1815 "Americans ... enjoyed the highest living standard in the world" (Conkin 1980, 3). Prosperity, however, was uneven as this stretch of American economic history witnessed several financial panics – 1797, 1819, 1837, and 1857 – a well as two depressions, one from 1807 to 1814 associated with the Embargo Act of 1807 and the War of 1812, and one in the 1870s, a spillover from a general worldwide deflation that affected prices in America but not production. Although "the longest in the nation's history," the depression of the 1870s was "in human terms ... one of the mildest" (Wiebe 1967, 1). Weaned on the Phillips curve, modern economists often equate deflation with negative growth and a shrinking level of national output (Rothbard 2002, 154–155). However, as one set of scholars noted that was not the case in the United States during the 1870s when the rate of growth of national output was 3 percent a year in current dollars but over 6 percent per year in real terms (Friedman and Schwartz 1963, 39).

The overall rate of long-term growth masks to some extent the regional differences in economic development between the various sections of the country during the long nineteenth century.

> In 1775, ... per capita wealth in the plantation colonies of the Chesapeake and the lower South was roughly twice that of New England and roughly 50 percent higher than in the middle Colonies. ... By 1840, per capita income in the northeastern United States was nearly twice that of the south, and by 1880 it was nearly three times as large.
>
> (Galenson and Menard 1977, 40)

This remarkable turnabout was the result of the transformation of the Northeast into an industrial juggernaut and not to a slowing of southern growth (Rothenberg 1988, 127), which prior to 1800 depended on the export of staples such as tobacco, sugar, rice, wheat, and indigo (Galenson and Menard 1977, 3). Then in 1793 Eli Whitney (1765–1825) invented the cotton gin and everything changed (Engerman 2000, 335); "cotton output ... catapulted from three million pounds in 1792 ... to more than thirty-six million pounds in 1800" (Wiltse 1961, 9–10). Worldwide demand for the fabric seemed limitless and so did the ability of American farmers to supply more. Technological change in the form of the widespread adoption in the antebellum period of a new variety of cotton dubbed the "Mexican hybrid" boosted both the yield and quality of American cotton (Olmstead and Rhode 2008, 98). As the South moved west, cotton became king, and the "Cotton South" was born. Covering an area of more than 200,000 square miles, the Cotton South ranged from the Carolinas to east Texas, with the five major cotton-producing states being South Carolina, Georgia, Alabama, Mississippi, and Louisiana (Ransom and Sutch 1977, xii). As valuable as slavery was to the economic well-being of the coastal South, the institution was even more important in the Cotton South, becoming the very backbone of the planation system.

Described as a 'factory in the field,' cotton plantations were large, complex enterprises that resembled the industrial firms of the times (Engerman 2000, 340). In addition to sizeable stock of physical capital, plantations were also deep in human capital, much of that invested in blacks who, as slaves, didn't just pick cotton but also became skilled in the many vocations and crafts needed to operate equipment or manage an organization. The value of this human capital was evident in the ranks of free blacks whose numbers increased from virtually zero in 1776 to over 300,000 by 1830 because of voluntary or legislated manumissions. Many among this group used the talents acquired as slaves to find gainful employment in the general economy or even start their own businesses (Johnson 1990). The importance of slavery to the economic well-being of the South is evident in the number of slaves in the region and their individual value prior to the Civil War. In 1800, there were about one million slaves the US, nearly all in the South representing about 40 percent of the region's overall population (Engerman 2000, 333). By 1860, there were about four million slaves in the United States, or about half of the South's population and nearly 13 percent of the country's total population. As the number of slaves increased so did their value per individual, reaching about $865 in 1860 (Ransom and Sutch 1977, 213), or approximately $130,000 in real, 2011 terms (Williamson and Cain 2015). The escalating value of slaves indicated that southern plantation owners expected the institution of slavery to continue indefinitely (Engerman 2000, 344), but the Civil War and the Emancipation Proclamation of 1863 redirected the trajectory of southern economics.

The material impact of the war on the South's economy while significant tends to be somewhat exaggerated: "stories of Sherman's march to the sea; the burning of Richmond, Atlanta, Columbia, and Charleston; ... and other ... incidents add to the popular image of widespread destruction" (Ransom and Sutch 1977, 40), as well they should for the physical devastation was extensive but not irreversible. For example, the transportation and manufacturing sectors in the South were quickly restored after the war and by 1870 operated close to pre-war levels (Ransom and Sutch 1977, 41). The same was not true for the plantation system, the cornerstone of the economy of the Cotton South. Emancipation meant the loss of the human capital necessary to run the system (Dowd 1956, 571), and most large farms were broken up into smaller agriculture units incapable of realizing the economies of scale germane to the success of plantations (Jones 1992, 77). The resources were still in place but the inability or unwillingness to use them differently put institutional and not physical restraints on southern economic development (Dowd 1956, 559), further diminishing the region's anemic rate of economic growth compared to that in other sections of the nation. Although the degree of inequality in the distribution of income and wealth within the United States during the early portion of the nineteenth century is a matter of debate (Soltow 1989, 5, 230–237), the increasing differentials in growth rates among the various sections of the country were particularly harsh on the economic wellbeing of American blacks (Soltow 1975, 144, 182) about 90 percent of whom lived in the South until the twentieth century (Engerman 2000, 361).

In contrast to the South which was inside the country but outside its economics mainstream (Robbins 1994, 146), other regions of the United States experienced buoyant growth throughout most of the nineteenth century. In the Northeast, the concurrence of the American Revolution and the Industrial Revolution was a fortunate happenstance. Unlike Europe where a "proto-industrial" period clearly preceded the Industrial Revolution, in the United States both occurred essentially simultaneously (Henretta 1988, 49, 87). Merchant capitalists readily embraced steam power, the engine driving the

Industrial Revolution, to consolidate a scattered putting-out production system into centralized, large-scale manufacturing facilities. More than just skilled manufacturers, eastern industrialists also became crafty marketers, establishing an energetic cadre of peddlers to sell their products to potential consumers in other regions of the nation, especially the South (Rainer 2005). The impact of industrialization was relentless. "In 1860, for the first time in American history, the output of factory, mill, shop, and mine exceeded in value that of the farm" (Normano 1943, 117). Market expansion encouraged more manufacturing specialization and growth, further propelling industrialization into the Midwest, notably along the Great Lakes via increased use of the area's waterways augmented with a network of canals (Engerman and Sokoloff 2000, 368). In the West, rapid and successful exploitation of natural resources, promoted by the development of railroads, created a period of dynamic economic expansion that began around 1860 and proceeded virtually unabated until World War I (Dowd 1956, 559–561). Commercially viable railroading began in the United States around 1830. In 1869, the first intercontinental rail line was completed and within twenty years, four more intercontinental routes were in operation. In the evolution of human history, water had been the principal medium for transporting people and their stuff over long distances; railroads turned land into a "second medium" for travelling great distances. In the vastness of the United States, the ability to move 'quickly' from one part of the country to another created the impression if not the reality of a fully integrated economic system.

Over the one hundred years following independence, the performance of the American economy was probably unmatched by any other nation on the planet (Gallman and Wallis 1992, 4, 16). The sources of this sustained expansion were many and include increasing literacy and education, as well as the ascendency of technology as applied to industrialization. From the last quarter of the eighteenth century through the 1840s, the literacy rate in America, already high by world standards, went from 50–75 percent of the adult population, depending on the section of the country, to around 80–90 percent (Soltow and Stevens 1981, 189–190). A number of factors drove the increase in literacy – rising levels of income and wealth, greater urbanization, work-related job requirements, and the widespread adoption of legal provisions for the schooling of both sexes, accompanied by a steady extension in the number of school days per year as well as the terminal age of students required to attend (Soltow and Stevens 1981, 55, 103–113). As literacy rose so did the production of books, pamphlets, and periodicals published in America. Journalism became a thriving profession, and newspapers, once almost exclusively partisan organs for specific political parties or ideologies, became commercialized market-driven sources of information, offering "wide-ranging content designed to appeal not just to voters but also to any and all potential readers" (Baldasty 1992, 36). The growth in the publication of books, pamphlets, and periodicals mirrored that in the newspaper industry, giving rise to an American literati that included the likes of Louisa May Alcott,

James Fennimore Cooper, Frederick Douglass, Ralph Waldo Emerson, Nathaniel Hawthorne, Herman Melville, and Walt Whitman (Nichols 1961, 32–33). An exclamation point for this literary eruption came in 1852 with the publication of Harriet Beecher Stowe's anti-slavery book *Uncle Tom's Cabin*, quite possibly the most influential novel ever written by an American. In its first year, the book sold 300,000 copies in United States alone (Gossett 1985, 164); relative to population size, a novel published today would have to sell over four million copies in a single year to achieve the same degree of regard.

Against this backdrop of continually improving levels of education and literacy, nineteenth-century Americans, ever the pragmatists, pursued the study of science, especially "when some clear utilitarian gain seemed likely" (Hindle 1956, 384). Generally, American science was less about discovery for its own sake and more about seeking out new and better "means for making and doing" (Hindle 1966, 4). In industry, this led to the development of the "American system of manufactures," an approach to production which relied on the use of interchangeable parts in labor-saving, assembly-line processes that insured the consistency of output, a critical characteristic of quality (Engerman and Sokoloff 2000, 378). This philosophy of practicality was also embedded in nineteenth-century educational institutions devoted to the study of engineering as evident in 1802 with the establishment of West Point, the publically funded military academy that focused its curriculum on the applications of engineering to military science. In 1824 the nation's first privately-funded engineering college, Rensselaer Polytechnic Institute, was founded, and the fusion of science and technology may have found its ultimate expression in 1861 with the formation of the Massachusetts Institute of Technology. Education for innovation also came to the farm with the 1862 passage of the Morrill Act which created land-grant colleges charged with applying science to agriculture, and then sharing the results as a public good with the farm sector as a way to bring best practices to an area of the economy not noted for initiating research (Nevins 1962).

Before there was baseball, one could argue that the Great American Pastime was inventing. The first patent statute in the United States was adopted in 1790; in the initial years of registration only a handful of patents were issued. By 1836, when the current patent examination process was established, the total number of patents issued had climbed to 10,000 (Anonymous 2003, 64), and thereafter steadily increased throughout the rest of the century. Dubbed the "golden age of independent inventors," the period after 1850 was an especially prolific time for creative individuals who were both practical and entrepreneurial (Engerman and Sokoloff 2000, 389). Indeed, many twentieth-century staples came into being in one form or another in the nineteenth century (Smil 2005, 6): the cash register, the telephone, peanut butter, the phonograph and records, the reaper, blue jeans, to cite a few. As fate would have it, three unrelated nineteenth-century inventions – the safety elevator, steel-frame building construction, and the electric light – would be at the core of the rise of the modern metropolis. In 1871 the Great Chicago Fire destroyed over 17,000 structures along the Lake Michigan shoreline, presenting a unique and wholly unanticipated opportunity for a grand experiment in urban renewal. Prior to the development of the three disparate breakthroughs, buildings usually had a maximum height of 5–7 stories for obvious reasons. When the three singular inventions were combined with other important nineteenth-century innovations, the high-rise became a reality (Smil 2005, 168), and that in turn made possible the urbanization of America, a distinctly twentieth-century phenomenon.

## Economic thought in the nineteenth century

The creation of the United States of America was essentially a two-stage process. The first stage was the successful prosecution of the war of independence; the second, and in hindsight clearly the more difficult stage, involved managing the peace in the years following the conflict. The nearly universal desire to form a new nation galvanized Americans against a common foe; organizing for peace required confronting with numerous internal tensions that had been put on hold during the war. In the process of working through these philosophical differences Americans discovered the wisdom in Walt Kelly's (1913–1973) aphorism "We have met the enemy and they are us." Some of these points of contention were regional, some were national, and many were complicated (Hudson 1974). On the issue of state's rights, for instance, residents of Charleston might share similar views as those in Richmond, but on the matter of tariffs, Charleston's preferences might match those found in Boston, Philadelphia, or other coastal cities. Reconciling competing perspectives usually entails compromise, which at its best requires making "hard choices" and "taking clear-cut positions" (Kammen 1972, 219). At its worst, compromise or its absence, often means deferring tough decisions until sometime in the future in the hope that changing circumstances will somehow produce more palpable options (Kammen 1972, 99). In certain instances, serendipity rewards or at least accommodates inaction – the near miraculous rate of economic growth throughout much of the nineteenth century obviated the pressing need for a coherent national policy regarding money and banking. In other circumstances, procrastination leads to unimaginable consequences: the issue of slavery and the Civil War. When discussing American economic thinking from 1787 to 1800 – a short, important, and immensely complicated period – it helps to adopt the historians' dichotomy of Republicans versus Federalists as long as one realizes that this oversimplification is sufficiently robust for a book whose scope is the history of economic thought and not history per se.

After the Treaty of Paris of 1783 ended the revolutionary war, the question arose as to who should actually run the new national government. Both Republicans and Federalists were suspect of the competency and trustworthiness of common folk to perform that task (Barlowe 2011, 3) as each subscribed to the view that "In all countries the wealthy will necessarily administer government, for they alone have the skill and leisure for this function" (Dorfman 1946, 298). For Thomas Jefferson, the titular head of the Republicans, and his followers, the wealthy class consisted of the landed gentry, especially those residing in the South, while for Alexander Hamilton, the principal spokesperson for the Federalists, the ruling elite would come from the emerging industrial capitalists living principally in the Northeast (Barlowe 2011, 5–10). The debate over political leadership set one group of wealthy white men against another. Neither side gave much if any consideration to the political significance of women, blacks, aboriginals, or the poor; these groups were invisible to Federalists and Republicans alike (Appleby 1984, 101–102). Besides disagreeing over who should rule, the two factions took exception with each other concerning the very purpose of the national government. Even though their philosophical precepts about liberty, the individual, and the state were generally similar (Nelson 1987, 8), the specific role of the national government was an issue of conflict. Republicans saw a strong national government as a potential threat to individual liberty and therefore wanted a relatively passive institution whose primary roles would be to protect personal freedom and referee disputes that pit private interest against the public good (Appleby 1984, 14–22). With a less sanguine view of the nobleness of the individual than that of Republicans, Federalists sought an active government that could harness human's baser instincts so as to promote the general well-being, thereby creating a prosperous society where individuals could more easily realize their full potential (Barlowe 2011, 6). In philosophical terms, the respective positions of the two sides on a number of practical issues were fluid to the point of being similar if not identical, save that the Republicans nearly always put the accent on the individual while the Federalists put it on society. These subtle yet important differences, particularly when it comes to economic policy, are reflected most clearly in the writings and activities of three individuals: Alexander Hamilton (1755–1804), Albert Gallatin (1761–1849), and Tench Coxe (1755–1824).

Alexander Hamilton was born in the British West Indies and immigrated to America in 1773. Two years later he volunteered to participate in the war of independence. A key contributor to *The Federalist Papers* published in 1788, Hamilton, because of his distinguished war record, had caught George Washington's attention long before the president appointed him the country's first Secretary of the Treasury in 1789 (Wilhite 1958, 230). Thomas Jefferson was also appointed to the same cabinet – Secretary of State – evidence that Washington was of no particular economic persuasion or simply lacked the acumen to distinguish between the competing schools of thought reflected in the Federalist/Republican debate (Normano 1943, 42). In any event, the imperial Washington, contrary to his status as a member of the South's landed gentry, sided with Hamilton's economics as revealed in a number of reports Hamilton wrote in the early 1790s, most notably the *Report on a National Bank* issued in 1790 and the *Report on Manufactures* of 1791 (Witzel 2006a, 405). That Hamilton produced the report on banking before the one on manufactures even though the latter was requested first probably indicates the relative importance he assigned to the two topics (Nelson 1987, 40). In these two reports, Hamilton made abundantly clear his preference for a strong federal government that would foster industrialization as the primary instrument for promoting national economic growth and stability; by contrast, the Republicans espoused a philosophy of agrarian sectionalism, operating under a weak national government, as the linchpins of a nostalgic desire to return to the status quo that existed before the war. While Republicans "warmly clasped" Adam Smith's invisible hand (Appleby 1984, 88), Hamilton and other Federalists rejected the idea that economic activity could somehow be self-regulating. Hamilton preferred managed laissez-faire economics to the Republican's unfettered variety, and critical to his vision of controlled market cybernetics were a strong central bank and a robust set of protective tariffs.

Through a combination of formal training and self-education, Hamilton became familiar with the major economic tracts of his time including *The Wealth of Nations* (Bowers 1967, 14). His personal economic philosophy, however, came more from his successful life as a lawyer and a businessman in New York than from any of the economics texts to which he was exposed. Just as a skilled basketball player is a good practical physicist or an accomplished cook is a good practical chemist, Alexander Hamilton became a good practical economist (Dunbar [1876] 1904, 7–8). He understood how the world he lived in worked, and came to the conclusion that a prudently administered system of money, banking, and credit was indispensable in promoting commerce and thus national economic growth and development. Specifically, an effective and efficient banking system would "augment the active or productive capital of a country: ... furnish pecuniary aid to the government, especially in emergencies; ... facilitate the payment of taxes; and ... stimulate trade, generate employment, and expand labor and industry" (Wilhite 1958, 238). Hamilton also realized that that same system was a two-edged sword and if left to its own devices could generate outcomes which, however beneficial for certain individuals, could wreak social havoc and undermine the nationalist agenda he sought to implement. In his report to the Congress on the National Bank, Hamilton proposed a privately owned, publically operated financial institution, basically a central bank, with the heft and authority to promote what today is recognized as the standard triptych of macroeconomic goals, namely, steady growth, stable prices, and full employment. To Republicans, Hamilton's national bank was the epitome of the kind of meddlesome government agency colonial American found so oppressive and had expressly prohibited in the constitution, or so they thought (Brands 2006, 53–54). President Washington sided with Hamilton's view and used his considerable influence to persuade those in Congress to follow his lead. In 1791, the First Bank of the United States became a reality and was given a twenty-year charter. In 1800 with the election of Thomas Jefferson as president, Republicans gained control of the White House and came to dominate nearly all branches of the federal government for a number of years. By 1811 when the bank's initial charter expired, Republicans under the leadership of then President James Madison did not renew it. Just five years later, however, the Republicans had to swallow their principles and create a Second National Bank, also with a twenty-year charter, to help with the financing of the public debt accumulated during the War of 1812 as well as with other fiscal matters. Eventually, the Republican's anti-national bank position prevailed. In 1836 the Republican President Andrew Jackson, who had little confidence in paper money and even less in banks, scuttled efforts to renew the charter of the Second National Bank (Brands 2005, 436–437, 455–471), effectively leaving the United States without a central bank for the duration of the long nineteenth century.

Hamilton's commitment to protective tariffs was a by-product of his belief that the economic future of the United States lay in industrialization. He sensed that the Industrial Revolution was just that, a revolution. While Republicans subscribed to an economy based on the export of agricultural goods and the products of extractive industries, Hamilton was committed to the idea that the growth of the American economy should rest on the expansion of manufacturing for domestic consumption.

> The expediency of encouraging manufactures in the United States, ... appears at this time to be pretty generally admitted. The embarrassments which have obstructed the progress of our external trade have led to serious reflections on the necessity of enlarging the sphere of our domestic commerce; the restrictive regulations, which in foreign markets abridge the vent of the increasing surplus of our agricultural produce, serve to beget an earnest desire that a more extensive demand for that surplus may be created at home; and the complete success which has rewarded manufacturing enterprise, in some valuable branches, conspiring with the promising symptoms which attend some less mature essays in others, justify a hope that the obstacles to the growth of this species of industry are less formidable than they were apprehended to be; and that it is not difficult to find, in its further extension, a full indemnification for any external disadvantages which are or may be experienced, as well as an accession of resources favorable to national independence and safety
>
> (Hamilton [1790] 1972, 1–2).

At the time Hamilton was writing, the American manufacturing sector was at the pupa stage and faced steep competition from European industries that were appreciably more advanced. Involving a classic infant-industry argument, he called for a system of protective tariffs reasoning that such a shield "was especially desirable and necessary to the establishment and development of factory manufacturing in the new American republic" (Wilhite 1958, 350). A second and in his mind equally prominent rationale for tariffs was Hamilton's vision of a strong federal government, a vision that would be realized only if the government had a sizeable and continuous stream of income, in other words tariffs, which at that time were the primary source of the national government's revenues (Nelson 1979, 973). For their part, Republicans disagreed with Hamilton's manufacturing/tariffs thesis on two counts; the manufacturing thesis was contrary to their notions of America having an agrarian-based economic system, and protective tariffs for American manufactures would invite European countries to retaliate with duties aimed at US farm products (Wang 1947, 24). Additionally, Republicans thought that America as a center of manufacturing was impractical, given its relatively high wage levels compared to those in Europe. To the later criticism, Hamilton, never noted for his compassion, had a ready reply: increase the supply of labor through the use of women, children, and more immigrants (Hamilton [1790] 1972, 19).

Many Republicans such as Jefferson and Madison spoke out against Hamilton's vision of the American economic system as revealed in the reports he wrote in the 1790s, but Albert Gallatin did much of the heavy lifting. Born in Geneva, Switzerland, he immigrated to the United States in 1780. A staunch Republican during the war, he was active in politics throughout most of the 1790s, first at the local level in Pennsylvania, then at the national level in both the US House of Representatives and the Senate, during which time he acquired a mastery of public finance. He served as Secretary of the Treasury from 1801 to 1813, filling "the same role for presidents Thomas Jefferson and James Madison that Alexander Hamilton, … had filled for George Washington" (McGraw 2012, 179). Sometimes portrayed as the economic counterpoint to Hamilton (McCraw 2012, 206–207), Gallatin's views were more nuanced than that. For instance, he supported both the First and Second National Banks, and eventually endorsed the idea of an American economy centered on manufacturing, a position even Thomas Jefferson, one of the most zealous proponents of agrarianism, came to embrace as evident in a letter he wrote in 1816.

> We have experienced what we did not then believe, that there exist both profligacy and power enough to exclude us from the field on interchange with other nations; that to be independent for the comforts of life we must fabricate them ourselves. We must now place the manufacturer by the side of the agriculturist. The former question is suppressed, or rather assumes a new form. Shall we make our own comforts, or go without them, at the will of a foreign nation? He, therefore, who is now against domestic manufactures, must be for reducing us either to dependence on that foreign nation, or to be clothed in skins, and to live like wild beasts in dens and caverns. I am not one of these; experience has taught me that manufactures are now as necessary to our independence as to our comfort.
>
> (Jefferson [1816] 2004, 269–270)

In a transportation report for Congress that Gallatin wrote in 1808, a report that ultimately spurred the construction of canals, roads, and eventually railroads, he expounded on the "importance and benefits of adequate transport facilities" for decreasing costs and increasing the competitiveness of American agriculture and manufacturing (Wilhite 1958, 381).

On the issue of tariffs, however, Gallatin was unbending in his opposition to Hamilton. His most important contribution on the matter was *The Free Trade Memorial* of 1831, a convention held in Philadelphia largely at Gallatin's behest. The purpose of the convention was succinctly stated in the preamble of the Memorial:

> the purpose of preparing and presenting to Congress a memorial setting forth the evils of the existing tariff of duties, and asking such a modification of the same as shall be consistent with the purposes of revenue, and equal, in its operation, on the different parts of the United States, and on the various interests of the same.
>
> (Gallatin [1831] 1972, 108)

The proceedings of the meeting became the basis of a report Gallatin, then president of the National Bank of New York, submitted to Congress in 1832 in favor of tariff reform and against protectionism, a document that "exhibits familiarity with the results of theoretical discussion, as well as the practical side of the question" (Dunbar 1904, 9). Where Gallatin truly differed from Hamilton was in the former's command of economics as it stood in the first half of the 1800s.

> Every nation takes a laudable pride in all that contributes to elevate its character; In every progress made in science, letters, arts, wealth, and power; in all that constitutes an advanced state of civilization. To substitute American for foreign industry whenever the substitution is advantageous is an object in which all cordially unite. But whether taking advantage of that general and patriotic feeling or carried away by it, the advocates of restriction contend that a trade in foreign commodities which, without regard to price, might be produced by domestic industry always interferes with that industry. They denounce and would proscribe that trade altogether, and thus in reality inflict the most serious injury on that object which they pretend to protect. Laws which do not trust the common sense of the citizen, which do not permit him to seek what he thinks the best market for the products of his industry, or which compel him to receive in exchange for these a less quantity of the objects he wants than without those laws he might have obtained, are evidently destructive of domestic industry. By free trade we mean that trade which we may carry free of any restrictions imposed by our own government. It is synonymous with free industry, and it is only because, and as far as, it promotes domestic industry we object to those restrictions.
>
> (Gallatin [1831] 1972, 142).

Among the preeminent "practical financiers" of the day only Gallatin "has claim to notice in connection with scientific theory" (Dunbar 1904, 9). Hamilton's economics was instinctive and sometimes unclear or even contradictory (Wilhite 1958, 255, 249), yet nonetheless effective given that his purpose was to influence policy makers and not advancement of the discipline. Gallatin also sought to sway decision makers, but as a disciple of Adam Smith and David Ricardo, he couched his arguments in terms of what were then the generally accepted principles of economics.

In 1804 the untimely death of Alexander Hamilton as a result of a duel transformed Tench Coxe from an affable bureaucrat into an important, if not the principal advocate for the industrialization of America. Born into a prominent, well-to-do Philadelphia family whose lineage included a noted lawyer who served as the Attorney-General of the province of Pennsylvania, Coxe was educated at the College of Philadelphia, the precursor of the University of Pennsylvania (Wilhite 1958, 211; Cooke 1978, 12–15). In the turbulent times prior to the War of Independence, he was perceived as a Loyalist (Dorfman 1946, 254), and for his alleged support of the British Crown, Coxe was referred to as "Mr. Facing Bothways," a character in the 1678 book *A Pilgrim's Progress* who could embrace mutually conflicting perspectives at the same time. Ironically, his empathy for competing points of view made Coxe the ideal voice for industrialization in the emerging arena of American politics. In 1787 he was instrumental in the formation of the Pennsylvania Society for the Encouragement of Manufactures and Useful Arts, and his work in public life promoting that cause was so impressive that Alexander Hamilton appointed him as the Assistant Secretary to the Treasury, where he became co-author with Hamilton of the 1791 *Report on Manufactures* (Crowden 2006, 183). Coxe also collected and published copious statistics on the country's commerce and manufacturing which "though crude by present statistical standards, constituted the major survey of the American situation of the time" (Kaplan 1931, 21). In contrast to Hamilton whose contemporaries and biographers alike described as an ambitious, prideful, overbearing evil genius (Cooke 1967, vii), Coxe was a good listener and showed respect for others even when he disagreed with them. For Coxe the choice for the American economy was not agrarian or industrial, but both. A moderate industrialist who recognized the importance of agriculture, he preached the gospel of a well-balanced economy (Wilhite 1958, 210), beginning in 1787 with his first major publication to that effect, *An Enquiry into the Principles of ... a Commercial System for the United States...* (Cooke 1978, 99), until he left public office in 1818. Thereafter, he continued to make the case for a diverse economic system in which farming and manufacturing played significant roles in his numerous correspondences with the major political figures of his time such as Thomas Jefferson and James Madison, and his copious data collections on the commerce and manufactures of the country at that time (Kaplan 1931, 21). Of the three – Alexander Hamilton, Albert Gallatin, and Tench Coxe – who collectively helped shape the American economy of the long nineteenth century, Hamilton was the visionary who saw the economic future of the United States more clearly than any of his contemporaries; Gallatin was probably the best economist of the lot (Dunbar 1904, 9); and ironically, the unassuming Coxe, the least well-known, may have had the greatest influence in the long run.

Paralleling the tectonic shifts in national economic policies occurring during the early nineteenth century were changes in American economics which, though not as seismic, were important nonetheless. This was especially true in higher education where prior to the early 1800s, economics or more accurately 'political economy,' was taught as part of a course in moral philosophy, a college class that served as the matrix of the social sciences in American higher education and was usually taught by the president of the institution (Hudson 1974, 16–17). Beginning around 1800 particularly among colleges in the Northeast, political economy was introduced into the curriculum as a stand-alone course usually taken after the class in moral philosophy (O'Connor 1944, 1). The teaching of political economy became an increasingly common practice across the growing number and types of American colleges and universities, spurring the writing of numerous textbooks crafted so as to bring "principles previously worked out by others within the easy comprehension of undergraduate students" (Dunbar 1904, 13). One such book, *The Elements of Political Economy* by Francis Wayland, President of Brown University, was published in 1837 and was widely used as a standard teaching text for several decades (Witzel 2006b, 897). By around 1850 the term 'economics' increasingly became the single-word descriptor of the course formerly labelled 'political economy' (O'Connor 1944, 3).

The ascendency of economics as a legitimate academic discipline was accompanied by a succession of American treatises on the subject. Written by lay or amateur economists, these works "dwelt on the practical politico-economic questions of the day and in common they essayed a revolt against the cosmopolitanism of the classical British school" (Kaplan 1931, 23–24). Among the more significant of these was Daniel Raymond's *Thoughts on Political Economy,* published in 1820 and reissued as a second edition in 1823 with the title *The Elements of Political Economy* (Seligman [1925] 1967, 134). A protectionist who endorsed the infant industry argument, Raymond (1786–1849) brought "zeal and ingenuity" to his discussions in opposition to slavery, banks, and free trade, but his "looseness of method" combined with illogical thinking and confusing definitions were reminiscent of American economic tracts that came before Adam Smith and not after (Dunbar 1904, 11). A trained lawyer, Raymond was not much at practical economics either; an unsuccessful businessman and newspaper publisher, he clearly was destitute at the time of his death (Conkin 1980, 78). Still, he developed the concept of economic nationalism and clearly understood the distinction between individual wealth and national wealth.

> a nation cannot supply itself with the necessaries of life, by loaning its money to other nations, neither can it by renting or selling its lands to

them. ... An individual is wealthy, because he can rent his lands, or loan his money ... A nation can [do] neither ... a nation, therefore, cannot be wealthy in that sense of the word in which an individual is wealthy, and any political economist, who applies the term wealth, to a nation, in the same sense in which it is applied to individuals, applies it erroneously ... upon the subject of political economy, or of national wealth.

(in Spiegel 1960, 58)

Raymond's writing influenced the thinking of the German-American economist Friedrich List and his late nineteenth-century notion of the "national system" (Seligman 1967, 134).

Other amateur economists who contributed to the growing literature of American economics included Jacob Newton Cardozo (1786–1873) and Thomas Cooper (1759–1839). Though he had little formal education, the American-born Cardozo was recognized as a talented writer at an early age. He became a staff writer for the *Southern Patriot*, a Charleston, South Carolina newspaper in 1816, and seven years later he bought the paper, serving as editor and publisher until 1845. In his capacity as editor at the *Patriot* and subsequent editorships, he had ample opportunities to express his views on a variety of matters including political economy (Crowden 2006). In 1826 he published *Notes on Political Economy*, basically an application of Ricardian/ Malthusian economics to the American South (Leiman 1969, 11–17). Unlike Cardozo, the English-born Cooper was well educated having studied the classics at Oxford University, and medicine and chemistry in London (Conkin 1980, 142). In 1794 he immigrated to America and for the next quarter-century was a farmer, lawyer, journalist, and a college teacher; in 1820 he began teaching at South Carolina College in Columbia (now the University of South Carolina), and a year later became president of the institution (Spiegel 1960, 78). As was the custom then, he taught the course in moral philosophy and in 1826 published *Lectures on the Elements of Political Economy*, a book "laden with opinions of subjects far beyond the scope suggested by the title" (McCann 2006, 175). Among these grassroots economist of this era was Henry C. Carey (1793–1879) who "lived well into the post-Civil War era" but "did his most creative work in political economy between 1835 and 1853" (Conkin 1980, 309).

The son of Mathew Carey, a wealthy Philadelphia publisher, lay economist, and himself the author of *Essays on Political Economy* (1822), an endorsement of Hamilton's protectionist policies (Conkin 1980, 77, 177), Henry Carey grew up in an intellectually rich environment in which the current topics of the day were vigorously debated among the noted political and literary illuminati who frequently visited his father's firm. In 1825 upon his father's retirement, the younger Carey became head of the family business which at the time "was probably the largest publishing house in America" (Kaplan 1931, 12). The business and social contacts associated with being one of the country's foremost publishers provided Carey a unique education, and nearly a decade later, having made a successful company even more prosperous, he retired from a life in commerce to devote his full time and energy to the study and development of economics in particular and social sciences in general. The first fruit of that effort was his book *Essay on the Rate of Wages* (1835), which expressed ideas that were embellished and expanded into a three-volume work, *Principles of Political Economy*, written between 1837 and 1840, and further refined and expanded in another three-volume work, *Principles of Social Sciences*, published in 1858 and 1859. The later work was subsequently translated into five European languages and Japanese, cementing his international reputation as the leading American economist of the time, especially among the Germans where he had a large and devoted following (Dunbar 1904, 14).

In his books and many pamphlets, Carey argued passionately and sometimes illogically for an American economic system, defined as an economy based on a "strong protective tariff, government aid to industry, investment in education and public works such as roads, canals, and railroads," which collectively would insure continuous domestic prosperity and democracy while promoting "American independence in an emerging British world economy" (Lewis 2006, 121). Unlike many of the American economists of his time, particular textbook writers who modeled their works along the lines of British thinking, Carey saw the world through a different lens.

> By contrast, there was his own system, a structure in which material conditions were important but not to the exclusion of every other aspect of human development. Of equal, or even greater, were the questions of moral and social growth. For man was more than an economic automaton, getting and begetting; he was also motivated by a desire for happiness and moral improvement.
>
> (Morrison 1986, 9).

He instinctively realized that the combination of Malthusian population theory and Ricardian diminishing marginal returns of land created a gloomy outlook for the prospects of the human condition (Spiegel 1960, 126), an observation that may have inspired the phrase 'dismal science,' a term Thomas Carlyle coined more than a decade later (Levy and Peart 2001). For Carey, the fundamental flaw in the thinking of British economists was the *a priori* nature of their methodology.

> Almost all approach the subject with a set of prejudices and instead of patiently collecting facts, and constructing theories therefrom, the theory is first constructed ... and then as many facts are taken as ten to support its, omitting all notice of those which have a contrary tendency.
>
> (Carey 1835, 7).

Eschewing deduction, Carey took an inductive approach, immersing himself in reams of data and, using a clever system of national income accounting, showed that American economic development was a direct and obvious contradiction to the woeful forecasts embedded in the supposedly universal principles of British economics of the time.

> Carey used his *Essay* to demonstrate the unparalleled economic achieve-ment of the youthful United States, and then to explain that achievement. After surveying a virtual avalanche of economic data drawn from a remarkably diverse range of sources, Carey concluded that American workers were easily the most efficient and best rewarded in the world. He estimated (an educated guess) that the provisions secured by eleven days of work by an American required sixteen days in England, eighteen in Holland, twenty-eight in France, thirty-eight in China, and seventy-four in India. In an even more elaborate estimate of national economic achievement, Carey awarded up to a hundred points to a country for a maximum achievement in five areas – security of person and property, freedom of action, freedom of commerce, habits of industry, and quality of productive capital (including land). On this scale, the United States achieved a total of 460 points (out of a possible 500, its largest debit being for restraints on commerce), Britain 400, Holland 315, France 225, China 135, and India only 75.
>
> (Conkin 1980, 263).

Carey believed that the prevailing school of American economic thought was an exiguous copy of British theory and thus not applicable to the unique system of economics found in the United States. If he had stopped with his empirical analysis and left it to those that followed to develop alternative economic models capable of explaining what he had observed and documented, Carey would probably still have a place of some prominence in the history of American economics. Instead, he tried to develop a competing paradigm to the British school, a model that "ultimately caused Carey no end of theoretical grief" and proved to be his undoing, at least with respect to his place in posterity (Morrison 1968, 270). He started out to disprove the classical model but ended up introducing a theory that was not materially different from the ones he sought to displace, replete with the kind of methodological lapses and deductive flaws he criticized others for committing (Morrison 1968, 274–275). "Great as was the influence that he exercised at the time, later generations have found but little of enduring value in his contributions to economic science …" (Seligman 1967, 141–142). And yet a case can be made for a contribution he made, however obliquely, to the arc of American thought outside of economics, namely the theory of American exceptionalism.

While a precise definition of the term remains allusive, American exceptionalism is the notion that a particular, if not peculiar, combination of circumstances and values distinguish the development of the United States from that which other nations have experienced (Heclo 2013, 29). This unique set of factors includes geographic location, laissez-faire economics, individualism, and historical good luck (Dunn 2013, 2; Heclo 2013, 30–31). American exceptionalism comes in two strains: a religious version that traces its roots to the New England Puritans under the leadership of John Winthrop and considers divine providence an integral aspect of American's success (Madsen 2011, 15–22); and a secular version which sees the triumphs of the United States as a product of more earthly reasons such as abundant supplies of natural resources (Gordon 2013, 86). Those who subscribe to the concept of American exceptionalism usually trace the roots of the idea to an obscure passage in *Democracy in America*, although a close reading of that passage suggests Tocqueville's comment about America being "entirely exceptional" is a left-handed compliment as he indicates that America is exceptional because of its singular focus "on caring for purely material things" at the expense of loftier pursuits such as "the study of the sciences, letters, and the arts" (Tocqueville 2000, 430). On the other hand, Carey like his father was genuine in his conviction that America was truly special (Ross 1991, 444–448). With regards to economics, Carey believed that the "American National System" as he called it, was unique and deserving of universal admiration and adoption. He also embraced the subliminal belief embedded in the concept of exceptionalism that the United States is not just different than other countries but also better (Baker 2011, 243). During Carey's time, the Civil War and the subsequent turmoil of the ten-year reconstruction period that followed disabused America of its infatuation with itself. Since then, however, the concept of American exceptionalism has witnessed several reincarnations including one in the 1980s during the presidency of Ronald Reagan (Hodgson 2009, 69–70, 176–177), and is still today a topic of discussion and debate among intellectuals.

## Other voices

In nineteenth-century America the economy was not the only thing expanding at a frenetic clip; knowledge was also growing briskly due to a combination of interrelated factors including rising literacy rates, the expansion of public education at all levels, rapid urbanization, and improving methods of communication and transportation. Formal education became increasingly the path to entry into various professions (Wiebe 1967, 121). As professionalization increased, affinity groups or associations formed among like-minded and similarly credentialed individuals. During the first half of the nineteenth century, these connections were largely local and often informal; by mid-century national organizations began to emerge (Burke 2012). The first prominent ones were those identified with long established professions: the American Medical Association began in 1847; the American Dental Association in 1859; and the American Bar Association in 1878. Science and mathematics also formed professional groups, beginning with an umbrella organization, the American Association for the Advancement of Science (1848), from which sprang more specialized associations: the American Chemical Society (1876);

the American Mathematical Society (1888); and the American Physical Society (1899). Humanists were also launching alliances including the Modern Language Association of America (1883) and the American Historical Association (1884). Social scientists began in one inclusive grouping – the American Social Science Association formed in 1865, then soon spun off specialized niches – the American Economic Association (1885), the American Psychological Association (1892), the American Political Science Association (1903), and the American Sociological Association (1905).

Today, heterodox economists generally consider the American Economic Association (AEA) the epicenter of American mainstream economics, an assessment with which most economists, regardless of their stripe, would agree. In 1885, things were different; the fledging organization had a decidedly revolutionary profile, indeed "there was a concern that the AEA might become a socialist organization" (Wible 2009, 1). To appreciate what was going on then, it might be best to recount the creation of the AEA through the prism of the conflict involving two of the main protagonists in the story, Richard Ely (1854–1943) and Simon Newcomb (1835–1909). After the Civil War "academicization" came to many fields including economics, the study of which "migrated from salons and learned societies to universities and other higher education establishments" (Fourcade 2009, 2). As economics became increasingly professional and academic, many young Americans, including Richard Ely, choose to pursue advanced economics degrees in Germany in part because of the limited number of doctoral economics programs in the United States, but more so to study the historical-school approach in economics then emerging in Germany as an alternative to the British tradition so popular in the United States (Normano 1943, 134). The two schools of economics differed in a number of ways, especially with respect to policy issues and methodology. In terms of policy, the main distinctions between the schools concerned their respective attitudes toward international trade and the role of government in economic affairs: the British school and its ardent followers in America believed in free trade and laissez-faire, while the German school was tolerant of protectionism and openly supportive of an active fiscal agenda for the national government. Regarding methodology, British economics was deductive and theoretical in that its methodology was to deduce economic actions that would be logically consistent with a few widely accepted principles of human behavior. In contrast, the German historical school was inductive and empirical, that is, given to formulating likely economic actions after observing persistent and recurring patterns evident in numerous observations of actual practices. British methodology slanted to the deterministic while German methodology leaned to the probabilistic (Ross 1991, 18). While Ely was the product of a new if not different approach to economics, Newcomb was clearly old school.

Simon Newcomb began his life in academe in 1861 with a teaching appointment at the US Naval Academy having earned a reputation as a highly regarded astronomer and mathematician following years of independent and formal study and working several jobs requiring practical applications of math, astronomy, and navigation (Emmett 2006, 658–659). Newcomb came to economics late in his teaching career, making it a secondary interest and something he taught occasionally. In 1884 he joined the faculty at the Johns Hopkins University and a year later published *Principles of Political Economy*, a well-received non-mathematical introductory text. In his professional publications by contrast, he displayed keen insights into his adopted discipline. His quantitative treatments of orthodox economics have led some to consider him "the first American mathematical economist" (Emmett 2006, 658). Newcomb quickly discerned the distinction between a flow and a stock (Spiegel 1991, 616) and

> he developed the idea of a wheel of wealth, designated by him as "societary circulation," made up of flows of money and goods and services running in opposite directions. [He] considered "demand as the director of industry," and in the monetary field he constructed an equation of exchange which served as the basis for the later work of Irving Fisher.
>
> (Spiegel 1991, 614–615)

He fervently believed in laissez-faire economics and was a devoted follower of social Darwinism, Herbert Spencer's theory of human behavior based on a fusion of biology and social thought. For Newcomb, the implications of Spencer's analysis dovetailed with the inferences of orthodox economics, especially the unequal distribution of income which Newcomb considered a 'natural' outcome of American industrial capitalism.

Richard Ely and many of the new young economists coming out of the German historical school saw things differently (Dorfman [1949] 1969, 205–206). The rise of industrialism in the United States and Western Europe had created a large and growing working class whose sole source of livelihood was their wages, making the economic well-being of this permanent underclass susceptible to the vagaries of the business cycle (Ross 1991, 57). During the cycle's upswings, jobs were plentiful, wages good, and incomes more than sufficient to provide for a decent standard of living. In the downturns, however, such as the depression of the 1870s, unemployment rose, noticeably so in growing urban areas. In the absence of economic safety nets or some other redundancies in the system, the loss of a job meant the loss of one's livelihood. As a result, the costs of general economic slumps that social Darwinists saw as inevitable fell hardest on those least able to absorb the blow. Ely and like-minded individuals thought that the implementation of appropriate social policies could negate these consequences or at least ameliorate them. To that end, Ely and some of his close colleagues set out to organize professional economists into a group which would lobby for political changes to do just that. Accordingly, they invited economists interested in forming a national association to gather at the next meeting of the American Historical Association set for early September, 1885, in Saratoga Springs, New York (Wible

2009, 31). The economists gathered there were presented with a platform that Ely and his followers hoped the new American Economic Association (AEA) would adopt. The proposed AEA was in part a reaction to the hegemony of the American Social Science Association formed in 1865 as an umbrella organization for all scholars and academics interested in promoting the social sciences (Haskell 2000, 16, 178–199).

Although just suggestive, the AEA's platform was unambiguously proactive.

PLATFORM

1   We regard the state as an educational and ethical agency whose positive aid is an indispensable condition of human progress. While we recognize the necessity of individual initiative in industrial life, we hold that the doctrine of *laissez-faire* is unsafe in politics and unsound in morals; and that it suggests an inadequate explanation of the relations between the state and its citizens.

2   We do not accept the final statements which characterized the political economy of a past generation; for we believe that political economy is still in the first stages of its scientific development, and we look not so much to speculation as to an impartial study of actual conditions of economic life for the satisfactory accomplishment of that development. We seek the aid of statistics in the present, and of history in the past.

3   We hold that the conflict of labor and capital has brought to the front a vast number of social problems whose solution is impossible without the united efforts of Church, state and science.

4   In the study of the policy of government, especially with respect to restrictions on trade and to protection of domestic manufactures, we take no partisan attitude. We are convinced that one of the chief reasons why greater harmony has not been attained, is because economists have been too ready to assert themselves as advocates. We believe in a progressive development of economic conditions which must be met by corresponding changes of policy.

(Ely 1886, 6–7)

To broaden the appeal of the new association, the platform was subsequently toned down so as to focus the emphasis of the AEA on service to the members and less on the advocacy for social causes. In this vein, Ely was passed over as the first president of the association in favor of Francis A. Walker, a Civil War hero, president of the Massachusetts Institute of Technology, and the preeminent American economist of the day. Ely was installed as the AEA's first secretary, ultimately serving as president from 1900–1901 (Spiegel 1960, 143–153). Despite these attempts to accommodate mainstream economists, the association still had its opponents, none more vociferous than Simon Newcomb.

Newcomb's opposition to the AEA was as much personal as it was professional. When he arrived at Johns Hopkins in 1884 Ely had already been there for three years; the two were diametric opposites and both of them at the same institution was the human equivalent of mixing water with oil. In his autobiography Ely described himself as a rebel (Ely 1938, 132); Newcomb was a snooty, status-conscious conservative. He favored a professional association for economists and with several like-minded colleagues was involved in the mid-1880s in creating the Political Economy Club (PEC), a private dining club modeled after an eponymous organization in London (Coats 1961, 625). While the AEA was open to anyone willing to pay membership dues, the PEC started with a select group of invited guests that even included Francis Walker and Richard Ely. Membership in the PEC was never large and those who regularly attended meetings represented such a narrow range of economic perspectives, the club "rapidly acquired the reputation of being a free trade clique" (Coats 1961, 627). The differences between the AEA and the PCE widened, becoming a chasm by the 1890s:

> Whereas the Political Economy Club continued to be a closed private club, many of whose members regarded themselves as custodians of "sound" economic doctrine, the A.E.A. from its inception aimed to recruit as many fee-paying members as possible, whether scholarly or not, and was almost equally acquisitive in its attitude to intellectual innovations.
>
> (Coats 1961, 634)

The friction between Ely and Newcomb was an extension of a larger issue over which the two were deeply divided, specifically the role of social scientists in society. Ely was symbolic of those who believed that "social scientists must take a moral stand on the controversial issues of overwhelming importance to the peace and security of ... society," whereas Newcomb was unflinching in his belief "that politization only subverts important academic values and diminishes the contributions that scholars can make to society if they confine themselves to their special fields of competence" (Furner 1975, 8). With respect to this and related issues, the two men engaged in heated exchanges in the mid-1880s, publishing articles in a number of prominent periodicals attacking each other's positions (Barber 1987, 182). These literary punches and counterpunches clearly showed that in "their approaches to political economy, the two men were at opposite poles" (Barber 1987, 180). Although Ely and Newcomb were in separate departments at Johns Hopkins, a single university was not big enough for both of them.

In the late 1880s Ely left for the University of Wisconsin, where with John R. Commons, a former student at Johns Hopkins, he built an economics program based on institutionalism, making the Madison campus home to a heterodox school of economics that thrived through the first third of the twentieth century. Newcomb continued to promote the Political Economy Club, including a stint as its president in the 1880s (Wible 2009, 11), but the gradual passing of old guard members and the growing popularity of the AEA caused the club to "dwindle into insignificance" in the mid-1890s (Coats 1961, 636). Newcomb acquiesced to the inevitable and joined the AEA 1894 (Barber 2003, 242). As for the American Economic Association, it remained steadfast in being apolitical and even after getting its voice – the *American Economic Review* began publishing in 1911 – the AEA's politics stayed as close to that of the median member as humanly possible.

## Crosscurrents

Utopias and their dual dystopias have been a part of the human story, fiction and nonfiction, for eons. Almost always embedded in these alternative blueprints for society are economic systems, usually implied but sometimes explained in such detail as to appear realistic and actually workable (Samuels 2003, 208). Historically, attempts to create real utopias have usually involved small groups of likeminded individuals who form a closed society based on a particular orientation or a shared philosophical focus. In the nineteenth century as a partial to the dark side of the Industrial Revolution, there were several small but concerted efforts, notably in Western Europe and subsequently transplanted to the United States, to create utopian settlements that would function within the framework of society as a whole and not as closed and cloistered communities. One such group of particular relevance to American history and especially the history of American economic thought was the Harmonists, a Christian-based sect founded in Iptingen, Germany in 1785. Also known as Rappists after their founder George Rapp (1757–1847), the Harmony Society was a communal organization that held all property in common, worked collectively and cooperatively in self-owned factories and farms, lived communally, and practiced celibacy, which meant population growth required attracting new members from the community at large (Wooster 1924, 2–4). In 1804, the Harmonist Society built a settlement in western Pennsylvania and set about creating the prosperous community of Harmony. Despite enjoying a considerable degree of economic success in Pennsylvania, the Society began a search for a larger and better farming site, and in 1815 moved its population of about 800 to the southwest corner of Indiana where the town of New Harmony was established (Wilson 1964, 33). A decade later, the Harmony Society decided to return to Pennsylvania and sold the New Harmony site to Robert Owen who took possession of the community in January of 1825.

A social reformer and committed socialist, Owen had already succeeded in developing a model industrial community at New Lanark, Scotland, a town of 1,500 which featured an eight-hour work day, a progressive educational system for children, and gender equality (Carmony and Elliot 1980, 162); his goal in acquiring New Harmony to replicate that success in Indiana. Physically, the town of New Harmony remained the same when ownership was transferred to Owen from the Harmonists: it consisted of 20,000 acres of land and had 180 structures that included "homes, dormitories, two churches, a lecture hall, four mills, a textile factory, a tanning yard, mechanics' shops, and a distillery and brewery" (Sutton, 5); philosophically, there was a quantum shift after Owen acquired the village as it when from being a religious community to a secular one. Owen was adamant that New Harmony be areligious, and he pushed the issue with such determination that he came across as anti-religious to many of the nearly one thousand individuals who flocked to the town when it became a secular commune (Sutton 2004, 7). In addition to religion Owen had other disputes with the residents of New Harmony such as his unwillingness to accept persons of color into the community (Wilson 1964, 118) which did not set well with utopians who were by and large abolitionists (Thomas 1965); those conflicts and the impending threat of financial insolvency soon convinced Owen to give up his interest in the village, which he did in 1827.

The demise of New Harmony, Indiana as a socialist commune was not the end of utopian socialism in nineteenth-century America, on the contrary. Between 1824 and the start of the Civil War in 1861, the United States witnessed the creation of at least nine phalanxes or communal utopias based on the writing of the French philosopher Charles Fourier (1772–1837), two Transcendentalists experiments in socialist communes, and five Icarian communes which also had French roots, that being the works of politician and journalist Etienne Cabet (Sutton 2004). All of these communes had a relatively short half-life and drew the contempt of so-called scientific socialists such as Karl Marx who the dubbed the communal socialist movement utopian for good reasons: their economics was blissfully naïve; their business acumen uneven; they thought that negative human attitudes such as racism and sexism would dissipate as soon as followers crossed the threshold separating the real world from the commune; and they believed that just having a commune would dissolve human conflict and consequently had no effective mechanisms for resolving strife whenever it arose. As the author of a history of one failed communal association in Northampton, Massachusetts observed: "The result was that the Association's members were a heterogeneous group, bound by no one allegiance save the ties of humanity, and then, as now, that was not enough" (McBee 1947, 66).

At the other end of the communitarian/libertarian spectrum stood the Transcendentalists. A philosophical and literary movement active in the thirty years prior to the Civil War, transcendentalism rested on the notion that humans can learn the purpose and meaning of life through their imagination and intuition and thus "transcend" or exceed the limits of acquiring self-knowledge using only logic and the senses (UShistory.org, 2016).

> As a whole, the transcendentalists were not systematic philosophers, bent on arranging the pattern of life into a logical sequence. Quite the contrary: they believed in living by inspiration. Believing that man and the universe

were God, they worshipped Him by trying to live in spiritual harmony with the great laws of nature – trying humbly to be good men. Their philosophy was little more than a collection of "thoughts," of individual aspirations and manifestations distilled from the sunshine and the mist over the river. They believed they were living the good life, not by accumulating knowledge or acquiring possessions, but by quickening their awareness of the beauties of nature and human nature.

(Atkinson 1937, xvi)

Unlike German transcendentalism, a philosophical doctrine based on a closely reasoned canon, American transcendentalism was a collection of individuals who shared a single belief in the superiority of intuitive knowledge to sensory perception and little else. As one of their number – James Freeman Clarke – put it: "We are called the like-minded because no two of us think alike" (Harding 2002, 3).

Prominent among those identified with transcendentalism were Ralph Waldo Emmerson, Margaret Fuller, and Walt Whitman, but arguably the most fascinating character associated with the philosophy was Henry David Thoreau.

Born "David Henry" on a small farm near Concord, Massachusetts, Thoreau (1817–1862) transposed his first two names while in college at Harvard University. After graduation he took a position as a school teacher but quickly left the profession because of his reluctance to administer corporal punishment (Robinson 2004, 30–31). He returned to Concord where he worked at a variety of jobs including pencil making, the family business, when he met and became friends with Ralph Waldo Emerson and other writers and intellectuals associated with transcendentalism. Over the next twenty-five years, Thoreau became a prolific writer of essays and articles on a host of topics ranging from natural history to philosophy and government. An arch individualist, he achieved a degree of literary notoriety with the publication of *Civil Disobedience* in 1849, although many of his works did not appear in print until after his death (Ashworth 1978, x). The Pulitzer Prize-winning historian Vernon Louis Parrington (1871–1929) dubbed Thoreau the "transcendental economist," and characterized his most famous book – *Walden* – published in 1854 and in print ever since as "the handbook of an economy that endeavors to refute Adam Smith and transform the round of daily life into something nobler than a mean gospel of plus and minus" (Parrington 1927, 400). In *Walden* Thoreau provides a detailed account of his personal experiment of living alone for two years, 1845–1847, in his self-constructed $10 \times 15 \times 8$ft 'house' on the northern shore of Walden Pond. The book is the story of his search for an "economy that would not hinder the highest spiritual development" (Ashworth 1978, x); appropriately, the first and longest chapter in this American classic is titled "Economy." Thoreau used the word economy in terms of its Greek origin – household management – and not in the contemporary sense of a system of precepts and institutions related to the processes of production, consumption, and distribution; nevertheless, his economics has societal implications and is not merely a prescription for individual behavior.

His motivation for writing *Walden* is reflected in his assessment of the human condition articulated in one of the most memorable sentences ever penned by an American writer: "The mass of men lead lives of quiet desperation" (Thoreau 1978, 6), a sad state that he attributes to preoccupation "with the factitious cares and superfluously coarse labors of life, that its finer fruits cannot be plucked by them" (Thoreau 1978, 8). A major source of these misplaced and time-consuming efforts is caring for the things that humans acquire and which ultimately 'acquire' them. As a case in point Thoreau notes "that men are not so much the keepers of herds as herds are the keepers of men" (Thoreau 1978, 58). As a student of life, he was perceptive enough to understand that the conquest of scarcity comes through wanting less, not acquiring more, a principle at the core of the economic systems common to many aboriginal groups prior to contact, as described in Chapter 2 of this book. Indeed, "the history of North American Indian tribes before or just at the point of their first contact with white men" was a major focus of his writings during the 1850s (Sattelmeyer 1988, 99), Thoreau believed that the division of labor created more problems than it solved; by his calculations, four months of work per year was more than enough in time and effort to provide everything an individual could require for a full, contemplative life (Thoreau 1978, 48, 51, 62).

> In short, I am convinced, both by faith and experience, that to maintain ones self on this earth is not a hardship but a pastime, if we live simply and wisely; as the pursuits of the simpler nations are still the sports of the more artificial. It is not necessary that a man should earn his living by the sweat of his brow, unless he seats easier than I do.
>
> (Thoreau 1978, 74)

While obviously a counter-culture perspective, this minimalist approach to economics has always resonated with certain segments of the American population.

Juxtaposed to the seemingly perpetual affection some segments of the American populous have for Thoreau's approach to economics, that of Henry George was like a one-stage rocket – a brilliant almost blinding flash – then nothing. In 1879 George published *Progress and Poverty*, one of the best-selling books ever penned by an amateur economist. Domestic sales quickly approached three million, and after being translated into numerous languages, additional sales overseas probably made George the most widely read American author to that point in time (Spiegel 1960, 154). In his heyday George's fame in America rivaled that of Mark Twain and Thomas Edison (Adams 2014). The notoriety transformed George into a public figure, a status he parlayed into a political career that included twice running for the mayor of New York

City. He came in second during his first campaign in 1886, finishing ahead of Theodore Roosevelt, a future US president; his second try for mayor in 1897 ended with his death just five days before the election. His demise also signaled the end of Georgism, the set of economic ideas and policies associated with him, but not before George had etched his name into the history of American economic thought.

George (1839–1897) was born in Philadelphia, one of ten children, in a family of modest means; his father owned and operated a small religious publishing business (King 1988, 83). He became an avid, lifelong reader which served him well as his formal education ended at age 14. George knocked around for several years working at a variety of nondescript jobs before settling in California in 1859 where he married and began a family in 1861. He then began a career in journalism, performing virtually every task associated with publishing a newspaper including writing editorials. In 1871 he and two partners started the ill-fated newspaper, the *San Francisco Daily Evening Post.* In that same year he published his first economics tract, *Our Land and Land Policy*, a 48-page pamphlet which laid out the basic theory George would subsequently expand upon in his magnum opus *Progress and Poverty* (King 1988, 84). The *Post* folded in 1875 and for the next four years, he worked as a state gas-meter inspector, a political job, while writing *Progress and Poverty*. In 1897, unable to find a mainstream publisher, George self-published 500 copies of his polemical book (Skousen 2016, 229). The book became an instant success, propelled in part by the nation's frustration and discontent with the depression of 1873–1878, an event known as the "Great Depression" until the 1930s when an even more severe economic downturn gripped the world (Irwin 2013, 39). A commercial edition of *Progress and Poverty* soon followed in January and was a run-away best seller, ultimately making him "the most widely read American writer on economic issues" (Spiegel 1991, 154).

The appeal of Georgism lay in the populist idea that an individual can own only what he or she creates or produces; land, being a natural resource, is thus communal property that everyone owns collectively. Land, however, *is* privately held, and as such is "the deepest source of social injustice" (Normano 1943, 146) because its price keeps rising as the human population grows, creating a windfall for those who 'commandeered' the fixed supply of land at the expense of the other members of society. For George, the private ownership of land was the principal cause of the ever increasing inequality in the distribution of income, itself a manifestation of the inherent evils of capitalism. To address this singular problem, George proposed a simple yet appealing solution, a single tax on the unearned value of unimproved land.

> The best tax is that which comes nearest to filling the three following conditions: That it bear as Lightly as possible upon production; That it can be easily and cheaply collected, and cost the People as little as possible in addition to what it yields the Government; That it bear equally – that is,

according to the ability to pay. The tax upon land better fulfills these conditions than any other tax it is possible to impose.

1  As we have seen, it does not bear at all upon production – it adds nothing to prices, and does not affect the cost of living.
2  As it does not add to prices, it costs the people nothing in addition to what it yields the Government; while as land cannot be hid and cannot be moved, it can be collected with more ease and certainty, and with less expense than any other tax.
3  A tax upon the value of land is the most equal of all taxes, not that it is paid by all in equal amounts, or even in equal amount upon equal means, but because the value of land is something which belongs to all, and in taxing land values we are merely taking for the use of the community something which belongs to the community, which by the necessities of our social organisation we are obliged to permit individual to hold.

(George 1999, 74)

At the zenith of George's popularity his fame in America rivaled that of Mark Twain and Thomas Edison (Adams 2014), but among economic professionals his vision of economics got mixed reviews. Alfred Marshall and some of his colleagues dismissed George out of hand, in part because "he did not clothe his thoughts in more modern methodologies" (Bryson 2011, xii). By contrast John Bates Clark and others found bright spots in George's economic analysis (Teilhac 1936, 118), but even those who took George seriously found shortcomings in his thinking. For example, Clark considered George's ideas of income distribution incomplete as they focused exclusively on rent to the near exclusion of the payments to other factors of production (Teilhac 1936, 172–174). Always suspicious of statistics (Bryson 2011, 10), George simply assumed that his single tax would generate enough revenue to fund the elaborate social justice program embedded in his economic thought, but critics were quick to note that given the relatively small magnitude of rent compared to other forms of income, the 'single tax' could not possibly create the resources necessary to support the grandiose welfare state that was Georgism (King 1988, 91, 103). Finally, the idea of a single tax was unoriginal as the Physiocrats had advanced a similar notion in the eighteenth century (Teilhac 1936, 155). While he had no lasting influence on mainstream economic theory per se, George did enhance the status of the profession for as a "representative of [the] American romantic national school, [his] brilliant fireworks served the popularization of political economy better than did many heavy volumes of academic erudition" (Normano 1943, 148)

Works by Henry George may seldom grace the reading lists for graduate-school economics classes but it would be a mistake to conclude that his spirit, if not his thoughts, has no impact on contemporary thinking. In 1925 with an endowment from its namesake, the Robert Schalkenach Foundation was founded "to promote public awareness of the social and economic reforms advocated by Henry George" (RSF). Among its many endeavors, the Foundation sponsors the *American Journal of Economics and Sociology*, a respected heterodox publication founded in 1941. A less solemn but more ubiquitous homage to Henry George can be found in thousands of living rooms across America and throughout the world. In 1904, Elizabeth Magie – a Washington, DC office worker, fervent board-game player and inventor, and ardent Georgist – patented the *Landlord's Game*, a board game she invented to "reflect her progressive views ... which centered on the economic theories of Henry George" (Pilon 2015, 18). The game's board consisted of a variety of squares showing, among other things, the costs and rental prices of various properties and real estate, a go-to-jail square, and a free parking space (Pilon 2015, 31). Parker Brothers, an American manufacturer of toys and board games, acquired the *Landlord's Game* in the mid-1930s, by which time its name had become *Monopoly*. The new owners tweaked the original game with several additions such as the iconic metal tokens, translated versions in numerous languages, and then heavily marketed the product as the self-described "world's favorite board game." Magie's original gave the game two sets of rules, an anti-monopoly set that rewarded wealth creation, and a cut-throat version in which the last remaining monopolist, having crushed all opponents, wins (Pilon 2015, 33). Parker Brothers opted for the latter alternative, an inadvertent but nonetheless obvious perversion of Henry George's core values.

## References

Adams, M. 2014. "Henry George: The Prophet of San Francisco (Part 1)." Progress (online).

Anonymous. 2003. "Organization and Functions of the Patent Office in 1936." *History of the Patent and Trademark Office Society*. Arlington, VA: Patent and Trademark Office Society: 54–68.

Appleby, J. 1984. *Capitalism and the New Social Order: The Republican Vision of the 1790s*. New York, NY: New York University Press.

Ashworth, J. 1978. "A Critical and Biographical Profile of Henry David Thoreau." In *Walden* (Henry David Thoreau). Danbury, CT: Grolier.

Atkinson, B. 1937. "Introduction." *Walden and Other Writings of Henry David Thoreau*. New York, NY: The Modern Library: vii–xxii.

Baker, T. 2011. "American Exceptionalism in American Intellectual Conversation, or How I Finally Submitted to Literary Criticism." In *American Exceptionalisms: From Winthrop to Winfrey* (S. Soderlind and J. T. Carson, Editors). Albany, NY: State University of New York Press: 243–253.

Baldasty, G.J. 1992. *The Commercialization of News in the Nineteenth Century*. Madison, WI: University of Wisconsin Press.

Barber, W. J. 1987. "Should the American Economic Association Have Toasted Simon Newcomb at its 100th Birthday Party?" *Economic Perspectives* 1(1): 179–183.

Barber, W. J. 2003. "American Economics to 1900." In *A Companion to the History of Economic Thought* (W. J. Samuels, J. E. Biddle, and J. B. Davis, Editors). Malden, MA: Blackwell: 231–245.

Barlowe, B. J. 2011. *Federalists vs. Republicans: The Nature of Man in a Republic 1787–1800*. Lynchburg, VA: Liberty University.

Bowers, C. G. 1967. "Hamilton: A Portrait." In *Alexander Hamilton, A Profile* (J. E. Cooke, Editor). New York, NY: Hill and Wang: 1–24.

Brands, H. W. 2005. *Andrew Jackson, His Life and Times*. New York, NY: Anchor Books.

Brands, H. W. 2006. *The Money Men: Capitalism, Democracy, and the Hundred Years' War Over the American Dollar*. New York, NY: W. W. Norton.

Bryson, P. J. 2011. *The Economics of Henry George: History's Rehabilitation of America's Greatest Early Economist*. New York, NY: Palgrave Macmillan.

Burke, P. 2012. *A Social History of Knowledge II: From the Encyclopedia to Wikipedia*. Cambridge: Polity Press.

Carey, H. C. 1835. *Essay on the Rate of Wages*. Philadelphia, PA: Carey, Lea, and Blanchard.

Carmony, D. F., and Elliot, J. M. 1980. "New Harmony, Indiana: Robert Owen's Seedbed for Utopia." *Indiana Magazine of History* 76: 161–261.

Coats, A. W. 1961. "The Political Economy Club: A Neglected Episode in American Economic Thought." *American Economic Review* 51(4): 624–637.

Conkin, P. K. 1980. *Prophets of Prosperity, America's First Political Economists*. Bloomington, IN: Indiana University Press.

Cooke, J. E. 1967. *Alexander Hamilton: A Profile*. New York, NY: Hill and Wang.

Cooke, J. E. 1978. *Tench Coxe and the Early Republic*. Chapel Hill, NC: University of North Carolina Press.

Crowden, R. 2006. "Jacob Newton Cardoza." In *The Biographical Dictionary of American Economists, Vol. 1* (R. B. Emmett, Editor). London: Continuum: 118–119.

Dorfman, J. 1946. *The Economic Mind in American Civilization, 1606–1865*. New York, NY: Viking Press.

Dorfman, J. [1949] 1969. *The Economic Mind in American Civilization. Volume Three, 1865–1918*. New York, NY: August M Kelley.

Dowd, D. F. 1956. "A Comparative Analysis of Economic Development in the American West and South." *Journal of Economic History* 16(4): 558–574.

Dunbar, C. F. [1876] 1904. "Economic Science in America, 1776–1876." *North American Review* January. In *Economic Essays by Charles Franklin Dunbar* (O. M. W. Sprague, Editor). London: Macmillan: 1–29.

Dunn, C. W. 2013. "Introduction: The Magnetism of American Exceptionalism." In *American Exceptionalism: The Origins, History, and Future of the Nation's Greatest Strength* (C. W. Dunn, Editor). Lanham, MD: Rowman & Littlefield: 1–7.

Ely, R. T. 1886. *Report of the Organization of the American Economic Association*. Publications of The American Economic Association. Vol. 1, No. 1 (March). American Economic Association: 5–37 (Online).

Ely, R. T. 1938. *Ground Under Our Feet: An Autobiography*. New York, NY: Macmillan.

Emmett, R. B. 2006. "Simon Newcomb." In *The Biographical Dictionary of American Economists, Vol. 2*. (R. B. Emmett, Editor). London: Continuum: 658–660.

Engerman, S. L. 2000. "Slavery and Its Consequences for the South in the Nineteenth Century." In *The Cambridge Economic History of the United States, Vol. II, The Long Nineteenth Century*(S. L.Engerman and R. E. Gallman, Editors). Cambridge: Cambridge University Press: 329–366.

Engerman, S. L. and Sokoloff, K. L. 2000. "Technology and Industrialization, 1790–1914." In *The Cambridge Economic History of the United States, Vol. II, The Long Nineteenth Century* (S. L. Engerman and R. E. Gallman, Editors). Cambridge: Cambridge University Press: 367–401.

Engerman, S. L. and Gallman, R. E., (eds). 2000. *The Cambridge Economic History of the United States, Vol. II, The Long Nineteenth Century.* Cambridge: Cambridge University Press.

Fourcade, M. 2009. *Economists and Societies: Discipline and Profession in the United States, Britain, and France, 18990s to 1990s.* Princeton, NJ: Princeton University Press.

Friedman, M., and Schwartz, A. J. 1963. *A Monetary History of the United States, 1867–1960.* Princeton, NJ: Princeton University Press.

Furner, M. O. 1975. *Advocacy & Objectivity: A Crisis in the Professionalization of American Social Science, 1865–1905.* Lexington, KY: University Press of Kentucky.

Galenson, D., and Menard, R. 1977. "Economics and Early American History." *The Newberry Papers in Family and Community History.* Chicago, IL: The Newberry Library.

Gallatin, A. 1972 [1831]. "Memorial of the Committee of the Free Trade Convention." In *State Papers and Speeches on the Tariff* (F. W. Taussig, Editor). Clifton, NJ: Augustus M. Kelley: 108–213.

Gallman, R. E., and J. J. Wallis. 1992. "Introduction." In *American Economic Growth and Standards of Living before the Civil War.* Chicago, IL: University of Chicago Press: 1–18.

George, H. 1999. "Our Land and Land Policy." In *Our Land and Land Policy: Speeches, Lectures, and Miscellaneous Writing by Henry George* (K. C. Wenzer, Editor). East Lansing, MI: Michigan State University Press.

Gordon, T. D. 2013. "Taking Exception to American Exceptionalism." In *American Exceptionalism: The Origins, History, and Future of the Nation's Greatest Strength* (C. W. Dunn, Editor). Lanham, MD: Rowman & Littlefield: 79–94.

Gossett, T. F. 1985. *Uncle Tom's Cabin and American Culture.* Dallas, TX: Southern Methodist University Press.

Haines, M. R. 2000. "The Population of the United States, 1790–1920." In *The Cambridge Economic History of the United States, Vol. II, The Long Nineteenth Century* (S. L. Engerman and R. E. Gallman, Editors). Cambridge: Cambridge University Press: 143–205.

Hamilton, A. 1972 [1790]. "Report on the Subject of Manufactures." In *State Papers and Speeches on the Tariff* (F. W. Taussig, Editor). Clifton, NJ: Augustus M. Kelley: 1–107.

Harding, W. 2002. "Transcendentalism." In *The Encyclopedia America* Vol. 27: Danbury, CT: Grolier.

Haskell, T. L. 2000. *The Emergence of Professional Social Science: The American Social Science Association and the Nineteenth-Century Crisis of Authority.* Baltimore, MD: The Johns Hopkins University Press.

Heclo, H. 2013. "Varieties of American Exceptionalism." In *American Exceptionalism: The Origins, History, and Future of the Nation's Greatest Strength* (C. W. Dunn, Editor). Lanham, MD: Rowman & Littlefield: 27–40.

Henretta, J. A. 1988. "The War for Independence and American Economic Development." In *The Economy of Early America: The Revolutionary Period, 1763–1790* (R. Hoffman, J. J. McCusker, R. R. Menard, and P. J. Albert, Editors). Charlottesville, VA: University of Virginia Press: 45–87.

Hindle, B. 1956. *The Pursuit of Science in Revolutionary America, 1735–1789*. Chapel Hill, NC: University of North Carolina Press.

Hindle, B. 1966. *Technology in Early America*. Chapel Hill, NC: University of North Caroline Press.

*Historical Statistics of the United States, Colonial Times to 1970: Part 1*. 1975. Washington, DC: Bureau of the Census.

Hodgson, G. 2009. *The Myth of American Exceptionalism*. New Haven, CT: Yale University Press.

Horner, J. 2006. "Henry George." In *The Biographical Dictionary of American Economists, Vol. 1* (R. B. Emmett, Editor). London: Continuum: 331–338.

Hudson, M. 1974. "Introduction." In M. J. O'Connor, *Origins of Academic Economics in the United States*. New York, NY: Garland: 5–27.

Irwin, N. 2013. *The Alchemists: Three Central Bankers and a World on Fire*. New York, NY: Penguin Press.

Jefferson, T. [1816] 2004. "Thomas Jefferson, Letter to Benjamin Austin." In *The Emergence of a National Economy: The United States from Independence to the Civil War* (M. Rutherford, Editor). London: Pickering & Chatto: 265–271.

Johnson, W. B. 1993. *The Promising Years, 1750–1830: The Emergence of Black Labor and Business*. New York, NY: Garland.

Jones, J. 1992. *The Dispossessed: America's Underclasses from the Civil War to the Present*. New York, NY: Basic Books.

Kammen, M. 1972. *People of Paradox: An Inquiry Concerning the Origins of American Civilization*. Ithaca, NY: Cornell University Press.

Kaplan, A. D. H., 1931. *Henry Charles Carey, A Study in American Economic Thought*. Baltimore, MD: The Johns Hopkins Press.

King, J. E., 1988. *Economic Exiles*. New York, NY: St Martin's Press.

Leiman, M. M. 1969. "The Economic Ideas of Jacob N. Cardozo." In *South Carolina Economists: Essays on the Evolution of Antebellum Economic Thought* (B. F. Kiker and R. J. Carlsson, Editors). Columbia, SC: Bureau of Business and Economic Research: 10–43.

Levy, D. M., and Peart, S. J. 2001. "The Secret History of the Dismal Science. Part 1. Economics, Religion and Race in the 19th Century." *Library of Economics and Liberty*. January 22 (Online).

Lewis, D. C., 2006. "Henry Charles Carey." In *The Biographical Dictionary of American Economists, Vol. 1* (R. B. Emmett, Editor). London: Continuum: 119–124.

Madsen, D. L. 2011. "Witch-hunting: American Exceptionalism and Global Terrorism." In *American Exceptionalisms: From Winthrop to Winfrey* (S. Soderlind and J. T. Carson, Editors). Albany, NY: State University of New York Press: 15–29.

McBee, A. E. 1947. *From Utopia to Florence: The Story of a Transcendentalist Community in Northampton, Mass. 1830–1852*. Smith College Studies in History, Vol. XXXII.

McCann, C. R., Jr. 2006. "Thomas Cooper." In *The Biographical Dictionary of American Economists, Vol. 1* (R. B. Emmett, Editor). London: Continuum: 173–177.

McCraw, T. K. 2012. *The Founders and Finance: How Hamilton, Gallatin, and Other Immigrants Forged a New Economy*. Cambridge, MA: Belknap Press.

Menard, R. R. 1996. "Economic and Social Development of the South." In *The Cambridge Economic History of the United States, Volume 1, The Colonial Era* (S. L. Engerman and R. E. Gallman, Editors). Cambridge: Cambridge University Press: 249–295.

Morrison, R. J. 1968. "Carey, Classical Rent, and Economic Development." *American Journal of Economics and Sociology* 27(3): 267–276.

Morrison, R. J. 1986. *Henry C. Carey and American Economic Development.* Transactions of the American Philosophical Society 76(3). Philadelphia.

Nelson, J. R., Jr. 1979. "Alexander Hamilton and American Manufacturing: A Reexamination." *Journal of American History* 65(4): 971–995.

Nelson, Jr., J. R.. 1987. *Liberty and Property: Political Economy and Policymaking in the New Nation, 1789–1812.* Baltimore, MD: The Johns Hopkins University Press.

Nevins, A. 1962. *The Origins of the Land-Grant Colleges and Universities.* Washington, DC: Civil War Centennial Commission.

Nichols, R. F. 1961.  *The Stakes of Power, 1845–1877.* New York, NY: Hill and Wang.

Normano, J. F. 1943. *The Spirit of American Economics.* New York, NY: John Day.

O'Connor, M. J. L. 1944. *Origins of Academic Economics in the United States.* New York, NY: Columbia University Press.

Olmstead, A. L., and Rhode, P. W. 2008. *Creating Abundance: Biological Innovation and American Agricultural Development.* New York, NY: Cambridge University Press.

Parrington, V. L., 1927. *Main Currents in American Thought: Volume II: The Romantic Revolution in American Thought, 1800–1860.* New York, NY: Harcourt, Brace.

Pilon, M. 2015. *The Monopolists: Obsession, Fury, and the Scandal Behind the World's Favorite Board Game.* New York, NY: Bloomsbury.

Price, J. M. 1988. "Reflections on the Economy of Revolutionary America." In *The Economy of Early America, The Revolutionary Period, 1763–1790* (R. Hoffman, J. J. McCusker, R. R. Menard, and P. J. Albert, Editors). Charlottesville, VA: University of Virginia Press: 303–322.

Rainer, J. T. 2005. "The 'Shaper' Image: Yankee Peddlers, Southern Consumers, and the Market Revolution." In *Cultural Change and the Market Revolution in America, 1789–1860* (S. C. Martin, Editor). Lanham, MD: Rowman & Littlefield: 89–110.

Ransom, R. L., and Sutch, Richard. 1977. *One Kind of Freedom: The Economic Consequences of Emancipation.* Cambridge: Cambridge University Press.

Robbins, W. G. 1994. *Colony and Empire: The Capitalists Transformation of the American West.* Lawrence, KS: University Press of Kansas.

Robinson, D. M. 2004. *Natural Life: Thoreau's Worldly Transcendentalism.* Ithaca, NY: Cornell University Press.

Ross, D. 1991. *The Origins of American Social Science.* Cambridge: Cambridge University Press.

Rothbard, M. N. 2002. *A History of Money and Banking in the United States: The Colonial Era to World War II.* Auburn, AL: Ludwig von Mises Institute.

Rothenberg, W. B. 1988. "The Emergence of a Capital Market in Rural Massachusetts, 1730–1838." In *The Economy of Early America, The Revolutionary Period, 1763–1790* (R. Hoffman, J. J. McCuster, R. R. Menard, and P. J. Albert, Editors). Charlottesville, VA: University of Virginia Press: 126–165.

RSF. The Robert Schalkenbach Foundation (online).

Sampson, R. E. 2003. *John L. O'Sullivan and His Times.* Kent, OH: Kent State University Press.

Samuels, W. J. 2003. "Utopian Economics." In *A Companion to the History of Economic Thought* (W. J. Samuels, J. E. Biddle, and J. B. Davis, Editors). Malden, MA: Blackwell: 201–214.

Sattelmeyer, R. 1988. *Thoreau's Reading, A Study in Intellectual History.* Princeton, NJ: Princeton University Press.

Seavoy, R. E. 2006. *An Economic History of the United States from 1607 to the Present.* New York, NY: Routledge.

Seligman, E. R. [1925] 1967. *Essays in Economics.* New York, NY: Augustus M. Kelley.

Skousen, M. 2016. *The Making of Modern Economics: The Livers and Ideas of the Great Thinkers* (Third Edition). New York, NY: Routledge.

Smil, V. 2005. *Creating the Twentieth Century: Technical Innovation of 1867–1914 and Their Lasting Impact.* New York, NY: Oxford University Press.

Soltow, L. 1975. *Men and Wealth in the United States, 1850–1870.* New Haven, CT: Yale University Press.

Soltow, L. 1989. *Distribution of Wealth and Income in the United States in 1798.* Pittsburgh, PA: University of Pittsburgh Press.

Soltow, L., and Stevens, Edward. 1981. *The Rise of Literacy and the Common School in the United States: A Socioeconomic Analysis to 1870.* Chicago, IL: University of Chicago Press.

Spiegel, H. W. 1960. *The Rise of American Economic Thought.* Philadelphia, PA: Chilton.

Spiegel, H. W. 1991. *The Growth of Economic Thought* (Third Edition). Durham, NC: Duke University Press.

Sutton, R. P. 2004. *Communal Utopias and the American Experience: Secular Communities, 1824–2000.* Westport, CT: Praeger.

Teilhac, E. 1936. *Pioneers of American Economic Thought in the Nineteenth Century* (translated by E. A. J. Johnson). New York, NY: Macmillan.

Thomas, J. L. 1965. "Antislavery and Utopia." In *The Antislavery Vanguard: New Essays on the Abolitionists* (M. Duberman, Editor). Princeton, NY: Princeton University Press: 240–269.

Thoreau, H. D. 1978. *Henry David Thoreau: Walden.* Danbury, CT: Grolier.

Tocqueville, A. de. 2000. *Democracy in America* (translated and edited by H. C. Mansfield and D. Winthrop). Chicago, IL: University of Chicago Press.

UShistory.org. 2016. *Transcendentalism, An American Philosophy.* US History Online Textbook.

Wang, W. T. 1947. "Economic Thought in a Transitional Period: A Study of Early American Protectionists." Master's Thesis. Urbana, IL: University of Illinois.

Wible, J. R. 2009. *Economics, Christianity, and Creative Evolution: Peirce, Newcomb, and Ely and the Issues Surrounding the Creation of the American Economic Association in the 1880s.* Durham, NH: University of New Hampshire.

Wiebe, R. H. 1967. *The Search for Order, 1877–1920.* New York, NY: Hill and Wang.

Wilhite, V. G. 1958. *Founders of American Economic Thought and Policy.* New York, NY: Bookman.

Wilson, W. E. 1964. *The Angel and the Serpent: The Story of New Harmony.* Bloomington, IN: Indiana University Press.

Wiltse, C. M. 1961. *The New Nation, 1800–1845.* New York, NY: Hill and Wang.

Williamson, S. H., and Cain, L. P. 2015. *Measuring Slavery in 2011 Dollars.* Measuring-Worth.com.

Witzel, M. 2006a. "Alexander Hamilton." In *The Biographical Dictionary of American Economists, Volume 1* (R. B. Emmett, Editor). London: Continuum: 404–407.

Witzel, M. 2006b. "Francis Wayland." In *The Biographical Dictionary of American Economists, Vol. 2* (R. B. Emmett, Editor). London: Continuum: 896–898.

Wooster, E. S. 1924. *Communities of the Past and Present.* New York, NY: AMS Press.

# 6 Economic thought in an era of abundance and anxiety, 1886–1928

## Introduction

In *The Instinct of Workmanship and the State of Industrial Arts*, Thorstein Veblen wrote "And here and now, as always and everywhere, invention is the mother of necessity" (Veblen 1922, 314). If there was ever a span of American history that gave substance to this insight it was the period 1886 to 1928. In less than 50 years the United States was transformed from a predominantly rural-based, agrarian society into an urban-industrial transcontinental country (Hughes and Cain 2007, 339). In no particular order, the catalysts for this rapid and complete metamorphosis included but were not limited to (a) an unprecedented wave of immigration which at its peak was, according to a headline in the *New York World* of April 29, 1906, creating new Americans at the rate of twelve a minute, (b) a plethora of technological breakthroughs that enabled the formation, development, and growth of the urban/industrial complex, (c) organizational changes in the structures of the business and governmental sectors that simultaneously diminished the sectional distinctions within the country while promoting a heightened sense of national identity and international importance, and (d) a reluctant acceptance on the part of the United States to shoulder the responsibilities of a leadership position in world affairs, even if that status was achieved as much by chance as by choice (Gordon 2016, 3–7).

Not only a time of transition that saw the United States go from a nation on the move to a genuine world power, the time period also witnessed an evolutionary shift in the standing of economics.

> The period from the late nineteenth century to the 1920s was dominated by methodological debates and the autonomization of economics from neighboring fields and scholarly enterprises. In this process of "academicization" or "disciplinarization," economics migrated from salons and learned societies to universities and other higher education establishments.
>
> (Fourcade 2009, 2)

With this change in status came elevated respect and as a consequence, the term 'economist' morphed from a self-described job title that any 'amateur' could appropriate into a bona fide profession.

## Economic, social, and political conditions

In 1889 four new states – North Dakota, South Dakota, Montana, and Washington – were added to the United States; a year later the designation of a "frontier line" was officially discontinued, signaling the end of the transcontinental expansion of the country (Seavoy 2006, 213). Although the westward extension of the nation technically ceased – it would be 1959 before Alaska and Hawaii achieved statehood – the population of America continued to grow, dramatically so in the 48 states that constituted the United States in 1912. In 1880 the population of continental America was just over 50 million; by 1930 it stood at nearly 123 million (Boyer *et al.* 2014, A-13). Immigration – primarily from northern and western Europe especially England, Ireland, and Germany prior to 1890, then mainly from southern and western Europe notably Italy and Poland thereafter – was the principal source of this growth, with over 28 million people coming to America in a fifty-year span (Boyer *et al.* 2014, A-15). The peak period of this flow was the first decade of the twentieth century when 8.7 million immigrated to the US. In the census of 1900, nearly one out every seven people in the country, roughly 14 percent, was an immigrant; "By 1910, immigrants and their U.S.-born children made up 35 percent of the population" (Whaples 2003, 168).

While the number of new Americans was growing, those who were already here began moving around at unprecedented rates as the structure of the US economy shifted to industrial from agricultural. Despite a doubling of workers in the farm sector to eleven million during the last half of the nineteenth century (Hughes 1970, 129), America witnessed a dramatic shift in sector shares of commodity production, from 49 percent in agriculture and 37 percent in manufacturing to nearly the reverse – 33 percent in agriculture and 53 percent in manufacturing by 1900, with mining and construction remaining nearly constant over the time period at about 14 percent of total commodity output (Rosenberg 1972, 88). The spectacular growth of the industrial sector in such a short period of time, often referred to as the 'Second Industrial Revolution,' (Hughes 1966, ix) was the magnet that attracted immigrants to the US in unprecedented numbers; it also precipitated two sizeable domestic migrations, one being "sons of northern farmers migrating to cities in search of employment" (Seavoy 2006, 223–224), and a second, smaller exodus of southern blacks northward. The later migration grew markedly after World War II as illustrated in Table 6.1, but clearly had its roots in the early twentieth century, especially the 1920s, when some 1.6 million blacks moved to industrial cities in the Northeast and Midwest. Urbanization and industrialization when hand-in-hand (Hughes 1966, ix): in 1880 26.3 percent of the US population lived in urban areas, and 73.8 percent lived in rural farm and nonfarm areas; by 1900, the split was 37.2 percent urban and the rest rural, and by 1930 urban stood at 56.2 percent, with rural at 43.8 percent (Gordon 2016, 98). The reasons for the symbiotic relationship between industrial development

*Table 6.1* Percentage of black Americans living in the South, 1890–2010

| Census Date | Percentage |
| --- | --- |
| 1890 | 90 |
| 1900 | 90 |
| 1910 | 89 |
| 1920 | 85 |
| 1930 | 79 |
| 1940 | 77 |
| 1950 | 68 |
| 1960 | 60 |
| 1970 | 53 |
| 1980 | 53 |
| 1990 | 53 |
| 2000 | 55 |
| 2010 | 57 |

Sources: Lemann 1991, 15; US Census Bureau.

and urban growth were two-fold: the considerable economies of scale associated with the industries that developed during the Second Industrial Revolution, and the spillover effects of an expanding industrial sector on satellite and service businesses in the local areas (Hughes 1970, 60), that is, or the economics of propinquity.

The rise of the urban/industrial complex from 1880 to 1930 witnessed an increase in the US population to 123 million from 50 million or at an annual rate of growth of about 1.75 percent per year; this sizeable and sustained expansion of population helped drive aggregate demand to new heights as reflected in the growth of national output which increased at about 3.5 percent a year over the time period under discussion despite a number of short-term economic downturns (Abramovitz and David 2001, 8). Economic development, however, was uneven across the various sections of the county, particularly in the Cotton South where growth was persistently less than the national average (Bensel 2000, 1–4). Nevertheless, the overall economy was not only getting bigger, it was also getting better on a per capita basis as output per person grew at an annual rate of about 1.7 percent (Rosenberg 1972, 9). On the supply side, new inventions and innovations were pulling economic growth with as much vigor as aggregate demand was pushing it. One of the major advances that powered economic development was the large-scale production and distribution of electricity. In 1880, "not a single American household was wired for electricity" (Gordon 2000, 5); two years later, the first commercial power plant came on line (Constable and Somerville 2003, 3). By 1920, 35 percent of US homes were electrified, and in 1930 about 70 percent of US homes had electricity (Novak 2013). In battery form, electricity had been used as a source of energy since the 1840s (Jonnes 2004, 44), so in a sense its widespread production and distribution during the Second Industrial Revolution was a difference of degree not kind. Nevertheless, a continuous, sizeable, and reliable supply of electricity had a profound effect on the nature of human life in general and economic activity in particular. As a dependable source of energy, it powered elevators making high-rise businesses and residences a reality, thus enabling urbanization and the dense concentration of work places and housing in relatively small areas. The nature of work itself began to change, becoming less craft-oriented and individualistic and more standardized, consistent, and mass produced. This boosted the annual rate of growth of output to 1.7 percent a year, a full half-percent higher than it had been from 1840 to 1880 (Rosenberg 1972, 9). On the other hand, electricity also created the night shift and the possibility of extending the work day beyond daylight hours. These and other implications for the working class did not go unnoticed as the skill set required of production workers diminished while round-the-clock work schedules became a realistic possibility. In response to these and other social and economic implications of the technology-driven Second Industrial Revolution, national unions such as the Knights of Labor and the American Federation of Labor which sought to represent general, unskilled workers began to emerge in the 1880s; there were other less constructive manifestations of the growing discontent in the labor sector such as the infamous Haymarket Affair that took place in Chicago in 1886, a violent reaction to the real or imagined threats associated with technological change.

The impact of electricity on the human condition was spectacular, indeed almost magical, but "the most tangible improvement in the everyday standard of living … came through the rapid spread after 1880 of running water, indoor plumbing, and urban sanitation infrastructure" (Gordon 2000, 59). Water has always been indispensable for human life, but as urbanization accelerated at the end of the nineteenth century, it became one of the most feared substances on the planet.

> Indoor plumbing was rare, especially in the countryside, and in cities it was inadequate at best. Tenements housing as many as 2,000 people typically had not one bathtub. Raw sewage was often dumped directly into streets and open gutters; untreated industrial waste went straight into rivers and lakes, many of which were sources of drinking water; attempts to purify water constantly fell short, and very few municipalities treated wastewater at all.
>
> As a result, waterborne diseases were rampant. Each year typhoid fever alone killed 25 of every 100,000 people (Wilbur Wright among them in 1912). Dysentery and diarrhea, the most common waterborne diseases, were the nation's third leading cause of death. Cholera outbreaks were a constant threat.
>
> (Constable and Somerville 2003, 38)

The plumbing revolution that began in America and other parts of the world in the late nineteenth century, with its numerous interrelated innovations – flush toilets, municipal systems to bring water to buildings and take sewage away, the use of chlorine to make drinking water safe – was extensive and expensive, but the benefits were immediate and obvious (Boyer *et al.* 2014, 574). In Chicago in the early 1890s for example, the incidence of typhoid peaked at 170 cases per 100,000 persons, but by 1918 and after a substantial and sustained investment in clean water, it had dropped to virtually zero (www.uic.edu/sph, 99). Similar outcomes were recorded nationwide and by 1940 "typhoid, cholera, and dysentery were for all practical purposes, non-existent in the United States and the rest of the developed world" (Constable and Somerville 2003, 39).

As the quality of life improved, the advent of mass production that took root in the 1880s and 1890s induced a response similar in magnitude on the demand side, which in turn became the foundation of the mass consumption society of the twentieth century. In the United States, the single product or service that most symbolized the rise of the consumer culture was arguably the automobile. "Of the 10,000 or so cars on the road by the start of the 20th century, three-quarters were electric or had external combustion steam engines" (Constable and Somerville 2003, 14); the development of an efficient, gasoline-burning internal combustion engine in the 1890s quickly changed the shape of transportation in the United States. In 1900 factory sales of passenger cars in the United States totaled just over 4,000; ten years later annual sales rose to 181,000. The airplane, which was invented at approximately this time, became one of the mainstays of the commercial transportation system in twentieth-century America; the automobile came to dominate the country's personal transportation market. Initially, cars were an expensive luxury but as their nominal and real price dropped after 1910 (Gordon 2000, 156), sales accelerated, reaching nearly two million by 1920 and rose to just less than 4.5 million in 1929, a level not exceeded until after World War II (Rosenberg 1972, 114). Widespread ownership of autos stimulated road construction across the country, which in 1904 had 154,000 miles of surface road, a number that rose to 276,000 by 1915, and reached nearly 700,000 in 1930 (Rosenberg 1972, 115). America's affinity for the motor vehicle spurred increases in the production of ancillary products such as petroleum, gasoline, service stations, and auto repair shops. While the embrace of the modern automobile was a worldwide phenomenon, in America owning a car took on the aspects of an obsession. In 1905, there were 79,000 registered motor vehicles in the United States, and about 81,000 in the United Kingdom, Germany, and France. By 1930, the US had over 26 million registered vehicles, more than five times the total for all of Europe (Landes 2003, 442). Besides transforming the nature of land transportation in the US, automobiles also proved to be a benefit to the country's public health system particularly in large urban areas. At the beginning of the twentieth century, over 25 million horses, about one horse for every three persons, powered much of America's local transportation, particularly in big cities (Constable and Somerville 2003, 14). In New York, for instance, 100,000 horses were used daily, a herd that collectively generated about 1,300 tons of manure and 25,000 gallons of liquid waste per day (bytesdaily, 2011). Some of the negative issues associated with this horse-dependent transportation system included flies, smell, and horse deaths – about 40 per day – but the real problem was the diseases linked to equine waste. By 1912, the number of motor vehicles in New York exceeded that of horses, and the continuing decline in the stock of horses, coupled with the improvements in water quality, decreased appreciably the incidences of many communicable diseases in New York City and other urban centers.

In addition to the new products and services driving American economic growth in the last third of the nineteenth century, novel ways of organizing and conducting business began to appear although their contributions to prosperity were a matter of debate at the time. Paramount among these emerging business structures was the mega-corporation, which represented a quantum shift in the very size and nature of business enterprises. It started with the intercontinental railroads but comparable organizational change quickly came to manufacturing, mining, and banking. The corporation as a vehicle of business formation was not new, but the scale of these enterprises increased vastly during the 1870s and 1880s, leading to considerable consolidations of market shares in various industries and the subsequent concentration of wealth and political influence. Even in the face of mounting agency costs – the risk that when owners delegate decision-making to intermediaries, these "agents and employees may fail to act diligently or may ... act in their own interests rather than in the interests of owners" (Rosenberg and Birdzell 1986, 231) – corporate size mushroomed in the constant search for economies of scale and the acquisition of monopoly status. The surge in size intoxicated business owners who sought to control market conditions by means not expressly prohibited by law. This period of American history became known as the Gilded Age, a term coined by Mark Twain to signify that the business world had become bright and shiny on the surface but was thoroughly corrupt underneath. Individual states simply lacked the heft to joust with large, well-financed national corporations or trusts, so attention turned to developing the federal government as a countervailing power to the monopolistic tendencies evident in the business sector. This represented a fundamental shift in the nature of the federal government whose primary peacetime function before 1900 was delivering the mail.

> The post office had more employees than any other department of the national government – 56,000 in 1880, 95,000 in 1890, and 136,000 in 1900. In 1880 the post office accounted for 56 percent of the employees of the national government, 61 percent in 1890, and 57 percent in 1900. In most years revenues made the post office self-supporting, or nearly so; and during these years it was the largest business in the United States.
>
> (Seavoy 2006, 215)

Despite its 'diminutive' size and limited scope, the federal government did take on the phenomenon of gigantism in business with the creation in 1887 of the Interstate Commerce Commission, a regulatory agency, and national legislation such as the Sherman Anti-Trust Act of 1890 (Bensel 2000). Nevertheless, some critics believed these and similar responses were too tepid and sought more fundamental change in the ways government at all level regulated business.

Some of those frustrated with the lack of effort on the part of the federal government to diminish the impact of national monopolies and trust turned to the political process as a means of redressing this perceived flaw. This change in focus became a popular national crusade which morphed into the Populist Party, an agrarian-based movement of the 1880s and 1890s, reflecting the farm sector's discontent with general economic conditions (McMath 1993, 3–17). The Populist Party also became a magnet for a variety of some long-simmering sectional grievances subliminally evident in the undertones of nationalism, xenophobia, and racism embedded in the populist movement (Boyer *et al.* 2014, 612). Although marginally effective during its relatively short half-life, the Populist Party became the catalyst for some fundamental political change, namely the consolidation of single-issue, often sectional political parties, into two large political entities, namely the Democrats (which subsumed the Populist Party), and the Republicans. Together, these two bodies became the nuclei of the two-party system that would come to dominate American politics in the twentieth century (Bensel 2008, 305). The bifurcation of the national political process became an important factor in the creation of a 'big government' capable of challenging the behemoths of the business world, but mere breadth alone was not sufficient to achieve success; depth in the form of resources, or at least access to resources, was also needed to get the job done (Hughes and Cain 2007, 36). That requirement was fulfilled with the adoption of the Sixteenth Amendment to the Constitution; passed by Congress in 1909 and ratified in 1913, it established the federal income tax, and historically speaking, was nearly as important as the Nineteenth Amendment that gave women the right to vote.

Prior to the adoption of the Sixteenth Amendment, the national government depended almost exclusively on tariffs and excise taxes for its revenues. With a national income tax in place, the federal government had the potential to acquire the wherewithal to fund a cadre of agencies and to staff these agencies with high-powered policy wonks capable of taking on their counterparts in big business, and the heft to impact national economic conditions not just local ones (Fawcett 2014, 257). As it is almost impossible to quantify the impact, positive or negative, of the political process on national economic development (Hughes 1966, 102), the efficacy of this approach has been a matter of debate ever since. More certain, however, was the transformation of sectional issues into national ones. Of particular note was the women's suffrage movement which had been committed to a state-by-state effort to advance its cause in the late nineteenth and early twentieth centuries. The existence of big political parties helped transform the right to vote for women into a national issue which ultimately translated into success with the ratification of the Nineteenth Amendment to the Constitution in 1920. A clearly unintended but nonetheless consequential benefit of big government involved the economics profession, for at about this time in US history, economists became 'indispensable' to successful policy-making in both government and business (Yarrow 2010, 28–29).

Many of the breakthroughs and innovations of the late 1800s and early 1900s were profound but not particularly flashy, e.g., insulin which was perfected around 1922 and considered the first wonder drug of the twentieth century (Bliss 1982). Other inventions were fascinating but at first blush did not pass the "so-what" test. Consider the phonograph and the movie camera, both invented by Thomas Edison, who in America was to the Second Industrial Revolution what Eli Whitney was to the first (Hughes 1966, 159–160). Initially, Edison considered the prototypes of what would become the phonograph and the movie camera engineering enigmas, that is, interesting technically but not necessarily commercially viable relative to other inventions that he was developing (Clark 1977, 149, 177). In due time and with further refinements, the two inventions would become the respective backbones of the recorded music and film industries, the dual cornerstones of the worldwide entertainment business in the twentieth century. Of course some breakthroughs during the Second Industrial Revolution were more about shifting attitudes rather than the invention of new technologies, a case in point particularly relevant to economics being the creation of the Federal Reserve System, America's central bank.

The essence of the convoluted story of central banking in the United States is probably best captured in a quotation often ascribed to Winston Churchill: "You can always count on Americans to do the right thing after they have tried everything else" (quoteinvestigator 2012). The Bank of North America – a private, commercial institution located in Philadelphia and chartered by Congress in 1781 – served as the nation's first, albeit *de facto* central bank during the 1780s (Michener 1906, 1–3) while a debate, often heated, over the wisdom of establishing a permanent central bank played out. On one side of the dispute were the agrarian interests of the coastal south, mainly located in the Charleston, South Carolina and the Virginia tidewater areas, while on the other side were the commercial interests of the coastal north, principally the urban areas of Philadelphia and New York. In a quintessential American political struggle of differing sectional viewpoints, the agrarian lobby with its desires for local control of monetary matters opposed the idea of a central bank and its objectives of monitoring and regulating national monetary conditions, goals that the commercial interests favoured (Wood 2015). In 1791 a grand compromise was achieved when the US Congress passed a bill creating the First Bank of the United States, a true central bank that was designed by Alexander Hamilton and modeled after the Bank of England (Kaplan 1999, 25–8). Part of the *quid pro quo* for establishing the bank was Congressional passage of the Residence Act of 1790 as amended in 1791, a statute that created the District of Columbia, a federal territory consisting of a one-hundred square mile tract of land donated by the states of Virginia and Maryland along the Potomac River that eventually would become Washington, DC, a permanent national capital to replace such temporary locations as Philadelphia and New York city, each of which having served as the nation's capital at various times during the country's early history (Lewis 1976, 4–7).

In 1811, the original twenty-year charter of the First Bank of the United States was allowed to lapse, but financial issues associated with financing the War of 1812 along with other monetary concerns led to the establishment of a Second National Bank of the United States in 1816. As was the case with the First Bank, the Second Bank was also given a twenty-year charter, and in 1836 history repeated itself and the bank's charter was not renewed. For the next 77 years the US economy operated with a central bank. During this time, an era before automatic stabilizers and federal government management of the business cycle, the multiplier/accelerator was especially pronounced (DeLong and Summers 1986, 680), leading to frequent economic panics as the ones in 1884, 1890, 1893, and 1907. The last of these was particularly acute and "persuaded American lawmakers to deal with their country's backward financial system" (Irwin 2013, 40). After several years of proposals, counter proposals, and compromise, a new central bank – the Federal Reserve System – came into being in 1913, with twelve regional units spread throughout the country so the System would be able to customize monetary policy to sectional needs (Hafer 2005, 127). As with its predecessors, each unit of the Fed, as the System came to be called, was supposed to be dissolved twenty years after being formed (Hafer 2005, 410), roughly 1933, which marked the depth of the Great Depression. Prudently, sense trumped sensibilities and without fanfare the existence of member banks, and thus the Fed, was prolonged indefinitely, a sure sign of America's coming of age.

## Mainstream

In the autumn of 1886, Frank Taussig, newly appointed Assistant Professor of Political Economy at Harvard University, taught for the first time the general introductory course in economics known to generations of students as "Ec. 11," (Schumpeter *et al.* 1941, 347). He would continue to do so, with a couple of notable interruptions, until his retirement neatly fifty years later. In that time, he would influence thousands as a teacher, text book author, editor of the *Quarterly Journal of Economics* (*QJE*) from 1896 to 1936, and writer of academic and popular articles and books. Schumpeter would eulogize Taussig as the "American Marshall" in the *QJE*, writing:

> Both succeeded in building up an organon of analysis that was classic in the sense in which that term applies to the theoretical physics of the 1890's – in the sense that conveys beauty and simplicity of lines as well as

technical limitation. Both made that organon serve a great historical vision and an ardent desire to solve the burning questions of their day.

(Schumpeter *et al.* 1941, 363)

Born in 1859 in St. Louis, Missouri to prosperous German immigrants, Taussig's father was a builder of railroad terminals. Arriving at Harvard University midway through his undergraduate education, Taussig transferred from Washington University. He departed for Europe following his completion of an AB in 1878 and spent six months at the University of Berlin studying Roman law and Political Economy. Returning to Harvard in 1880 with the intention to enroll in law school, he was sidetracked by an offer of the position of Secretary to the University President. The opportunity would give him an intimate knowledge of the University's administration and internal politics, experience which would serve him well in later years. The secretarial appointment was part-time, and Taussig filled the remaining hours studying toward a PhD in Political Economy, which he finished in 1883 with a dissertation on the history of the US tariff (Emmett 2006d, 813). He had taken over instruction of undergraduate students during Professor Charles Dunbar's leave of absence the previous year. In the fall of 1883 Taussig entered the law school at Harvard and was offered a professorship of Political Economy ahead of his graduation three years later, upon which he formally became a member of faculty. It is perhaps worth noting that, through all this, Taussig maintained a passion for playing the violin, performing in string quartets and other ensembles throughout these years – he was a highly accomplished musician, and later a dedicated family man (Schumpeter *et al.* 1941, 348). He was the very image of a happy, prosperous, and highly productive Victorian academic, and the archetype of an extraordinary gentleman.

As the United States emerged from the crucible of the Civil War, there came the growing recognition of the need for serious consideration of economic problems. An earlier era had resisted ideas of diminishing returns and laissez-faire because of the seemingly boundless frontier in the former case and the interests of New England industrialists in protectionist trade policy in the latter case (Haney 1939, 718). In the 1870s at most American colleges and universities political economy was a single course requiring no special quali-fications of the instructor save a suitable textbook. Charles Dunbar had been appointed the first chair of Political Economy at Harvard University in 1871, and Graham Sumner was appointed to the same position at Yale University the following year. The 1880s would see a proliferation of courses in Political Economy in the US (Johnson 2014, 4), spurred in part by a growing interest in the possibilities of social and economic reforms. Although this interest cut across a diverse population, most students, including Taussig, were well-educated young white men from upper-middle class backgrounds.

The influence of the English classical political economists, particularly David Ricardo and John Stuart Mill, placed the otherwise conservative Taussig and his fellow economists in the Progressive camp in the American academic scene of the late nineteenth century. At that time colleges still taught the Common Sense philosophy propagated by Sir William Hamilton after the Presbyterian Scottish philosopher Thomas Reid and expounded by President James McCosh of Princeton University. "The clerical rulers of the colleges had use only for a philosophy which could be authoritatively taught and on which students could easily recite. It must cast no doubts upon the literal interpretation of the Bible and the allied system of New England morals" (Dorfman 1934, 18–19). The staunchly religious conservatives of the era could not abide the influence of Darwinian biology as it slowly made its way through the academy. Early popular economics textbooks in the United States were written by religious ministers, Francis Wayland being the most famous example (Bateman and Kapstein 1999, 250). As the need for well-trained professionals became increasingly apparent the dearth of high quality instruction in the United States would send many students across the Atlantic in search of better opportunities.

As with many students of his generation, Taussig studied in Germany. The universities at Berlin, Heidelberg, and Leipzig were popular with Americans studying abroad in the late nineteenth century, and the economists of the German historical school were on the cutting edge of methodological development in the social sciences. The most influential German historicists were Adolph Wagner, Gustav Schmoller, and Joseph Conrad, and although their ideas emerged from the metaphysical philosophy of Hegel, they prioritized empirical methods (Schäfer 2001, 933). The practical application of economic theory at the Royal Bureau of Statistics in Berlin was a particular source of wonder for American students. Unlike the English economists, the German historicists eschewed laissez-faire doctrine and emphasized progressive social activism (Johnson 2014, 3). Schmoller, who for many years carried on the famous *Methodenstreit* ("Battle of Methods") against his Austrian rival, Karl Menger, rejected Ricardo altogether (Ekelund and Hebert 2007, 234). The inclusion of sociology, psychology, ethics, institutions, and culture in the study of economics would have an important influence on many American economists in the era before the New Deal.

The ideological pluralism of the era is especially obvious in the emerging literature appearing in newly established academic journals. The *Journal of Political Economy*, the *Quarterly Journal of Economics*, and the *Political Science Quarterly* published articles pertaining to a wide range of subjects and embracing diverse perspectives (Persky 2000, 95). The distinguishing characteristic of American economics was not an ideological one, but rather a focus on empirical research and practical applications (Johnson 1977, 19). It cannot be overstated that economics in this era became a literary enterprise; no longer the obscure subject of a few authors, economics would become its own specialized genre, engaging thousands of readers across the nation and requiring the production of a tremendous self-referential body of work. Economics became the province of those who had time to read and interact within the milieu of academic publishing.

In 1888 Taussig published *The Tariff History of the United States*, a work based on his dissertation. The book established him as a leading figure in economics, particularly regarding tariffs and international trade (Schumpeter *et al.* 1941, 342). His use of the historical method was exemplary of the period – economic histories formed the largest category of economic dissertations during this era (Johnson 2014, 8). While certainly the theoretical developments of the period were important, much of the work in economic research was concerned in laying the groundwork of the conception of the US *as an economy*, and doing basic economic research.

In 1901, Taussig, now the Henry Lee Professor of Economics at Harvard University, found himself unexpectedly unable to work, and left on a long absence abroad, returning two years later to academic life (Schumpeter *et al.* 1941, 350). Upon full recovery in 1905 he began work on a textbook. The result of his labor, *Principles of Economics* (1911) would become a standard text in American and English classrooms. The textbook was a presentation of classical and post-classical economic thought – the neoclassical framework that would come to dominate the academic scene was not part of Taussig's thinking. As late as 1921 Taussig would write "No one supposes that economics is an accurate science, or that the neat arithmetic or diagrammatic illustrations, the mathematical equations and deductions, conform to the facts of the market. They stand only for tendencies ..." (Taussig 1921, 411). Like J. S. Mill's *Principles of Political Economy* the book concerns itself first with "Production" and then with "Distribution." Moreover, Taussig demonstrates the influence of the institutionalists, writing of "that leisure class, which in modern times adopts many of the traditions of feudalism. The growing democratization of society may be expected to change this, and to raise the dignity and self respect of labor of all kinds, manual and mental" (Taussig 1920, 12). In his later years, he would write books on entrepreneurs and industrial organization, works having more in common with institutionalists than marginalists (Bruce 2005, 209).

Taussig's second absence from Harvard, from 1917 to 1919, occurred during and on account of, the First World War. He was hired by the Wilson administration to run a commission on the tariff, a role naturally suited to him. Afterwards he took part in the Price Fixing Board of the War Industries Commission, and took part in the Paris peace conference of 1918 (Emmett 2006d, 812). He returned to the university upon his resignation from the government. The war laid bare the need for more and better quality economic data, and thus the need for more and better trained economists. The following decade would see further expansion in economics programs in American academia, and an ever increasing number of professional economists working in both the public and private sectors. Taussig would remain, throughout the 1920s and early 1930s, at the forefront of the profession, a towering figure considered the dean of American economists. He retired from Harvard in 1935, and died a few years later, in 1940.

Taussig had come to political economy in no small part due to the efforts of Charles Dunbar, Harvard's first Professor of Political Economy, and a well-known expert on money and banking policy. As the founding editor of the *Quarterly Journal of Economics* Dunbar wrote the journal's first lead article, "The Reaction in Political Economy," in which he positioned the mainstream of American economic thought as being between the extremes of laissez-faire and Populist sentiment:

> behind this practical tendency in favor of a more effective use of the authority of the State, lies what seems to be regarded as the chief theoretical characteristic of the new movement, "the reunion of ethics with political economy." The power of society is to be directed by a keen sense of duties, scientifically defined and recognized. The obligation to consider other and higher aims than the mere enriching of the community, the duty of treating the laborer as something more than a certain amount of energy to be made effective by the administration of certain doses of capital, the constraint of Christian brotherhood, are to be enforced as a part of the teachings of political economy. And thus, it is to be declared, a new life is to be given to a science which has hitherto regarded man as living by bread alone. Without wasting time upon a needless defense of the older political economy, against charges certainly not based upon any real examination of the uses to which economic truth has been held to be applicable, it must be remarked that a good deal of the current talk of an ethical political economy appears to contemplate merely the infusion of emotion into economics. But, after all, can there be any doubt that even the most generous emotions must find their place, not in reasoning, but in the use of the results of reasoning? Is there any doubt that our sympathy with the aspirations of the working classes in their centuries of effort, or our zeal for whatever shall bring masses of society into the full light and warmth of modern civilization, is and must always be altogether foreign to the question as to the causes which determine wages? Both in the pulpit and in the press, it sometimes seems to be assumed that really humane economists may be expected to avoid any conclusions which unpleasantly recognize the persistence of moral as well as physical evil.
>
> (Dunbar 1886, 23–24)

Dunbar had another famous student, one J. Laurence Laughlin, who had studied under Dunbar at Harvard while pursuing his bachelor's degree in History in the early 1870s. Laughlin received one of the first PhDs granted in the United States, his dissertation written with Henry Carter Adams at Johns Hopkins University in 1876 (Emmett 2006c, 546). He returned to Harvard University in 1878 where he worked as instructor of Political Economy for the next ten years. He did a brief stint as a manager for the Philadelphia Manufacturers Mutual Fire Insurance Company, a period Laughlin would later recall as one in which he did virtually no work whatsoever, where he acquired an investment income that would continue throughout the rest of his life (Nef 1934, 780). He resumed his academic career with an appointment to Cornell

University's philosophy department. Sitting in his office in the autumn of 1890, a tall, quiet man shuffled into his office wearing a coonskin hat and announced to the Professor that his name was Thorstein Veblen. When Laughlin was appointed to head the department of Political Economy at the newly formed University of Chicago in 1892 he took Veblen with him. Laughlin was the formal editor-in-chief of the new *Journal of Political Economy*, but it was Veblen who performed a great deal of the editorial work during the journal's early years.

In many ways Laughlin's career was parallel to that of Taussig. He was a professor and department head at an elite University, editor of an influential journal, and an important contributor to the economic debates of the time. Like many of his colleagues, Laughlin was a defender of the gold standard and a "hard money" advocate, in opposition to the Free Silver movement championed by William Jennings Bryan. Laughlin argued originally in favor of a decentralized banking system, developing the "real bills" doctrine in which commercial bills allowed banks to expand and contract the money supply in accordance with prevailing business conditions (Mehrling 2002, 210). After the establishment of a central bank gained broad public support following the Panic of 1907, Laughlin became a leading figure among supporters of the new Federal Reserve System.

To understand the debates that would culminate in the creation of a central bank in the United States it is necessary to understand the state of American banks after the Civil War. The banking system in the US was based on the 1863 National Currency Act which established the "greenback" dollar, and the 1864 National Banking Act, which created the system of federally regulated national banks. The Civil War had necessitated the suspension of the gold standard, and a massive increase in the money supply in the form of greenbacks. State backed notes were taxed out of existence to make room for the national bank notes, which were backed by federally issued 2 percent government bonds. Even after the redemption of the greenbacks and restoration of the gold standard in 1879, the money supply continued to be constrained by the availability of government bonds. The pyramiding of reserves in New York City banks meant that a liquidity crisis in one place could drive up interest rates on Wall Street and cause a nationwide panic (Mehrling 2002, 207–208). More recent research has shown that many of the financial panics during this period were caused by adverse credit conditions around the cotton harvest, which could place a strain on the country's financial system because of the large volume of cash transactions involved in harvesting cotton and the importance of cotton in American export markets (Hanes and Rhode 2012, 3). Laughlin's aim with the real bills doctrine was to preserve a decentralized banking system in the US by making the supply of currency more elastic. Banks would be able to issue commercial bills, the quantity of which would be adjustable with the needs of the bank's customers in the business community.

On the other side of the debate – disregarding the free silver advocates – stood Irving Fisher, who argued in favor of a central banking institution able to adjust the money supply as necessary. He met Laughlin to discuss the latter's *Principles of Money* at a meeting of the American Economic Association in 1904, and would go on to write *The Purchasing Power of Money* (1911) in response to Laughlin's arguments for the real bills doctrine (Mehrling 2002, 211). Supporting the Quantity Theory of Money, Fisher argued that the money supply ought to be adjusted to the state of the economy, and that a central bank would be the best way to stabilize domestic prices. Because he was able to conceptualize such a bank using sophisticated mathematics, his work pointed towards the possibility of scientific management of the economy. Between these two important influences on the formation of central banking in US there was a crucial third voice – Paul Warburg, a German banker at the Wall Street firm of Kuhn, Loeb and Company.

For Wall Street, and also Europe, the matter of utmost importance was the control of international gold reserves, and keeping the periodic crises in the US from disturbing European commerce. To this end, Warburg proposed a system of national commercial bills, with a central bank to set the discount rate. He would become the chief spokesman for the Aldrich Bill, the forerunner of the Federal Reserve Act, which was defeated in 1912. The legislation was taken up by Democrats in the following year, after the Republican Party had suffered defeat in the 1912 elections. The core of Warburg's proposals remained, but Laughlin's emphasis on the maintenance of support for independent banks supplying credit to agricultural, industrial, and commercial interests, became essential elements in the legislation. The establishment of 12 regional reserve banks, as opposed to just one central institution, came directly out of Laughlin's influence. Additionally, the economist who wrote much of the Federal Reserve Act itself was a student of Laughlin, J. Parker Willis (Caporale 2003, 322). Despite the critical influence of Laughlin's ideas, in practice, the New York Federal Reserve, under the leadership of Benjamin Strong, would work along lines closer to those laid down by Warburg, and more aligned with the interests of Wall Street generally (Mehrling 2002, 212).

The development of social science at Yale University was led early on by Graham Sumner, who worked in both political economy and sociology and tended to treat the two subjects separately. His work in sociology was deeply influenced by the work of the social Darwinist Herbert Spencer. An immigrant to the US, born in 1840 to a poor English family, Sumner was educated at Yale University and Oxford University, and began his career as an Episcopal minister before moving into academia. During the 1870s he would author an early history of money, while participating in debates over the theory of evolution. Essentially a conservative in political economy, Sumner long held to the doctrine of laissez-faire, problematic in New England, where many well-established industrial fortunes were made possible by tariffs on imported goods. Towards the end of his life, he began to reverse his position on free trade, in favor of arguments that it could be used by government to rein in the power of the trusts. He would continue to teach at Yale, even after a serious stroke in 1907, until his death in 1910 (Witzel 2006a, 801).

Among Sumner's students at Yale University were two future giants of the field: Arthur Hadley and Irving Fisher. Fisher was the son of a Congregationalist minister in upstate New York and something of a mathematical prodigy, completing a PhD in Math and Economics in 1891 with a dissertation on general equilibrium theory that paralleled contemporary work by Walras. Fisher became an assistant professor of Math in 1892 but moved to the department of Political Economy in 1895 and made full professor three years later (Dimand 2006a, 284). He spent the rest of his career at Yale, until his retirement in 1935. As an economist, he would prefigure the coming century in economics, developing work around the use of indices, and theorizing macroeconomics as a system of constrained maximization problems (Tobin 2005, 20). He even went as far as to build a hydrostatic machine with flows and cisterns to demonstrate the principle of general equilibrium in the early 1890s. The device was unfortunately destroyed en route to the 1893 Columbian Exposition in Chicago. Fisher established himself early in his career with *Appreciation and Interest* in 1896, which explored the relationship between the price level and interest rates familiar to students today as the Fisher Equation (Dimand 2006a, 285). After nearly dying of tuberculosis in 1898 he would devote a part of his considerable energies to advocating for healthy living and reform. He had few graduate students and spent much of his time producing a vast literature for academic journals and popular publications, as well as publishing a monthly subscription report on business conditions to compete with the Harvard Business Service. Additionally, he would become immensely wealthy during the 1920s through his invention of the rolodex index card filing system. He would lose his fortune in the stock crash of 1929 that he famously and incorrectly predicted would be a brief recession.

Fisher was known as an inveterate reformer, advocating abstinence from alcohol and tobacco, dietary reforms and improvements in hygienic practice (Tobin 2005, 21). He was also a passionate eugenicist. The eugenics movement was an extension of Darwin's evolutionary theories to society, and many American economists in this period subscribed in one way or another to it (Leonard 2005, 208). In essence it advocated breeding policies with the aim of producing a superior society through the promotion of "good genes." Taussig belonged to the Eugenics Society at Harvard University, along with many of the school's most respected faculty members. He wrote that the "human race could be immensely improved in quality, and its capacity for happy living immensely increased, if those of poor physical and mental endowment were prevented from multiplying" (Cohen 2016). Progressive reformers were also taken in by the eugenicist movement and argued that minimum wage policies were a way to exclude weaker individuals from the workforce (Leonard 2005, 213). Today the eugenicist movement is remembered as pseudo-intellectual racism, but at the time it was considered part of the study of human biology.

Arthur Twining Hadley, son of a Professor of Greek at Yale University, taught at Yale for a few years in the early 1880s before moving to the University of Pennsylvania. Hadley became a renowned scholar of railroad economics, pioneering the concept of price discrimination, as well as the theory of monopolies. He also published a textbook in 1896 which would become a standard text in classrooms, the first to overtake Wayland's textbook in the United States, and written somewhat in response to Marshall's textbook (Kline 2006, 400). Hadley was critical of Marshall's reliance on static analysis, and emphasized the limitations of the static model. Together with Taussig, Laughlin, and Sumner, Hadley formed what was known as the "old school" of political economy in the US, as the four of them refused to join the American Economic Association in 1886, although only Laughlin would remain outside of the organization (Normano 1943, 136). Among the more conservative founding members of the AEA was its first President, General Francis Amasa Walker, then also President of the Massachusetts Institute of Technology.

The General's father, Amasa Walker, was a successful Massachusetts businessman and politician. Francis Walker lectured in political economy at Oberlin College in the 1840s and then at Harvard University in the 1850s. He wrote an early economics text, *The Science of Wealth*, published in 1865 (Gani 2006, 869). He became a General fighting for the Union in the Civil War, and would go on to supervise the United States Census in 1870 (Witzel 2006c, 876). He was considered an authority on social statistics in the United States and would act as something of an elder statesman in political economy during the late nineteenth century. As the first President of the American Economic Association (AEA), Walker helped to establish the organization as a moderate force that eventually became the dominant paradigm in American economic thought. In return, AEA would name its highest honor for him. Although he endorsed the laissez-faire and classical economics generally, he was remembered for his attack on the orthodox wage-fund theory. Walker argued that the entrepreneur was the benefactor rather than the exploiter of labor, and that the "captain of industry" was responsible for opening new sources of wealth (Normano 1943, 127). He died in 1897 at the age of 56.

The group of economists who provided the impetus for the formation of the AEA were known as the "New School," and included Richard Ely and Henry Carter Adams, of John Hopkins University, Edwin R. A. Seligman and John Bates Clark from Columbia University, and Simon Patten from the University of Pennsylvania. Patten had completed his PhD at the University of Halle in Germany in 1878 and would find his way into the faculty at Pennsylvania ten years later where he would play an important role in the founding of the Wharton School of Business. He was beloved as a teacher, and a prolific, if eccentric, author. His thought was characterized by a faith in social progress and the dynamism of human institutions (Namorato 2006, 680). He was a critic of the classical political economists, and rejected their theories of population, rent, and profit, regarding competition as an unacceptable standard of industrial regulation and developed ideas of state-directed social planning (Normano 1943, 152). Although a reformer, his emphasis, following the Austrian school, was on consumption and production rather than distribution. Something of a romantic nationalist, he advocated for social cooperation towards the development of social prosperity. He died in 1922, leaving no recognizable magnum opus, despite a large body of work and considerable influence on his contemporaries.

Columbia University was one of the era's three major mainstream institutions in political economy (the other two being Harvard University and the University of Chicago), and it boasted three of its most influential economists: Seligman, Clark, and Mitchell. Clark was easily the intellectual giant of the three, contributing the most influential theoretical works of the period, and providing the groundwork for American neoclassical economics. Born in Rhode Island in 1847, Clark attended Amherst College as an undergraduate with plans to enter religious ministry before he discovered political economy. Among the first Americans to seek out an education in Germany, he began studying under Karl Knies at the University of Heidelberg in Germany in 1873. On his return to the US in 1875, he was appointed Professor of Political Economy at Carleton College in Minnesota, where among his students he took especial notice of a young Thorstein Veblen (Henry 2006, 138). Prior to 1886, Clark's writings were characteristic of the Christian socialist thinking of the era. However, in the late 1880s he wrote a series of journal articles that indicated a change in his thought and adopted a softer tone towards oligopolies. Clark would migrate to Smith College and then to Amherst before finally settling at Columbia University in 1895, where he would establish himself as the leading academic economist of the era with the publication of *The Distribution of Wealth* in 1899. The view brought forth in *The Distribution of Wealth* is summarized in an 1891 article, "Natural Law in Political Economy," thus:

> The basic laws of economics are natural and universal; socialists have seized on a faulty theory to advance their position on the exploitation of workers and attack capitalism; the law of distribution guarantees that, under competition, "working man, working instrument, productive agent of any sort, would get under natural law what he or it is worth to society;" thus, with the discovery of the current theory of distribution, "socialism would lose its case and retire from court."
>
> (Henry 2006, 142)

Although Clark would write against socialism, his analysis in many ways was a response to the writing of Henry George's *Progress and Poverty* and the Populist movement of the 1890s. Among the points asserted by George was that the wage of the laborer was set by the marginal productivity of farm land. In crafting his response, Clark sought to discover a situation in which all production would return to labor, and in doing so developed the idea of the "zone of indifference" on the fringes of capitalism. Capital which has been exhausted – that is, which has already provided its natural return on investment – could be used by workers to generate income. The forces of free competition would equalize wages at the extensive margin of the no-rent capital goods and the intensive margin of the last worker hired (Persky 2000, 99). In showing that neoclassical economics could be reconciled with progressive goals, Clark rejected the once mainstream doctrine of laissez-faire.

In *The Distribution of Wealth*, Clark named five dynamic forces on society: (1) population growth; (2) capital accumulation; (3) technological change; (4) organizational change; and (5) the multiplication and refinement of human wants and needs (Persky 2000, 105). These dynamic forces were disruptive to the static equilibria developed in the book, although the lack of a formal dynamic analysis was admitted by Clark to be a major shortcoming of the work. However, static neoclassical analysis provided the foundation for his marginalist approach and was of course the basis of his response to Populist thought. Later critics, such as George Stigler and Paul Samuelson, would say that Clark had made neoclassical economics a "made-to-order foil for the diatribes of Veblen" (Persky 2000, 100). Nevertheless, by emphasizing the normative standard of free competition, Clark would provide a role for progressive government action while simultaneously limiting it, and make neoclassical economics adaptable in ways that institutionalism was not.

The American Economic Association named its annual award for the best American economist under 40 the John Bates Clark Medal, in honor of Clark's early support of the organization. Awarded biennially from 1947 to 2009, and annually since 2010, winners include several Nobel laureates, including inaugural medalist Paul Samuelson, as well as Milton Friedman, James Tobin, Kenneth Arrow, Robert Solow, Gary Becker, Joseph Stiglitz, and Paul Krugman, which means that roughly 20 percent of the American recipients of the Economics Nobel had previously won the John Bates Clark Medal. Although Clark's legacy today is somewhat overshadowed between those of the English neoclassicists and the American institutionalists, his work forms a crucial bridge between conservatives and progressives. He would provide the theoretical foundations of American economics in the early twentieth century while his Columbia colleagues provided the bricks and mortar of empirical methodology.

E. R. A. Seligman was the progressive lion of the Columbia University economics faculty. Born in Manhattan to a prominent banking family, he spent nearly his entire academic career, from his student days onwards, at Columbia University. As a boy, he was educated privately at home, tutored by a young Horatio Alger (Mehrotra 2006, 758). His graduate education was completed at the University of Heidelberg and afterwards he became the one of the first instructors of public finance in the United States. Besides teaching graduate seminars in public finance, financial history, and the political economics of finance, Seligman was active in reform movements, an advisor to New York State government, and editor of the *Political Science Quarterly*. Building on Clark's marginalist theories, he pioneered the development of progressive income taxes in the early years of the twentieth century, and wrote New York state's income tax law in 1911 (Johnson 2014, 13). Moreover, Seligman advocated a progressive view of government as a part of modern society. Taxes were not simply a payment for protection from harm, but an obligation of citizenship.

Public finance in the United States was developed within economics departments in the first half of twentieth century. Afterwards both public policy and finance would become independent academic fields (Rutherford 2006, 176). However, the study of the business cycle and the labor market would remain within the field of economics. The United States Department of Labor was formed at the beginning of President Woodrow Wilson's administration in 1913, and the Bureau of Labor Statistics, which had been formed independently in 1884, was incorporated therein. Royal Meeker was appointed Commissioner of the Bureau, which by 1920 had developed into the forerunner of the modern statistical agency, producing the monthly industrial employment reports which form the basis for the contemporary unemployment numbers (Goldberg and Moye 1985, 81). The development of business cycle models would have a major impact on government institutions from the 1930s onward, leading to the creation of the most widely-cited macroeconomic statistic of them all: Gross Domestic Product.

Wesley C. Mitchell (1874–1948) was the most empirically focused of the three major economists at Columbia University in this period. A student of both Laughlin and Veblen at Chicago in the 1890s, Mitchell had little use for the theoretical arguments of his time and spent his career in the development of statistical methods (Dimand 2006b, 630). Although his academic career at Columbia spanned decades, he would become best known as the founding research director of the National Bureau of Economic Research (NBER). The NBER would emerge from Mitchell's first major work, *Theory of the Business Cycle*, published in 1908, and the interests of the business community in establishing a coordinated center for calculating the basic parameters of the business cycle. The work pioneered by Mitchell would be built upon in the 1930s by Simon Kuznets, who would later recognize Mitchell as his most important intellectual forebear. Mitchell recognized the extraordinary nature of his work at the time, saying to an audience at the American Statistical Association's annual meeting in 1918:

> In physical science and in industrial technique ... we have emancipated ourselves ... from the savage dependence upon catastrophes for progress ... In science and in industry we are radicals – radicals relying on a tested method. But in matters of social organization we retain a large part of the conservatism characteristic of the savage mind ...
>
> (Burns 1952, 5)

More than perhaps any other figure of the period, Mitchell seemed to marry the socially conservative elements of academic institutions with the far-reaching consequences of their development. Together with fellow Columbia professors philosopher John Dewey, historians Charles Beard and James Harvey Robinson, as well as fellow economist Alvin Johnson, Mitchell founded the

New School for Social Research in New York City in 1918 as a protest of Columbia president Nicholas Murray Butler's firing of junior faculty who voiced pacifist views (Dimand 2006b, 633). Mitchell also maintained a working relationship between the NBER and the institutionalists at the University of Wisconsin, lending his considerable empirical resources to the leading progressives of the era (Rutherford 2006, 166).

The First World War would bring with it the need for more and better trained economists, and by the 1920s economics programs in the United States were considerable larger and better endowed than they had been when the people running them had been students themselves (Johnson 2014, 4). At Harvard, Allyn Young was a rising star in the faculty of Economics. A student of Richard Ely at the University of Wisconsin, Young completed his PhD in 1902 and worked as a professor at Western Reserve University, Dartmouth College, Stanford University, and Cornell University, among others, before becoming a part of the War Trade Board in 1917. He arrived at Harvard in 1920 and taught there until 1927 when he left to teach at the London School of Economics (Sandilands 2006, 912). Considered on his way to becoming a major figure in the field by his colleagues, Young died abruptly in 1929 when he was 52 years old.

The other major figure to come out of Harvard was Taussig's star pupil, Jacob Viner. He was Laughlin's last appointment at the University of Chicago in 1916. Viner shared the editorship of the *Journal of Political Economy* with his colleague Frank Knight from 1928 to 1946. At Chicago Viner taught the Price Theory class, known as the best economics class in the United States in the 1920s and 1930s (Emmett 2006e, 861). Paul Samuelson would write that there "has never been a greater neoclassical economist than Jacob Viner" (1977, 9). At Chicago, he developed the ideas that would form the basis of Milton Friedman's monetary theories (Nerozzi 2009, 598). He left academe in the late 1930s to serve as special assistant to the United States Secretary of the Treasury. In 1946 he joined the faculty at the Princeton University Center for Advanced Studies and remained there until his death in 1970.

The University of Chicago would boast several of the major figures in economics in the 1920s, including Paul Douglas. A 1921 graduate of Columbia University, Douglas would become most famous for his *Theory of Wages* (1934), which included the equation that is today familiar to economics students as the Cobb-Douglas production function, used to examine the marginal productivity of inputs. Douglas hit upon the production function while estimating coefficients for a least squares regression of statistical data in 1927, and published his results as "A Theory of Production" in the *American Economics Review* the following year. Among the paper's critics would be Douglas' Chicago colleague Frank Knight, but Douglas' work represented a milestone in the increasing statistical sophistication of the economics profession (Biddle 2012, 235). After working in the Roosevelt Administration as part of the Consumer Advisory Board under the National Recovery Act, Douglas would become involved in politics, first as alderman for the Hyde Park neighborhood of

Chicago, and later as a United States Senator from Illinois. During World War II he would enlist in the Marines and was wounded at Iwo-Jima. He served three terms as Senator, and would end his career teaching economics at the New School for Social Research in New York City (Ashbury 2006, 223).

Frank Knight is perhaps the apotheosis of this period. Raised on a farm in rural Illinois, Knight began his academic career as a scholar of German language before studying economics and philosophy at Cornell University. His doctoral dissertation, written in 1916 and published in 1921 as *Risk, Uncertainty, and Profit* was hailed as an instant classic and the final piece of the Marshallian neoclassical revolution in economics. Lionel Robbins and Fredrich von Hayek used the book as the text for their price theory classes at the London School of Economics (Emmett 2006b, 518). At the center of Knight's conception of the economy was the entrepreneur, who coordinated the disparate scarce resources of the economy into the production process and was therefore justifiably rewarded with profits. A professor of economics at the University of Chicago from 1928 until 1952, he was the dominant voice in the department prior to the ascension of Milton Friedman. Knight was one of the last major economists to rely on nonmathematical exposition and spent much of his career refining the conceptual terminology of economics (Leigh 1974, 584). His philosophical approach would lead him to emphasize the importance of ethics and history in the study of economics as opposed to focusing solely on the analysis of empirical evidence.

## Other voices

While much of the economics taught in the United States in this period came from sources in England, Germany, and Austria, there arose a genuinely American school of thought. Institutionalism was developed from influences both domestic and foreign and incorporated elements of sociology, psychology, and Darwinian evolution.

> the "institutional economists" regard human motives as largely instinctive, and criticize those economists who assume rational self-interest as a dominant motive. All center attention upon the institution (habits, customs, legal forms), regarding it as the chief factor in governing human behavior. Both the institution and behavior are regarded as phases of an evolutionary process, but the changes in the two are considered as non-synchronous. Accordingly, there is a tendency to see a need of eliminating maladjustments and classes of interest, and therefore to advocate social control over institutions.
>
> (Haney 1939, 742)

The institutionalist school of thought would be the subject of discussion at the AEA's 1914 meeting. It would also be an important influence on the "New Deal" policies of the Roosevelt administration in the 1930s.

In an age of giants, Thorstein Veblen had the reputation as a giant slayer. He was held in high esteem by many of the leading economists of the era, including Taussig, Laughlin, and John Bates Clark. Veblen's caustic wit was frequently directed at Clark's marginal utility analysis, but emerged out of his unique life experiences. Veblen was the son of Norwegian immigrants, born in 1857 on his parent's Wisconsin farm. The family moved to Minnesota while Thorstein was still young, and he grew up on a homestead carved out of the frontier wilderness. He was intellectually voracious from an early age, devouring every book he could get his hands on and mastering several languages. He attended Carleton College in Minnesota, where he first encountered J. B. Clark and then went on pursue philosophy at Johns Hopkins University and Yale (Adil 2006, 844). Despite his obvious talent, Veblen failed to secure a teaching appointment, and spent several years in his twenties listlessly reading on his father's farm. Eventually he met Laughlin at Cornell University, who took him along to the University of Chicago the following year. Veblen was the *de facto* editor of the *Journal of Political Economy* in its first 14 years (Dorfman 1934, 95), as well as being an instructor. In the late 1890s he published a series of articles in the *Quarterly Journal of Economics* which anticipated his first, and most famous, book: *The Theory of the Leisure Class*.

> [*Theory of the Leisure Class*] reads as if it were a saga, as if, in accordance with saga traditions, the underlying motif constantly before the listener were the inevitable doom of the industrially advanced, democratic community, through the functioning of the heroic characters who are thrown up as an effective leisure class by conditions supposed to make for peace, and who go also to their destruction.
>
> (Dorfman 1934, 174–175)

A wide-ranging criticism of economics, *Theory of the Leisure Class* was a savage indictment of upper-class culture in the Gilded Age. The class of people alluded to in the title were characterized as purposely unproductive consumers, the vestige of barbarian culture. The analysis pointed to the evolution of institutions, defined in the book as "habits of thought" (Veblen 1922, 88), as crucial in economic development. It was a hit among students of political economy, and made Veblen something of a star. The ideas in *Theory of the Leisure Class* would continue to preoccupy Veblen for the rest of his career, in various forms. In his authoritative biography of Veblen, Dorfman would write:

> Veblen's analysis is concerned with the dominance of modern capital … The never-ending competitive accumulation of wealth for the sake of competitive expenditure of life and substance, so that there may be further competitive accumulation of wealth … capital is the objective, and the consequence is a steady elimination and repression of the one end conceded by sober, civilized mankind as the only undisputed end …

modern corporation finance leads to the repression and elimination of material welfare. The factors that are ostensibly only the means of life have become the ends of life, to the destruction of civilized humankind.

(Dorfman 1934, 396)

Veblen left Chicago for Stanford University, where he would teach until heading for the opposite coast to take a position in the Wilson administration analyzing the economic outcomes of World War I. After a brief stint as an editor at the magazine *The Dial*, Veblen took up a position at the New School in New York. He was not a talented lecturer, being painfully shy and soft spoken. Nevertheless, he attracted admirers (including a surprising number of romantic partners) throughout the last 30 years of his life, dying in 1929. Of his contemporaries, he is easily the most well-known today in popular culture, and *Theory of Leisure Class* is still in print and the subject of much discussion. His influence reached across the social sciences and beyond, and his work was foundational for the emerging Institutionalist school of economics. Veblen was an iconoclast, however, and had limited direct influence over the development of economics within the academy.

Richard Ely was among the most influential economists of this era. After studying at Columbia University and the University of Halle in Germany, he did his PhD in Heidelberg under Knies. He was appointed to a professorship at John Hopkins University in 1881, where he helped lay the foundations for the American Economic Association (Emmett 2006a, 254). In 1892 he took a professorship at the University of Wisconsin, where he would stay until 1925, building the economics department there into one of the most important and influential in the United States, and the focal point for the development of institutionalism. Ely's views could be described as Christian Socialism – he was sympathetic to the labor union movement, but deeply committed to traditional morality. Towards the end of his career he would develop agricultural economics, founding a center for the study of land economics that he moved from Wisconsin to Northwestern University in Illinois.

Ely was a colleague of Adams' at John Hopkins University in the early 1880s, and together they helped to launch the American Economic Association (AEA). The founding of the Association helped set off something of an American *Methodenstreit* – progressives, influenced by German historical economics, advocated for reform and regulations, while the conservatives attempted to stay true to the laissez-faire doctrine of the classical economists. Over time the AEA would moderate, and become the definitive mainstream organization of economists. It would retain a pluralistic character in the first half of the twentieth century, publishing neoclassical economists alongside institutionalists in its journal, the *American Economic Review* (*AER*), in addition to putting out individual monographs and studies.

Among Ely's students at John Hopkins University was John Commons, who would become a distinguished colleague at the University of Wisconsin in 1904. Commons, who did not finish his PhD, would establish a reputation as a radical while teaching economics in the 1890s, eventually being fired from the University of Syracuse for his political leanings. Ely hired Commons to supervise research for a multi-volume history of American labor, then a part of Ely's American Bureau of Industrial Research. Commons thrived in Wisconsin, helping to draft the Civil Service Law of 1906 and the Public Utilities Act of 1907 for the state legislature (Rutherford 2006, 164). He was also involved in developing workers' compensation legislation in Wisconsin that would become the benchmark for the entire country. In 1909 Commons was asked by the Carnegie Foundation to lead its labor history project when their lead researcher, Carroll Wright, died unexpectedly. Commons would combine the efforts of the American Bureau of Industrial Research with the Carnegie Foundation, and become involved with the Pittsburg Survey on labor conditions funded by the Russell Sage Foundation. The additional funding and research opportunities allowed Commons to involve Wisconsin graduate students and gave him considerable independence from Ely, which would fuel a bitter dispute between the two. Commons gradually became the dominant figure at Wisconsin, and when Ely at last left for Northwestern University in 1925, Commons took over altogether. Between 1926 and 1931, he would supervise 31 graduate dissertations, and many of his students would become highly influential. They included Alvin Hansen, an early leader of American Keynesianism; major labor economists Selig Perlman, Ira Cross, and Sumner Slichter; Harold Groves, Elizabeth Brandeis, and Paul Rauchenbush, who together first created unemployment insurance in Wisconsin under the Groves Act; and Edwin Witte, who worked for the Roosevelt administration, taught at Wisconsin, and is considered the father of Social Security (Rutherford 2006, 172).

Economics at the University of Wisconsin started off as a heterodoxy of elements culled from neoclassicists, historicists, and Christian socialists. Under the leadership of Richard Ely, an empirical approach was emphasized in combination with a reformist attitude as well as John Bates Clark's marginalist theory. With the rise of Commons, the department became definitively institutionalist, with an emphasis on labor laws, arbitration and mediation, issues of industrial accident insurance and unemployment compensation. After the New Deal, much of this research would move into schools of public policy, public administration, and industrial relations. With neoclassical theory innovations in imperfect output and factor markets and the arrival of Keynesian macroeconomics, institutionalism's influence began to fade, but is nonetheless still evident in the landscape of contemporary American economics.

## Crosscurrents

In Chicago in May of 1886, a bomb exploded amidst a detachment of policemen at a gathering of labor activists. Sixty-six policemen were injured by the blast and seven would eventually die of their wounds. The police fired their guns into the crowd, wounding two hundred. Eight anarchists were convicted and sentenced to death for throwing the bomb, and four were hanged the following year. The events caused an international sensation, and would become known as the Haymarket Affair (Zinn 2003, 271). It brought forth a powerful reaction from the American ruling class – socialism and labor unions would be under fierce attack in the US in the closing years of the nineteenth century. Revolutionary socialism, however, scarcely existed outside of small communities in major urban centers. Only in 1905 was a distinctly American version of revolutionary organization formed, also in Chicago: The Industrial Workers of the World (IWW), later known as the Wobblies. Among the organizers was Eugene V. Debs, who had been a leader with the American Railway Union. The Wobblies, although never very numerous, spread throughout the country, organizing workers everywhere they went, often utilizing a pocket-sized song book of music "to fan the flames of discontent" (Zinn 2003, 331). It is interesting to note that Joe Hill, pictured within the songbook, author of many of the original lyrics therein, having been executed in Utah, would be a crucial influence on Woody Guthrie, who would in turn serve as a model for the Nobel laureate Bob Dylan, considered perhaps the most influential lyricist of the second half of the twentieth century.

In 1900, W. E. B. DuBois published his visionary work *The Souls of Black Folk*, which included estimates of the contribution of black people to the economy, noting how much less was received in payment as was produced in profits. As many of the leading economists of his generation, DuBois did post-graduate work in Germany, studying in Berlin and Heidelberg. The influence of the German historicists would set DuBois apart among his contemporaries, Booker T. Washington in particular, and put him in opposition to the many academics that supported biological theories of racial differentiation. It would also put him at odds with the many progressives who ascribed to a race-based view of society. He foresaw that the "color line" would become one of the central social conflicts of the twentieth century, was deeply influential to the late Civil Rights movement, and remains relevant today.

*The Souls of Black Folk* is often remembered for its prophetic observation that the "problem of the twentieth century is the problem of the color line" (DuBois 1953, 23). Buried within the pages of this slim volume one finds astute economic analysis of the conditions of southern poverty in the era. Describing the Black Belt of Georgia, DuBois writes

> The country is rich, yet the people are poor. The keynote of the Black Belt is debt; not commercial credit, but debt in the sense of continued inability on the part of the mass of the population to make income cover expense. This is the direct heritage of the South from the wasteful economies of the slave *regime*; but it was emphasized and brought to a crisis by the Emancipation of the slaves. In 1860, Dougherty County had six thousand slaves, worth at least two and a half millions of dollars; its farms were estimated at three millions,–making five and a half millions of

property, the value of which depended largely on the slave system, and on the speculative demand for land once marvelously rich but already partially devitalized by careless and exhaustive culture. The war then meant a financial crash; in place of the five and a half millions of 1860, there remained in 1870 only farms valued at less than two millions. With this came increased competition in cotton culture from the rich lands of Texas; a stead fall in the normal price of cotton followed, from about fourteen cents a pound in 1860 until it reached four cents in 1898. Such a financial revolution was it that involved the owners of the cotton-belt in debt.

(DuBois 1953, 105–106)

Although there was tremendous variety in economic thought during this turbulent period, a great deal of it would prove shallow, evaporating with the emergence of the Great Depression and the New Deal. In particular, the ideological backlash to the industrialization of the US proved, for all its ferocity, to have little staying power. This backlash came in the form of three uprisings, the first, known as the Greenback movement, emerged in the 1870s; it was followed by the better-known Populist movement, active in the 1880s and 1890s; and later echoed by the Non-Partisan movement of the 1910s (Normano 1943, 154). At the height of its influence, agrarian Populism saw through the passage of the Interstate Commerce Act of 1887 and the Sherman Anti-Trust Act of 1890. Both pieces of legislation were aimed at constraining the burgeoning power of Wall Street over the American economy, and neither were especially successful in their intended effects (Normano 1943, 156). Populism peaked in 1896, with the Presidential campaign of William Jennings Bryan – famous today for its "Cross of Gold" stump speech, in which Bryan advocated for bimetallist money.

Along with the Populist movement sprung up a wide ranging utopian literature, the most well-known title being *Looking Backward* by Edward Bellamy, published in early 1888. The novel imagines itself as a retrospective from the year 2000, and predicts the perfection of society in the process. It was an enormous commercial success in its day, and inspired politically minded "Bellamy Clubs" throughout the US. The utopian view essentially envisioned national socialism, with a welfare state, strong labor rights, and nationalized industry (Normano, 160). The genre would grow to include hundreds of books and pamphlets, with its own vibrant counter-literature, and its influence would reach Europe. Unlike earlier romantic thinkers, Bellamy did not blame industry for society's ills so much as desire to harness its productive potential in the service of ordinary people.

No less influential was the journalistic literature known as "muckraking," such as Upton Sinclair's *The Jungle*, set in the meat packing plants of Chicago, or Ida Tarbell's *History of the Standard Oil Company*, which helped establish the field of investigative journalism. Such works helped focus the nation on its economy, with a special focus on the *distribution* of wealth, as opposed its production. Although Henry George's land tax ideas remained influential in this period, the newer literature reflected the growing urban population in the US, which was interested in legal equality and public services. Tarbell's criticism of Standard Oil was paired with an interest in scientific management and efficient production techniques (Witzel 2006b, 807). As with so many of the thinkers in this period, her position reflected the growing interest in reform and the gradual ebb of the revolutionary tide.

## References

Abramovitz, M., and David, P. A. 2001. *Two Centuries of American Macroeconomic Growth from Exploitation of Resource Abundance to Knowledge-Driven Development*. Stanford, CA: Stanford Institute for Economic Policy Research (online: accessed 24 August 2016).

Adil, M. 2006. "Veblen, Thorstein B., (1857–1929)." In *The Biographical Dictionary of American Economists* (Ed. R. Emmett). New York: Continuum: 844–852.

Ashbury, A. D. 2006. "Douglas, Paul Howard, 1892–1976." In *The Biographical Dictionary of American Economists* (Ed. R. Emmett). New York: Continuum: 223–224.

Bateman, B. W., and Kapstein, E. B. 1999. "Retrospectives: Between God and the Market: The Religious Roots of the American Economic Association." *Journal of Economic Perspectives* 13(4): 249–257.

Bensel, R. 2000. *The Political Economy of American Industrialization, 1877–1900*. Cambridge: Cambridge University Press.

Bensel, R. 2008. *Passion and Preferences: William Jennings Bryan and the 1896 Democratic National Convention*. Cambridge: Cambridge University Press.

Biddle, J. 2012. "Retrospectives: The Introduction of the Cobb-Douglas Regression." *Journal of Economic Perspectives* 26(2): 223–236.

Bliss, M., 1982. *The Discovery of Insulin*. Chicago, IL: University of Chicago Press.

Boyer, P. S., *et al.* 2014. *The Enduring Vision: A History of the American People*. Boston, MA: Wadsworth, Cengage.

Bruce, K. 2005. "Frank W. Taussig's Institutionalism." *Journal of Economic Issues* 39 (1): 205–220.

Burns, A. 1952. "Introductory Sketch." In *Wesley Clair Mitchell: The Economic Scientist* (A. Burns, Editor). Cambridge, MA: National Bureau of Economic Research: 1–54.

bytesdaily. 2011. The Great Horse Manure Crises of 1894. Blogspot.com/2011/07.

Caporale, B. 2003. "The Influence of Economists on the Federal Reserve Act." *Scottish Journal of Political Economy* 50(3): 311–325.

Clark, R. W. 1977. *Edison: The Man Who Made the Future*. New York, NY: Putnam.

Cohen, A. 2016. "Harvard's Eugenics Era." *Harvard Magazine* 118(4): 48–52.

Constable, G., and Somerville, B. 2003. *A Century of Innovation: Twenty Engineering Achievements That Transformed Our Lives*. Washington, DC: Joseph Henry Press.

DeLong, J. B., and Summers, L. H. 1986. "The Changing Cyclical Variability of Economic Activity in the United States." In *The American Business Cycle: Continuity and Change* (R. J. Gordon, Editor). Chicago, IL: University of Chicago Press: 679–734.

Dimand, R. 2006a. "Fisher, Irving (1867–1947)." In *The Biographical Dictionary of American Economists* (Ed. R. Emmett). New York: Continuum: 284–291.

Dimand, R. 2006b. "Mitchell, Wesley Clair (1874–1948)." In *The Biographical Dictionary of American Economists* (Ed. R. Emmett). New York: Continuum: 630–636.

Dorfman, J. 1934. *Thorstein Veblen and His America*. New York, NY: Augustus M. Kelley.

Du Bois, W. E. B. 1953. *The Souls of Black Folks*. New York, NY: Blue Herron Press.

Dunbar, C. F. 1886. "The Reaction in Political Economy." *Quarterly Journal of Economics* 1(1): 1–27.

Ekelund, R., and Hebert, R. 2007. *A History of Economic Theory and Method* (Fifth Edition). Long Grove, IL: Waveland Press.

Emmett, R., (ed.). 2006. *The Biographical Dictionary of American Economists: Vols. 1 & 2*. New York, NY: Continuum.

Emmett, R. 2006a. "Ely, Richard Theodore (1854–1943)." In *The Biographical Dictionary of American Economists* (Ed. R. Emmett). New York: Continuum: 253–256.

Emmett, R. 2006b. "Knight, Frank Hyneman (1885–1972)." In *The Biographical Dictionary of American Economists* (Ed. R. Emmett). New York: Continuum: 517–522.

Emmett, R. 2006c. "Laughlin, James Laurence (1850–1933)." In *The Biographical Dictionary of American Economists* (Ed. R. Emmett). New York: Continuum: 546–548.

Emmett, R. 2006d. "Taussig, Frank William (1859–1940)." In *The Biographical Dictionary of American Economists* (Ed. R. Emmett). New York: Continuum: 812–814.

Emmett, R. 2006e. "Viner, Jacob (1892–1970)." In *The Biographical Dictionary of American Economists* (Ed. R. Emmett). New York: Continuum: 859–862.

Fawcett, E. 2014. *Liberalism, The Life of an Idea*. Princeton, NJ: Princeton University Press.

Fourcade, M. 2009. *Economists and Societies: Discipline and Profession in the United States, Britain, and France, 1890s to 1990s*. Princeton, NJ: Princeton University Press.

Gani, M. 2006. "Walker, Amasa (1799–1875)." In *The Biographical Dictionary of American Economists* (Ed. R. Emmett). New York: Continuum: 869–875.

Goldberg, J., and Moye, W. 1985. *The First Hundred Years of the Bureau of Labor Statistics*. Washington, DC: United States Bureau of Labor Statistics.

Gordon, R. J. 2000. *Does the "New Economy" Measure Up to the Great Inventions of the Past?* Cambridge, MA: National Bureau of Economic Research: Working Paper 7833.

Gordon, R. J. 2016. *The Rise and Fall of American Growth: The US. Standard of Living Since the Civil War*. Princeton, NJ: Princeton University Press.

Hafer, R. W. 2005. *The Federal Reserve System, An Encyclopedia*. Westport, CT: Greenwood Press.

Hanes, C., and Rhode, P. 2012. *Harvest and Financial Crises in Gold-Standard America*, NBER Working Paper 18616: www.nber/papers/w18616 (online: accessed 30 November 2016).

Haney, L. 1939. *History of Economic Thought* (Third Edition). New York, NY: Macmillan.

Henry, J. 2006. "Clark, John Bates (1847–1938)." In *The Biographical Dictionary of American Economists* (Ed. R. Emmett). New York: Continuum: 138–146.

Hughes, J. 1970. *Industrialization and Economic History: Theses and Conjectures*. New York, NY: McGraw-Hill.

Hughes, J. 1966. *The Vital Few: American Economic Progress and Its Protagonists*. Boston, MA: Houghton Mifflin.

Hughes, J. and Cain, L. P. 2007. *American Economic History* (Seventh Edition). Boston, MA: Pearson/Addison Wesley.

Irwin, N. 2013. "The Federal Reserve was created 100 years ago. This is how it happened." *The Washington Post Wonkblog*. December 21 (online).

Johnson, H. 1977. "The American Tradition in Economics." *Nebraska Journal of Economics and Business* 16(3): 17–26.

Johnson, M. 2014. "Progressivism and Academic Public Finance, 1880–1930." *History of Political Economy* 46(1): 1–32.

Jonnes, J. 2004. *Empires of Light: Edison, Tesla, Westinghouse, and the Race to Electrify the World.* New York, NY: Random House.

Kaplan, E. S. 1999. *The Bank of the United States and the American Economy.* Westport, CT: Greenwood Press.

Kline, A. 2006. "Hadley, Arthur Twining (1856–1930)." In *The Biographical Dictionary of American Economists* (Ed. R. Emmett). New York: Continuum: 398–402.

Landes, D. S. 2003. *The Unbound Prometheus: Technological Change and Industrial Development in Western Europe from 1750 to the Present* (Second Edition). Cambridge: Cambridge University Press.

Leigh, A. H. 1974. "Frank H. Knight as Economic Theorist." *Journal of Political Economy* 82(3): 578–586.

Lemann, N. 1991. *The Promised Land: The Great Black Migration and How It Changed America.* New York, NY: Alfred A. Knopf.

Leonard, T. C. 2005. "Retrospectives: Eugenics and Economics in the Progressive Era." *Journal of Economic Perspectives* 19(4): 207–224.

Lewis, D. 1976. *District of Columbia: A Bicentennial History.* New York, NY: Norton.

McMath, Jr., R. C. 1993. *American Populism; A Social History, 1887–1898.* New York, NY: Noonday Press.

Mehrling, P. 2002. "Retrospectives: Economists and the Fed: Beginnings." *Journal of Economic Perspectives* 16(1): 207–218.

Mehrotra, P. 2006. "Seligman, Edwin Robert Anderson (1861–1939)." In *The Biographical Dictionary of American Economists* (Ed. R. Emmett). New York: Continuum: 757–762.

Michener, J. H. 1906. *The Bank of North America, Philadelphia, a National Bank, Founded in 1781.* New York, NY: R. G. Cooke.

Namorato, M. 2006. "Patten, Simon Nelson (1852–1922)." In *The Biographical Dictionary of American Economists* (Ed. R. Emmett). New York: Continuum: 678–682.

Nef, J. 1934. "James Laurence Laughlin (1850–1933)." *Journal of Political Economy* 42(1): 1–5.

Nerozzi, S. 2009. "Jacob Viner and the Chicago Monetary Tradition." *History of Political Economy* 41(3): 575–604.

Normano, J. F. 1943. *The Spirit of American Economics.* New York, NY: John Day.

Novak, M. 2013. "How the 1920s Thought Electricity Would Transform Farms Forever." *Gizmode* (Blog): June 3.

Persky, J. 2000. "The Neoclassical Advent: American Economics at the Dawn of the 20th Century." *Journal of Economic Perspectives* 14(1): 95–108.

quoteinvestigator. 2012. Exploring the Origins of Quotations (online).

Rosenberg, N. 1972. *Technology and American Economic Growth.* New York, NY: Harper & Row.

Rosenberg, N. and Birdzell, Jr., L. E. 1986. *How the West Grew Rich: The Economic Transformation of the Industrial World.* New York, NY: Basic Books.

Rutherford, M. 2006. "Wisconsin Institutionalism: John R. Commons and his Students." *Labor History* 47(2): 161–188.

Samuelson, P. A. 1977. "Jacob Viner, 1892–1970." *Journal of Political Economy* 80(1): 5–11.

Sandilands, R. 2006. "Young, Allyn Abbott (1876–1929)." In *The Biographical Dictionary of American Economists* (Ed. R. Emmett). New York: Continuum: 912–914.

Schafer, A. R. 2001. "W. E. B. DuBois, German Social Thought, and the Racial Divide in American Progressivism, 1892–1909." *Journal of American History* 88(3): 925–949.

Schumpeter, J. A., Cole, A. H., and Mason, E. S. 1941. "Frank William Taussig." *Quarterly Journal of Economics* 55(3): 337–363.

Seavoy, R. E. 2006. *An Economic History of the United States from 1607 to the Present.* London: Routledge.

Taussig, F. W. 1920. *Principles of Economics, Vols. 1 & 2* (Second Edition). New York, NY: Macmillan.

Taussig, F. W. 1921. "Is the Market Price Determinate?" *Quarterly Journal of Economics* 35(3): 394–411.

Tobin, J. 2005. "Irving Fisher (1867–1947)." *American Journal of Economics and Sociology* 64(1): 19–42.

*UIC SPH*, uic.edu/sph/prepare/courses. n.d. "(7) Typhoid Fever." Chicago, IL: University of Illinois at Chicago: School of Public Health: 95–109.

Veblen, T. 1899. *Theory of the Leisure Class*: Available at http://moglen.law.columbia.edu/LCS/theoryleisureclass.pfd (online: accessed 30 November 2016).

Whaples, R. 2003. "United States, Modern Period." In *The Oxford Encyclopedia of Economic History. Vol. 5* (J. Mokyr, Editor-in-Chief). New York, NY: Oxford University Press: 167–174.

Witzel, M. 2006a. "Sumner, William Graham (1840–1910)." In *The Biographical Dictionary of American Economists* (Ed. R. Emmett). New York: Continuum: 800–802.

Witzel, M. 2006b. "Tarbell, Ida Minerva (1857–1944)." In *The Biographical Dictionary of American Economists* (Ed. R. Emmett). New York: Continuum: 806–808.

Witzel, M. 2006c. "Walker, Francis Amasa (1840–1897)." In *Liberalism, The Life of an Idea*. Princeton, NJ: Princeton University Press: 876–878.

Wood, J. H. 2015. *Central Banking in a Democracy: The Federal Reserve and its Alternatives.* London: Routledge.

Veblen, T. 1922. *The Instinct of Workmanship and the State of the Industrial Arts*:New York, NY: B. W. Huebsch.

Yarrow, A. 2010. *Measuring America: How Economic Growth Came to Define American Greatness in the Late Twentieth Century.* Amherst, MA: University of Massachusetts Press.

Zinn, H. 2003. *A People's History of the United States.* New York, NY: Harper Perennial.

# 7 Economic thought from the Great Depression through the golden age of economic growth, 1929–1973

## Introduction

This chapter begins in the year of the Wall Street crash and ends in the year in which the Bretton Woods system broke down. In between there was a decade of deep depression and faltering recovery (1929–1941), four years of world war (1941–1945) and almost three decades of sustained prosperity, the so-called 'golden age' of post-war American – and indeed global – capitalism (1945–1973). There were equally dramatic changes in the nature of American economics, which was completely transformed. By 1973 formal modeling and rigorous econometric techniques were the norm, rather than the preserve of a small minority as had been the case in 1929. The earlier pluralism of ideas and methods had given way to an increasingly monolithic neoclassical mainstream, which was exerting great influence over the ways in which economics was taught and practised all over the world. This is covered below. For most of the period the 'Other Voices' and 'Crosscurrents' were operating in an increasingly difficult intellectual and institutional environment. At the very end of the period, however, there were some indications that dissident ideas were beginning to revive.

## Economic, social, political conditions

In 1930 the population of the United States was 122.8 million, 11.6 percent of whom had been born overseas. By 1970 total US population had risen to 203.3 million, but the virtual cessation of mass immigration for two decades after 1929 meant that only 4.8 percent were now foreign-born, the lowest proportion ever recorded (Hughes and Cain 2011, 558). It was an increasingly urbanized population, with the proportion employed in primary production (agriculture, forestry, and fishing) falling from 17.4 percent in 1940 to a mere 3.1 percent in 1970. Those working in the secondary sector (manufacturing, construction, and transport) rose from 39.0 percent in 1940 to an all-time high of 41.0 percent in 1950, before beginning a slow but steady and continuing relative decline to 35.8 percent in 1970. Employment in the tertiary sector rose steadily, from 43.5 percent of total employment in 1940 to

61.1 percent in 1970, by which time the United States was well on the way to becoming a service economy (Hughes and Cain 2011, 567).

Both total output and output per head of population were higher in 1973 than they had been in 1929, with per capita GDP rising from $6,899 to $16,689, or by 142 percent. This was in contrast to a dramatic decline between 1929 and 1933, when GDP per head of population fell by an astonishing 31 percent, to $4777 (Maddison 2006, table 2c), primarily the result of a collapse in business investment in the aftermath of the Wall Street crash. The extent of the decline in investment in the United States during the Great Depression understandably attracted considerable international attention. In his *General Theory of Employment, Interest and Money* John Maynard Keynes presented data from the Russian-born American economic statistician Simon Kuznets that revealed how 'net capital formation suffered an appalling collapse after 1929, falling in 1932 to a figure no less than 95 per cent below the average of the quinquennium 1925–1929' (Keynes 1936, 104). In current dollars, net investment had peaked at $25.48 million in 1929, falling to $11.01 million in 1931 and to an astonishing low of $1.24 million in 1932 (Keynes, 103). If Kuznets's data had been graphed in a diagram they would have justified a very old cliché – net investment had indeed fallen off a cliff. Unemployment also rose dramatically, peaking as a percentage of the workforce in the high or low twenties (depending on whether the many millions engaged in emergency relief projects are counted as having been gainfully employed).

Recovery from the Great Depression began in 1933 but soon faltered, with a second sharp (but relatively short-lived) downturn in 1937–1938. When the United States entered the war in 1941 per capita GDP was already almost 20 percent above the 1929 level, and (uniquely among the combatants) it continued to grow rapidly during the war, reaching a peak in 1945, when it was 40 percent higher still (Maddison 2006, table 2c.). The quarter of a century that followed the end of the WWII has often been described as the 'golden age' of capitalism, with rapid growth, strong booms, and weak recessions (Marglin and Schor 1990). GDP grew at an annual average rate of 3.93 percent between 1950 and 1973, compared to 2.84 percent between 1913 and 1950; the corresponding figures for GDP per capita are 2.45 percent and 1.61 percent respectively. Growth in per capita GDP in the 'golden age' was the fastest ever recorded in the United States (Maddison 2006, tables A-1e and A-1d).

There was also sustained improvement in real wages and salaries with an average growth rate of 4.5 percent between 1948 and 1966 and a still impressive 3.0 percent from 1966 to 1979 (Kotz 2015, table 4.12). Unemployment was much lower than it had been in the 1930s, averaging 4.8 percent between 1949 and 1973. This was significantly higher than in some Western European countries, but still relatively close to full employment (Kotz 2015, table 4.15). In the boom years of the late 1960s unemployment fell below 4 percent for several years (Kotz 2015, 64, fig. 3.2).

This period has also been characterized as an age of 'regulated capitalism' in Kotz (2015, table 3.1) who provides a useful summary of the ideas and institutions of this new era. Keynesian ideas and theories were dominant, both nationally and globally. The role of the government in the economy was greatly increased, with a welfare state financed through progressive taxation, high levels of government provision of public goods and services, strong anti-trust enforcement and strict regulation of industry and (especially) finance, together with a firm commitment to full employment and low inflation. Labor enjoyed increased power relative to capital, with a major role for collective bargaining and a large proportion of stable, long-term employment. Finance was subordinated to production, both as a matter of corporate culture and through tight government regulation of the banking system.

Strict regulation applied also to international economic relations. At the 1944 Bretton Woods conference the Roosevelt administration had agreed to fix the value of the dollar in terms of gold and of the other major trading currencies. This reflected a conscious decision to resolve the so-called 'policy trilemma' that all governments face: they can have any two of fixed exchange rates, an autonomous monetary policy, and free international capital movements, but not all three. For the next three decades both Democratic and Republican administrations accepted the need for controls over international capital movements. When the Bretton Woods system collapsed in 1973 and the value of the dollar was left to the vicissitudes of the market, capital controls were no longer necessary and the powerful and dangerous process of financialization (discussed in Chapter 8) was soon under way.

In 1950 the economic dominance of the United States was beyond all dispute. It accounted for 27.3 percent of world GDP, up from 18.9 percent in 1913; even in 1973 its share of global output had fallen only slightly, to 22.1 percent (Maddison 2006, table 8b). In individual industries the American preponderance was even greater. World steel production in 1950 totalled 192 million tons, of which 47.7 percent came from the North American Free Trade Agreement countries, that is, the United States, Canada, and Mexico – in this case, overwhelmingly from the United States; the corresponding figures for 1970 are 601mn tons, of which 22.6 percent was from NAFTA, and for 2013 a massive 1607mn tons, of which only 7.3 percent was produced by NAFTA (Anonymous 2014). Throughout the period covered in this chapter the American worker was easily the most productive in the world. In 1929 GDP per capita had been 40 percent higher than the Western European average; in 1950 it was more than double, and even in 1973 the United States still enjoyed a 38 percent advantage over Western Europe (Maddison 2006, table 2c).

## The mainstream

Although with hindsight the severity of the Great Depression made the triumph of Keynesian macroeconomics almost inevitable, the victory of the new ideas was actually a complex and protracted process, which is documented in considerable detail in two books published to commemorate the

60th anniversary of the *General Theory* (Barber 1996; Colander and Landreth 1996). As will be shown below, the institutionalists – who were still very influential in Roosevelt's America – had little time for any form of macro-economics, while many of the more conservative neoclassical economists continued to defend the postulates of what Keynes had described as "classical economics." Thus Frank Knight "insisted that the cause of high unemployment was not deficient demand but the real wage being too high, and real wage resistance by workers" (Cristiano and Fiorito 2016, 75).

This implied that downward flexibility in wages (and prices) was a good thing, and was probably a necessary condition for the restoration of prosperity. Other non-Keynesian macroeconomists, however, took the opposite position on this question. The most prominent was Irving Fisher, whose *Booms and Depressions* (1932) set out a 'debt-deflation theory' in which it was precisely the collapse of the price level (which fell by 26 percent between January 1930 and April 1933) that explained the depth of the Great Depression. Deflation involved a redistribution of wealth from borrowers to lenders, so that Fisher's argument implied that there was an asymmetry between debtors, who could be required to reduce their spending when their resources fell, and creditors, who could not be forced to increase their spending when their resources rose. Thus it was consistent with the principle of effective demand, whether Fisher acknowledged it or not, and in the mid-1950s the future Post Keynesian theorist Hyman P. Minsky would begin to develop an original and compelling version of the *General Theory* that relied heavily on the relationship between debtors and creditors (see Chapter 8, p. 229).

Other non-Keynesian macroeconomists maintained that it was the series of bank failures in 1930–1933, and the associated sharp decline in the stock of money, that was responsible for the severity of the Depression. This involved a significant revision of the conventional Quantity Theory to allow for contractions in the stock of money to affect output and employment as well as the price level, and to that extent it diverged from what would later become known as 'monetarism' (p. 183). It attracted the support of both Irving Fisher and the young Milton Friedman, and led the conservative Chicago theorist Henry C. Simons to propose a surprisingly radical change in the entire monetary system. Simons called for the replacement of fractional reserve banking by '100% money,' in which for every dollar lent a dollar would be held in reserve. This was a position previously associated with monetary cranks and heretics, not mainstream economists. For Fisher, however, it

> might afford the banks the only escape from nationalization. For if, in another decade, we should have another depression like the one we have just been passing through, the banks would probably find themselves permanently in the hands of the government. It would be better for the banks to give up gracefully their usurped function of minting money (in the form of bank notes and chequebook money) and be content to

conduct their strictly banking business, unmolested and uninterfered with by booms and depressions – so largely of their own making.

(cited by Barber, 92)

It never came to this, although the banks did have to accept the strict separation of their retail and more speculative wholesale activities that was imposed by the Glass-Steagall Act of 1933, which was repealed in 1999. Fiscal policy in the New Deal was equally unadventurous. Despite Keynes's efforts to interest Roosevelt in a huge programme of deficit-financed public works, it was not until the severe (and unexpected) recession of 1937–1938 that Keynesian ideas had much impact in Washington, where the President's attachment to the principle of balanced budgets constituted a powerful barrier to their acceptance. The renewed downturn in economic activity in 1937, which was largely the result of ill-advised measures of fiscal austerity, did more than anything else to increase Keynes's influence in the United States, among both policy-makers and academic economists. Ironically, though, his ideas proved even more influential after full employment had been restored, via his analysis of *How to Pay for the War* (1940) and the first faltering economic projections of the problems that would confront the post-war economy. By this time a remarkably impressive formal presentation of the Keynesian model had been published by the young Paul Samuelson (1915–2009), who combined the multiplier with the accelerator principle in a simple but impressive explanation of the economy's proneness to recurrent business cycles. He also provided an invaluable teaching version of simple Keynesian theory in the form of the now-commonplace income-expenditure diagram that he invented (Samuelson 1939).

The most influential convert to Keynesian macroeconomic theory, however, came from a previous generation. This was the Harvard University professor Alvin H. Hansen (1887–1975), who abandoned his earlier support for deflationary policies in his *Fiscal Policy and Business Cycles* (1941) and urged the need for the government to respond to recession by stimulating effective demand. The corresponding principles of 'functional finance' were soon enunciated by Abba P. Lerner (1903–1982) in his book *The Economics of Control* (1944). Macroeconomic policy should be directed towards the maintenance of full employment without demand inflation, Lerner argued; nothing else matters. If it is held by the nation's own citizens, the national debt is not a burden on posterity. It is not a burden on the nation, nor is it a sign of national poverty. The interest on the national debt is not a burden on the nation. The nation cannot be forced into bankruptcy. This is because neither the nation nor the government is an ordinary business concern, and fiscal policy should not be treated as if it were. Lerner's argument on all these questions reads as well today as it did over seventy years ago (King 2015).

The Great Depression and the New Deal were only two of the forces that transformed American economics after 1933. Equally important were the flood of refugees from Hitler's Germany, the huge expansion of the military in the Second World War, and the rapidly increasing use of mathematical models and advanced statistical techniques. These developments were closely related. First, there were the European immigrants. Two of the most notable figures arrived before the establishment of the Nazi regime. Joseph Schumpeter (1883–1950), author of *Business Cycles* (1939) and the posthumously published *History of Economic Analysis* (1954), spent the last two decades of his life at Harvard. Probably his most influential book was *Capitalism, Socialism and Democracy* (1942), in which he argued that Marx was right, for as Schumpeter saw it, a socialist form of society would inevitably emerge from the equally inevitable decomposition of capitalist society. Schumpeter regretted the expected demise of capitalism, but like many of his contemporaries in the 1940s did not believe that it could be prevented.

The Hungarian-born John von Neumann (1902–1957) moved to the United States in 1931, where he was based at Princeton University but worked extensively for the US government. Von Neumann's *Theory of Games and Economic Behavior* (1944), co-authored with another émigré, the Austrian Oskar Morgenstern (1902–1977), was not fully appreciated for some years but eventually established game theory at the very heart of microeconomic analysis. Von Neumann was a genuine polymath, who made original contributions in pure and applied mathematics, computer science, and physics as well as economics. He was also a pioneer in the integration of mathematical economics into the military, serving *inter alia* as a principal in the Manhattan Project, a consultant to the Central Intelligence Agency and a member of the Scientific Advisory Group of the US Air Force.

Between 1933 and 1941 a steady stream of Europeans arrived in the US. The authoritative two-volume study edited by Harald Hagemann and Claus-Dieter Krohn (1999) (sadly not translated into English) has entries on over 300 German-speaking refugee economists, many of whom ended up in the United States. The Austrian émigrés are described by Craver (1986), and more general accounts of the migration are provided (in English) by Hagemann (2005, 2011) and Mongiovi (2005). Outside the mainstream there were a number of significant economic theorists, including the Austrian subjectivists Fritz Machlup (1902–1983) and Ludwig von Mises (1881–1973) and the Marxists Paul Baran (1910–1964) and Adolph Lowe (1893–1995). Many of the mainstream immigrants left a mark on the development of American economics, including the development economists Albert Hirschman (1915–2007), Bert Hoselitz (1913–1995) and Paul Rosenstein-Rodan (1902–1985); the public finance theorists Gerhard Colm (1897–1968) and Richard Musgrave (1910–2007); the trade theorists Gottfried Haberler (1900–1995) and Wolfgang Stolper (1912–2002); the economic historian Alexander Gerschenkron (1904–1978); and the economic statistician Simon Kuznets (1901–1985), a refugee from Lenin rather than Hitler, having moved from his native Russia to the United States with his family in 1922. Kuznets's pioneering work in the definition and measurement of national income led him to an extensive study of the empirical evidence on comparative economic growth, culminating in his *Modern Economic Growth* (1966).

Probably the most important of all the Europeans, however, were the mathematical theorists and econometricians Jacob Marschak (1898–1977), Gerhard Tintner (1907–1983), Tjalling Koopmans (1910–1985) and Abraham Wald (1902–1950). As Director of the Cowles Commission, which was based first at the University of Chicago and then at Yale University, Marschak was especially important in developing the foundations of econometrics and in encouraging the formalization of economic theory. His team at Cowles included the future Nobel laureates Kenneth Arrow (1921–2017), Trygve Haavelmo (1911–1999) and Lawrence Klein (1920–2013). Haavelmo was only a temporary migrant, taking refuge in the United States for the duration of WWII and soon returning to his native Norway – not, however, before he had published two path-breaking papers in 1943 and 1944 that demonstrated how mathematical statistics could provide both a rigorous foundation for econometric estimation and reliable quantitative answers to policy questions.

By 1945, however, the formalization of American economics had not got very far. This can be seen very clearly from the contents of a typical issue of the *American Economic Review*, then as now the country's leading academic journal. The September 1944 *AER* was a relatively slim volume. Just over 100 of its 250 pages were taken up by six main papers. The lead article was devoted to a pressing policy issue, the disposal of surplus war property. Then there was an analysis of the national output at full employment in 1950, which involved the use of descriptive statistics and informal projections, and an empirical and descriptive article on the future economic prospects of Palestine. The remaining two papers were contributed by Leon Trotsky's former secretary, the Russian émigrée Raya Dunayevskaya (1910–1987). One was her translation of a 30-page article on the teaching of economics in the Soviet Union, from the Russian-language journal *Under the Banner of Marxism*, and the other was her own analysis of this 'new revision of Marxian economics.' The editors promised further discussion of the Soviet article in the December issue. None of these six main articles was concerned with neo-classical economics, and none contained a single equation or diagram. The same was true of three of the four brief 'communications,' which dealt with the official British White Paper on full employment and the work of the US Labor Board. Ironically, the only theoretical piece in the entire issue was contributed by Kenneth Boulding (1910–1993), whose later career revealed that his sympathies lay with evolutionary and institutional rather than neo-classical economics. Boulding's brief note on the incidence of profits taxation did include two elaborate diagrams, but there were no equations.

All this was soon to change, and the most important single actor in the process of disciplinary transformation was undoubtedly Paul Samuelson. Between 1937 and 1940 Samuelson was employed as a Junior Fellow at Harvard University, where he wrote "a series of papers that changed the basis on which theoretical debates were conducted in several fields: consumer theory (revealed preference), the theory of international trade (the Heckscher-Ohlin-Samuelson model), Keynesian economics, and the business cycle." However, "he was considered a specialist in a field called 'mathematical economics' in which posts were so difficult to find that his teachers feared that he might never land an academic position" (Backhouse 2015, 327). Samuelson had just completed his PhD at Harvard where Joseph Schumpeter was his mentor, but he did not get along well with his head of department, one Harold Burbank, who was hostile to economic theory in general and mathematical economics in particular. Samuelson found employment at the Massachusetts Institute of Technology because a vacancy had arisen when staff were lost through preparations for war.

Samuelson had the last laugh. His thesis was eventually published in 1947 as *Foundations of Economic Analysis*, which revealed the influence of the Harvard physicist Edwin Bidwell Wilson in its extensive use of differential, difference, and integral equations. He formalized the problem of dynamic analysis in both macroeconomics and microeconomics, together with a codification of the principles of welfare economics. For decades the book was a core graduate text "and, for many economists, defined the way to do economic theory" (Backhouse 2015, 327). More than any other theorist, Samuelson was responsible for the acceptance of mathematical tools as the essence of the economist's method.

In the process he also transformed the status of economics at MIT, which in 1940 involved primarily the provision of service teaching for engineers but by the early 1970s was ranked top among the world's economics departments. MIT now led the world in growth theory, macroeconomics, public economics, finance, development economics, and urban economics, and would soon add energy and environmental economics to the list. By the end of the century no fewer than thirteen Nobel Laureates in economics were connected with MIT, including Samuelson, Robert Solow, and Franco Modigliani (1918–2003), along with future central bank governors from Israel (Stanley Fischer, PhD, 1969), the Eurozone (Mario Draghi, PhD, 1977), and the United States (Ben Bernanke, PhD, 1979). In addition to its excellence in pure – that is to say, mathematical – theory, there was also an important policy dimension to economics at MIT (Cherrier 2014).

Samuelson had always been interested in the application of economic theory to the real world, and while at Harvard University in the late 1930s he had worked on policy questions with the entirely non-mathematical Alvin Hansen, who like Samuelson was a liberal Democrat. Not surprisingly *Economics* (1948), *the* first-year principles textbook that appeared in the year after *Foundations* and is still in print, "expresses a very different view of economics – more institutional and data-driven" (Backhouse 2015, 347). It was written in a highly accessible, almost conversational style, was well produced, and had abundant illustrations. Samuelson took a deliberately 'centrist' position, 'writing around' his conservative detractors in the McCarthy era rather than confronting them, and pursuing a 'harmonist ideal' in all the early editions of the book (Elzinga 1972; Pearce and Hoover 1995). In the early 1970s he responded to his critics on the radical left, modifying both the tone and the content of the book to make it more palatable to them (Skousen 1997). *Economics* sold millions of copies in the United States, was translated into many languages and had a significant effect on economics teaching all over the world. It was a major factor in the continuing Americanization of economics education.

Possibly because of his commitment to policy applications, Samuelson was never greatly interested in the Walrasian model of general equilibrium that became so influential in American economics after 1950. Here the critical analytical advance came in a single paper co-authored by his brother-in-law, the New York-born Kenneth J. Arrow, and the Frenchman Gerard Debreu (1921–2004), which appeared in *Econometrica* in 1954 with the title "Existence of an Equilibrium for a Competitive Economy." Arrow had already achieved distinction with the publication of *Social Choice and Individual Values* (1951), based on his Columbia University PhD dissertation, which used symbolic logic to demonstrate a fundamental 'impossibility theorem': the choices of individuals cannot be combined through a system of democratic voting into a single unambiguous social choice. Debreu, originally educated in mathematics, was a member of the Bourbaki group of young theorists who attempted to reconstruct the logical foundations of mathematicians in early post-war Paris, publishing their work under the collective name of the imaginary genius 'Henri Bourbaki.' He was a very strange individual (Düppe 2012). Debreu came to the United States on a Rockefeller Fellowship and worked for the Cowles Foundation in Chicago and Yale University before moving to the University of California at Berkeley in 1960. Arrow spent most of his long career at Stanford University, giving the Arrow-Debreu formulation of Walrasian theory a certain West Coast flavor.

The 1954 paper was notable for its use of topological methods that were hitherto unknown in economics, bringing to the subject a degree of mathematical rigor that had not been seen before. Arrow and Debreu demonstrated that the mere counting of equations and unknowns was not sufficient to prove the possibility of simultaneous equilibrium in all markets in a perfectly competitive economy. This also required the existence of forward markets in all goods and services, for every period until the end of human existence. This conclusion seemed to many critics to cast severe doubt on the relevance of Walrasian theory to the real world, not least because it appeared to rule out any rational motive for the use of money. Moreover, the *existence* of general equilibrium was only part of the analytical problem, and arguably the least important part. As we shall see in the following chapter, questions concerning the *uniqueness* and the *stability* of equilibrium would preoccupy theorists in the late 1970s and 1980s, and would eventually lead to the effective abandonment of Walrasian theory as the core of neoclassical economics (p. 211).

The Arrow-Debreu model was undoubtedly an important milestone in the process whereby "economics became a mathematical science" (Weintraub

2002). After 1954 its two creators followed rather different intellectual trajectories. Debreu continued to concentrate his energies on the modeling of general equilibrium; his *Theory of Value: An Axiomatic Analysis of Economic Equilibrium* (1959) constituted a further landmark in the growing sophistication of mathematical economics. Arrow was more interested in the application of economic theory and published extensively on health economics, social investment, learning by doing, and the understanding of economic growth. But he did return to pure theory with his *General Competitive Analysis* (1971), co-authored with the German-born British theorist Frank Hahn, which aimed to show that the highly formalized Walrasian model did in fact have significant practical relevance to real-world economic problems.

This leads us to the development of empirical techniques. The early history of formal quantitative empirical research in economics is more a European than an American story. The term "econometrics" was coined in 1926 by Ragnar Frisch, a Norwegian, and "it could be said in 1930 that all mathematical economists in the United States could be counted on the fingers of one hand" (Bjerkholt 2015, 1176). Although the Econometric Society was established at a small meeting of 16 people at the joint annual meetings of American Social Science Associations (including the American Economic Association) in December 1930 in Cleveland, Ohio, with Irving Fisher as the inaugural President, seven out of the ten Council members resided in Europe and its first conference was held in Lausanne, Switzerland in September 1931 without American participation. While the Society's journal *Econometrica* was published in the United States with the support of the businessman Alfred Cowles, who became its business manager, Frisch was the founding Editor and most of the early papers came from European authors. Between 1933 and 1939 further meetings of the Society were held only in Europe, in Leyden, Oxford, Warsaw, and Elsinore. The role of European migrants to the United States in the rapid development of econometric methods after 1939 has already been noted. The transformation of empirical and policy research in the 1940s and 1950s was at least as rapid as the contemporaneous changes in economic theory.

These radical changes in the nature of American economics were profoundly affected by the Second World War and the Cold War that soon followed it. The new techniques of linear programming, activity analysis, and decision theory were extremely useful to the US military, and the work of the economists who developed them was often financed by the federal government and its agencies (Amadae 2003; Mirowski 2002). As already noted, John von Neumann in particular was a pioneer in the integration of mathematical economics into the military.

Mainstream economists were immensely proud of these developments. Here is George Stigler (1911–1991), not himself particularly distinguished in formal theory or in econometrics, giving his presidential address to the American Economic Association, appropriately enough in Chicago, in December 1964:

It is a scientific revolution of the very first magnitude – indeed I consider the so-called theoretical revolutions of a Ricardo, a Jevons, or a Keynes to have been minor revisions compared to the vast implications of the growing insistence upon quantification. I am convinced that economics is finally at the threshold of its golden age – nay, we already have one foot through the door.

(Stigler 1975, 56)

Stigler was a microeconomist, but the spread of quantitative methods was equally important in macroeconomics. Indeed, as Marion Fourcade suggests, the entire period from the 1930s to the 1960s was characterized by the emergence of economics as "a technique of government (symbolized by the twin innovations of national accounting and macroeconomic modeling) and, more generally, as a tool for the exercise of public expertise" (Fourcade 2009, 2). At all levels government was also the major source of finance for the economics profession,

This was not just a question of econometrics. The same period saw the formulation of a distinctive version of Keynesian macroeconomic theory described by its advocates as 'the Keynesian-neoclassical synthesis' (or 'the neoclassical synthesis' for short), and by its opponents as 'the Bastard Keynesian model' that was intended, or so Joan Robinson alleged, to "put Keynes to sleep." This Old Keynesian or Old Neoclassical Synthesis, as we shall call it to distinguish it from the New Neoclassical Synthesis that will be discussed in the following chapter (p. 215), had three components. Two of them – the Phillips Curve model of inflation, and the Solow-Swan theory of economic growth – were only formulated in 1956–1958.

The first component of the Old Keynesian Synthesis, however, began life a full 20 years earlier. This was the IS-LM model of the Keynesian system (De Vroey and Hoover 2004). It was a genuinely multiple discovery, for which credit (or discredit) belongs to no fewer than nine individuals: "Although often attributed solely to Hicks, and sometimes called the Hicks-Hansen model after Hansen later institutionalised Hicks's formulation within the profession, it would be more accurately called the Harrod-Meade-Hicks-Reddaway-Champernowne-Lange-Timlin-Modigliani-Hansen ISLM model to indicate the broader range of its originators, contributors and institutionalizers from 1936 to 1953" (O'Donnell and Rogers 2016, 349). Of these, the first five were British and the last four American, though Oskar Lange (1904–1965) was Polish by birth (and subsequent domicile) and Franco Modigliani (1918–2003) was an Italian who immigrated to the USA in 1939. Mabel Timlin (1891–1976) was the least well-known of the nine while Hansen was easily the most prominent of the Americans. The Old Neoclassical Synthesis was subsequently propagated by American Keynesians like Gardner Ackley (1915–1998), author of the best-selling graduate textbook, *Macroeconomic Theory* (1961), which was translated into several languages, went into a number of editions, and was widely regarded as the standard advanced macro text in the 1960s and early 1970s.

The IS-LM model allowed the simultaneous determination of the level of output and the rate of interest, and its depiction in a simple two-dimensional diagram made it a very effective teaching device. In the model, the demand for money is a function of income and the rate of interest, through Keynes's transactions and speculative motives. Investment is a function of the rate of interest, through the marginal efficiency of capital schedule, and income depends on investment via the multiplier. Keynes himself regarded IS-LM quite favorably, and if his Cambridge (UK) followers were not greatly impressed, nor did they raise serious objections to it. Franco Modigliani extended the analysis to the labor market, adding an aggregate production function and a labor supply function to the IS-LM equations and showing that underemployment equilibrium requires either a liquidity trap or downward rigidity in money wages. For Modigliani, like Hicks, Keynes had provided only a special case of a more general neoclassical theory. It was not until the 1960s that the Post Keynesians whose views will be discussed in below (pp. 190–1) began to object that the Old Keynesian Synthesis "has no role for the principle of effective demand, relies on Say's law and has at its core a theory applicable only to imaginary real exchange economies" (O'Donnell and Rogers 2016, 352). Indeed, it was precisely the status of IS-LM as the apparent macroeconomic corollary of the now-dominant Walrasian general equilibrium theory that had increased its appeal to many mainstream theorists.

The second component of the Old Neoclassical Synthesis was a theory of economic growth, which allowed the analysis to be extended into the long run. The Russian-born American growth theorist Evsey Domar (1914–1997) and the British economist Roy Harrod (1900–1978) combined the Keynesian multiplier with the accelerator principle to derive a model of demand-driven growth in which the level of output (and hence also employment) is inherently unstable (Domar 1957; Harrod 1948). In the Harrod-Domar model the economy is precariously balanced on a knife-edge, with the slightest departure from equilibrium leading either to ever-increasing unemployment or to a rapid rate of wage and price inflation. In 1956 Robert Solow proposed an alternative, more obviously neoclassical model of economic growth that did not (like the Harrod-Domar model) assume fixed proportions between capital and labor; a similar model was being developed in Australia, quite independently of Solow, by Trevor Swan. In the Solow-Swan growth model, stable growth with full employment and low inflation is secured by introducing a monotonic, twice differentiable neoclassical production function that permits continuous substitution between labour and capital in response to changes in the wage rate relative to the rate of profit. The influence of John Bates Clark was evident here.

Both IS-LM and Solow-Swan dealt with real income, and had nothing directly to say about inflation. But the price level was rising continuously (if relatively slowly) after 1945, and this exposed an obvious hole in the Keynesian macro model. The third component of the Old Neoclassical Synthesis involved the explanation of inflation by means of the Phillips Curve, which was invented in 1958 by the British-based New Zealander A. W. (Bill) Phillips on the basis of his interpretation (and econometric modeling) of the historical data on the relationship between unemployment and the rate of increase in money wages. It was introduced to an American audience by Samuelson and Solow in a very widely-read article in the May 1960 issue of the *American Economic Review*. The Phillips Curve had neoclassical credentials of sorts, since it depicted changes in the price of labor that varied inversely with the amount of excess supply in the labor market. It was widely regarded as constituting a sort of macroeconomic budget constraint, or a 'menu for policy choice.' In the United States of the 1960s, on the assumption that the relative shares of wages and profits remained constant, price stability required wages to go up by no more than 2.5 percent per annum, which was regarded as the long-term trend rate of productivity growth. The Phillips Curve revealed that this required the unemployment rate to fall no lower than 5–6 percent, unless efforts were made to shift it through antitrust legislation or direct controls over wages and/or prices. If policy makers wished to reduce unemployment to 3 percent, they would have to accept a higher rate of price inflation, probably 4–5 percent. This interpretation of the Phillips Curve seems to have rested on a number of misunderstandings (Forder 2014), but it was very widely accepted at the time.

The 'freshwater economics' taught at the University of Chicago was both less abstract than the 'saltwater economics' of the eastern and western seaboards and also more overtly political. Between the world wars the Chicago economics department was not at all monolithic, with the quasi-institutionalist Paul Douglas (1892–1976) and the Walrasian market socialist Oscar Lange coexisting in relative harmony with theorists such as Frank Knight and Jacob Viner who were favorably inclined towards the Marshallian version of neoclassical theory. After 1945 this diversity of opinion soon vanished. Douglas became a US Senator in 1948 and Lange left academic life to work for the communist government of his native Poland, leaving the new generation of Milton Friedman (1912–2006), George Stigler, and their younger colleagues to make a strong and largely unchallenged case both for neoclassical economics and for corporate capitalism.

In his memoirs Friedman explained how his friend and teacher, the future institutionalist Arthur Burns (1904–1987), had introduced him to the work of Alfred Marshall: "Arthur was a great admirer and thorough student of Marshall's *Principles of Economics*, and we spent many a pleasant hour then and in later years discussing the precise interpretation to be placed on passages from that magnificent book" (Friedman and Friedman 1998, 30). Friedman's own students were also exposed to Marshall, from the course in 'structure of neoclassical economics' that he taught at Columbia University in 1939–1940 through his long-running Chicago lectures on price theory (Hammond 2010) to his 1976 book on *Price Theory,* where the *Principles* comes at the head of the recommended reading list on the fundamental topics of demand, supply, and distribution and there are 19 index references to Marshall, well ahead of Keynes (12), Knight (8), Hicks, Stigler, and Slutsky.

There was an important methodological dimension to this respect for Marshall. It involved the critical University of Chicago distinction between "analysis which is formally valid and analysis which is a characteristic of substantive hypotheses" (Hirsch and de Marchi 1990, 19). The latter, which Friedman and his Chicago colleagues endorsed, was associated with Marshall; the former, which they rejected, was linked to Léon Walras. As Steven Medema has noted, the University of Chicago approach

> follows Marshall in the melding of theoretical and empirical work, and, like Marshall, considers both to be necessary for doing good economics and each to be incomplete without the other. The empirical strand solidified the Marshallian tendencies of Chicago as against the Walrasian approach, and the theoretical strand was a Marshallian counterpart to the perceived atheoretical empirical work of the institutional tradition in the first half of the twentieth century.
>
> (Medema 2015, 52)

Thus Friedman's approving reference in his Presidential address to the American Economic Association to Walras's equations of general equilibrium was totally out of character (Friedman 1968, 8). This insistence on empirical (and policy) content is probably even more important than the second methodological claim associated with Friedman, the irrelevance of the truth of the assumptions made by economists: only the truth of the predictions that follow from the assumptions needs to be considered. This 'as if' methodology has proved remarkably appealing, and also exceptionally controversial (see Wong 1978).

Even more than Marshall, Friedman and his University of Chicago colleagues emphasized the free market policy implications of the economic theory that they espoused. In *Free to Choose*, Friedman quoted the well-known passage from John Stuart Mill's *On Liberty* asserting that "the only purpose for which power can be rightfully asserted over any member of a civilized community against his will, is to prevent harm to others." Friedman took this to imply that

> Economic freedom is an essential requisite for political freedom. By enabling people to cooperate with one another without coercion or central direction, it reduces the area over which political power is exercised. In addition, by dispersing power, the free market provides an offset to whatever concentration of political power may arise. The combination of economic and political power in the same hands is a sure recipe for tyranny.
>
> (Friedman and Friedman 1980, 2–3)

It is not at all clear that Mill would have gone this far (Claeys 2013), and the assumptions that are required to justify this position are very demanding indeed (van Horn and Mirowski 2009). Under the leadership of Friedman and Stigler, however, the Chicago school integrated its microeconomics, methodology, and political theory in the claim that even the most concentrated product markets behaved in practice as if they were perfectly competitive, and so denied any need for extensive government regulation of corporate activity.

Stigler was sometimes described as Chicago's 'Mr. Micro,' by contrast with Friedman as 'Mr. Macro,' although his interests were never restricted to macroeconomics. He certainly did become the most prominent and effective critic of the neoclassical synthesis. In the Old Keynesian theoretical framework, it will be recalled, changes in the stock of money affect the rate of interest but not (directly) the inflation rate. This drew strong criticism from 'monetarists' like Friedman, who insisted on the continuing relevance of the Quantity Theory, as articulated by Marshall and subsequently formalized by Irving Fisher; on the importance of inflationary expectations; and on the need for the Federal Reserve to apply a strict zero-inflation rule limiting the rate of growth of the money stock to the expected rate of growth of real output.

All this was set out with brutal clarity in Friedman's Presidential address in December 1967 (Friedman 1968). In the Quantity Equation $MV = PT$, causation runs (only) from left to right and $V$ and $T$ are assumed to be constant, so that changes in $M$ have a direct and almost immediate effect on $P$. The Phillips Curve is unstable in the short run, since it will shift with every change in inflationary expectations, and it is vertical in the long run. There is thus no usable trade-off between inflation and unemployment. It follows that monetary policy must concentrate exclusively on controlling inflation, without any concern for the level of employment (which is in any case determined by the level of the real wage). This was the return of pre-Keynesian macroeconomics with a vengeance. In *A Monetary History of the United States, 1867–1960* published in 1963, Friedman and Anna J. Schwartz explained the severity of the Great Depression in monetarist (and clearly anti-Keynesian) terms, as the result of the Federal Reserve's inaction in the face of the bank failures of the early 1930s, which had led to a sharp and damaging contraction in the money supply. Until the acceleration of inflation in the late 1960s, however, monetarism remained a minority position, and as late as 1971 the Republican President Richard Nixon declared himself (and everyone else) to be a Keynesian. As inflation continued to accelerate in the early 1970s, Friedman's ideas rapidly increased their influence, although by 1973 it was still too early to describe monetary policy in the United States as unequivocally monetarist in nature.

The free market liberalism promoted by Friedman, Stigler, and their American colleagues at the University of Chicago was reinforced by the British-born Ronald Coase (1910–2013), who demonstrated that, on certain (somewhat implausible) assumptions, external costs and benefits could be internalized in voluntary contracts between the affected parties, eliminating the need for either regulation or Pigovian taxes and subsidies (Coase 1960).

The Coase Theorem subsequently became a key element in neo-liberal economics, although Coase later distanced himself from some of the more extreme political conclusions that the Chicago school derived from it. A closely related development was the emergence of the new discipline of economics and law, which applied marginalist economic theory to the study of legal principles and their application in the courts. The most prominent figure here was Richard Posner, who combined his role as a judge in the US Court of Appeals in the Seventh Circuit in Chicago with lecturing duties at the University of Chicago Law School. Posner was the author of an influential text, *Economic Analysis of Law* (1973), which went into its eighth edition in 2010.

By the early 1970s the range of problems to which neoclassical microeconomics appeared to offer solutions was steadily expanding. From the early 1950s, models of rational choice were being applied to political behaviour, most notably by the 'public choice' theorist James M. Buchanan (1919–2013). In *The Calculus of Consent: Foundations of Constitutional Democracy* (1962), co-authored with Gordon Tullock, Buchanan used neoclassical economics, including game theory, to interpret and predict the behaviour of politicians and public servants. It was assumed that politicians and bureaucrats pursue their own self-interest rather than the public good, and thus need to be constrained by constitutional rules to prevent them from manipulating economic policy for short-term political ends. In some ways this was a straightforward application of the principles of pressure group politics, long-established in the American political science literature, and there was no reason why 'public choice' theory might not appeal to the American left. Much of the discussion of government policy in Baran's and Sweezy's classic Marxian text *Monopoly Capital* (1966), for example, could be interpreted in this way. But Buchanan himself was a convinced conservative, who advocated constitutional rules to prevent the use of deficit financing and favored flat rather than progressive taxation. Buchanan influenced the thinking of Margaret Thatcher and Ronald Reagan, and was also influential in the so-called 'tax revolt' of the 1970s and 1980s. He spent most of his academic life at Virginia Polytechnic Institute (where he established the Center for the Study of Public Choice, which continues to promote his ideas), and the nearby George Mason University. Buchanan was awarded the Nobel Prize in 1986.

Both liberal and conservative critics of 'public choice' theory objected to the way in which it dismissed altruistic motives and denied both the significance of concern for the well-being of others and the very notion of public service. And there was another analytic issue: pressure groups were by their very nature *collective* organizations, whose very existence was difficult to reconcile with the assumption of the relentless pursuit of *individual* utility maximization. An influential contribution to the discussion of this problem was made by Mancur Olson (1932–1998), who argued in *The Logic of Collective Action* (1965) that only pressure groups with small numbers of members were likely to prove effective. In large groups the strong incentive to take a free ride would inevitably undermine their effectiveness. Why pay for benefits ('public goods') that you would receive even if you did not pay? This is best interpreted as a *reductio ad absurdum*: the survival of large groups (trade unions, employer associations, local and national business lobbies) suggests that there is something wrong with the underlying theoretical assumptions of the free rider principle. As the institutionalists had always maintained, social norms cannot be reduced to simple outcomes of the pursuit of individual self-interest.

At about this time, economists began invading what had previously been considered the domain of the other social sciences, which were seen as ripe for takeover. "A political scientist," in words attributed (entirely plausibly) to George Stigler, "is someone who thinks that the plural of anecdote is data" and has therefore failed to appreciate the explanatory power that is wielded by formal models of constrained maximization. In addition to political scientists, social psychologists, sociologists, and anthropologists now found their theoretical terrain under threat from the irresistible advance of the new 'economics imperialism.' Under the leadership of Gary Becker (1930–2014), neoclassical economic modeling was applied to education (via the concept of 'human capital'), crime (since the criminal could be seen as a rational, utility-maximizing entrepreneur), and the family (with the popular metaphor of the 'marriage market' being taken literally and feminists being enraged by the idealization of male domestic tyranny).

Becker took his undergraduate degree at Princeton University, where Jacob Viner is reported to have described him as the most brilliant student that he had ever taught. He then moved to the University of Chicago for his PhD, where he was supervised by Friedman and influenced by the labor economist H. Gregg Lewis (1914–1992) and the education economist Theodore W. Schultz (1902–1998). Becker was the first to apply neoclassical theory to the problem of racism in *The Economics of Discrimination* (1957). His *Human Capital* (1964) was immensely influential not only in the economics of education but also in labor economics, where it was used to explain wage differentials and the extent of inequality in the distribution of individual incomes from employment. After spending the 1960s in New York, at Columbia University and the National Bureau of Economic Research, Becker returned to Chicago, where he published *The Economic Approach to Human Behavior* (1971) and *A Treatise on the Family* (1981). He was awarded a Nobel Prize in 1992.

By the 1960s, inter-disciplinary cooperation was giving way to invasion tactics. The success of the economics imperialism project is still hotly debated. Some of its advocates were absolutely convinced of its triumph:

> The power of economics lies in its rigor. Economics is scientific; it follows the scientific method of stating a formal refutable theory, testing the theory, and revising the theory based on the evidence. Economics succeeds where other social sciences fail because economists are willing to abstract.
>
> (Lazear 2000, 102)

A similar conclusion but an entirely different judgement came from the Marxists Ben Fine and Dimitri Milonakis, who were especially critical of the 'new style' of economics imperialism in which "the non-economic, and previously neglected aspects of the economic, are addressed as the response to market imperfection" (Fine and Milonakis 2009, 119). This has proved to be "a more successful economics imperialism by breadth of subject matter and influence, and encroachment on other disciplines" (Fine and Milonakis 2009, 12; 119–120). They describe the new economics imperialism as "devilish" (110), and its practitioners as "parasitic, arrogant, ignorant and contemptuous" of their colleagues in other disciplines (123). They also accuse mainstream economics of "plunder" (84, 166) and of "asset-stripping" (153) the intellectual resources of the other social sciences.

The imperialists were often fiercely resisted and with considerable success. Neoclassical models were indeed sometimes used in political science, sociology, anthropology, and social psychology, but only on the disciplinary fringes. The authoritative history of the social sciences since 1945 edited by Roger Backhouse and Philippe Fontaine reveals that economics is unique in having a single dominant mainstream. There has never been such a thing as 'orthodox psychology' or 'orthodox political science,' and in those disciplines where functionalism might once have aspired to such hegemony (sociology and social anthropology), its supremacy proved to be temporary. Economic geography, too, "at least since the early 1960s, has been multi-paradigmatic, at every scale of that concept" (Backhouse and Fontaine 2010, 175). The failure of economics imperialism is confirmed by the eminent University of Chicago sociologist Neil Smelser, a long-standing colleague of Becker's. If anyone in the social sciences might be expected to reveal the impact of intellectual colonization it would be Smelser, whose research has always had economic themes at the center of its subject-matter, yet there is not the slightest sign of such subjugation anywhere in his autobiography, and few references to economists in the index (Smelser 2014).

Economics imperialism did, however, begin to extend its reach from the academic journals into popular culture and ideology. The University of Chicago was again at the center of this movement, with the best-selling book by Milton Friedman and his wife, Rose Friedman (1910–2009), *Free to Choose* (1980), being used as the basis for an influential television series promoting neo-liberal ideas. It was also shown on British television, where it had "an enormous impact" on public opinion (Cockett 1994, 152). For many years, in fact, Friedman had enjoyed a high public profile in Britain, where a free market pressure group known as the Institute of Economic Affairs published his work in its series of Occasional Papers, including *The Counter-Revolution in Monetary Theory* (1970) and *Inflation and Unemployment* (1976), which was the text of his Nobel Prize lecture. He dined privately with the then opposition leader Margaret Thatcher in 1978 (Cockett 1994, 173), and monetarist ideas dominated the macroeconomic policy decisions of the first term of her Conservative government (1979–1983).

Chicago economics had been introduced to Europe much earlier. In 1947 the first meeting of the Mont Pèlerin Society included a contingent from Chicago, including Friedman, Stigler, Aaron Director (1901–2004), and Frank Knight, the last-named being appointed as the only American among its five Vice-Presidents; Friedman served as President in 1972 (Cockett 1994, 115, 118). The Mont Pèlerin Society was an important channel for the dissemination in Western Europe of what would later be known as neoliberal ideas (van Horn and Mirowski 2009). However, it was dominated not by Friedman but by another prominent Chicago personality, Friedrich von Hayek, and it will be encountered again later in this chapter, and again in Chapter 8, when the role of Austrian economics in the United States is considered.

An impression of the main characteristics of American economics at the end of the time period covered in this chapter can be gained from the December 1973 issue of the *American Economic Review*, which begins with a tribute by Don Patinkin to the recently-deceased Frank Knight. A glance at the first four substantive papers is enough to indicate the massive changes that had taken place in the discipline since the mid-1940s. C. Scott Clark's "Labor Hoarding in Durable Industries" has 38 equations and three tables that summarize author's econometric estimates of them. Gregory C. Chow's "Problems of Economic Policy from the Viewpoint of Optimal Control" has a mere 25 equations, but as the title suggests it is equally and unequivocally neoclassical. The third paper, by Rudolph G. Penner and William L. Silber, which deals with "The Interaction between Federal Credit Programs and the Impact on the Allocation of Credit," offers some relief, with no algebra and just four diagrams (twice as many, it will be recalled, as could be found in the entire September 1944 issue of the journal). Formalism is restored in the fourth paper, in which Abram Bergson begins his discussion of "Monopoly Welfare Losses" with a couple of diagrams but then provides 22 equations in the body of the text and another 25 in the Appendix that provides proof of the derivation of equations (18) and (22). And so the issue continues. One suspects that few of the *AER*'s 1944 readers would have been able to make much sense of any of it, or would have been interested enough to try.

## Other voices

Although it was already beginning to fade, the single most important alternative voice was that of the institutionalists. The rapid and continuous decline in the fortunes of institutional economics after 1940 has been described in great detail by Yuval Yonay (1998). The accompanying transformation of American economics more generally, *From Interwar Pluralism to Postwar Neoclassicism*, to use the title of one important book of essays (Morgan and Rutherford 1998), was the result of several factors that proved unfavorable to the progress of institutionalism. To some extent it was simply a question of personalities: the post-1945 generation of institutionalists was not in the same league as John R. Commons and Wesley Mitchell, as is evident from the briefest encounter with the work of the most prominent of them, Clarence E. Ayres (1891–1972), whose books on *The Theory of Economic Progress* (1944) and *Toward a Reasonable Society* (1961) were not especially enlightening.

The Keynesian revolution was another factor that reduced their influence. Institutionalism had no systematic or convincing alternative to the new macroeconomics, and its explanation of the Great Depression emphasized microeconomic failings rather than the principle of effective demand. Thus in his 1935 analysis of 'Major Causes of the Depression', the leading institutionalist Gardiner C. Means (1896–1988) placed more emphasis on developments that had reduced economic flexibility than on the restriction of purchasing power. Most important was the "increasing concentration of economic activity into great administrative organisations which resulted in inflexible administered prices ... which have in themselves also impeded economic adjustments" (Means [1935] 1992, 80).

This 'structuralist' interpretation pointed less to an anti-Keynesian than to an essentially non-Keynesian explanation of the slump (Barber 1996). The problem was not that there was no connection between imperfect product markets and deficient effective demand. Indeed, some Post Keynesian and Marxian theorists would soon argue that a decline in competition was indeed likely to have serious macroeconomic consequences. A coherent theory of capital accumulation and the realization of surplus value were needed to establish precisely what the connection was, and this the institutionalists lacked.

Structuralists like Means and Rexford Tugwell (1891–1979) were important in the early stages of the New Deal, exerting a considerable influence over the National Recovery Administration and the Agricultural Adjustment Administration before fading from the scene (see Tugwell 1982). In one way their indifference or hostility to Keynesian ideas was a continuing advantage for the remaining institutionalists, since in the 1940s and 1950s it served to preserve their influence over conservative Americans in public life, who were themselves to a greater or lesser extent hostile to Keynesian thought. Thus the institutionalist Arthur F. Burns served as Chair of the Council of Economic Advisers in the Eisenhower presidency (and then as Chairman of the Federal Reserve under Nixon), and it was not until John F. Kennedy moved into the White House in 1961 that Keynesians like Samuelson, Ackley, and Arthur Okun (1928–1980) were able to exercise any great political influence in Washington (the latter two serving as President of the Council of Economic Advisers in 1964–1968 and 1968–1969 respectively). These eminent neoclassical Keynesians were acknowledged as proficient economic modelers, and by the 1960s the absence of formal proficiency – or any interest in this sort of work – was serving to rapidly reduce the political influence of the remaining institutionalist thinkers.

By far the most prominent institutionalist in the third quarter of the twentieth century was in fact also a convinced Keynesian, though not of the neoclassical variety. This was John Kenneth Galbraith (1908–2006), who was born in Canada and educated in agricultural economics before moving to the United

States in 1931. During the Roosevelt administration Galbraith worked for the various federal government agencies, most prominently in 1941–1943 as deputy head of the Office of Price Administration, where he was responsible for price control. In 1949 he settled back into an academic career at Harvard University, where he spent the final six decades of his life, with time out as Ambassador to India in the early 1960s.

Galbraith was an accomplished writer and broadcaster, whose popular 1977 television series *The Age of Uncertainty* inspired Milton Friedman to respond with the even more successful pro-capitalist *Free to Choose*. His first major book was also his best. In *American Capitalism: The Concept of Countervailing Power* (1952) he criticized the focus of mainstream economists on the virtues of competitive markets, emphasizing instead the much greater significance of economic and political power. Monopolistic exploitation was prevented not by competition between producers but by the exercise of countervailing power by other interests, including suppliers, customers, and (especially) trade unions. Galbraith's best-seller, *The Affluent Society* (1958) pointed to the paradox of "private affluence and public squalor," citing a typical middle-class family that was accustomed to drive in its smart air-conditioned new car on pot-holed roads through inner cities made ugly by litter and blighted buildings to picnic on beautifully packaged food by a polluted stream.

None of his many subsequent publications achieved quite the same success, although *The New Industrial State* (1967) was an influential account of the separation of ownership and control and the growing power of corporate managers. This was, of course, a long-established theme in institutionalist thought, having been explored in great depth by Adolph A. Berle (1895–1971) and Gardiner Means in *The Modern Corporation and Private Property* (1932). It had also been taken up by the maverick Marxist (and later Cold War conservative) James Burnham (1905–1987), whose book on *The Managerial Revolution* (1941) had a more apocalyptic tone, arguing that free market capitalism was being transformed into a new and illiberal form of class society. Like Berle and Means, Galbraith never established a clear analytical connection between uncompetitive product markets and the macroeconomic difficulties that they might cause; his total lack of interest in formal (or even informal) modeling made this impossible for him. Additionally, he seems not to have recognized the importance of the post-1973 financialization of American (and soon also of global) capitalism, which will feature prominently in the following chapter. Nevertheless, he did help propagate Keynesian ideas among the educated public, and in 1977 offered financial support for the fledgling *Journal of Post Keynesian Economics*. He was probably the last celebrity from outside the mainstream of the economics profession to be elected President of the American Economic Association. This was in 1971, when he invited another eminent maverick, the English Post Keynesian Joan Robinson, to give the last ever Richard T. Ely lecture to be delivered by a non-orthodox economist (Robinson 1972).

In the period covered by this chapter the term 'Post Keynesian' was often used chronologically, to refer to any post-1936 work in macroeconomics that was broadly consistent with the *General Theory*. By the mid-1970s it had come to be used predominantly to refer to a particular school of thought that was critical of the Old Keynesian ideas of the neoclassical synthesis. In the United States the most important pioneer of Post Keynesian thinking was Sidney Weintraub (1914–1983), who in his early career had been an orthodox Keynesian, using the IS-LM model and publishing in all the best mainstream journals. This changed in the late 1950s under the influence of the continuing cost-push (that is, wage-push) inflation that Weintraub believed to be inconsistent with the neoclassical synthesis. A critical influence on his thinking was the brief stagflationary episode of 1957–1958, when unemployment and inflation rose simultaneously. This led him to reject what he now termed the 'Classical Keynesian' model, especially the new Phillips Curve approach to modeling inflation, in which inflation and unemployment were inversely related. Weintraub insisted on returning to Keynes's aggregate supply-aggregate demand model of output and employment, which was set out in the *General Theory* (Keynes 1936, chapter 3).

Weintraub's innovation concerned the price level ($P$), which in his model was determined by the simple wage-cost mark-up equation: $P = kW/A$, where $W$ is the average money wage-rate, $A$ is the average product of labor and $k$ ($>1$) is the mark-up, equal to the inverse of the wage share in GDP. The empirical evidence, Weintraub believed, showed the wage share (and hence $k$) to be roughly constant over time. If the equation is expressed in terms of annual rates of change, $\dot{P} = \dot{W} - \dot{A}$, it reveals the rate of price inflation ($\dot{P}$) to be equal to the rate of growth of money wages ($\dot{W}$) minus the rate of growth of labor productivity ($\dot{A}$). Causation runs from right to left, and since $\dot{A}$ depends largely on the long-run development of technology and can be taken as given we have a simple wage-push theory of inflation. There are equally clear implications for economic policy. Weintraub was a consistent and energetic supporter of a wages policy to combat inflation by keeping $\dot{W}$ equal to $\dot{A}$. In the early 1970s he advocated a tax-based incomes policy (TIP) that would impose a tax surcharge on excessive wage increases and replace the inefficient direct controls that had been imposed by the Nixon administration.

Although he titled one of his books *Classical Keynesianism, Monetary Theory and the Price Level* (1961), Weintraub was not an accomplished monetary theorist. This aspect of the Post Keynesian critique of Old Keynesian macroeconomics was provided by his student Paul Davidson (b. 1930), whose *Money and the Real World* (1972) attempted to recover the core of Keynes's theory of money, which he believed to have been effectively discarded from the neoclassical synthesis. Above all, Davidson argued, Keynes's *finance motive* for holding money had disappeared from the mainstream models of theorists like Don Patinkin (1922–1995) and James Tobin (1918–2002), who implicitly assumed that Say's Law operated and involuntary unemployment did not exist (Patinkin 1956; Tobin 1971). Davidson attacked the three central axioms of what he, like Weintraub, termed 'Classical Keynesian' theory. These were *ergodicity* (the future can be reliably inferred from the past); *gross substitution* (price flexibility insures that all markets clear); and the *neutrality of money* as assumed in the well-known 'classical dichotomy': money affects prices, not output and employment, which depend only on the 'real' factors of tastes and technology.

Davidson insisted that Keynes himself believed all three axioms to be false. The existence of fundamental uncertainty means that we live in a non-ergodic world where the future cannot be reliably inferred from the past. The axiom of gross substitution is simply false, since price and wage flexibility does not guarantee full employment, and money is not neutral; it affects output and employment. From this Keynes derived the principle of effective demand, summarized in Davidson's aggregate supply-aggregate demand diagram, which had been described in words (but not drawn) in the *General Theory*. It is quite different from the mainstream textbook version, which is drawn in price level-real GDP or inflation-real GDP space. In contrast, in Davidson's version, the vertical axis measures expected sales proceeds and planned spending, while the level of employment is measured on the horizontal axis. The intersection of the aggregate demand and aggregate supply curves gives the point of effective demand, which determines the level of employment; this is normally less than the full employment level. As with Keynes and Weintraub, Davidson insisted that the principle of effective demand had very clear policy implications. Monetary policy should be directed at the achievement and maintenance of full employment, reinforced where necessary by expansionary fiscal policy. Inflation should be combated by means of wages policy.

The microeconomic components of *Money and the Real World* were also taken directly from Keynes and were thus essentially neoclassical or, as Davidson would insist, Marshallian in nature. In this and many other respects he was a 'fundamentalist Keynesian' (King 2002, chapters 5, 10). Neither Davidson nor Weintraub took much interest in the macroeconomic implications of oligopoly in the product market. This distinguished them not only from institutionalists such as Galbraith and Means but also from the second variant of Post Keynesian macroeconomics, associated with the Polish economist Michał Kalecki (1899–1970). Kalecki spent eight years in New York working at the United Nations (1946–1954) but had no contact with Weintraub and exercised no influence over him or Davidson. The Kaleckian variant of Post-Keynesian theory was not influential in the United States until at the very least the mid-1970s (Kalecki 1943, 1954). A third variant, the 'financial instability hypothesis' developed by Hyman P. Minsky (1919–1996), was still under construction, and will also be discussed in the following chapter. In 1973, the year after the publication of *Money and the Real World*, 'Post Keynesianism' was effectively synonymous with the 'fundamentalist Keynesian' macroeconomics of Weintraub and Davidson.

A third alternative voice came from the behavioral economists, who argued that neoclassical theory was also open to criticism for its neglect of scientific psychology. Yet another refugee from Hitler's Europe, the Hungarian-born George Katona (1901–1981), took issue with the Old Neoclassical Synthesis on precisely these grounds (King 2016). Trained in Germany in experimental psychology, and himself an advocate of the *Gestalt* school and the author of a well-received text on *Organizing and Memorizing* (1940), Katona directed a Cowles Commission project on business reactions to wartime price controls before settling at the University of Michigan, where from 1946 until his retirement in 1972 he was Director of the Survey Research Center in the Institute for Social Research. His most important contribution to empirical macroeconomics came in the regular surveys of consumer spending intentions that he organized.

At the theoretical level, Katona tried to cut through the boundaries that separated economics and psychology. In *The Psychological Analysis of Economic Behavior* (1951) and *The Powerful Consumer* (1960) he argued that the study of spending, saving, investing, and setting prices and output levels had much in common with research into learning, thinking, voting, and cooperating with others. He was critical of Keynes for (supposedly) regarding current income as the only significant determinant of consumption expenditure, ignoring the role of expectations and refusing to take account of consumers' purposeful adaptation to changing circumstances. Katona was equally opposed to Milton Friedman's permanent income hypothesis, which revealed a similar neglect of the evidence on real-world decision-making by consumers. His own work was praised by such leading (Old) Keynesians as Lawrence Klein, James Tobin, and Gardiner Ackley (a colleague at the University of Michigan), all of whom recognized the potential contribution of psychology to the modeling and econometric forecasting of consumption spending.

Even more than Katona, Herbert A. Simon (1916–2001) was a formidable polymath, who held chairs at Carnegie-Mellon University, first in Administration and Psychology and then in Computer Science and Psychology, not in Economics. He, too, applied the principles of psychology to economics, but concentrated on the microeconomic aspects of human behaviour. Much more than Katona, Simon emphasized the limitations that are imposed on rationality in economic decision-making by the cost of obtaining information about alternative opportunities in a world where the future is fundamentally uncertain. 'Economic man' could not behave in the precisely rational, calculating, utility-maximizing way that neoclassical economists insisted on modeling. Instead economic agents are forced to look for satisfactory rather than optimal outcomes: they are 'satisficers' rather than maximizers. In *Administrative Behavior* (1947) Simon applied these ideas to the study of corporate and governmental bureaucracies, while *Models of Man* (1957) provided many applications to microeconomics of his central principle of 'bounded rationality.' Simon's autobiography, *Models of My Life* (1991), is unusually accessible and informative about these ideas and their implications (*inter alia*) for economics.

Both Katona and Simon saw themselves as critics of mainstream economic theory, rather than mere reformers of it, and they are sometimes described as

Old Behavioral Economists to distinguish them from the more accommodating New Behavioral Economics that will be discussed in the following chapter. But they were generally regarded as friendly critics. As we have seen, Katona's work was praised by some of the leading (Old) Keynesians of his generation, while Simon was awarded the 1978 Nobel Prize in economics.

## Crosscurrents

As noted earlier, one of the most striking features of American 'exceptionalism' was the absence of a mass socialist movement (pp. 120–1). This was reflected in the lack of any significant original work in Marxian political economy right down to the 1930s, when the severity of the Great Depression and the contemporaneous success of Stalin's forced industrialization of the Soviet Union aroused the interest of a small but influential minority of American intellectuals. By far the most important of the young Marxian economists was Paul M. Sweezy (1910–2004), who taught for several years at Harvard University, where he tutored for and earned the respect of Joseph Schumpeter. Anticipating that he would not be offered a tenured position, Sweezy resigned from Harvard in 1947; coming from a wealthy New England family, he did not need the salary. In 1949 he established the *Monthly Review* as a journal of Marxist economics and politics, independent of the Communist Party but broadly supportive both of the Communist movement and of the Soviet model of socialist economic development.

Sweezy's *Theory of Capitalist Development* (1942) was the first major book on economics to come from the pen of an American Marxist, and it displays quite remarkable scholarship, providing both a lucid introduction to Marx's own economic thought and a comprehensive survey of Marxian theories of economic crisis from the late nineteenth century down to the late 1930s (Howard and King 1992, chapters 1, 7). For the first time the ideas of German and Austrian theorists like Otto Bauer, Ladislaus von Bortkiewicz, Henryk Grossman, Rudolf Hilferding, and Rosa Luxemburg were made accessible in English. Sweezy himself advocated an underconsumptionist theory of the tendency to secular stagnation which – like Alvin Hansen, but for very different reasons – he believed to be confronting the capitalist system. In the new monopoly stage of American capitalism, he maintained, consumption tends to fall as a proportion of total output: the profit share of capitalists rises, but capitalists spend a decreasing proportion of their incomes, while workers (who spend everything that they get) receive a declining share of net output. Thus capital accumulation runs ahead of consumer expenditure, the expected profitability of new investment falls, actual investment expenditure declines, and profitable growth comes to an end. This tendency to stagnation is offset to some extent, Sweezy concedes, by the growth of unproductive spending, both peaceful (on advertising and other costs of distribution) and violent (military spending, which increases the danger of war). The monopoly stage of capitalism is therefore characterized domestically by increasing levels of waste and internationally by rising political tension and the growing danger of inter-imperialist war.

The other prominent Marxian economist in this period was the Russian-born Paul Baran (1910–1964), who came to the United States in 1939 after spending several years in Germany and Poland. After studying at Harvard University where he first met Sweezy, Baran found employment in a variety of jobs before settling down in 1949 on the West Coast, at Stanford University. Here he was burdened with an unusually heavy teaching load, but he kept his job throughout the years of McCarthyite repression, when it seems he was the only tenured Marxian economist in any American university. His book *The Political Economy of Growth* (1957) made a great contribution to the burgeoning literature on the causes of underdevelopment in the post-colonial world (Howard and King 1992, chapter 9). For Baran the growing gap between rich and poor countries – the center and the periphery – was due to the large and constantly increasing transfer of surplus production from the underdeveloped world to the core capitalist countries of North America and Western Europe. In the nineteenth century the rapid accumulation of capital in the center was largely due to its exploitation of the periphery, and Baran believed that the process of decolonization after 1945 had made little or no difference. The transfer of surplus had continued through the repatriation of profits from overseas investments, with the collaboration of the *comprador* (client) bourgeoisie in the former colonies, supported by the imperialist states of the advanced capitalist world, above all the United States. The rich countries of the center had a strong incentive to restrict growth in the periphery, which might threaten their interests. Underdevelopment, Baran concluded, and not development, was the inevitable outcome.

This was, in effect, a critique of some earlier Marxian theories of imperialism that even Marx himself had seen as a progressive force, albeit a very dangerous one. It revealed the influence on Baran of Lenin and the Marxism of the Third International, but he was not an uncritical adherent to the Moscow line. Also sympathetic to the 'Critical Theory' of the Frankfurt School, Baran was concerned with the increasing irrationality of capitalism, not just as an economic system but also as a form of social life. This broader perspective was evident when Baran and Sweezy worked together in the 1950s and early 1960s, first on articles for *Monthly Review* and then in writing *Monopoly Capital* (1966), probably the most widely-read book on Marxian economics ever to appear in the English language. It told a distinctly American and rather idiosyncratic (though immensely readable) story, which made no use of the labor theory of value and rejected the law of the falling rate of profit. Instead Baran and Sweezy defined the 'economic surplus' as the difference between what a society produces and the costs of producing it, and set out a 'law of rising surplus.' This was a variant of Sweezy's earlier underconsumption model, in which real wages lagged behind the growing productivity of labor and the problem of absorbing the surplus was solved only through increasing levels of wasteful expenditure. The most important outlet for the surplus was, once again, also the most dangerous: expenditure on armaments. It was only the economic, political, and military predominance of the United States, Baran and Sweezy maintained, that had prevented the resumption of inter-imperialist warfare after 1945.

When *Monopoly Capital* appeared Sweezy had been out of academia for almost two decades. Before the emergence of the New Left in the mid-1960s, there were few if any Marxian economists other than Baran employed in American universities. The changes that followed will be described in detail in the following chapter (pp. 229–30). Those changes included the foundation of the Union for Radical Political Economics (URPE) in 1968. This was a non-dogmatic, open-ended and pluralist organization, with the choice of 'Radical' rather than 'Marxist' in the title being deliberate, and it soon attracted sub-stantial support among students and young professors. In the 1950s, however, the climate was much less hospitable (Lee 2009, chapter 3), and two of the best young Marxian economists, Richard Goodwin (1913–1996) and Lawrence Klein, left the United States for the dreaming spires of Cambridge University and Oxford University respectively. Goodwin spent the 29 years after his arrival in 1951 in Cambridge, publishing sparsely on the margins of Marxian and Post Keynesian theory before enjoying a late Italian renaissance in the 1980s at the University of Siena (Goodwin 1970, 1982). Klein had already published a comparative analysis of the Marxian and Keynesian macro-economic models – in the *Journal of Political Economy*, no less – coming down in favor of the former (Klein 1947). When he returned home in 1958 it was as a moderate orthodox Keynesian. Klein was an outstanding econome-trician, and his Nobel Prize, which he received in 1980, was a reward for his work in Old Keynesian modeling.

A link of sorts between Marxian and Austrian economics was established when Joseph Schumpeter was a graduate student at the turn of the century in Red Vienna, with Bauer and Hilferding on the socialist left and Ludwig von Mises on the pro-capitalist right. Mises migrated to the United States in 1940 and spent the rest of his life there, but was never fully assimilated and never held a tenured academic position. He did travel widely, lecturing at Ivy League universities and speaking to business groups across the country. Between 1945 and 1949 he had a series of temporary appointments at New York University and continued to run a weekly seminar there (financed by the pro-market Volker Fund) until his retirement in 1969, at the age of 88. Although he was an adviser to the Chamber of Commerce and closely associated with the right-wing Foundation for Economic Education, Mises was "never more than a peripheral figure in American academic circles" (Vaughn 1994, 64). His treatise on *Human Action* (1949) sold more copies to business professionals and conservative intellectuals than it did to university professors, establishing Mises as an influential advocate of those opposed "to Keynesian economics and interventionist policy coupled with a steadfast belief in the superiority of free markets for economic prosperity and individual freedom" (Vaughn 1994, 67). As described in the following chapter (pp. 226–7), two of his students,

Murray Rothbard and Israel Kirzner, would play a central role in the revival of Austrian economics that began in 1974, the year after his death.

Another major figure in Austrian economics – Friedrich von Hayek (1899–1992) – arrived in America at the end of 1949. His migration reflected a desire for a cheap divorce rather than political persecution. After a brief spell in Arkansas, Hayek moved to the University of Chicago, where he spent the next twelve years holding a chair in Social and Moral Sciences, not economics, before returning to Europe in 1962. Hayek's interests were already turning away from economic theory, and his American publications reflected his growing preoccupation with political theory and the constitutional order (Hayek 1960). His influence over free market economists in the United States was a largely indirect one, operating via Switzerland and the Mont Pèlerin Society that he founded there in 1947. The Society served as a rallying point for free market liberals – the term 'neoliberal' is anachronistic in the period covered by this chapter – in Western Europe and the United States. Before 1973, however, there were very few prominent American economists who would have described themselves as Austrian, and little sign of a distinctively Austrian school.

Apart from the fledgling ecological economics community, consideration of which will be deferred to the following chapter (p. 232), the only other cross-current of any real significance in the period between 1929 and 1973 was provided, towards the end, by feminist economics. Together with the emergence of a militant feminist movement in the 1960s and early 1970s came a revival of interest in the way in which women were treated (or more commonly ignored) by economists and their relative absence from the economics profession. The new self-proclaimed feminist economists criticized the mainstream for its inadequate and inaccurate depiction of women and their economic activities, which save for a few instances were not included at all. Feminist economists called for women to be integrated into the discipline and its theories (Hewitson 1999). This strategy of 'add women and stir' would soon be challenged by a new generation of more radical feminists, as we shall see in the next chapter (pp. 231–2).

## References

Ackley, G. 1961. *Macroeconomic Theory.* New York, NY: Macmillan.

Amadae, S. M. 2003. *Rationalizing Capitalist Democracy: The Cold War Origins of Rational Choice Liberalism*, Chicago, IL: University of Chicago Press.

Anonymous 2014. "Entwicklung der Weltweiten Stahlproduktion" ['Development of World Steel Output'], *Der Kurier* [Vienna]. 21. August.

Arrow, K. J. 1951. *Social Choice and Individual Values.* New York, NY: Wiley.

Arrow, K. J., and Debreu, G. 1954. "Existence of an Equilibrium for a Competitive Economy." *Econometrica* 22(3): 265–290.

Arrow, K. J., and Hahn, F. 1971. *General Competitive Analysis.* San Francisco, CA: Holden-Day.

Ayres, C. E. 1944. *The Theory of Economic Progress.* Chapel Hill, NC: University of North Carolina Press.

Ayres, C. E. 1961. *Toward a Reasonable Society: The Values of Industrial Civilization.* Austin, TX: University of Texas Press.

Backhouse, R. 2015. "Revisiting Samuelson's Foundations of Economic Analysis." *Journal of Economic Literature* 53(2): 326–350.

Backhouse, R., and Fontaine, P., (eds). 2010. *The History of the Social Sciences Since 1945.* Cambridge: Cambridge University Press.

Baran, P. A. 1957. *The Political Economy of Growth.* New York, NY: Monthly Review Press.

Baran, P. A., and Sweezy, P. M. 1966. *Monopoly Capital: An Essay on the American Economic and Social Order.* New York, NY: Monthly Review Press.

Barber, W. J. 1996. *Designs within Disorder: Franklin D. Roosevelt, the Economists, and the Shaping of American Economic Policy, 1933–1945.* Cambridge: Cambridge University Press.

Becker, G. S. 1957. *The Economics of Discrimination.* Chicago, IL: Chicago University Press.

Becker, G. S. 1964. *Human Capital: A Theoretical and Empirical Analysis, with Special Reference to Education.* New York, NY: National Bureau of Economic Research.

Becker, G. S. 1971. *The Economic Approach to Human Behavior.* Chicago, IL: University of Chicago Press.

Becker, G. S. 1981. *A Treatise on the Family.* Cambridge, MA: Harvard University Press.

Berle, A. A.Jr., and Means, G. C. 1932. *The Modern Corporation and Private Property.* New York, NY: Macmillan.

Bjerkholt, O. 2015. "How it all Began: The First Econometric Society Meeting, Lausanne, September 1931." *European Journal of the History of Economic Thought* 22(6): 1149–1178.

Buchanan, J. M., and Tullock, G. 1962. *The Calculus of Consent: Foundations of Constitutional Democracy.* Ann Arbor, MI: University of Michigan Press.

Burnham, J. 1941. *The Managerial Revolution.* Harmondsworth: Penguin.

Cherrier, B. 2014. "Towards a History of Economics at MIT, 1940–1972." In *MIT and the Transformation of American Economics* (E. R. Weintraub, Editor). Durham, NC: Duke University Press: 15–44.

Claeys, G. 2013. *Mill on Paternalism.* Cambridge: Cambridge University Press.

Coase, R.H. 1960. "The Problem of Social Cost." *Journal of Law and Economics* 3: 1–44.

Cockett, R. 1994. *Thinking the Unthinkable: Think Tanks and the Economic Counter-Revolution, 1931–1983.* London: HarperCollins.

Colander, D. and Landreth, H. 1996. *The Coming of Keynesianism to America: Conversations with the Founders of Keynesian Economics.* Cheltenham and Northampton, MA: Elgar.

Craver, E. 1986. "The Emigration of the Austrian Economists." *History of Political Economy* 18/1: 1–32.

Cristiano, C., and Fiorito, L. 2016. "Two Minds that Never Met: Frank H. Knight and John M. Keynes Once Again." *Review of Keynesian Economics* 4(1): 67–98.

Davidson, P. 1972. *Money and the Real World.* London: Macmillan.

Debreu, G. 1959. *Theory of Value: An Axiomatic Analysis of Economic Equilibrium.* New York, NY: Wiley.

De Vroey, M., and Hoover, Kevin D., (eds). 2004. *The IS-LM Model: Its Rise, Fall, and Strange Persistence.* Durham, NC: Duke University Press.

Domar, E.S. 1957. *Essays in the Theory of Economic Growth.* New York: Oxford University Press.

Düppe, T. 2012. "Gerard Debreu's Secrecy: His Life in Order and Silence." *History of Political Economy* 44(3): 413–449.

Elzinga, K. 1972. "The Eleven Principles of Economics." *Southern Economic Journal* 38(4): 861–879.

Fine, B. and Milonakis, D. 2009. *From Economics Imperialism to Freakonomics: The Shifting Boundaries between Economics and Other Social Sciences.* London; New York, NY: Routledge.

Forder, J. 2014. *Macroeconomics and the Phillips Curve Myth.* Oxford: Oxford University Press.

Fourcade, M. 2009. *Economists and Societies: Discipline and Profession in the United States, Britain and France, 1890s to 1990s.* Princeton, NJ: Princeton University Press.

Friedman, M. 1968. "The Role of Monetary Policy." *American Economic Review* 58(1): 1–17.

Friedman, M., and Friedman, R. 1980. *Free to Choose: A Personal Statement.* New York, NY: Harcourt Brace Jovanovich.

Friedman, M., and Friedman, R. 1998. *Two Lucky People: Memoirs.* Chicago, IL: University of Chicago Press.

Friedman, M., and Schwartz, A. J. 1963. *A Monetary History of the United States.* New York, NY: National Bureau of Economic Research.

Galbraith, J. K. 1952. *American Capitalism: The Concept of Countervailing Power.* Boston, MA: Houghton Mifflin.

Galbraith, J. K. 1958. *The Affluent Society.* Boston, MA: Houghton Mifflin.

Galbraith, J. K. 1967. *The New Industrial State.* Boston, MA: Houghton Mifflin.

Goodwin, R. M. 1970. *Elementary Economics from the Higher Standpoint.* Cambridge: Cambridge University Press.

Goodwin, R. M. 1982. *Essays in Economic Dynamics.* London: Macmillan.

Hagemann, H. 2005. "Dismissal, Expulsion, and Emigration of German-speaking Economists after 1933." *Journal of the History of Economic Thought* 27(4): 405–420.

Hagemann, H. 2011. "European Emigrés and the 'Americanization' of Economics." *European Journal of the History of Economic Thought* 18(5): 643–671.

Hagemann, H., and Krohn, H.-D., (eds). 1999. *Biographisches Handbuch der deutsch-sprachigen wirtschaftswissenschaftlichen Emigration nach 1933* (Vols. 1 & 2). Munich, DE: K. G. Saur.

Hammond, J. D. 2010. "The Development of Post-war Chicago Price Theory." In *The Elgar Companion to the Chicago School of Economics* (R. B. Emmett, Editor). Cheltenham and Northampton, MA: Edward Elgar: 7–24.

Harrod, R. F. 1948. *Towards a Dynamic Economics.* London: Macmillan.

Hayek, F. von. 1960. *The Constitution of Liberty.* Chicago, IL: University of Chicago Press.

Hewitson, G. 1999. *Feminist Economics: Interrogating the Masculinity of Rational Economic Man.* Cheltenham and Northampton, MA: Edward Elgar.

Hirsch, A., and de Marchi, N. 1990. *Milton Friedman: Economics in Theory and Practice.* Ann Arbor, MI: University of Michigan Press.

Howard, M. C., and King, J. E. 1992. *A History of Marxian Economics: Volume II, 1929–1990,* Basingstoke: Macmillan; Princeton, NJ: Princeton University Press.

Hughes, J., and Cain, L. 2011. *American Economic History* (Eighth Edition). Boston, MA: Addison Wesley.

Kalecki, M. 1943. *Studies in Economic Dynamics.* London: Allen & Unwin.

Kalecki, M. 1954. *Theory of Economic Dynamics: An Essay on Cyclical and Long-run Changes in Capitalist Economy.* London: Allen & Unwin.

Katona, G. 1940. *Organizing and Memorizing: Studies in the Psychology of Learning and Teaching.* New York, NY: Columbia University Press.

Katona, G. 1951. *Psychological Analysis of Economic Behavior.* New York, NY: McGraw-Hill.

Katona, G. 1960. *The Powerful Consumer: Psychological Studies of the American Economy.* New York: McGraw-Hill.

Keynes, J. M. 1936. *The General Theory of Employment, Interest and Money.* London: Macmillan.

King, J. E. 2002. *A History of Post Keynesian Economics Since 1936.* Cheltenham and Northampton, MA: Edward Elgar.

King, J. E. 2015. "A Post Keynesian Critique of Swabian Housewife Logic." In *Europe in Crisis* (A. Bitzenis, N. Karagiannis and J. Marangos, Editors), Basingstoke: Palgrave Macmillan: 29–43.

King, J. E. 2016. "Katona and Keynes." *History of Economics Review* 64(1): 64–75.

Klein, L. R. 1947. "Theories of Effective Demand and Employment." *Journal of Political Economy* 55(2): 108–132.

Kotz, D. M. 2015. *The Rise and Fall of Neoliberal Capitalism.* Cambridge, MA: Harvard University Press.

Kuznets, S. 1960. *Modern Economic Growth.* New Haven, CT: Yale University Press.

Lazear, E. 2000. "Economic Imperialism." *Quarterly Journal of Economics* 115(1): 99–146.

Lee, F. S. 2009. *A History of Heterodox Economics: Challenging the Mainstream in the Twentieth Century.* London and New York: Routledge.

Lee, F. S., and Samuels, W. J., (eds). 1992. *The Heterodox Economics of Gardiner C. Means: A Collection*, Armonk, NY: M.E. Sharpe.

Lerner, A. P. 1944. *The Economics of Control: Principles of Welfare Economics.* New York: Macmillan.

Maddison, A. 2006. *The World Economy.* Paris: OECD.

Marglin, S. A., and Schor, J. B., (eds). 1990. *The Golden Age of Capitalism: Reinterpreting the Postwar Experience.* Oxford: Clarendon Press.

Means, G. [1935] 1992. "The Causes of the Great Depression." In *The Heterodox Economics of Gardiner C. Means: A Collection* (F. S. Lee and W. J. Samuels, Editors). Armonk, NY: M. E. Sharpe: 73–92.

Medema, S. 2015. "The 'Subtle Process of Economic Reasoning': Marshall, Becker, and Theorizing about Economic Man and Other-Regarding Behavior." In *Research in the History of Economic Thought and Methodology* 33 (L. Fiorito*et al.*, Editors). Bingley: Emerald Group Publishing: 43–73.

Mirowski, P. 2002. *Machine Dreams: Economics Becomes a Cyborg Science.* Cambridge: Cambridge University Press.

Mongiovi, G. 2005. "Emigré Economists and American Neoclassical Economics, 1933–1945." *Journal of the History of Economic Thought* 27(4): 427–437.

Morgan, M. S., and Rutherford, M., (eds). 1998. *From Interwar Pluralism to Postwar Neoclassicism.* Durham, NC: Duke University Press.

O'Donnell, R., and Rogers, C. 2016. "ISYM: A General Theory-compatible Replacement for ISLM." *Cambridge Journal of Economics* 40(1): 349–364.

Olson, M. 1965. *The Logic of Collective Action: Public Goods and the Theory of Groups.* Cambridge, MA: Harvard University Press.

Patinkin, D. 1956. *Money, Interest, and Prices: An Integration of Monetary and Value Theory.* New York, NY: Row, Peterson.

Pearce, K. A., and Hoover, K. D. 1995. "After the Revolution: Paul A. Samuelson and the Textbook Keynesian Model." In *New Perspectives on Keynes* (A. F. Cottrell and M. S. Lawlor, Editors). Durham, NC: Duke University Press: 183–216.

Posner, R. 1973. *Economic Analysis of Law.* Boston, MA: Little Brown.

Robinson, J. 1972. "The Second Crisis of Economic Theory." *American Economic Review: Papers and Proceedings* 62(2): 1–10.

Samuelson, P. A. 1939. "A Synthesis of the Principle of Acceleration and the Multiplier." *Journal of Political Economy* 47(6): 786–797.

Samuelson, P. A. 1947. *Foundations of Economic Analysis.* Cambridge, MA: Harvard University Press.

Samuelson, P. A. 1948. *Economics.* New York, NY: McGraw-Hill.

Samuelson, P. A., and Solow, R. M. 1960. "Analytical Aspects of Anti–inflation Policy." *American Economic Review: Papers and Proceedings* 50(2): 177–194.

Schumpeter, J. A. 1939. *Business Cycles, Vol. 1 & 2.* New York, NY: McGraw-Hill.

Schumpeter, J. A. 1942. *Capitalism, Socialism and Democracy.* New York: Harper.

Schumpeter, J. A. 1954. *History of Economic Analysis.* London: Allen & Unwin.

Simon, H. A. 1947. *Administrative Behavior.* New York, NY: Macmillan.

Simon, H. A. 1957. *Models of Man.* New York, NY: Wiley.

Simon, H. A. 1991. *Models of My Life.* New York, NY: Basic Books.

Skousen, M. 1997. "The Perseverance of Paul Samuelson's Economics." *Journal of Economic Perspectives* 11(1): 137–152.

Smelser, N. J. 2014. *Wanderlust in Academia.* http://escholarship.org/uc/item/9j2082pm (online: accessed 9 March 2015).

Stigler, G. J. 1975. *The Citizen and the State.* Cambridge: Cambridge University Press.

Sweezy, P. M. 1942. *The Theory of Capitalist Development.* New York, NY: Oxford University Press.

Tobin, J. 1971. *Essays in Economics.* Amsterdam, NL: North-Holland.

Tugwell, R. G. 1982. *To the Lesser Heights of Morningside: A Memoir.* Philadelphia, PA: University of Pennsylvania Press.

Van Horn, R., and Mirowski, P. 2009. "The Rise of the Chicago School of Economics and the Birth of Neoliberalism." In *The Road from Mont Pèlerin: The Making of the Neoliberal Thought Collective* (P. Mirowski and D. Plehwe, Editors). Harvard, MA: Harvard University Press: 139–178.

Vaughn, K. 1994. *Austrian Economics in America: The Migration of a Tradition.* Cambridge: Cambridge University Press.

Von Mises, L. 1949. *Human Action: A Treatise on Economics.* Chicago, IL: Regnery.

Von Neumann, J., and Morgenstern, O. 1944. *Theory of Games and Economic Behavior.* Princeton, NJ: Princeton University Press.

Weintraub, E. R. 2002. *How Economics Became a Mathematical Science.* Durham, NC: Duke University Press.

Weintraub, S. 1961. *Classical Keynesianism, Monetary Theory and the Price Level.* Philadelphia, NJ: Chilton.

Wong, S. 1978. *The Foundations of Paul Samuelson's Revealed Preference Theory: A Study by the Method of Rational Reconstruction.* London: Routledge & Kegan Paul.

Yonay, Y.P. 1998. *The Struggle over the Soul of Economics: Institutionalist and Neoclassical Economics in America between the Wars.* Princeton, NJ: Princeton University Press.

# 8 Economic thought from stagflation and sustained growth to the Great Recession and beyond, 1974–2017

## Introduction

In 1973, the end of the Bretton Woods system of fixed exchange rates in favor of a floating dollar was a necessary but by no means sufficient condition that marked the beginning of the 'age of neoliberalism,' which may or may not be coming to an end. As an ideology, neoliberalism can be defined as the belief that all social problems have a market solution, or at least a solution in which market processes feature prominently. As a social practice, it is the application of this doctrine to an ever-expanding area of life in the real world, through privatization, deregulation, and the introduction of market-mimicking arrangements in areas where genuine markets are not possible (Howard and King 2008).

The ideas and institutions of neoliberal capitalism are neatly summarized by David Kotz (2015, 42, table 2.1). Globally, such thinking invites the removal of barriers to the movement of goods, services, capital, and money (but not labor) across national boundaries. Domestically, neoliberalism diminishes the role of the government in the economy, greatly reducing the regulation of markets, increasing the privatization or contracting out of previously state-run activities, and downplaying the management of aggregate demand management, while cutting taxes for the well-to-do and spending on social welfare programs. The power of capital relative to labor has increased significantly, and the influence of finance is greater than ever before. Internationally, the 'Washington Consensus' established the authority of the International Monetary Fund, the World Bank and the World Trade Organization (formerly the General Agreement on Tariffs and Trade), and with it the general application throughout the developing world of free market policies favorable to the interests of American multinational enterprises (Anderson 2013). American economics has contributed to this metamorphosis while simultaneously analyzing its impacts, both good and bad.

## Economic, social, and political conditions

The population of the United States grew by almost 60 percent between 1970 and 2015, to 320.1 million from 203.3 million, with about 75–80 percent living in urban areas; the world population grew somewhat faster, to 7.2 billion from 3.7 billion, so that the American share fell, to 4.4 percent from 5.5 percent. Mass immigration had resumed after a 50-year hiatus, increasing the foreign-born population from 4.8 percent of the total in 1970 (a historic low) to 10.4 percent in 2000 (Hughes and Cain 2011, table 28.1, 558). In 2007 the primary sector accounted for a mere 0.7 percent of total employment, down from 3.1 percent in 1970. The relative decline of secondary employment (manufacturing, construction, and transport) continued, from 35.8 percent of the total to only 22.6 percent. The tertiary sector accounted for 76.8 percent of all jobs in 2007, compared with 61.1 percent in 1970: more than three-quarters of all Americans now work in the service sector (Hughes and Cain 2011, table 28.6, 567). Many of these service activities involve information technology, and the value of intellectual property is growing faster than the value of material assets such as land, buildings, and machines.

Total output also continued to grow, but not as rapidly as might have been expected: the performance of the American economy in the age of neoliberalism has not been especially impressive. GDP grew at an average annual rate of 3.0 percent both in the crisis years of 1973–1979 and in the subsequent period 1979–2007 that ended with the onset of the Great Recession; this was clearly less than the average growth rate of 4.0 percent in 1949–1973. The slowdown in labor productivity growth was even more pronounced, from 2.8 percent in 1949–1973 to 1.1 percent in 1973–9 and 2.0 percent in 1973–2007 (Kotz 2015, 90, 92, figs 4.2, 4.5). Unemployment, however, was significantly higher, averaging 6.8 percent in 1973–1979 and 6.1 percent in 1973–2007, compared to an average of 4.8 percent during the golden era. It rose to 10 percent in late 2009 before falling back to just over 5 percent at the end of 2016 (Kotz 2015, 156, fig. 5.9; 102, fig. 4.15). One unambiguous improvement was the steady and continuing decline in inflation, from a peak of 8.8 percent per annum in the years 1975–1980 to 3.1 percent per annum in 1990–1995 and a mere 2.4 percent per annum in 1995–2000, with only a very slight increase, to 2.5 percent, in 2000–2004 (Hughes and Cain 2011, table 30.1, 626). This led Ben Bernanke and many others to describe the period beginning *c.* 1990 as 'The Great Moderation.'

The continuing growth in productivity was not reflected in the average hourly earnings of non-supervisory workers, which reached a peak of $20 in 1972 and then declined to $17 in the late 1990s before recovering to $19 by 2007 (Hughes and Cain 2011, 100, fig. 4.13; all in 2011 dollars). Thus the age of neoliberalism was also an age of growing inequality in both income and wealth. The substantial increase in inequality in the distribution of *wealth* has been documented in detail by Thomas Piketty, who was born in France but was trained in the United States, in his best-selling book *Capital in the Twenty-First Century* (Piketty 2014). Every measure of the distribution of *income* tells a similar story: it has become very much more unequal since the early 1970s. Not surprisingly the share of labor in GDP, which had been roughly constant in the golden age, fell steadily thereafter, most sharply early in the twenty-first century when between 2000 and 2007 real corporate profits rose by 5.3 percent per annum, while real wages and salaries grew by only 0.4 percent annually (Kotz 2015, 99, fig. 4.12). The share of the top 1 percent of the American people, which had been roughly constant at about 10 percent of total income from the early 1950s to the late 1970s, rose continuously to reach 24 percent by 2007. In the same time period the share of the top 0.1 percent increased from 3 percent to 12 percent (Kotz 2015, 98, fig. 4.11). After a brief hiatus at the peak of the Great Recession in 2008–2009, most indices of inequality in income and in wealth have continued to increase since 2010 (Ruccio 2017).

The adverse consequences of this increase in inequality are also well documented (Pressman 2016, chapter 3). To appreciate them fully it is necessary to take account of the other significant development in the age of neoliberalism: *financialization.* As Damon Silvers has shown, the financial deregulation of the late twentieth century can be traced to the deregulation of currency markets after the collapse of the Bretton Woods system. It was most pronounced in the United States, where the weakening or elimination of banking regulation soon spread to the equity and housing markets, with the destruction of the New Deal housing finance system giving rise first to the Savings and Loan crisis and then to the perilous innovation of mortgage securitization. By the late 1990s the lax enforcement and then the repeal of the Glass-Steagall Act was producing "the phenomenon of regulatory holes, or true shadow markets," in which "financial activity escapes oversight entirely" (Silvers 2013, 441). Pressure from financial industry lobbyists meant that the financial derivatives market soon became entirely unregulated, while decisions by both Congress and the Supreme Court greatly weakened the rights of investors to take action against underwriters, lawyers, and accountants.

Thomas Palley argues convincingly that in the era of neoliberalism the notion of 'regulatory capture' applies to macroeconomic policy institutions no less than to their microeconomic counterparts: to central banks as well as to industry regulators. Palley notes that there is a strong element of circular causation here, with economic ideas and economic activities having a strong mutual influence upon each other. He is especially critical of the way in which the Federal Reserve has been "protected by its patronage of academia, which includes its own revolving door with university economics departments" and "buys the Federal Reserve intellectual cover and legitimacy" (Palley 2013, 640).

Financialization was closely connected to the growth in inequality, since Americans with low incomes and low (or zero, or negative) wealth continued to increase their consumption expenditure by reducing their saving or, in many cases, by dis-saving, going heavily into debt. Consumer spending as a percentage of disposable personal income reached a low of 86 percent in 1982 and then rose steadily, reaching a peak of 95 percent in 2005. Over the same period household debt rose from 65 percent of household disposable income to over 125 percent before falling sharply in the wake of the Great Recession, but it was still equal to 100 percent of annual income in 2012 (Kotz 2015,

110, table 4.19; and 111, table 4.20). The underlying cause of the Great Recession that put a brutal end to the 'Great Moderation' was financial fragility, made worse by deregulation. The proximate cause was the collapse of the housing market, which led to falling consumption expenditure, the collapse of housing investment, and the fall in financial derivative values that caused the failure of Lehman Brothers in September 2008. Just like the Great Depression of the 1930s, the crisis was 'made in America,' and was transmitted to the rest of the world through declining trade, capital flows, and expectations (Eichengreen 2015). Its impact – or rather, its surprising lack of impact – on economic theory will be considered later in this chapter.

The United States was still the world's largest economy, notwithstanding the events of September 11, 2001, a date seared into the American psyche. In 1998 the US produced 21.9 percent of world GDP, almost twice as much as China, with nearly five times the population. Per capita output was still 34 percent higher than that of Japan, the next most productive major economy, and 53 percent higher than in Western Europe; this was an even larger difference than in 1973, when the American advantage had been only 45 percent (calculated from data in Maddison 2006, table A1-c, 185; table 3.6, 130). The continuing rapid growth of China did close the gap substantially in the next two decades, and early in 2016 it was reported that Beijing had become the "billionaire capital of the world," with 100 billionaires living there compared to 95 in New York (Anon 2016).

It would, however, be a mistake to underestimate the continuing supremacy of the United States in the world economy in the second decade of the twenty-first century. In 2014 its GDP ($17.4 trillion) was still 70 percent greater than that of China ($10.3 trillion), and also larger than that of Japan, Germany, the United Kingdom, France, and Brazil, the next five national economies combined (Nixey 2015). Of the world's 100 largest companies at the end of 2015, 54 had their headquarters in the United States, compared with 26 in Europe and 17 in Asia. US dominance was most pronounced in the information technology sector, with the world's three largest companies all being American IT companies: Apple (with a total share value of $596 billion), Google ($531billion) and Microsoft ($447 billion) (Anon 2014). None of them, it should be noted, was a manufacturing enterprise in the traditional meaning of that term, and they all reflected the increasing dominance of intellectual over material property.

## The mainstream

In 1997 the Nobel Laureate Robert M. Solow was asked to contribute to a symposium on "American academic culture in transformation: fifty years, four disciplines," organized by the American Academy of Arts and Sciences. He reflected at some length on the great changes that had taken place in academic economics since he enrolled as a freshman in an elementary economics course at Harvard College in 1940. The introductory textbooks that he used there were written by Frederic Garner and Alvin Hansen, and by Sumner H. Slichter. They were distinguished authors, two of them on the Harvard faculty. As noted in the previous chapter, Hansen was (*inter alia*) a pioneer of Keynesian macroeconomics, while Slichter was a well-regarded labor economist. Yet their texts would appear very strange to the modern economics student. "Even a quick physical comparison of a good contemporary elementary text with Garner and Hansen and Slichter tells us something," Solow observed. A modern textbook is "sprinkled with diagrams, tables, even simple equations, whereas the older ones present page after page of unbroken prose" (Solow 1997, 40). The two 1940 texts each contained just one equation, the Quantity Equation. Instead of algebra they were "long on classifications – kinds of goods, kinds of industries, kinds of labor – and on descriptions of public and private institutions," together with "very sensible discussions of economic policy, and serious looks at recent history as it would be seen by an economist" (Solow 1997, 41).

In contrast, Solow notes that the typical 1997 text "presents and uses economic analysis as a tool to be directly applied to contemporary or historical situations. The student is shown how to map real events into the categories that appear on the axes of the diagrams or the terms of the equations. The older texts are simply more discursive ... the authors ruminate more than they analyze" (Solow 1997, 41). Thus the modern text "treats economics as a collection of analytical tools to be applied quite directly to observable situations," so that the discipline has become "a self-consciously technical subject, no longer a fit occupation for a gentleman scholar" (Solow 1997, 41–42).

Up to this point almost no-one would disagree with the story that Solow tells. His argument becomes more contentious when he denies that there has been since 1940 "a sweeping victory for 'formalism' in economics," which has therefore "lost contact with everyday life [and] has become more self-involved and less relevant to social concerns as it became more formal (and more mathematical)" (Solow 1997, 42). Not so, Solow maintains. Formalist economics has indeed grown and prospered since 1940, but it does not represent the majority of the economics profession. What most economists do is model-building "which is an altogether different sort of activity." For Solow a model is nothing more or less than "a deliberately simplified representation of a much more complicated situation ... The idea is to focus on one or two causal or conditioning factors, exclude everything else, and hope to understand how just these aspects of reality work and interact" (Solow 1997, 43).

The crucial word here is 'reality.' Far from being unworldly, Solow maintains, "modern model-builders are obsessed with data" (Solow 1997, 57). This is because models "compete on the basis of their ability to give a satisfying account of some facts." Thus they depend on data: "technique and model-building came along with the expanding availability of data, and each reinforces the other." There is another partner in this evolutionary spiral: "the development of new methods of data analysis and statistical inference," which was manifested in "the explosion of econometrics from an esoteric minority task to an essential part of a PhD dissertation" (Solow 1997, 47).

For Solow it was an historical accident – albeit a very fortunate one – that "the spread of model-building coincided in time with the development and diffusion of Keynesian economics," so that "the heyday of Keynesian economics provides a wonderful example of the interplay among theory, the availability of data, and the econometric method" (Solow 1997, 47). Keynes had supplied the theory, Simon Kuznets the national accounting data, and the early members of the Econometric Society the methods of modeling and analysis (see Chapter 7). Increasingly, Solow suggests, this emphasis on modeling has taken economics away from the other social sciences, which may not be such a bad thing: "sociology may be right to stay away from model-building as a mode of thought" and to preserve its own methods of theorizing, even if this makes communication with economists more difficult. "Adjacent territories may adopt different track gauges for good and sufficient reasons, but their railroads will have problems at border crossings" (Solow 1997, 55).

For the most part Solow concludes that economists themselves have not succumbed to "the style of explanation they see (or think they see) in physics" (Solow 1997, 55), even though both disciplines deduce equilibrium conditions from first principles and make heavy use of differential and finite difference equations. This is because economic laws are not like those of physics: "the part of economics that is independent of history and social context is not only small but dull." There is a much closer resemblance with the work of biologists, whose "keen observation and shrewd generalizations" are also regarded as real virtues (Solow 1997, 58).

An intriguing alternative story to that of Solow is told by an economist of a later generation. The Canadian-born economic historian William Lazonick (b. 1945) spent a year taking a master's degree at the London School of Economics in 1968–1969, where "the neo-classical guru was Harry Johnson, the Canadian-born economist who brought the Chicago school to Britain." Johnson, Lazonick recalls,

> preached the static theory of the market economy. But Johnson and his followers really believed in the efficacy of market coordination. Hence they made clear their substantive assumptions of how the world works rather than, as was becoming increasingly the trend among American liberal economists, hiding their ideological orientation behind the scientific facade of mathematical formulae … their candour and consistency made it possible to discern the key issues that a critical perspective had to address.
>
> (Lazonick 2000, 411)

Then, in the fall of 1970, Lazonick went to Harvard to study for his PhD. In some ways it was refreshingly different from the Chicago-dominated London School of Economics:

I found that, quite apart from the iconoclast Galbraith, there were some 15 to 20 students and four faculty members in the Harvard Economics Department who, in opposition to neo-classical orthodoxy, had styled themselves as 'radical economists'. Indeed, in 1970, compared with what came later, the tenured faculty of the Harvard Economics Department was a heterodox bunch.

(Lazonick 2000, 414–415)

This description applied principally to the older generation of the Harvard faculty, born in the first two decades of the century, including several prominent figures that we encountered in the previous chapter: James Duesenberry (1918–2009), Alexander Gerschenkron (1904–1978), John Kenneth Galbraith (1908–2006), Albert Hirschman (1915–2007), Simon Kuznets (1901–1985), Richard Musgrave (1910–2007), and Wassily Leontief (1906–1999). "Yet," Lazonick continues

a narrow-minded, and somewhat cynical, neo-classicism was already asserting its domination over the graduate curriculum and new faculty appointments. At the LSE, those who taught neo-classical theory appeared to really believe that individualism exercised through impersonal markets leads to optimal economic outcomes. At Harvard, however, the neo-classical professors did not really seem to believe the free-market story, and substituted mathematics for substance in what they taught … With the important exception of Stephen Marglin (a tenured prodigy turned 'radical'), the offerings in economic theory at Harvard in the early 1970s were exercises in obfuscation of not only the real world economy but also the foundations of neo-classical economic thought.

(Lazonick 2000, 415)

Several extremely important issues are raised by these two very contrasting, accounts. First is the significance of the desire to emulate the methods and successes of the natural sciences, sometimes described as "physics envy," which has been emphasized by Philip Mirowski in *More Heat than Light* (1989) but is often denied by those more sympathetic to mainstream economic theory, including Solow. The second question concerns the distinction between 'formalism' and 'technical' thinking that is emphasized by Solow (1997, 57), and the connection between formalism and 'analysis,' a word that Solow uses repeatedly without defining it. The third issue concerns the 'economics imperialism' project that Gary Becker launched in the 1960s, endorsed by his Chicago colleagues, and taken up by many neoclassical theorists with the aim of applying economic models and methods of analysis to problems previously considered to be the preserve of the other social sciences. This was a truly American invention: no European economist had tried to colonize the other social sciences in this way, although there had always been interest in the economic dimensions of non-economic behavior since Malthus had written on population and the earliest economists had studied the acquisition of skills and the returns that they brought. It can be argued that Becker has something in common with the Marxists, since for him, being determines consciousness! Becker's ambition, however, was much greater: the *reduction* of all social phenomena to neoclassical microeconomics, including but not confined to the family, crime, and social interaction.

Economics imperialism has been judged an outstanding success by both supporters (Lazear 2000) and opponents (Fine and Milonakis 2009), and the resulting self-confidence that has characterized mainstream economists has often been noted (Fourcade, *et al.* 2015). However, a recent authoritative history of the social sciences since 1945 reveals economic imperialism to have been much less successful than this implies, with the disciplines of anthropology, human geography, political science, social psychology, and sociology retaining both substantive and methodological autonomy (Backhouse and Fontaine 2010). The alternative to Becker was cooperation with the other social sciences, as practised by advocates of several of the Crosscurrents that will be considered below, including institutionalists, (Old) behavioral economists, radicals, and Marxists.

As noted in Chapter 7, it was not long before economics imperialism began to extend its reach from the academic journals into popular culture and ideology. The University of Chicago was again at the center of this movement, with the best-selling book by Milton Friedman and his wife, Rose Friedman (1910–2009), *Free to Choose*, being used as the basis for an influential television series promoting neo-liberal ideas. Galbraith's *Age of Uncertainty*, televised in 1977, had presented the history of economics from a broadly social democratic, Keynesian perspective, but it was much less influential than the *Free to Choose* series, which was made in reaction to it. Eventually a successful Hollywood film was made starring an economist. This was Ron Howard's *A Beautiful Mind* (2001), featuring the brilliant but deeply troubled game theorist John Nash (1928–2015), whose eponymous theorem was one of the most influential products of the post-von Neumann era in game theory. Some years later Charles Ferguson's *Inside Job* (2010) took a much less sympathetic look at the prominent American macroeconomic theorists who had given a clean bill of health to the Icelandic banking system just before what, with hindsight, was its inevitable collapse. Ferguson's film brought to mind Marx's (1872) denunciation of many of the economists of his day as "hired prize-fighters of the bourgeoisie."

There is a further and very interesting question in the history of economic thought, already answered in the negative by Solow: has there been a smooth and more or less continuous movement towards formalism in economics since the late nineteenth century (as argued, for example, by Mirowski 1989, 2002), with the United States lagging behind until *c.* 1940, when the European immigrants moved it forward? Certainly by the early 1970s there was no trace of any surviving American exceptionalism in this context. Ten years later the 1973 Nobel laureate Wassily Leontief (1906–1999) was complaining bitterly that formalism had been taken much too far:

Not having been subjected from the outset to the harsh discipline of systematic fact-finding, traditionally imposed on and accepted by their colleagues in the natural and historical sciences, economists developed a nearly irresistible predilection for deductive reasoning ... Year after year economic theorists continue to produce scores of mathematical models and to explore in great detail their formal properties; and the econometricians fit algebraic functions of all possible shapes to essentially the same sets of data without being able to advance, in any perceptible way, a systematic understanding of the structure and the operations of a real economic system.

(Leontief 1982, 104–105)

This criticism was widely accepted, and at the end of the twentieth century led to the emergence, at first in Europe, but soon achieving considerable support in the US, of a movement campaigning for a "Post-Autistic Economics" (Fullbrook 2003).

It seems that already in 1982 Leontief's critique was beginning to have some effect. Thus David Colander, Richard Holt and Barkley Rosser (2004) have identified a major shift away from formalism (or at least from pure theory) to applied and empirical and/or policy-driven work, which began around 1980 and continued into present century, with clear evidence of this transformation being found in the contents of leading journals like the *American Economic Review* (see also Hamermesh 2013). Indeed, the sociologist Marion Fourcade denies that economics was ever in any real danger of losing touch with the real world. Beginning in the early 1970s, she suggests, there was "a massive expansion of the business applications of economics ... turning economic knowledge into a successful corporate activity" (Fourcade 2009, 2). By contrast with their British and French counterparts, American economists are "market professionals," not public-minded elites or technocrats. There has been a systematic "commercialization of economic ideas and tools" in the United States, and "economics has produced a vast array of practical instruments that are widely used in policy and business (in finance and law, for instance)." Formalism has been only a small part of this process, Fourcade maintains, as can be seen from the success of the informal sub-disciplines of economics and law and public choice, based at the Universities of Chicago and Virginia, not Massachusetts Institute of Technology or the University of California, Berkeley (Fourcade 2009, 8–9).

One final, closely related issue concerns the almost total absence of politics in Solow's account of the transformation of academic economics, apart from a brief reference to the role of the Great Depression and World War II in his discussion of the rise of Keynesian economics. Solow can be criticized for focusing on the internal and neglecting the external influences on the evolution of economic thought in the era of neoliberalism, laying him open to criticism both from the right – both the Austrian and the Chicago schools would emphasize the revolt against 'big government' – and the left, since Marxists would insist on ideological dimension of the revival of free market economics in the Reagan years. Fourcade, too, notes that economic knowledge "has been more 'market-oriented', both cognitively and professionally, than elsewhere" in the world, not least because of its tenacious defence of competitive markets (Fourcade 2009, 9).

It would, however, be wrong to exaggerate these differences. Almost no-one would deny the growing internationalization (read, Americanization) of economics in the period covered in this chapter. As early as 1985, when Mark Blaug published his book on *Great Economists since Keynes*, 78 of his 100 subjects were American by birth or adoption, while 12 were British, eight were European and one came from Canada and one from Japan. This growing American dominance of the global profession was reflected in increasing numbers of international students and teaching staff migrating to the United States, growing pressure on overseas economists to publish in English, and the spread of the American model of economics education, at every level, from first-year textbooks upwards (Elliott *et al.* 1998; Fourcade 2006). To take just one example, in 2010 the University of Melbourne adopted the three-essay requirement for a PhD in economics that had long operated in Ivy League institutions in the US, giving up the single, book-length dissertation requirement that it had inherited from the British and European university systems. Other top-level Australian universities will almost certainly feel compelled to follow suit very soon.

One way of charting the increasing influence of America over the global discipline of economics is by examining the nationality and long-term residence of recipients of the Nobel Prize in economics since the first award was made in 1969. Of the 77 people so honored (all but one of them male) down to 2016, 45 were born in America and another 19 were immigrants, born overseas but spending a large part of their careers in the US; the remaining 13 were European. However, these numbers mask a continuously increasing American predominance. In the first eleven years of the Prize (1969–1979) it was much more evenly distributed between the American-born (five out of 17), immigrants (five) and Europeans (seven). Since 1980, Americans have won 41 (out of 58), immigrants 15 and the Europeans just six. In the twenty-first century the process of Americanization has continued to advance, the corresponding numbers being 25 (out of 32), ten and one (the 2014 laureate, the Frenchman Jean Tirole, is so far the only European to have been so honored in the twenty-first century). For full details see http://nobelprize.org/nobel-prizes/economics.

There is, of course, always a substantial time-lag between the intellectual achievements that are being honored and their recognition by the Swedish Nobel committee: rarely less than 20 years, and sometimes substantially more. (The unenviable record is held by the Moscow-born American scholar Leonid Hurwicz, who at the age of 90 shared the 2007 Prize for work that he had published half a century earlier, and who understandably complained that it had come rather late in the day.) Assuming an average delay of perhaps

30 years in the award of the Prize, we can interpret the Americanization of the Nobel after 1980 as recognition of the country's dominance (in fact, its increasing dominance) over the world of academic economics since 1950. Before then non-Americans had been much more influential, and this was reflected in the early awards to the Europeans Jan Tinbergen and Ragnar Frisch (1969), J. R. Hicks (1972), Gunnar Myrdal (1974), Leonid Kantorovich (1975), and James Meade and Bertil Ohlin (1977), and to the immigrants Simon Kuznets (1971), Friedrich Hayek (1974), Tjalling Koopmans (1975), and W. Arthur Lewis (1979). The first Nobel laureates to be unambiguously American, born and bred, were Paul Samuelson (in 1969), Kenneth Arrow (in 1972), Milton Friedman (in 1976), and Herbert Simon (in 1978).

As stated in Chapter 7, Arrow was one of the leading practitioners of Walrasian general equilibrium theory. Ironically, the year in which he was honored by the Nobel committee also saw the publication of the first paper in a series that fatally undermined the entire Walrasian project (brief bibliographies are provided by Kirman (1989) and Rizvi (2006)). Gerard Debreu and two colleagues, the American Hugo Sonnenschein and the Yale-trained Argentinian Rolf Mantel (1935–1999) demonstrated that almost nothing could be said *a priori* about the excess demand functions that were generated by such models, and therefore there was no reason to expect the existence of a unique equilibrium. The problem arose because of the profound individualism that underpinned the Walrasian treatment of tastes and preferences. As Kirman explained:

> The basic artifact employed is to find individuals each of whose demand behaviour is completely independent of the others. This independence of individuals' behaviour plays an essential role in the construction of economies generating arbitrary excess demand functions. As soon as it is removed the class of functions that can be generated is limited. Thus making individual behaviour dependent or similar may open the way to obtaining meaningful restrictions.
>
> (Kirman 1989, 137–8)

The replacement of methodological individualism by a social theory of consumption behavior was a step too far for the great majority of neoclassical theorists. Instead the Debreu-Mantel-Sonnenschein theorem, sometimes described as the 'anything goes theorem,' led to a very different outcome. By the early 1990s general equilibrium models had been quietly abandoned by the great majority of US microeconomists, just as (ironically) they were being incorporated into the core of macroeconomic theory.

General equilibrium was rapidly replaced by game theory as the principal theoretical framework for the analysis of microeconomic problems. It shared the most important characteristics of Walrasian modeling, above all the assumptions of methodological individualism, instrumental rationality, and certainty-equivalence, so that goals and constraints were known, at least probabilistically, and the standard procedures of constrained maximization could be applied. There was an explosion in the literature on game theory after 1970, with major developments including the distinction between cooperative and non-cooperative games, static and dynamic games, games played with and without complete information, and the analysis of learning in games. Game theory was increasingly applied to policy questions, above all in the fields of industrial organization, competition policy, and legal decisions in anti-trust cases, and the auctioning of various forms of public assets. It also served as an inspiration for the development of evolutionary and experimental economics, two of the 'Other Voices' that will be considered below.

The applications of the theory of games were extended beyond market behavior to sport, family life, social issues, and political philosophy, making game theory a powerful agent of economics imperialism. This extension, however, was not entirely successful. As the authors of one survey concluded, the "ambitious claim that game theory will provide a unified foundation for all social science seems misplaced," since "people appear to be more complexly motivated than game theory's instrumental model allows" and "a part of that greater complexity comes from their social location." This social determination of preferences represents "a challenge to the type of methodological individualism which has had a free rein in the development of game theory" (Hargreaves Heap and Varoufakis 1995, 260).

At this level of high theory, the driving force behind the change in approach from general equilibrium models to game theory was largely internal, derived from the analytical problems encountered in the course of mathematical modeling, and had no external and even less a political dimension. In the softer fields of applied and policy-oriented microeconomics, the situation was very different, since the political context was, as it had always been, extremely important. The neoliberal credo was that all social problems had a market solution, and where markets did not exist they had to be created. The University of Chicago economist Ronald Coase (1910–2013), himself a British immigrant, had demonstrated that under certain conditions 'any externality can be internalised through a suitable allocation of property rights and contracting between their owners, so that the Pigovian complex of taxes and subsidies becomes unnecessary' (Howard and King 2008, 140, referring to Coase 1960). The Coase Theorem was interpreted – though not, perhaps, by its creator – as implying that government failure was always worse than market failure. Taken in conjunction with the notions of rent-seeking behavior by public servants and 'regulatory capture' of the relevant public institutions by private vested interests, it allowed mainstream economics to be used to advocate light regulation, self-regulation, and thoroughgoing deregulation of labor markets and utilities as well as the financial sector. In the early years of the twenty-first century the adverse macroeconomic consequences of neoliberal deregulation would become painfully evident.

In the mid-1970s, however, Chicago macroeconomics was increasingly in the ascendancy. The simultaneous increase in unemployment and inflation was very difficult for (Old) Keynesians to explain, and appeared to confirm

Milton Friedman's long-standing critique of the Phillips Curve, and his objection to its use as a menu for policy choice, that was discussed in the previous chapter (Forder 2014). If the long-run Phillips Curve was indeed vertical, and the long run was reached in months rather than years, there was no point in using monetary or fiscal policy to reduce unemployment, since this would be successful only temporarily and would come at the cost of an accelerating inflation rate. The 'natural' rate of unemployment – later denoted as the non-accelerating inflation rate of unemployment, or NAIRU – could not be avoided by the use of Keynesian macroeconomic policies, and especially not by irresponsible laxity in monetary policy. Discretionary monetary policy should therefore be replaced by a strict monetary rule: to achieve and maintain a stable price level, the money supply should increase by no more than the expected rate of productivity growth. Fortunately, the Federal Reserve was independent of the federal government, and could implement this rule without political interference. This was the 'monetarist' message, which by 1980 had become increasingly influential not only in the United States but also in Western Europe and Australasia.

In fact this was Monetarism Mark I (Snowdon and Vane 2005, chapter 4). By the late 1970s it was already succumbing to friendly criticism from the free market right, with the emergence of what soon came to be known as Monetarism Mark II. There was a methodological dimension to this important generational change. Friedman's version of monetarism had always been rather light on theory, with the Quantity Theory defended mainly on empirical grounds: the velocity of circulation was roughly constant, Friedman claimed, and in the Equation of Exchange ($MV = PT$) causation ran principally (though not exclusively) from left to right, so that changes in the money stock ($M$) caused changes in the price level ($P$). These propositions were derived from his interpretation of the empirical evidence, rather than from any rigorous theoretical analysis of individual behavior. In this respect Friedman claimed (correctly) to have something in common with Keynes, since both men did their macroeconomics from the top down, not from the bottom up.

The second generation of Chicago monetarists, led by Robert Lucas, did it the other way round, insisting on the provision of 'microfoundations' for macroeconomic theory (King 2012). If macroeconomic models were not based on the assumption of rational, utility-maximizing behavior by individuals, there could be no guarantee that these relationships would be stable over time, no reason to have confidence in econometric estimates of the relevant parameters, and hence no grounds on which to expect policies based upon such estimates to be successful. This was especially important for the analysis of inflation, since it led to the replacement of the old monetarist assumption of 'adaptive expectations' by the new assumption of 'rational expectations,' first articulated in 1961 by John Muth (1930–2005) and vigorously advocated by Lucas and other self-proclaimed 'New Classical' theorists such as Thomas Sargent, Finn Kydland, and Edward Prescott. The 'New Classical' label was intended as a dig at Keynes, but also as a reaffirmation of

Say's Law and the principle that there was no such thing as involuntary unemployment (Snowdon and Vane 2005, chapters 5–6).

It was somewhat ironic that these neo-liberal macroeconomists took up general equilibrium modeling just as it was being discarded by their colleagues in microeconomics. The new Dynamic Stochastic General Equilibrium (DSGE) models focused on individual consumers of a very particular type: representative agents with rational expectations, who maximized lifetime utility in an economic environment that was characterized by random shocks. Fluctuations in economic activity resulted from their individual utility-maximizing decisions, which led them first to increase and then to reduce their supply of labor to the market. Changes in the money supply were irrelevant to the analysis of economic fluctuations, since they affected only the price level and had only a transient influence on output and employment. This soon led to the emergence of 'real business cycle theory,' where the intended opposite of 'real' was not 'unreal' but 'monetary.' It involved a dramatic shift in the focus of macroeconomic theory, as can be seen from a graduate-level text published by Princeton University Press that contained the following statement by the (British) author: "including labor caused only minor changes to the previous results … we shall also exclude labor where appropriate and feasible" (Wickens 2008, 83). This proved to be almost always; there was no entry in the index of the book for 'unemployment.'

For many theorists, macroeconomics without unemployment has proved to be a step too far. By the 1990s, however, representative agents with rational expectations – delightly acronyminized as RARE microfoundations – were widely accepted by mainstream macroeconomists, including many of those who were now describing themselves as 'New Keynesians,' to distinguish themselves from Old Keynesians like Samuelson and Solow (Snowdon and Vane 2005, chapter 7). The most important of the New Keynesians were Paul Krugman and Joseph Stiglitz, who rejected the assumption of perfect markets that was implicit in New Classical macroeconomics and argued instead that labor and product markets were imperfect, and this meant that prices and money wages tended to be inflexible downwards. There were good reasons why profit-maximizing employers might not offer work to unemployed people who were prepared to undercut their existing workforce, especially the potential withdrawal of the workers' goodwill towards their employer and the reduction in effort levels that this would induce in circumstances where the employee inevitably knew more than the employer about the practicable level of effort that could be supplied. This gave 'insiders' a significant advantage over 'outsiders,' and meant that there was no compelling reason to expect the labor market to clear. The New Keynesians concluded that involuntary unemployment was the most important consequence of the asymmetries in information that gave rise to imperfect markets (Stiglitz 1987).

This was a travesty of Keynes, who had maintained in chapter 19 of the *General Theory* that downward flexibility in prices and wages should be discouraged. These arguments, however, constituted an important element of the New Neoclassical Synthesis that had emerged by the late 1990s, in which

> a simple three-equation model has replaced the old IS-LM apparatus of the original neoclassical synthesis. The first is an aggregate demand curve, making real output a negative function of the rate of interest; this is the old IS curve slightly reconfigured. The second is a downward-sloping short-run Phillips curve, making the inflation rate a negative function of the output gap (itself closely and positively related to the unemployment rate). The novelty lies with the third equation, which replaces the LM curve and makes the real short-run interest rate a positive function of the central bank's expected inflation rate; this is the 'Taylor rule' for monetary policy.
>
> (King 2015, 26)

The treatment of the savings-investment relationship in the New Neoclassical Synthesis is essentially pre-Keynesian, with equality between savings and investment being established by changes in the rate of interest, not output and employment. There is also a serious problem with the incorporation of money into the analysis, since the continuing underlying assumption of rational expectations eliminates the possibility of default and undermines any need for agents to demand payment in money rather than creditors' IOUs. In the canonical text, Michael Woodford's *Interest and Prices* (2003), there is no index entry for 'banks' or 'banking,' and money is treated as a friction or imperfection (Rogers 2006). The great majority of New Classicals and New Keynesians, however, now agreed on the need for RARE microfoundations, accepted the Taylor Rule as the basis for macroeconomic policy, and at least implicitly rejected Keynes's irreducibly macroeconomic principle of effective demand.

The sub-field of labor economics provides a revealing case study in the changes in US academic economics that were already under way when the period covered in this chapter was beginning, and have gone much further since 1973. The subject area of this speciality is unusually broad, initially encouraging both theorists and empirical researchers to take a multi-disciplinary rather than a narrowly economic approach, with particular interest being shown in cooperation with the discipline of industrial relations. This cooperation benefited both parties, giving rise both to valuable work by economists like John T. Dunlop (1914–2003), Clark Kerr (1911–2003) and Lloyd Reynolds (1910–2005), who offered a synthesis of institutionalist and neoclassical ideas, and also contributed to what has been described as "the golden age of industrial relations" in the fifteen years after 1945 (Kaufman 1993, chapter 5).

After the publication of Gary Becker's *Human Capital* (1964), however, this changed very rapidly. The intellectual focus of industrial relations had always been the study of problems in the employment relationship and methods to resolve these problems. When labor economists abandoned any interest in institutionalism and began to apply neoclassical ideas to labor issues without reservation or qualification, the tacit assumption was that "free markets have no 'problem' that needs reform, and industrial relations has little intellectual justification" (Kaufman 1993, 123). The result was a rapid "hollowing out" of industrial relations (Kaufman 1993, chapter 6), in what seems to have been the most significant success of the economics imperialism project. Once again these intellectual changes were linked to changes in the real world, with the rise of neoliberalism in the labor market, the collapse of union membership and with it union power, a continuing decline in labor market regulation, the growth of inequality and – the most obvious phenomenon of all – a steady decline in the real value of the minimum wage. Once again the causation ran both ways, with theoretical developments encouraging deregulation and deregulation appearing to confirm the success of the new economics (Mishel *et al.* 2012).

At the level of research and advanced theory the turning-point for labor economics was the early 1960s. Undergraduate teaching took much longer to adapt, as can be seen by comparing two textbooks, one published at the very beginning of the period covered by this chapter and the other in widespread use at the end. In the introduction of *The Economics of Work and Pay*, author Albert Rees (1921–1992) notes that the 'institutionalist tradition' that had dominated labor economics before 1945 had its "intellectual roots ... in the law and a sociological rather than an economic theory."

> In the past ten to fifteen years, however, a new and active interest in labor economics has grown up among scholars interested in applying the tools of economic theory to labor problems. The key figures in this analytical approach to labor economics have been H. Gregg Lewis, Melvin Reder, Gary Becker, William Bowen, and Jacob Mincer.
>
> (Rees 1984, viii)

All but one of these theorists had strong Chicago connections, as did Rees himself, having studied for his doctorate there and chairing the economics department between 1962 and 1966 before moving to Princeton University. Rees's commitment to an unregulated 'free market' in labor was rather more qualified than that of Becker and his other colleagues, but he is included with them in Kaufman's list of "neoclassical restorationists" (Kaufman 1993, 122).

Rees describes his book as an attempt to survey "his now rich and extensive literature" (Rees 1984, viii). Its 239 pages of text are divided into six parts, dealing with the supply of labor, the demand for labor, labor markets and labor mobility, economic aspects of trade unions, the wage structure, and macro-economic aspects of the labor market. There are 25 diagrams and 19 statistical tables, but almost no mathematics – two equations defining the internal rate of return on human investment and applying it to the determination of wage differentials (Rees 1984, 172–173) – and absolutely no econometrics.

One of the most widely used texts in labor economics in the second decade of the twenty-first century, now in its 11th edition, is *Modern Labor Economics: Theory and Public Policy* by Ronald G. Ehrenberg and Robert S. Smith (2012). It runs to 650 pages. In addition to a large number of diagrams and tables, it has equations in 12 of the 16 chapters, each of which ends with a set of problems (many of them quantitative) for the reader to solve; almost fifty pages are devoted to the solutions to these problems. Econometrics is introduced in the first chapter, with a set of problems designed to introduce a simple regression equation relating wages to the age of the individual worker; an appendix includes a detailed account of linear regression techniques, along with a discussion of the omitted variable problem. In all these respects it is a very different text from that of Albert Rees.

Labor economics, of course, was a long-established sub-discipline. Perhaps the most important new field for the employment of neoclassical modeling techniques was provided by financial theory, which was in its infancy in 1945 but expanded rapidly thereafter. "The institutional rise of finance as an intellectual powerhouse within economics follows from the establishment of a teaching base in business schools in the second half of the twentieth century" (Fourcade *et al.* 2015, 105). By 2004 there were almost as many economists with PhDs teaching in the top 20 business schools as there were in the top 20 economics departments – 549 compared with 637 – and nine post-1990 Nobel laureates were among them. This deepening involvement with business led to increased pay for economists, together with "new connections and consulting opportunities, and often different politics as well" (Fourcade *et al.* 2015, 105).

The new economics of finance drew heavily on mainstream economic theory, combining the standard analysis of profit-maximizing firms with the New Classical notion of rational expectations to generate highly technical analyses of financial market behavior, which proved also to have extremely large and wide-ranging real-world applications. Without the Capital Asset Pricing Model developed by Fischer Black (1938–1995), Harry Markowitz, Merton Miller (1923–2000), and William Sharpe and others, there would have been no explosive growth of the market for financial derivatives. Equally important was the Efficient Market Hypothesis articulated by the University of Chicago theorist Eugene Fama, according to which prices in financial markets always fully reflect available information. This led Fama and other free marketeers to make "the fatal elision from the true statement that financial markets are subject to random disturbances and therefore impossible to predict, to the false statement that they should be left to regulate themselves" (King 2009, 390). This *faux pas* thereby provided the intellectual justification for dismantling the New Deal regulatory structure of the financial system after 1980, culminating in the repeal of the Glass-Steagall Act in 1999 and enabling the explosive and very largely unregulated growth of those markets. In this way the new economic theory of finance played an important part in establishing the new economic world of financialized neoliberalism (Silvers 2013).

Many established branches of economics flourished throughout the period under review, but others did not. Courses in economic history are seldom offered today as part of an economics degree in any major university, and research in the 'new economic history' is essentially a form of applied econometrics, using data from the distant (or not-so-distant) past (Lyons *et al.* 2008). Similarly, students are rarely exposed in any depth to the methodology and philosophy of economics, as once was the case. In fact the Friedman-Samuelson generation was the last in which leading theorists took a deep interest, and actually published in the methodology of the subject (however, see Hands 2015 for a more positive assessment).

The history of economic thought has also disappeared from the undergraduate syllabus and is rarely prominent in graduate teaching or as the subject of doctoral research; the widespread adoption of the three-essay doctorate has been especially unfavorable to the history of economic thought, which lends itself to the traditional book-length dissertation. Research in the area is rarely, if ever, published in the leading journals, as once was the practice. In its increasingly complete lack of interest in its own intellectual history, economics is again distinguishing itself from the other social sciences. Few sociologists, for example, would consider their students' education to be complete without some exposure to the ideas of Karl Marx, Max Weber, and Talcott Parsons.

The one institutional exception to this general rule is Duke University, home to the Center for the History of Economic Thought and to an important and steadily growing archival collection, and the host of regular international conferences in the sub-discipline. Duke is the last bastion of graduate teaching and doctoral research in the history of economic ideas in any leading US university. One of the two specialist journals in the area, *History of Political Economy*, has been published by Duke University Press since its inception in 1969, edited for the first 41 years by the Canadian-born Craufurd D. Goodwin. (The other is the *Journal of the History of Economic Thought*, the official organ of the History of Economics Society since 1990, which began as the Society's newsletter in 1974.) *History of Political Economy* is an excellent journal, but it has a paltry number of paid subscriptions, 376 at the last count, compared with more than 20,000 for the *American Economic Review. HOPE* has come to rely increasingly on overseas – principally European – contributors, as can be seen from a comparison of the country of residence of the authors of articles published in volume 15 (1983) and volume 47 (2015). The earlier volume had 19 American and 14 non-American authors (eight Europeans, three Australians, two Israelis and one Canadian), while the later one had just four US authors and 16 Europeans, together with one each from Japan and Lebanon. Outside Duke, it seems, there may be no future at all for the history of economic thought, at least if it is continued to be seen as a branch of economics. This has led some to suggest that young scholars should instead look for jobs (and outlets for their work) in departments (and journals) devoted to the history of science, a proposal that provoked fierce resistance (compare Schabas 1992 and Kates 2013).

## Other voices

Here we outline the progress of five research programs that developed outside mainstream economics, but were close enough to it to be regarded by the end of the period as actual or potential components of its cutting edge: (new) behavioral economics, experimental economics, evolutionary economics, complexity economics, and neuroeconomics. These are distinct programs, but they also overlap to a greater or lesser degree, as we shall see.

The key figures in the early development of 'new behavioral economics' were Amos Tversky (1937–1996) and Daniel Kahneman, both of whom were trained in Israel, where Tversky studied cognitive psychology and Kahneman specialized in the psychology of vision and attention. They began to collaborate on the application of psychology to economics in 1969, and over the next decade published the results of extensive research that "introduced the idea that although rational individuals should adhere to the normative theories of logic, Bayesian updating, and expected utility calculation in their decision-making, individuals in fact systematically and predictably deviate from these norms" (Heukelom 2014, 98). They took up Herbert Simon's notion of 'bounded rationality,' which implied that limited cognitive ability made it impossible for individuals to maximize utility and added three additional arguments. The first was an emphasis on the framing and context of decisions, which led people to take short cuts and develop biases that caused them to make errors in their decision-making; this was compounded by the absence of the competitive market pressures that compelled firms to maximize profits by avoiding such cognitive errors wherever possible. Second, they drew on the experimental evidence of 'bounded willpower,' by which they meant that individuals often made choices that they themselves realized – at the time and/or subsequently – not to be in their best interests. Third, Tversky and Kahneman stressed the relevance of 'bounded self-interest,' which involves a willingness to sacrifice one's own utility to help others, and means that considerations of altruism and fairness (and also punishment and revenge) often play a role in individual decision-making (Sent 2004).

These behavioral insights were soon applied by theorists like Richard Thaler to problems of consumer choice, self-control, and savings behavior, in addition to labor economics and law and economics. In the 1980s and early 1990s Thaler cooperated with Tversky and Kahneman in the behavioral economics programs of the Alfred Sloan Foundation and the Russell Sage Foundation. New journals were launched – the *Journal of Economic Behavior and Organization* in 1980 and the *Journal of Economic Psychology* in the following year – and the Society for the Advancement of Behavioral Economics was established in 1982. Thaler was also involved in the most important extension of the new behavioral economics – its application to financial decisions – creating a new and highly influential literature on 'behavioral finance.' This involved a rejection of the efficient market hypothesis on the grounds that it was impossible for the value of financial assets to reflect 'true value,' since market players never have complete information and are unable to process all the information that they do possess. Various cognitive biases, and the over-projection of current feelings into the future, generate unsustainable increases in asset values as a result of 'irrational exuberance,' the title of a widely read book Robert Shiller published in 2000, before crashing to be replaced by what might be an equally protracted period of equally unwarranted pessimism.

Behavioral finance seemed to have wider implications. The New Keynesian theorist George Akerlof entitled his Nobel Prize acceptance speech "Behavioral Macroeconomics and Macroeconomic Behavior" (Akerlof 2002). There had been some efforts to construct a behavioral macroeconomics in the 1980s, but little had come of them. Thus, the publication of Akerlof's and Shiller's book *Animal Spirits* (2009) was a potentially very important event. An ambitious work, as can be seen from the subtitle: "How Human Psychology Drives the Economy, and Why It Matters for Global Capitalism," the book began with a long and glowing endorsement of Keynes, but it was profoundly non-Keynesian in several important respects, notably its neglect of business investment decisions. This reflected the overwhelming bias of the behavioral economics literature, which is slanted towards the study of individual – rather than organizational – behavior (Jefferson and King 2010–2011).

How then did the new behavioral economics differ from the old and apparently more heretical version developed by Herbert Simon that was identified as a crosscurrent in the previous chapter? In fact it was much closer to the mainstream than Simon's work had been. Kahneman and Tversky were always 'much less hostile' to the established theory than Simon. "In fact, they were in favour of current practice in economics ... and they only meant to suggest that a few adjustments be made to improve it" (Heukelom 2014, 127). The new behavioralists also believed neoclassical welfare economics to be entirely correct as a normative theory, despite its weaknesses as a descriptive analysis, and they developed a form of 'libertarian paternalism' in which people were encouraged to change their decision-making processes so that their real preferences could be satisfied, which in many cases only required that they be given a 'nudge' in the right direction (Thaler and Sunstein 2009). Thus the new behavioral economics was correctly seen as being safer than the old as a career choice for young economists (Sent 2004).

Many of the new behavioral economists made extensive use of experiments in their research. Any discussion of the growth of experimental economics must begin, however, by drawing an important distinction between 'natural' and 'controlled' (or laboratory) experiments. In a sense economists have always been concerned with the former, just as seismologists study the effects of earthquakes and vulcanologists learn from volcanic eruptions, even though neither phenomenon can be reproduced in a laboratory. In their well-received book on the economic consequences of labour market regulation, *Myth and Measurement: The New Economics of the Minimum Wage* (1995), David Card and Alan Krueger treated legislated increases in state and federal minimum wage rates as the equivalent of dramatic natural events like earthquakes and volcanic eruptions. They offered striking new evidence, revealing that mono-psonistic imperfections in the labor market often nullified or even reversed the supposed employment-reducing consequences of higher minimum wages (the two labor economics texts discussed above (pp. 216–17) made little or nothing of the implications of monopsony in the labor market). The authors explicitly described this evidence as the outcome of a series of natural experiments (Card and Krueger 1995, 17–18; 397–398).

Laboratory experiments by economists go back at least to the 1930s, and were increasingly used in the early post-WWII years (Friedman and Sunder 1994, chapter 9; Roth 1995). One of the most influential practitioners of experimental economics, Vernon L. Smith conducted his first experiments in 1962 but was discouraged from repeating them for a decade due to the lack of interest they generated in the wider profession. Only in the 1980s did experimental economics become firmly established, with the provision of substantial research finance by the National Science Foundation and the increasing authority of three economics departments that specialized in laboratory-based experimental research. The first of these was at the University of Arizona, under Smith, the second was at the California Institute of Technology, led by Charles Plott; and the third was Northwestern University, under Stanley Reiter (1925–2014). It is generally agreed that "the period between the early 1980s and the early 1990s marked a watershed in the history of experimental economics" (Lee 2016, 192).

There were several, only loosely related, reasons for its rapid growth of in this period. First, and probably most important, was the collapse of the Walrasian general equilibrium project in microeconomics that was discussed in the previous section. This encouraged young economic theorists to look for alternative forms of cutting-edge research, one of which proved to be laboratory experimentation (Rizvi 2005). Second, the very rapid progress in information technology after 1970 made it easier and cheaper to use computers in the course of experiments. Third was the familiar theme of 'physics envy': many economists had long regretted their apparent inability to conduct genuinely scientific experiments, and once the opportunity finally arose they seized it enthusiastically.

Finally, as we have seen, one profoundly important consequence of the abandonment of general equilibrium modeling was the resurgence of game theory, which proved to be especially suitable for experimentation. An author-itative handbook of experimental economics published in 1995 included chapters on coordination problems, bargaining experiments, industrial organi-zation, experimental asset markets, and the design of auctions, all of which were heavily game-theoretic in nature (Kagel and Roth 1995). It also dealt at some length with questions of public policy, including the regulation of compe-tition and the provision of public goods. The policy lessons that could be drawn from experimental economics helped to cement its growing intellectual respectability, which was confirmed in 2002 when Vernon Smith shared the Nobel Prize with Daniel Kahnemann.

Psychology was not the only scientific discipline on which economists began to draw. Biology provided the inspiration for several strands of 'evolutionary economics' that emerged in the 1970s and 1980s. The term itself needs to be used with care. Since the early twentieth century, Veblen and other institutionalists had complained that neoclassical economics was not and could not easily become an 'evolutionary science'. As we shall see below, when the institutionalists set up their own professional association they called it the Association for Evolutionary Economics (AFEE), but this was not what the former Chicago economist Jack Hirshleifer (1925–2005) had in mind when, at the 1976 conference of the American Economic Association, he spoke about the strong similarities between economics and biology.

Hirshleifer began by suggesting that "the various social sciences devoted to the study of man, economics among them, constitute but a sub-division of the all-encompassing field of sociobiology" (Hirshleifer 1978, 238), citing as an authority the recently published and immensely influential text by E. O. Wilson (1975). Just like economists, biologists stressed the role of competition and the importance of strategies to promote success that relied, in effect, upon constrained optimization to reach equilibrium – or, as the biologists would say, adaptation along paths of change that led to solution states. Further analogies were suggested "by terminological pairs like species/industry, mutation/innovation, mutualism/exchange, and evolution/progress" (Hirshleifer 1978, 239). Admittedly, things were a bit more complicated in the economic world, where Adam Smith's 'invisible hand' required constraints on competition to be imposed by the law of property, enforced by the state. "The fundamental fact," however, "is *the selfishness of the gene*" (Hirshleifer 1978, 240; original stress). Here Hirshleifer was alluding to the title of another contemporary bestseller, by Richard Dawkins (1976).

In the 1980s and 1990s the University of Chicago-based version of evolutionary economics that drew on Dawkins and Wilson was extremely influential, not least because it was individualistic and reductionist in nature. The reductionism soon found its way into both New Classical and New Keynesian macroeconomics in the form of an insistence on 'microfoundations,' the requirement that all statements relating to the macroeconomy must be derived from ('reduced to') propositions about the maximizing behavior of individuals, often drawing explicit parallels with the 'selfish gene.' The apparent success of the microfoundations project was illusory (King 2012), but not before a great deal of confusion had been generated. Applied to microeconomic questions, evolutionary economics in the Hirshleifer mould continues to attract considerable interest. However, this was not the only way in which economics was being linked with the life sciences.

Biology and mathematics combined to stimulate the development of 'complexity economics,' a branch of the science of complexity centred on the Santa Fé Institute in Arizona and largely financed in its early stages by Citibank. Complexity theory is inherently multidisciplinary, and is 'seen as not just revolutionizing economics but revolutionizing all the social sciences via the creation of a unified theory of the social sciences that is the equivalent of field theory in physics' (Thornton 2015, 16). The fundamental conception is of a complex theory of an economic system dominated by evolutionary change processes that are adaptive and self-organizing. This system generates non-linearities, path dependence, and emergent properties, which cannot be reduced to their component parts, positive feedback loops, and increasing returns to scale. Unlike neoclassical theory, complexity economics deals with processes that occur in historical, not logical, time. It only became possible with advances in information technology that allowed the numerical simulation of dynamic equation systems for which analytical solutions could not be obtained, and it soon attracted the interest of at least one major mainstream theorist, Kenneth Arrow (Anderson *et al.* 1998).

Two of the most influential advocates of complexity in economics are the former Marxists Samuel Bowles and Herbert Gintis. Their book *A Cooperative Species* (2011) provides a formal analysis of cooperation, which they interpret as evidence of real concern for the wellbeing of others rather than the pursuit of self-interest disguised as altruism. People try to uphold social norms, value ethical behavior for its own sake, and have genuine feelings of pride, shame, and guilt. Bowles and Gintis explain these traits as the product of human evolution, drawing on anthropology and neuroscience to argue that our earliest ancestors benefited from cooperation. They maintain that natural selection favors non-selfish behavior, since it operates at the level of the group rather than the individual (still less the gene). Altruistic cooperation is still necessary in the twenty-first century, especially in the production of goods and services where quality is difficult to monitor, and it will never be entirely replaced by private contract or government regulation: "where the invisible hand fails, the handshake may succeed" (Bowles and Gintis 2011, 211). In the formal demonstration of these conclusions, they make heavy use of complexity theory.

However, the enthusiasm Bowles and Gintis displayed is not universally shared. For its critics, complexity economics "seems guilty of an old-fashioned misconception in equating the use of computers and mathematics with better science" (Thornton 2015, 19). Its advocates seem to be guilty of the ancient offence of applying the methods of the natural sciences to economic problems where they are simply not appropriate. Moreover, Arrow aside, there seems to be "scant evidence of complexity gaining traction in research, teaching or policy" (Thornton 2015, 22).

The fifth and final new approach was that of 'neuroeconomics,' which drew heavily on developments in neuroscience: "the imaging of brain activity and other techniques to infer details about how the brain works" (Camerer *et al.* 2005, 9). It was no longer necessary to regard the human brain as a 'black box' and to infer its operations from individual behavior, using 'as if' assumptions about conscious maximization that were commonplace in neoclassical theory in the 1950s and 1960s. It could now be seen from brain imaging that human behavior involved "fluid interaction between controlled and automatic processes and between cognitive and affective systems," so that it was not "the product of cognitive deliberation alone" (Camerer *et al.* 2005, 11). This enhanced the economist's understanding of inter-temporal choice and decision-making under risk and uncertainty, and also had important implications for game theory and the study of labour market (Camerer *et al.* 2005, 39–53).

As with new behavioral economics, there was ground for disagreement about the exact relationship between these new ideas and existing mainstream economic theory. Colin Camerer and his co-authors distinguish the 'incremental' from the 'radical' version of neuroeconomics. The incremental approach involves adding variables to, and suggesting specific functional forms for, the conventional account of decision-making. Drug addiction, for example can be explained in terms of dynamic cross-partial effects in utility for bundles of commodities. The radical approach asks how economics might have developed if the findings of neuroscience had been available from the outset. Nineteenth- and early twentieth-century economic theorists might have gone in a very different direction if they had known that models of deliberative utility maximization subject to precise constraints were unable to handle either automatic or emotional processing of information by the human brain. On the other hand, there is also increasing evidence of a reverse influence, in which economic models of the brain are beginning to influence the conduct of neuroscience:

> Many neuroscientists are now using the most basic elements of rational choice theory to explain what they see. Ironically, they are taking up rational choice theory at the same time as more and more economists are moving away from rational choice toward a behavioural view anchored in limits on rational willpower and greed.
>
> (Camerer *et al.* 2005, 54)

Ironic but not quite economics imperialism as it involves the exercise of soft power rather than acts of deliberate intellectual aggression.

Some observers argue that all these developments represented a new pluralism in American economics while providing evidence of *reverse* imperialism. Economics was now importing new ideas, techniques, and research agendas from biology, neuroscience, and cognitive psychology, disciplines recognized as being increasingly "ripe for harvest" (Camerer *et al.* 2005, 9). In the process, the new 'dissenters,' or 'heterodox mainstreamers,' were abandoning much of the intellectual apparatus of the old mainstream. They recognized that individuals are socially embedded, not atomistic; accepted that economic processes are evolutionary rather than mechanical; and acknowledged that individuals and socio-economic structures are mutually dependent, so that methodological individualism was futile and the quest for 'microfoundations' was bound to fail (Colander *et al.* 2004; Davis 2008).

Against this, critics maintained that the new ideas were being absorbed into mainstream theory in ways that insured that no threat was posed to its core tenets. A process of 'bastardization' was under way, similar to that which had accompanied the incorporation of Keynes's macroeconomics into the mainstream of American economics in the 1940s. This could be seen in all the new streams of thought, perhaps most clearly in the case of behavioral economics, since the 'new behaviorism' was essentially individualistic and carried the comforting implication that in many cases economic agents needed only to be 'nudged' in the right direction to obtain something approaching the instrumentally rational behavior postulated by traditional neoclassical theory. Far from constituting a set of genuinely progressive new research programs, the 'other voices' in fact represented a new, more subtle, and rather sinister form of economics imperialism (Fine and Milonakis 2009).

Entirely disconnected from these controversies, there were still some advocates of the old Chicago way of doing economics which avoided elaborate mathematical modeling in favor of informal empirical observation and elegant literary exposition of the case for largely unregulated free markets. The most eloquent practitioner of this approach was Deirdre McCloskey who in a previous incarnation had been the economic historian Donald McCloskey. A stern opponent of the mysterious Chinese Jewish theorist known as 'Max U s.t.c.', McCloskey has written at great length on the merits of the market, emphasizing the many ways in which it has encouraged the development of ethically desirable behavior (McCloskey 2006, 2010). Attacking liberal critics of the market such as Richard Sennett (1998) and Robert Putnam (2000), who maintain that extending the domain of the market has crowded out virtue and destroyed community values, McCloskey claims that the opposite is true. Everyone is equal in the marketplace, so that engagement in market transactions discourages favoritism, hierarchy, and sectarianism, promoting instead universal values. Market participants learn to become independent, self-reliant, and responsible citizens, often displaying the related virtues of enterprise and alertness. They develop tolerance and respect for the preferences of others – 'the consumer is always right' – in an environment characterized by generalized trust and trustworthiness (McCloskey 2006, 2010). For McCloskey these are the most important lessons to be learned from competitive markets, and they have little or nothing to do with the formal modeling of equilibrium outcomes for utility-maximizing automatons.

## Crosscurrents

One consequence of a changing mainstream and the emergence of the "other voices" was the further marginalization – if we might be permitted to use this term – of institutionalism and Post Keynesian economics, whose leading advocates found it more and more difficult to debate directly with the mainstream and to publish in the leading journals. For this reason we have moved these two schools of thought to the 'crosscurrents' section, along with the Marxists and the Austrians, who have always been there. Two further 'crosscurrents' to emerge after 1973 were those of feminist economics and ecological economics, making six in all.

The revival of Austrian economics began in 1974, when the delightfully named Institute for Humane Studies sponsored a week-long conference at South Royalton, Vermont. The two most influential participants were Murray Rothbard (1926–1995), whose libertarian politics were important in the launching of an Austrian 'movement' in economics in the 1970s, and the London-born Israel Kirzner, whose work (unlike Rothbard's) was consciously directed at a mainstream audience. In *Competition and Entrepreneurship* (1973) and *Discovery and the Capitalist Process* (1985), Kirzner argued that

> Neoclassical economics had a theory of equilibrium prices, but it had no accepted theory of how these prices were attained. Kirzner set out to show that an Austrian theory of markets as entrepreneurial processes could fill this gap and provide deeper understanding of markets as well.
>
> (Vaughn 1994, 101)

Although there were sharp internal divisions on some important issues, the Austrians were united in their emphasis on purposeful human action and their opposition to the positivist philosophy of knowledge that underpins mainstream economics and looks only at the observable consequences of human behavior. Instead the Austrians stressed the importance of "praxeology, verbal deductive economics, no use of mathematics, limited use of econometrics, suspicion of macroeconomics, [and] specific theories of entrepreneurship, capital and business fluctuations, and money" (Vaughn 1994, 107).

Thus Austrian economists focused upon the study of competition as a 'market process' of discovery, which "depicts an economy that is continually evolving as people design new products and production processes, and gain information about their economic activities and the activities of others" (Holcombe 2014, 21). The outcome of this market process is the creation of spontaneous order, which is seen as "the result of human action but not human design" (Holcombe 2014, 4), and has clear policy implications:

> For many reasons, the way that the Austrian school understands the market process leads its members to favor capitalism and free markets. This is not an ideological position but rather one that follows directly from the economic analysis of the school.
>
> (Holcombe 2014, 105)

Outsiders would dispute the non-ideological nature of these conclusions, but there is no doubt that Austrian economics did profit from the rapid progress of neoliberal ideas and the discrediting of all forms of socialism in the wake of the disintegration of the Soviet empire after 1989.

In 1974 Rothbard had helped to set up the Cato Institute, a libertarian think tank that also promoted Austrian ideas, and he had also launched two publications, *Libertarian Forum* and *The Journal of Libertarian Studies* (Boettke *et al.* 2016, 32–33). By the 1980s there were three universities offering PhD programs in Austrian economics: New York University (under the leadership of Kirzner), George Mason University (where the Center for Market Processes was set up in 1980), and Auburn University (in association with the Ludwig von Mises Institute, which was established at Auburn in 1982). In 1987 the Mises Institute set up the *Review of Austrian Economics*, which soon became the leading academic journal in the field; the *Quarterly Review of Austrian Economics* began publishing in 1998. Organizationally, Austrian economics has struggled. "The only Austrian school program that has thrived into the twenty-first century is the one at George Mason University, which is the academic center of the Austrian school in the early twenty-first century." As for the Mises Institute, it "is well established, and offers conferences and student programs promoting the Austrian school, but it is no longer associated with any university and does not offer a degree program" (Holcombe 2014, 101).

John Kenneth Galbraith continued to be an inspiration to the institutionalists. A couple of years after its publication, his *New Industrial State* (1967) was, as William Lazonick reminds us, "quickly becoming what I would suppose is the most widely read book written by a twentieth-century economist" (Lazonick 2000, 414). Galbraith, however, had not been deeply involved in the establishment of the Association for Evolutionary Economics (AFEE) in 1965 or in the launch, two years later, of its quarterly *Journal of Economic Issues*, whose editor for a decade after 1972 was Warren J. Samuels (1933–2011). One of the most influential personalities in institutional economics in the final quarter of the twentieth century, Samuels was the author of the two-volume *Essays on the Economic Role of Government* (1992) and editor of several collective volumes in which the political and social background to economic issues received detailed attention.

Questions of class, gender, and corporate power had always been emphasized by the institutionalists, creating strong links with other cross-currents in what was coming to be known as 'heterodox economics' (we shall return to the precise meaning of this new concept at the end of this section). Some advocates of the 'cactus school', heavily influenced by Clarence Ayres of the University of Texas, became critical of both AFEE and the *Journal of Economic Issues* under Samuels's editorship for becoming too diffuse and open-ended and thereby failing to promote institutionalist ideas (Rutherford 2013). In 1979 they established the Association for Institutional Thought (AFIT), which continues to hold sessions at the annual meetings of the Western Social Science Association, although its journal, the *Review of Institutional Thought*, ceased publication after only three issues in 1981, 1982, and 1986. Meanwhile in 2016 the *Journal of Economic Issues* published its 50th volume, with more than 100 articles and 1,200 pages in the four issues.

Many members of AFEE did develop links with other strands of heterodox economics, including feminism, Post Keynesianism, and radical-Marxian political economy. In *Economics, Power and Culture* (1995), James Ronald Stanfield (b. 1945) argued the need for a 'radical institutionalism' to expose what Charles Whalen described as a society in which powerful corporate interests dominate not only economic processes but also politics and the overall culture. The standard economics of individual choice is left in tatters by the institutional economics of power and culture.

(Whalen 1996, 247)

The "Welcome" page on the AFEE website suggests that Stanfield's influence has been substantial:

The intellectual heritage of AFEE is that of the Original Institutional Economics (OIE) created and developed by early twentieth-century economists such as Thorstein Veblen, John R. Commons, and Wesley Mitchell. Over recent decades, this legacy has evolved to address such contemporary issues as:

- The role of diverse cultures in economic performance.
- Domestic and international inequalities of income.
- The roles of social, economic and political power in shaping economic outcomes.
- Globalization and the increasing weight of multinational corporations in the international economy.
- The need for expanding use of modern technologies to relieve want.
- The urgent need for awareness of the impact of new technology on the biosphere.
- The ways in which economic thought is affected by and affects always changing economics.(www.afee.net consulted 13 June 2016).

Two of the more important younger institutionalists to take up these challenges, both of whom died young, were Frederic S. Lee (1949–2014) and Robert Prasch (1958–2015). Lee, who also made a significant contribution to Post Keynesian price theory, published an influential and provocative *History of Heterodox Economics* (2009), while Prasch was the author of the lucid and insightful *How Markets Work: Supply, Demand and 'the Real World'* (2008).

The formal separation of Post Keynesian theory from the neoclassical Keynesian branch of the mainstream was confirmed in 1978 when the first issue of the *Journal of Post Keynesian Economics* appeared. The new journal was edited by Paul Davidson and Sidney Weintraub and then, after the latter's death in 1983, by Davidson alone. Although he continued to advocate the 'fundamentalist Keynesian' strand of Post Keynesian theory ('it's all in the *General Theory*'), Davidson never denied space in the journal to those who approached the macroeconomic problems of the late twentieth century from a different perspective (King 2002). These included Alfred S. Eichner (1937–1988), author of *The Megacorp and Oligopoly* (1976) and *The Macrodynamics of Advanced Market Economies* (1988), who was heavily influenced by the ideas of Michał Kalecki and therefore stressed the role of corporate pricing decisions and the link between market power and deficient effective demand. From the 1980s onwards Kaleckian models became increasingly influential among American Post Keynesians. There was a close connection between the Post Keynesian analysis of the macroeconomic implications of corporate power and that of the institutionalists, with theorists such as Eichner and Lee publishing in both the *Journal of Post Keynesian Economics* and the *Journal of Economic Issues.*

One highly distinctive Post Keynesian voice was that of Hyman P. Minsky (1919–1996), whose book *John Maynard Keynes* (1975) offered an interpretation of Keynes that Minsky elaborated on in later work, including *Can 'It' Happen Again? Essays on Instability and Finance* (1982). Minsky's 'financial instability hypothesis' was derived from his understanding of the underlying causes of the Great Depression and revealed the influence of Irving Fisher, whose debt-deflation theory was discussed in the previous chapter. For Minsky the analysis of corporate debt was the central problem in macroeconomic theory. In his 'Wall Street vision,' the crucial economic relationship is that between investment banker and client, not factory-owner and worker. His 'representative agent' is a financial capitalist. Borrowing and lending are the crucial transactions, and the expectations of lenders and borrowers fluctuate, often dramatically, in a regularly repeated cyclical process. Depression gives way to confidence, which grows into exuberance and excitement before collapsing into despair. These mood swings are reflected in financial transactions, as caution is replaced first by optimism and then by euphoria.

In the early stages of an upswing, *hedge finance* is the general rule: borrowers are able to make both scheduled interest payments and the necessary repayments of principal from the cash flows generated by their activities. Eventually *speculative finance* becomes more typical, and profit flows are sufficient only to meet interest bills and possibly a proportion of principal commitments. As the boom nears its end, *Ponzi finance* appears, with borrowers unable even to pay interest without incurring further debts in order to do so. *Financial fragility* now increases rapidly, and soon the cycle turns down in a spiral of bankruptcies, 'fire sales' of assets at greatly reduced prices, falling profit expectations, and declining profit flows, before confidence recovers and the entire process begins all over again. In the late 1970s Minsky came to recognize that Kalecki's theory of profits was needed to complement his analysis of debt, providing a theory of the firm's resources to match his own account of its financial commitments (Wray 2015).

As discussed in the previous chapter, the distinctively American brand of Marxian economics that Paul Baran and Paul Sweezy developed in the 1950s and early 1960s not only focused on the power of the capitalist corporation but also paid close attention to the social, cultural, and ideological dimensions of US capitalism. Sweezy (who died in 2004) ended up as a left social democrat, regarding the abolition of capitalism as impracticable for the foreseeable future and instead arguing for a large public sector and a substantial redistribution of income and wealth within the existing social order. While his earlier work remains influential, the final, non-economistic, chapters of *Monopoly Capital* have something in common with the post-modern Marxism proposed by David Ruccio, Jack Amariglio, Antonio Callari, Steven Resnick, and Richard Wolff (1996), which represents yet another, distinctively American attempt to reformulate Marxian political economy. It is a 'non-deterministic' version of Marxism that draws also on American post-analytic epistemology and on French post-structuralism and emphasizes decentered, multiple, endogenous subjectivities and social processes rather than objective laws of motion. Post-modern Marxists reject the traditional Marxian view that the base (economy) and superstructure (politics, culture, and the rest of society) must be analyzed hierarchically, and reinterpret the labor theory of value as a class analysis of the mutual determination of production and exchange. Thus, over-determination and difference are crucial concepts. Post-modern Marxists pay great attention to questions of race, gender, and exploitation within the family and other institutions. They maintain that there is no single 'logic of capital,' but rather open-ended, conjunctural trajectories of capitalist corporations. The relationship between the 'real' economy and the monetary system is one of complex interaction, not one-directional causation.

A further innovation has seen the emergence of a Marxian variant of environmental economics, which had been anticipated by Sweezy in some of his final articles. Writers like Paul Burkett, Michael Perelman, and John Bellamy Foster have argued that Marx was not an anti-ecological thinker, but rather that ecology was central to his thought. The legacy of Hegelian Marxism, Foster suggests, was to deny the possibility of applying dialectical reasoning to nature, as Engels had unconvincingly attempted in his *Dialectics of Nature*. On Foster's interpretation, however, "Marx's world-view was deeply, and indeed systematically, ecological" (Foster 2000, viii). For Marx, the alienation of human labor was closely connected to the alienation of human beings from nature.

Finally, the *Analytical Marxists* made a conscious effort to apply the standards of (Anglo-Saxon) analytical philosophy to Marxism, and to eradicate Hegelian influences, or at least Hegelian modes of expression, from Marxian thought. If nothing else, this improved the clarity of the arguments. Some Analytical Marxists went too far, however, when they adopted a strong version of the principle of methodological individualism and combined it with the theory of rational choice, taken directly from neoclassical economics. Rational Choice Marxists such as John Roemer claimed that all propositions in Marxian political economy must be expressed in terms of, indeed, reduced to statements about the maximizing behavior of rational individuals. This required a substantial revision of the theory of exploitation, with class antagonism between capitalists and wage-labourers largely disappearing from the analysis. The legacy of Analytical Marxism remains disputed, but few have been convinced by its insistence of the need to provide microfoundations for Marxian economics (Veneziani 2012). Throughout this period, Marxian economics in the United States has been much more open-ended and more multi-disciplinary than was ever the case in Western Europe.

The two remaining 'crosscurrents' were only beginning to be heard in 1973. Feminist economics and ecological economics have something else in common: their rejection of efforts to incorporate them into the mainstream as particular sub-branches or applications of neoclassical analysis. Thus Suzanne Bergeron distinguishes

> two overlapping stages of feminist analysis. The first stage is associated with writers in the 1960s and 1970s who were primarily concerned with issues such as the relative absence of women from the economics profession, the failure of economists to incorporate women's economic activities into their models, and the inaccurate depiction of women in the few cases in which they were explicitly considered (e.g. the new home economics). The feminist solution to these problems was to integrate women into both the discipline and its theories. This approach has been referred to as the 'add women and stir' strategy because it leaves the existing neoclassical framework relatively unchallenged.
>
> (Bergeron 2001, 496)

It also takes gender and the household as *givens*, rather than social constructs, whereas it could be argued as many cultural anthropologists have that both are *outcomes* of social processes and the exercise of political power (Danby 2007).

As Bergeron notes, the second stage of feminist economic theory paid serious attention to these questions. It

> began in the late 1970s and early 1980s, when feminist scholars in many disciplines began to argue that the primary problem was not that women were omitted from existing theoretical frameworks, but that the experiences of women were distorted by the frameworks themselves. In economics, this led to an increasing concern with the masculinist biases of the core assumptions of neoclassical economics, especially regarding the inadequacies of the theory of individual optimizing behavior in terms of explaining women's (and men's) experiences.
>
> (Bergeron 2001, 496)

This came in a review of Gillian Hewitson's *Feminist Economics: Interrogating the Masculinity of Rational Economic Man* (1999), which applied poststructuralist ideas to economic issues, "borrowing and transforming ideas from Foucault, Lacan, Althusser and Derrida to explore questions of gender, subjectivity and knowledge production" (Bergeron 2001, 495). These were live issues in the work of the International Association for Feminist Economics (IAFFE), established in 1992, and in the journal *Feminist Economics*, which began publication three years later. This second stage, however, involved more than a change in methodology. Feminist economists now began to extend their subject matter to macroeconomic theory and economic development and to make connections with other heterodox schools, notably institutionalism and Post Keynesian economics (van Staveren 2010).

In the process they had challenged the very nature of the mainstream conception of 'economic activity' and its measurement, in a way not greatly different from the contemporaneous critique of ecological economists. If labor was itself a produced input, why was the cost of producing it (in the household, predominantly by the unpaid labor of women) not included in GDP, which purported to be a measure of total output? Were non-marketed activities like child care labor of no economic value whatsoever? Was not the economic system dependent on social and environmental systems, which mainstream economists neglected at their peril? Perhaps, as argued by Herman Daly (2006), GDP should be replaced by the notion of 'throughput,' which tracks the flow of matter and energy from the environment through the economic subsystem of production and consumption back to the environment as waste.

Ecological economists rejected the mainstream insistence that environmental policy be treated as a straightforward application of neoclassical welfare economics, with large market failures that needed to be corrected by appropriate Pigovian taxes and subsidies (Gowdy and Erickson 2005). This involved the extension of market relations to previously non-market environmental 'goods,' and probably also the 'enclosure of the commons,' so that private ownership could provide the relevant incentives for their conservation. All this raised huge questions. Is it possible to put a price on nature? Is it ethically proper to do so? If not, how can we make rational decisions about the conservation of endangered ecosystems, or individual species that are threatened with extinction, or the future of the entire planet? Is 'green growth' a feasible alternative to an environmentally sustainable steady-state economy (Dale *et al.* 2016)? As with the feminists, the ecologists also came to recognize the importance to them of macroeconomic analysis, and began to explore the common ground that they shared with the Post Keynesians (Holt *et al.* 2010).

Five of the six crosscurrents that have been considered in this section share a strong – and fully reciprocated – suspicion of the mainstream: its increasing formalism, its growing intolerance of dissent, and its neoliberal insistence on the virtues of the free market. (Austrian economics is in a rather different position, since Austrians agree with the mainstream on this most important third point). This has tended to bring the five dissenting schools together, though the extent and depth of their cooperation is a contentious question. Early in the new century, Frederic Lee claimed that there was now a community of heterodox economists who formed "a pluralistic integrative whole" with "much in common that is positive (as opposed to holding only a critique of mainstream economists in common)" (Fred Lee 2009, 202). Against this it can be argued that the divisions between the various heterodox schools – not to mention their sometimes profound internal conflicts – render Lee's vision of a single, coherent heterodox economics that is separate from the mainstream entirely unrealistic. The alternative is pluralism, which involves the acceptance of a substantial and irreducible diversity of perspectives, methods, and techniques of analysis in which the 'other voices' cooperate on specific issues but retain their own separate identities and remain as distinct and largely independent schools of thought.

In 2004 Lee established the online *Heterodox Economic Newsletter*, which has appeared at roughly monthly intervals since then with comprehensive details of publications, conferences, and seminars from the United States and around the world (http://heterodoxnews.com). Lee also helped to compile the first online *Heterodox Economic Directory* in the following year. Its sixth edition, published in March 2016, listed 26 heterodox PhD programs around the world, nine of them in the United States (at American University; Colorado State University; Michigan State University; New School University; University of California, Riverside; University of Massachusetts, Amherst; University of Massachusetts, Boston; University of Missouri, Kansas City; and University of Utah). There were also 32 Masters and 64 undergraduate programs, of which seven and 43, respectively, were American. Of the nine regular heterodox conferences listed in the *Directory*, the majority were held in the United States, but only a minority of the 11 regular summer schools, most of which were European. The *Newsletter* itself is now edited in Austria at the University of Linz, confirming that the globalization of academic economics has not been confined to the mainstream.

### Economics in the United States in 2016 and beyond

In June 2016 the American Economic Association website boasted of its "more than 20,000 members." Interestingly, this was rather less than the "peak of over 26,000, including [non-member] subscribers" that had been attained in 1983, though much greater than the 4,145 members in 1945 (Coats 1985, 1717: n. 32). The publishing activities of AEA, however, have continued to expand. In 1973 the *American Economic Review* ran to five parts per year, with a total of 1,137 pages; by 2015 it was publishing monthly, with no less than 3,797 pages in that year's twelve issues. The *Journal of Economic Literature* was launched by the AEA in 1969 to remove book reviews and related material from the *AER*, and in 1987 the *Journal of Economic Perspectives* began publication, to provide a non-technical journal for undergraduate students and the general educated reader. No fewer than four additional new journals were established in 2008, specializing in applied economics, economic policy, micro and macro, bringing the total number of AEA publications to seven.

The profession that the AEA represents remains highly distinctive by comparison with the other social sciences. First, it is relatively insular, as evidenced by the paucity of inter-disciplinary citations in economics journals by comparison with political science and sociology journals, and by surveys revealing that economists place little value on inter-disciplinary knowledge (this is further, indirect, confirmation of the failure of the economics imperialism project). Second, economics is more hierarchical than the other social sciences, with the top five departments having a high degree of control over publications and appointments, and economists being much more concerned with rankings of departments and journals than their colleagues in the other social sciences. Almost three-quarters of the non-appointed members of the AEA's council come from the top five departments (Fourcade *et al.* 2015, 100).

Economics also remains more monolithic than the other disciplines, though there is, as we have seen, some dispute as to whether this is now changing. The economic methodologist Wade Hands (2015) argues that since 2000 the state of stable equilibrium in economic theory that had lasted for the half-century after 1945, with mainstream and heterodox ideas facing off against each other, has begun to collapse. Hands sees several of the 'other voices' that were identified above – (new) behavioral economics, evolutionary economics, experimental economics, and neuroeconomics – generating a welcome pluralism in the discipline. He cautions, however, that these developments are most evident in microeconomics, while the future of macroeconomics is much less certain.

Indeed, the failure of the Great Recession to induce any profound change in macroeconomic theory has interested many commentators. Philip Mirowski invokes the theory of cognitive dissonance to explain how neoliberalism survived the Great Recession not just unscathed but actually strengthened. Neoliberals responded to the crisis just as social psychologists would have predicted: "Contrary evidence did not dent their worldview" (Mirowski 2013, 357). Instead they redoubled their efforts to capture the economics profession – not that they had to try very hard. They also "resorted to industrial-scale manufacture of ignorance about the crisis, based on the time-tested tobacco strategy" (Mirowski 2013, 358), which involved "the injection of surplus noise into public discourse concerning the crisis" (Mirowski 2013, 300). In all this a number of prominent academic economists played a major role.

At the other end of the political spectrum, some American economists are at last beginning to take an interest in the massive growth of inequality in income and wealth that has occurred since the 1970s, which has had a social and political impact the equal of its influence on economics. This has been recognized by mainstream economists including Jeffrey Sachs, in *The Price of Civilization* (2011), and by some on the fringes of the mainstream such as Joseph Stiglitz, in *The Price of Inequality* (2012). Thomas Piketty's *Capital in the Twenty-first Century* (2014) was a runaway bestseller; its French author was educated and for some years worked in the United States and the book, which makes extensive use of neoclassical theory, was published by Harvard University Press. Nevertheless the growth in inequality has not been adequately explained in mainstream theory, since narratives that focus largely on the consequences of labor-saving technical progress or a supposedly inevitable increase in the capital-output ratio are not convincing (King 2017). Changes in social and especially political power are a crucial part of the explanation for the growth in inequality, which suggests that there may well be some mileage left in the (old) Institutionalism and in both radical and Marxian political economy.

In *The Great Divide* (2015), Stiglitz comes close to the Post Keynesian position on the macroeconomic consequences of growing inequality, which he sees as an important factor contributing to financialization and to increasing financial instability, a major cause of the crisis of 2007–2008. His voice, however, remains a minority one. In 2009 the Cato Institute paid for a full-page advertisement opposing the Obama administration's fiscal stimulus plan to combat the Great Recession. It was signed by over 200 economists, including the Nobel laureates James Buchanan, Eugene Fama, Edward Prescott, and Vernon Smith and the Chicago stalwarts John Cochrane, Deirdre McCloskey, and Allan Meltzer. It is worth quoting in full:

> Notwithstanding reports that all economists are now Keynesians and that we all support a big increase in the burden of government, we the undersigned do not believe that more government spending is a way to improve economic performance. More government spending by Hoover and Roosevelt did not pull the United States economy out of the Great Depression in the 1930s. More government spending did not solve Japan's 'lost decade' in the 1990s. As such, it is a triumph of hope over experience to believe that more government spending will help the U.S. today. To improve the economy, policymakers should focus on reforms that remove impediments to work, saving, investment and production. Lower tax rates and a reduction in the burden of government are the best ways of using fiscal policy to boost growth.

Evidently this controversy has yet to run its course.

## References

Akerlof, G. A. 2002. "Behavioral Macroeconomics and Macroeconomic Behavior." *American Economic Review* 92(3): 11–33.

Akerlof, G. A., and Shiller, R. 2009. *Animal Spirits: How Human Psychology Drives the Economy, and Why It Matters for Global Capitalism.* Princeton, NJ: Princeton University Press.

Anderson, P. 2013. "American Foreign Policy and its Thinkers." *New Left Review* n.s. 85: 5–167.

Anderson, P. W., Arrow, K. J., and Pines, D., (eds). 1988. *The Economy as an Evolving Complex System.* Reading, MA: Addison-Wesley.

Anon. 2014. "Zehn wilde Börsenjahre bringen Apple nach ganz oben" ["Ten wild years on the stock market bring Apple right to the top"]. *Frankfurter Allgemeine Zeitung.* 29 August.

Anon. 2015. "54 der am höchsten bewerteten Firmen sitzen in den USA, 26 in Europa und 17 in Asien" ["54 of the world's most highly-valued firms are based in the USA, 26 in Europe and 17 in Asia"]. *Die Presse* [Vienna], 30 December.

Anon. 2016. "Financial Brief." *Guardian Weekly.* 4 March.

Backhouse, R. E., and Fontaine, P., (eds). 2010. *The History of the Social Sciences Since 1945.* Cambridge: Cambridge University Press.

Bergeron, S. 2001. "Review of Hewitson (1999)." *Review of Radical Political Economics* 33(4): 495–508.

Blaug, M. 1985. *Great Economists Since Keynes*. Brighton: Wheatsheaf.

Boettke, P. J., Coyne, C. J., and Newman, P. 2016. *The History of a Tradition: Austrian Economics from 1871 to 2016*. George Mason University Working Paper in Economics no. 16–18.

Bowles, S., and Gintis, H. 2011. *A Cooperative Species: Human Reciprocity and its Evolution*. Princeton, NJ: Princeton University Press.

Camerer, C., Loewenstein, C., and Prelec, D. 2005. "Neuroeconomics: How Neuroscience can Inform Economics." *Journal of Economic Literature* 43(1): 9–64.

Card, D., and Krueger, A. B. 1995. *Myth and Measurement: The New Economics of the Minimum Wage*. Princeton, NJ: Princeton University Press.

Coase, R. 1960. "The Problem of Social Cost." *Journal of Law and Economics* 3(1): 1–44.

Coats, A. W. 1985. "The American Economic Association and the Economics Profession." *Journal of Economic Literature* 23(4): 1697–1728.

Coats, A. W., (ed.). 1996. *The Post-1945 Internationalization of Economics*. Durham, NC: Duke University Press.

Colander, D., Holt, R. P. F., and Rosser, J. B. 2004. *The Changing Face of Economics*. Ann Arbor, MI: University of Michigan Press.

Dale, G., Mathai, M. V., and Puppim de Oliveira, J., (eds). 2016. *Green Growth: Ideology, Political Economy and the Alternatives*. London: Zed Books.

Daly, H. 2006. *Beyond Growth*. Washington, DC: Beacon Press.

Danby, C. 2007. "Political Economy and the Closet: Heteronormativity in Feminist Economics.' *Feminist Economics* 13(2): 27–53.

Davis, J. B. 2008. "The Turn in Recent Economics and the Return of Orthodoxy." *Cambridge Journal of Economics* 32(3): 349–366.

Dawkins, R. 1976. *The Selfish Gene*. Oxford and New York, NY: Oxford University Press.

Ehrenberg, R. G., and Smith, R. S. 2012. *Modern Labor Economics: Theory and Public Policy*. Boston, MA: Prentice Hall.

Eichengreen, B. 2015. *Hall of Mirrors: The Great Depression, the Great Recession, and the Uses – and Misuses – of History*. New York, NY: Oxford University Press.

Eichner, A. S. 1976. *The Megacorp and Oligopoly: Micro Foundations of Macro Dynamics*. Cambridge: Cambridge University Press.

Eichner, A. S. 1988. *The Macrodynamics of Advanced Market Economies*. Armonk, NY: M.E. Sharpe.

Elliott, C., Greenaway, D., and Sapsford, D. 1998. "Who's Publishing Whom? The National Composition of Contributors to Some Core US and European Journals." *European Economic Review* 42(1): 201–206.

Fine, B., and Milonakis, D. 2009. *From Economics Imperialism to Freakonomics: The Shifting Boundaries between Economics and Other Social Sciences*. London and New York, NY: Routledge.

Forder, J. 2014. *Macroeconomics and the Phillips Curve Myth*. Oxford UK: Oxford University Press.

Foster, J. B. 2000. *Marx's Ecology: Materialism and Nature*. New York, NY: Monthly Review Press.

Fourcade, M. 2006. "The Construction of a Global Profession: the Transnationalization of Economics." *American Journal of Sociology* 112(1): 145–194.

Fourcade, M. 2009. *Economists and Societies: Discipline and Profession in the United States, Britain and France, 1890s to 1990s.* Princeton, NJ: Princeton University Press.

Fourcade, M., Ollion, E., and Algan, Y. 2015. "The Superiority of Economists." *Journal of Economic Perspectives* 29(1): 89–114.

Friedman, D., and Sunder, S. 1994. *Experimental Methods: A Primer for Economists.* Cambridge: Cambridge University Press.

Friedman, M., and Friedman, R. 1980. *Free to Choose: A Personal Statement.* New York, NY: Harcourt Brace Jovanovich.

Fullbrook, E., (ed.). 2003. *The Crisis in Economics: The Post-Autistic Economics Movement – The First 600 Days.* London: Routledge.

Galbraith, J. K. 1967. *The New Industrial State.* Boston, MA: Houghton Mifflin.

Gowdy, J., and Erickson, J. 2005. "The Approach of Ecological Economics." *Cambridge Journal of Economics* 29(2): 207–222.

Hamermesh, D. 2013. "Six Decades of Top Economics Publications: Who and How?" *Journal of Economic Literature* 51(1): 162–172.

Hands, D. W. 2015. "Orthodox and Heterodox Economics in Recent Economic Methodology." *Erasmus Journal for Philosophy and Economics* 8(1): 61–81.

Hargreaves Heap, S., and Varoufakis, Y. 1995. *Game Theory: A Critical Introduction.* London and New York, NY: Routledge.

Heukelom, F. 2014. *Behavioral Economics: A History.* New York, NY: Cambridge University Press.

Hewitson, G. 1999. *Feminist Economics: Interrogating the Masculinity of Rational Economic Man.* Cheltenham: Edward Elgar.

Hirshleifer, J. 1978. "Competition, Cooperation, and Conflict in Economics and Biology." *American Economic Review* 68(2) Papers and Proceedings: 238–243.

Holcombe, R. 2014. *Advanced Introduction to Austrian Economics.* Cheltenham and Northampton, MA: Edward Elgar.

Holt, R. P. E., Pressman, S., and Spach, C. L., (eds). 2010. *Post Keynesian and Ecological Economics: Confronting Environmental Issues.* Northampton, MA: Edward Elgar.

Howard, M. C., and King, J. E. 2008. *The Rise of Neoliberalism in Advanced Capitalist Economies: A Materialist Analysis.* Basingstoke: Palgrave Macmillan.

Hughes, J., and Cain, L. 2011. *American Economic History* (Eighth Edition). Boston, MA: Addison Wesley.

Jefferson, T., and King, J. E. 2010–2011. "Can Post Keynesians Make Better Use of Behavioral Economics?" *Journal of Post Keynesian Economics* 33(2): 211–234.

Kagel, J. H., and Roth, A. E. 1995. *The Handbook of Experimental Economics.* Princeton, NJ: Princeton University Press.

Kates, S. 2013. *Defending the History of Economic Thought.* Cheltenham: Edward Elgar.

Kaufman, B. E. 1993. *The Origins and Evolution of the Field of Industrial Relations in the United States.* Ithaca, NY: ILR Press.

King, J. E. 1988. *Economic Exiles.* Basingstoke: Macmillan.

King, J. E. 2002. *A History of Post Keynesian Economics Since 1936,* Cheltenham: Edward Elgar.

King, J. E. 2009. "Economists and the Global Financial Crisis." *Global Change, Peace and Security* 21(3): 389–396.

King, J. E. 2012. *The Microfoundations Delusion: Metaphor and Dogma in the History of Macroeconomics.* Cheltenham: Edward Elgar.

King, J. E. 2015. *Advanced Introduction to Post Keynesian Economics*. Cheltenham: Edward Elgar.

King, J. E. 2017. "The Literature on Piketty." *Review of Political Economy* 29(1): 1–17.

Kirman, A. 1989. "The Intrinsic Limits of Modern Economic Theory: The Emperor Has No Clothes." *Economic Journal* 99(395): Supplement: Conference Papers (1989): 126–139.

Kirzner, I. M. 1973. *Competition and Entrepreneurship*. Chicago, IL: University of Chicago Press.

Kirzner, I. M. 1985. *Discovery and the Capitalist Process*. Chicago, IL: University of Chicago Press.

Kotz, D. M. 2015. *The Rise and Fall of Neoliberal Capitalism*. Cambridge, MA: Harvard University Press.

Lazear, E. 2000. "Economic Imperialism." *Quarterly Journal of Economics* 115(1): 99–146.

Lazonick, W. 2000. "William H. Lazonick (b. 1945)." In *Exemplary Economists, Volume I: North America* (R. E. Backhouse and R. Middleton, Editors). Cheltenham and Northampton, MA: Edward Elgar: 409–433.

Lee, F. 2009. *A History of Heterodox Economics: Challenging the Mainstream in the Twentieth Century*. London: Routledge.

Lee, K. S. 2016. "Mechanism Designers in Alliance: A Portrayal of a Scholarly Network in Support of Experimental Economics." *History of Political Economy* 48(2): 192–223.

Leontief, W. 1982. "Academic Economics." *Science* 217(4555): 104–107.

Lyons, J. S., Cain, L. P., and Williamson, S. H., (eds). 2008. *Reflections on the Cliometrics Revolution: Conversations with Economic Historians*. London and New York, NY: Routledge.

Maddison, A. 2006. *The World Economy*. Paris, FR: OECD.

McCloskey, D. N. 2006. *The Bourgeois Virtues: Ethics for an Age of Commerce*. Chicago, IL: University of Chicago Press.

McCloskey, D. N. 2010. *Bourgeois Dignity: Why Economics Cannot Explain the Modern World*. Chicago, IL: University of Chicago Press.

Minsky, H. P. 1975. *John Maynard Keynes*. New York, NY: Columbia University Press.

Minsky, H. P. 1982. *Can "It" Happen Again? Essays on Instability and Finance*. Armonk, NY: M.E. Sharpe.

Mirowski, P. 1989. *More Heat than Light: Economics as Social Physics, Physics as Nature's Economics*. Cambridge: Cambridge University Press.

Mirowski, P. 2002. *Machine Dreams: Economics Becomes a Cyborg Science*. Cambridge: Cambridge University Press.

Mirowski, P. 2013. *Never Let a Serious Crisis Go To Waste: How Neoliberalism Survived the Financial Meltdown*. London and New York, NY: Verso.

Mishel, L. *et al.* 2012. *The State of Working America* (Twelfth Edition). Ithaca, NY: ILR.

Nixey, J. 2015. "Is Russia Still a Key World Power?" www.bbc.com/news/world-europe-34857908 (online: accessed 21 December 2015).

Palley, T. 2013. "Monetary Policy and Central Banking After the Crisis: The Implications of Rethinking Macroeconomic Theory." In *The Handbook of the Political Economy of Financial Crises* (M. H. Wolfson and G. A. Epstein, Editors). Oxford and New York, NY: Oxford University Press: 624–643.

Piketty, T. 2014. *Capital in the Twenty-First Century*. Cambridge, MA: The Belknap Press of Harvard University Press.

Prasch, R. E. 2008. *How Markets Work: Supply, Demand and "the Real World".* Cheltenham and Northampton, MA: Edward Elgar.

Pressman, S. 2016. *Understanding Piketty's Capital in the Twenty-First Century.* London and New York, NY: Routledge.

Putnam, R.D. 2000. *Bowling Alone: The Collapse and Revival of American Community.* New York, NY: Simon & Schuster.

Rees, A. 1984. *The Economics of Work and Pay.* New York, NY: Harper & Row.

Rizvi, S. A. T. 2005. "Experimentation, General Equilibrium and Games." In *The Experiment in the History of Economics* (P. Fontaine and R. Leonard, Editors). London and New York, NY: Routledge: 50–70.

Rizvi, S. A. T. 2006. "The Sonnenschein-Mantel-Debreu Results after 30 Years." In *Agreement on Demand: Consumer Theory in the Twentieth Century* (P. Mirowski and D. W. Hands, Editors). Durham, NC: Duke University Press: 228–245.

Rogers, C. 2006. "Doing Without Money: A Critical Assessment of Woodford's Analysis.' *Cambridge Journal of Economics* 30(2): 293–306.

Roth, A. E. 1995. "A Brief History of Experimental Economics." In *The Handbook of Experimental Economics* (J. H. Kagel and A. E. Roth, Editors). Princeton, NJ: Princeton University Press: 4–21.

Ruccio, D. F. 2017. "Class and Trumponomics." *Real-World Economics Review* 78: 62–85, http://www.paecon.net/PAEReview/issue78/Ruccio78.pdf.

Ruccio, D., Amariglio, J., Callari, A., Resnick, S., and Wolff, R. 1996. "Non-determinist Marxism: The Birth of a Postmodern Tradition in Economics." In *Beyond Neoclassical Economics: Heterodox Approaches to Economic Thought* (F. E. Foldvary, Editor). Cheltenham: Elgar: 134–147.

Rutherford, M. 2013. "Warren Samuels, the *Journal of Economic Issues*, and the Association for Evolutionary Economics." *Research in the History of Economic Thought and Methodology* 31A: 61–72.

Sachs, J. 2011. *The Price of Civilization: Reawakening American Virtue and Prosperity.* New York, NY: Random House.

Samuels, W. J. 1992. *Essays on the Economic Role of Government, Vols. 1 and 2.* Basingstoke: Macmillan.

Schabas, M. 1992. "Breaking Away: History of Economics as History of Science." *History of Political Economy* 24(1): 187–203.

Sennett, R. 1998. *The Corrosion of Character: The Personal Consequences of Work in the New Capitalism.* New York, NY: Norton.

Sent, E. 2004. "How Psychology Made Its (Limited) Way Back into Economics." *History of Political Economy* 36(4): 735–760.

Shiller, R. J. 2000. *Irrational Exuberance.* Princeton, NJ: Princeton University Press.

Silvers, D. 2013. "Deregulation and the New Financial Architecture." In *The Handbook of the Political Economy of Financial Crises* (M. H. Wolfson and G. A. Epstein, Editors). Oxford and New York, NY: Oxford University Press: 430–446.

Snowdon, H., and Vane, H. R. 2005. *Modern Macroeconomics: Its Origins, Development and Current State.* Cheltenham: Edward Elgar.

Solow, Robert M. 1997. "How Did Economics Get That Way and What Way Did It Get?" *Daedalus* 126: 39–58.

Stanfield, J. R. 1995. *Economics, Power and Culture: Essays in the Development of Radical Institutionalism.* New York, NY: St. Martin's Press.

Stiglitz, J. 1987. "The Causes and Consequences of the Dependence of Quality on Price." *Journal of Economic Literature* 25(1): 1–48.

Stiglitz, J. 2012. *The Price of Inequality*. New York, NY: Norton.

Stiglitz, J. 2015. *The Great Divide*. London: Allen Lane.

Thaler, R. H., and Sunstein, C. R. 2009. *Nudge: Improving Decisions about Health, Wealth and Happiness* (Revised Edition). New York: Penguin.

Thornton, T. 2015. "The Changing Face of Mainstream Economics?" *Journal of Australian Political Economy* 75: 11–26.

Van Staveren, I. 2010. "Post-Keynesianism Meets Feminist Economics." *Cambridge Journal of Economics* 34(6): 1123–1144.

Vaughn, K. 1994. *Austrian Economics in America: The Migration of a Tradition*. Cambridge: Cambridge University Press.

Veneziani, R. 2012. "Analytical Marxism." *Journal of Economic Surveys* 26(4): 649–673.

Whalen, C. J. 1996. "Review of Stanfield (1995)." *Eastern Economic Journal* 22(2): 247–249.

Wickens, M. 2008. *Macroeconomic Theory: A Dynamic General Equilibrium Approach*. Princeton, NJ: Princeton University Press.

Wilson, E.O. 1975. *Sociobiology*. Cambridge, MA: The Belknap Press of Harvard University Press.

Woodford, M. 2003. *Interest and Prices: Foundations of a Theory of Monetary Policy*. Princeton, NJ: Princeton University Press.

Wray, L. R. 2015. *Why Minsky Matters: An Introduction to the Work of a Maverick Economist*. Princeton, NJ: Princeton University Press.

# Name index

# Subject index

For Product Safety Concerns and Information please contact our EU
representative GPSR@taylorandfrancis.com
Taylor & Francis Verlag GmbH, Kaufingerstraße 24, 80331 München, Germany